the road to

MALPSYCHIA

the road to

MALPSYCHIA

humanistic psychology
and our discontents

JOYCE MILTON

ENCOUNTER BOOKS
SAN FRANCISCO

First edition published in 2002 by Encounter Books, an activity of Encounter for Culture and Education, Inc., a nonprofit tax exempt corporation.

Encounter Books website address: www.encounterbooks.com

Manufactured in the United States and printed on acid-free paper.

The paper used in this publication meets the minimum requirements of ANSI/NISO Z39.48-1992 (R 1997) *(Permanence of Paper)*.

FIRST EDITION

Library of Congress Cataloging-in-Publication Data

Milton, Joyce.
    The road to Malpsychia : humanistic psychology and our discontents / Joyce Milton.
    p.   cm.
    Includes bibliographical references and index.
    ISBN 1-893554-46-5 (alk. paper)
    1. Humanistic psychology—History—20th century.   I Title.
BF204.M54 2002
150.19'8—dc21

                                          2002018837

10   9   8   7   6   5   4   3   2   1

Contents

The Road to Eupsychia

Although it's hard to imagine now, the great fear of American college students in the early 1960s was that we were repressed. Pop sociology books like William Whyte's *The Organization Man* warned that corporate culture was transforming managers and executives into the white-collar equivalents of assembly line workers. Vance Packard's *The Hidden Persuaders* claimed that advertisers were using subliminal messages to create a nation addicted to the consumption of tacky mass-produced goods. In the realm of fiction, Sloan Wilson's bestseller *The Man in the Gray Flannel Suit* depicted suburbia as a spiritual desert where ambitious couples sacrificed family values in the pursuit of status symbols. In 1957, novelist Norman Mailer gained attention for an essay entitled "The White Negro," expressing his envy of ghetto blacks who were sufficiently uninhibited to commit violent acts. As Mailer saw it, the younger generation faced a choice: "One is hip or one is square. One is a rebel or one conforms, one is a frontiersman in the Wild West of American nightlife, or else a square cell, trapped in the totalitarian tissues of American society, doomed willy nilly to conform if one is to succeed."

To be precise, this horror of conformity was limited to the segment of the population that considered itself intellectually sophisticated. Many of us were only dimly aware of such ideas during our high school years. We had grown up watching *Leave It to Beaver* and *Ozzie and Harriet*.

The creators of these shows took it for granted that wholesome family life was the norm. And, for a great many of us, it was so. The Cleavers and the Nelsons might be more articulate than our parents. They lived in better houses and never seemed to have money problems. But these were improvements that we could reasonably hope to make when it was our turn to be parents ourselves.

In school, our teachers and guidance counselors preached the mantra of *adjustment*. The remedy for unhappiness was to study the popular kids and do as they did. Those of us with a cynical turn of mind were contemptuous of this advice. Personally, I was pretty sure that nothing I did would ever turn me into cheerleader or majorette material. Nor did I want to be a cheerleader or a majorette—a possibility that no adult ever seemed to consider. Still, the opportunities for expressing one's uniqueness seemed to be limited. Some of us sneaked cigarettes at the bus stop and huddled behind the bleachers at football games, sucking on oranges injected with vodka. Mostly, we borrowed our parents' cars and drove around looking for action. But there was no action. The title of the movie *Rebel Without a Cause* captured our dilemma perfectly.

It was only after we arrived at college that we discovered that our teenage boredom was fraught with significance, a symptom of the malaise of civilization in the modern era. Our reading lists bristled with books on the problem of alienation. Important works of literature dealt with the dilemma of the outsider, the stranger adrift in a world he never made. Art and literature that aspired to ideals of truth and beauty were hopelessly middlebrow—pap for middle-class audiences too self-satisfied to grasp the nature of the crisis. In my freshman political science class we read the works of the neo-Marxist sociologist C. Wright Mills, who described America as a mass society of "cheerful robots," governed by a faceless "power elite." Like many radicals at the time, Mills saw the breakup of big institutions as the key to social change, and independent intellectuals like himself as the necessary catalysts. Until his death in 1962 at the relatively early age of fifty-six, Mills embodied his own ideal of the intellectual ruffian. A professor at Columbia University, he drove a BMW motorcycle, wore work boots in the classroom, and exuded contempt for his colleagues. His rudeness was the stuff of legend. Mills' biographer, Irving Louis Horowitz, observes of his subject: "He responded to others' claims that his behavior was boorish by behaving even more outlandishly.... Mills' personal style led to a near unanimous negative consensus about him." The notion that one could improve society by acting on one's selfish impulses was powerfully seductive.[1]

There seemed little chance that intellectuals of our professors' generation would ever enjoy real influence. The urbane, ironic Adlai Stevenson, so admired on campus, had twice failed miserably as a presidential candidate, and politicians ritually expressed their disdain for "eggheads." Students, however, were emboldened by the suggestion that political struggle was an outgrowth of the search for personal authenticity. According to the 1962 Port Huron Statement, the founding document of Students for a Democratic Society, the main impetus behind SDS was disillusionment. Having grown up enjoying material plenty and personal freedom, the authors of the statement were shocked to discover that racial inequality and poverty were still in existence. The persistence of these problems was proof of "the hypocrisy of American values." With hindsight, the SDS organizers expressed an amazing confidence that they could succeed where their elders had failed. Their goals included reforming the social order and making work more creative and less "stultifying," but also remaking human relationships to address the problems of "loneliness, estrangement and isolation." Moreover, the statement went on portentously, "Our work is guided by the sense that we may be the last generation in the experiment with living."

Such outsize goals were justified, in part, by early successes of the civil rights movement. In reality, the movement represented the culmination of decades of social change and years of patient organizing, but one would never guess this from watching the evening news. College students were integrating lunch counters and bus stations; and in Birmingham, Alabama, high school kids defied the snarling police dogs and high-pressure fire hoses of Sheriff Bull Connor and his deputies. Jim Crow laws that had stood since the Reconstruction era were being swept away. The lesson we gleaned was that amazing things could happen if young people simply refused to accept the status quo.

On the individual level, freeing oneself from the programming of middle-class morals and habits was more problematical. The dominant idea of the self at the time was heavily influenced by Freudian psychology—or, frequently, Freudianism as derived from second-hand sources like magazine articles, literary criticism and Hollywood movies like *Spellbound* and *David and Lisa*. Supposedly, our personalities were formed in infancy by experiences that we no longer consciously remembered. It was possible that some tragedy of toilet training gone awry or an unresolved Oedipal conflict had rendered us incapable of experiencing life authentically. Sex was the great test. Apart from the hurdle of having any at all and the usual worries about pregnancy, there was the fear that the act might expose us as frauds, too robotically bourgeois to enjoy life's earthier pleasures. Boys, I suppose, worried about performance. We girls feared that we might be unable to have orgasms, or at least the right kind of orgasms. Worse, as Freudians like Helene Deutsch warned us, our intellectual inclinations might render us permanently incapable of adjusting to the female role.

Marijuana was another truth test. In the early Sixties it was quite possible to go through high school without ever hearing a lecture about drugs. It never occurred to our teachers that we would be faced with that particular temptation. Suddenly, however, it seemed that in the waning moments of every party, someone would produce a single bedraggled-looking joint. This was always an anxiety-provoking moment. Passing the joint was a ritual, accompanied by much sucking of air and elaborate care not to bogart the sacred object, which threatened to disintegrate before making its way around the circle. Failure to get a buzz was not a good sign. Bill Clinton may or may not have been telling the truth when he claimed that during his grad student days he smoked grass but didn't inhale, though the "I can't inhale" excuse was a common way of deflecting the suspicion that you were one of those people who were *too uptight to get high.* In terms that a sax player like Clinton would understand, not getting high signaled a lack of emotional chops.

At the other extreme, there was always the worry that you might get *too* high and learn things about yourself that you didn't want to know. Freudian psychology posited the existence of the deep unconscious, the root cellar of the mind, where secrets were left to rot and molder like last year's potato crop. It was dangerous to poke around in there without professional guidance.

The drugs, in time, became more potent. In my experience this happened in the early part of 1965, when one of my boyfriend's fraternity brothers returned from a vacation with some thai sticks given to him by a high school friend who had been stationed in Southeast Asia. Around the same time, LSD made its first known appearance on campus, appropriately enough at the house of the independent fraternity Tau Alpha Omega, whose unofficial slogan was "TAO is the Way." Few of us thought of these substances as belonging in the same category as illegal drugs like heroin or cocaine, exotic substances known only by their evil reputations. Experimenting with psychedelics, as they came to be called, was more in the nature of recreational anthropology or, perhaps, an unsupervised psychology experiment. It turned out that under the right conditions, anyone could get high. And—for many, at least—it was fun! Certainly very few people found themselves pondering dark secrets about their misadventures with toilet training.

Drugs were a great social leveler. It no longer mattered how you looked, what kind of clothes you wore, who your family was or what high school you had attended. You didn't even need to develop social skills, because you could always have a party in your own mind. In short order, the world seemed to divide itself between "straights" and "heads." The former were hung up on dualistic thinking, judgmentalism, habits, schedules—all sorts of things that kept them perpetually anxious and wary. The heads were more spiritual and mellow. They didn't care about money or success, an indifference that seemed to infuriate those stuck in the other camp. In one sense at least, the heads were right. The straights, which included most everyone of the older generation, were fascinated by the unconscious, but it was a mysterious realm that they knew about almost exclusively from second-hand accounts. The heads, on the other hand, were like tourists who hitchhiked through the Khyber Pass and returned, exhilarated, to pronounce the journey completely safe.

Many parts of the country must have been on a similar schedule, because 1965 was the year that the youth culture underwent a seismic shift. The touchstone event occurred at the Newport Folk Festival that summer, when Bob Dylan plugged in his Fender guitar and wailed, "Ain't gonna work on Maggie's farm no more." The folkie purists booed. Electronic amplification was one of the artifacts of consumerism that we were supposed to be against. But the heads loved it. The old-style social rebels—politicos, folkies and the Beats—wore black turtlenecks and sat around in dank bars and coffeehouses, immersed in the doleful strains of "The Lonesome Death of Hattie Carroll" and "Peat Bog Soldiers."

The hippies wore bright colors and danced in the streets. It wasn't necessary to worry about repression when you could join Mr. Tambourine Man for a trip on his magic swirling ship. Even alienation, a favorite topic of college course reading lists, no longer seemed worth brooding about. Hillary Clinton expressed the new outlook in her now famous

Wellesley commencement speech when she dismissed conventional politics practiced as "the art of the possible" and called instead for the discovery of "more immediate, ecstatic and penetrating modes of living." As she put it, "We're not interested in social reconstruction; it's human reconstruction."

It was the dawning of the Age of Aquarius. Something called "flower power" would put an end to war, violence and even petty jealousies. People would live together communally and in peace. Couples could enjoy the freedom of open marriages. Like Tinkerbelle, all we had to do was close our eyes, envision a better world, and utopia would arrive. John Lennon expressed it best: Send out vibes of peace and love, and the world will come together. *Imagine* and it will come true.

The euphoria lasted for a few years. But, contrary to predictions, bad things kept on happening—notably the assassinations of Martin Luther King Jr. and Bobby Kennedy. For those who had bought into the promise of flower power, these events weren't just tragic, they were apocalyptic. Some few retreated in a conspiracy-hunting mode—the Oliver Stone syndrome. Some followed the lead of the Black Power movement and narrowed their focus, devoting themselves to causes based on identity politics. Most, in time, tried to move on by improvising a personal morality based on a compromise between the promise of human reconstruction and the reality of living in a world where actions still had consequences. In the beginning, this process was known as "selling out," though as the ranks of the purists thinned the phrase lost its currency. In the longer run, it gave rise to a fascination with the law, the court system and government regulation. Nothing was exactly immoral anymore, but some things might be indictable or, failing that, grounds for a civil suit. For a surprising number of Baby Boomers, the search for more ecstatic and penetrating modes of living soon led to law school.

Opinions about the Sixties are deeply divided and likely to remain so. Some see this as an era of liberation, whose gains were snuffed out— or nearly so—by conservative backlash. For others, it was an eruption of radical madness, the source of all that is wrong with America today. Regardless of their point of view, histories of the decade tend to concentrate on politics, treating the emergence of the New Left as the main story and reducing the psychedelic revolution and the human potential movement to background. But for all the noise they made, the committed activists were a very small group, never more than a few thousand. Most of the students who demonstrated against the war in Vietnam had no interest in launching a political revolution. When the activists began to talk about "bringing the war home," their support melted away.

For every committed New Left activist there were thousands who dropped acid, and tens of thousands affected by the human potential movement, which promised to show us how to "get high without drugs" through encounter groups, communal living, or guru-led religious movements. Even the New Left itself was less about politics than about authenticity. James Miller's history of the movement, *Democracy Is in the Streets,* quotes SDS founder, Sharon Jeffrey, as recalling, "In the beginning, we were about discovering self-worth."[2] When the New Left began to disintegrate, some activists simply switched over to another branch of the human potential movement. One notable defector was Rennie Davis, an organizer of the demonstrations at the 1968 Democratic convention in Chicago. Davis traveled to India and returned as a disciple of the teenage guru Maharaj-Ji, who taught that "God is the filter on your carburetor."

The usual view of the Flower Power era is that a great shift in consciousness just happened—touched off, perhaps, by drugs, and without any mainstream historical roots. This is the version suggested by the 1998 film *Pleasantville.* A couple of teenagers fall into a time warp and arrive in the blandly conformist village of Pleasantville, causing it to morph from black and white into color, and opening up dazzling, if sometimes troubling, vistas of self-awareness. Sex is discovered, along with passion, art, independent thinking and, eventually, violence.

That is pretty much how I remember it. Rationally, however, I know it can't have been so. Americans in the Fifties may have watched black and white television, but they lived in color. They experienced the gamut of emotions and even had fun—perhaps more than we do today. Marilyn Monroe standing over a subway grating and Elvis rotating his pelvis on the *Ed Sullivan Show* inspired as many erotic fantasies as Britney Spears, though she has to work harder.

Certainly, the utopian illusions of the Age of Aquarius didn't spring full-blown into the minds of the psychedelic generation with that first toke of grass. Whether or not we realized it, we were part of a mass experiment in applied psychology. In the 1950s, behaviorists told children they must adjust to the values of the majority and strive to be "normal."

Meanwhile, intellectuals submitted to psychoanalysis and adapted its insights to their own fields, from literary criticism to sociology. Freud was radical in offering a secular, medicalized model of personality, yet he didn't directly challenge social norms any more than behaviorists did. In the traditional view of the self, the rational mind is the referee in a battle between conscience and desire. In Freudian terms, the struggle is between the superego and the id. When this goes awry, the result is repression, leading to neuroses and mental illness. Still, the id cannot be allowed to rule. Suppressing its desires is the price we pay for civilization. Freudianism accepted prevailing mores, but also changed along with them. Dr. Benjamin Spock's best-selling *Baby and Child Care,* which introduced American parents to "penis envy" and the "Oedipus complex," warned that making a child feel guilty about masturbation might be traumatizing and lead to lifelong sexual inhibitions.

While Freudian concepts were settling into popular culture, academic psychology was in flux. The horrors of Nazism led some to reexamine the ideas of Alfred Adler, who had stressed the human drive to dominance. The émigré psychoanalyst Erich Fromm borrowed from Marx to elaborate his theory that late-stage capitalism was creating "authoritarian personalities" and anxiety-ridden masses who submitted to their domination. Fromm and Karen Horney, author of the influential book *The Neurotic Personality of Our Time,* drew from anthropologists Ruth Benedict and Margaret Mead to indict Western civilization and the patriarchal family as causes of mental dysfunction. Fritz Perls established the Gestalt Therapy Institute along with Paul Goodman, author of *Growing Up Absurd.* Despite a grudge against Freud, who had dismissed him as a nonentity, Perls claimed to be merely correcting and extending the master's ideas; yet he was opening the door to a host of anti-intellectual influences. Freud's ideas may have been essentially unverifiable, but psychoanalysis at least encouraged a reasoned examination of the patient's life. Gestalt therapy, by contrast, claimed that insights could arise from throwing off cultural conditioning and expressing whatever one felt at the moment.

By the 1960s the stage was set for a radically simplified view of human nature, influenced by existentialism but with a unique American spin. To maximize one's potential, one had to throw off the distorting influences of society and discover and nurture one's innate good self. While psychology and psychiatry as taught in the universities would remain splintered, the new concept of the self quickly gained popular acceptance, filling the void left by the erosion of traditional religious values and disillusionment with Marxism. The new theory described human nature as it ought to be, not necessarily as it was. Supposedly, once the detritus of repressive social institutions and moral codes was swept away, people would be free to develop their inborn goodness. "Authentic" human beings would build a society without hypocrisy, prejudice or exploitation.

These ideas emerged from a school of thought known as humanistic psychology. Harvard psychologist Timothy Leary, though he operated on the fringes of the movement, became its high-pressure salesman. When it came to popularizing a new way of seeing the self, the psychedelic drugs he advocated worked a lot faster than the usual method of spreading ideas. But Leary was just offering a more daring take on the ideas of others. Brandeis University psychologist Abraham Maslow, the chief theoretician of humanistic psychology, had already laid the foundation for the revolution with his theory of self-actualization.

In August 1960, two years before the publication of *Toward a Psychology of Being*, which would establish him as a counterculture guru, Maslow offered a blueprint for the dawning of the Age of Aquarius in an interview broadcast over the Pacifica Radio network. During a leisurely conversation with his friend Frank Manuel, Maslow speculated that America might be on the brink of creating a "realistic" utopia, which he called Eupsychia—the land of healthy psyches. In contrast to earlier utopias, it would reflect the needs and desires of all people, including women.

Maslow's intellectual roots were in the left. As late as 1960 he still believed that Marxian socialism, even in "fairly authoritarian" varieties, was the best form of government for underdeveloped countries. But in pondering the future of American society, he worried about many of the same trends that preoccupy today's social conservatives, including the nihilism of modern art, the debasement of popular culture, and the reflexive anti-Americanism of so many in academia. And, like them, Maslow blamed these ills on "cultural relativism"—the belief that standards of right and wrong are the product of a particular culture.

As a young man, Maslow had befriended Margaret Mead and Ruth Benedict, who made a life's work of spreading the message of cultural relativism. Maslow admired both women, especially Benedict, and he did postdoctoral fieldwork among the Blackfoot Indians under her supervision. He agreed that Americans could learn important lessons from other cultures, but didn't accept the idea that good and evil varied from place to place. He told the Pacifica audience: "Instead of cultural relativity, I am implying that there are basic, underlying standards which are cross-cultural, which transcend cultures and which are broadly human." In the past, the human race "looked for guiding values, for principles of right and wrong outside of [itself], to a God, to some sort of sacred book, to a ruling class"; but it was no longer possible for educated people to read the scriptures literally or believe in revealed truth. The problem with the social sciences, on the other hand, was that they were morally neutral, offering "no criterion for criticizing, let us say, the well-adjusted Nazi in Nazi Germany."[3]

Maslow believed he had the solution to this conundrum. He proposed that some absolute values are rooted in human biology. We are all born with "innate instincts" for good, which reach their highest expression in certain individuals who successfully complete a process he called self-actualization. By studying the lives of these people, "the best of humanity," and following the dictates of "the God within," we can discover a universal set of values.

Maslow's optimism set him apart from the relativists and the neo-Freudians. He could rail against the malign influences of "our cockeyed society," but still maintain a deep faith in the promise of American life. As he noted in his journal around this time, people in many parts of the world struggled to get enough to eat. Being absorbed with the challenge of survival, they weren't ready to search for higher values. But the United States stood atop the "hierarchy" of world societies because it could afford to satisfy the basic physical and emotional needs of all its citizens, including the need for self-esteem.

During the Pacifica broadcast, Maslow described Eupsychia as an imaginary desert-isle kingdom of a thousand self-actualized individuals. As his listeners could guess, he hoped to see America remade on the eupsychian model. Affluence, he thought, made people less selfish and freed them to concentrate on the pursuit of higher values. It wasn't necessary to have a plan for the ideal society, for once people set aside mistrust and competitiveness, institutions would transform themselves. This sounded much like Flower Power: Believe that people are good and it will become so. And the message was delivered in avuncular, reassuring tones by the chairman of the Brandeis University psychology department, a scholar whose theory of human motivation was being applied in fields ranging from education to corporate management.

Chapter 1

The Rise of
Relativism

When Abe Maslow was a young man, cultural relativism was the cutting edge of social science. The originator of the concept, Franz Boas, chairman of the Department of Anthropology at Columbia University, was a towering figure. An outspoken opponent of racism and anti-Semitism, "Papa Franz" fought to put anthropology on a more scientific basis. He became a mentor to talented Jews and women, giving them a chance to further their careers at a time when the doors of academia were largely closed to them. For better or worse, he also personified the belief that the true intellectual must be a cosmopolitan, upholding the interests of science and universal humanitarian principles over parochial concerns such as loyalty to community or country.

Born in 1858, Boas grew up in Germany, where he studied science, philosophy and geography before signing up for an Arctic surveying expedition in 1883. During the course of this adventure, he lived among the Eskimos of Baffin Island, learned their language, and came away convinced that "although the character of their life is so rude as compared to civilized life, the Eskimo is a man as we are; that his feelings, his virtues, and his shortcomings are based in human nature, like ours."[1]

Eighteen months after this return home from the Arctic, Boas emigrated to the United States, where he joined his uncle Dr. Abraham Jacobi, a prominent New York City pediatrician. Settling at last on the field of anthropology, he finished his doctorate and did fieldwork among the Indians of the Pacific Northwest. Boas was far from the first white scholar to admire primitive peoples and appreciate the often tragic consequences of their contacts with contemporary civilization. What set Boas apart from other researchers was less his attitude toward other cultures than a grudge against his own. He came from a family that regarded social revolution almost as a duty. Dr. Jacobi, in an earlier life, had been a friend of Marx and Engels and had served time in jail for his part in the Revolution of 1848. Boas himself explained:

> My parents had broken through the shackles of dogma.... Thus, I was spared the struggle against religious dogma that besets the lives of so many young people.... The psychological origins of the implicit belief in the authority of tradition, which was so foreign to my mind and which shocked me at an earlier time, became a problem that engaged my thoughts for many years. In fact, my whole outlook upon social life is determined by the question: how can we recognize the shackles that tradition has laid upon us? For when we recognize them, we are also able to break them.[2]

When Boas joined the faculty of Columbia University in 1896, American anthropology was controlled by the Darwinists—more accurately known as cultural evolutionists because their school of thought actually predated Darwin. The cultural evolutionists sought to explain the social and biological forces underlying historical trends. Typical of the school was Henry Lewis Morgan, who saw societies as evolving from a state of savagery (nomadism) through barbarism (agriculture, with the clan as the primary social unit) and on to civilization (marked by the development of writing, codified laws and monogamy). Central to the evolutionist way of thinking was the belief that civilization was progressing toward ever more humane forms of social organization. Almost inevitably, it glorified Anglo-Saxon culture and values as the acme of human accomplishment so far.

Cultural evolutionism certainly had its shortcomings. Like so much social science theory, it was a thick stew concocted out of meager scraps of fact and large helpings of dubious supposition. At the time, the science of genetics was in its infancy, which didn't prevent the proponents of cultural evolutionism from making sweeping statements about race and heredity, whose importance they greatly overestimated. At times their rhetoric was blatantly racist, especially when they got involved in political debates like the controversy over immigration from Central and Southern Europe that happened to be raging during Boas's early years at Columbia. Those of us who attended school during the 1950s may recall using outdated textbooks that reprinted William Z. Ripley's comparison of the long-headed (and, thus, presumably superior) Nordics, the round-skulled Alpines, and the positively beetle-browed Mediterranean type. Darwinist biologist H. S. Jennings warned that interracial marriage could lead to physically deformed offspring, and the popularizer Madison Grant, a lawyer by training, published a remarkably bigoted screed called *Passing of the Great Race,* which went so far as to suggest that Jesus Christ may have been of Nordic stock.

As a Jew and a Central European, Boas took such claims personally. But he seems to have been at least as incensed by the spirit of Anglo-Saxon triumphalism that animated so many of his colleagues, men he considered second-rate provincials at best. He took on the evolutionists by advancing the equally extreme position that culture was purely a social construct, which owed nothing whatsoever to differences in race or heredity. The debate between the evolutionists and Boas is often discussed in terms of the nature vs. nurture conundrum. An evolutionist would argue, for example, that factors like the social status of women or the centrality of the family unit are influenced by biological differences between the sexes. The Boasian would counter that only environmental factors matter, and he would not be surprised to discover individual cultures in which women hold power and parents feel no particular attachment to their own children.

But perhaps the most important byproduct of the triumph of Boasian anthropology was that it stripped away the faith in the inevitability of progress that had done so much to fuel the optimism and energy of early-twentieth-century America. The Boasian school made no distinctions between "higher" and "lower" cultures. Nor did it attempt to explain why some civilizations flourish and expand while others remain localized or disappear altogether. What can't be explained often comes to seem illegitimate and even criminal, if only by default. And there are indications that this is what Boas himself believed. In an 1894 speech to the anthropology section of the American Association for the Advancement of Science, Boas portrayed Western civilization as a kind of cancer, uniquely destructive in its impact. Whereas in earlier times, meetings of cultures may have been relatively benign, Boas explained, the spread of "the culture represented by the modern white" had given the world little beyond the proliferation of lethal diseases and a flood of cheap, mass-produced goods. Moreover, "the rapid dissemination of Europeans over the whole world cut short all promising beginnings which had arisen in various regions."[3]

The notion that cultural clashes were once benign would no doubt come as news to victims of the Mongol hordes, Viking raiding parties or the armies of Rameses the Great. Nor is it clear why "white" civilization, uniquely, should be held responsible for wiping out cultures that never existed but might, theoretically, have come into being. The suggestion that the spread of Western civilization had tragic implications was exactly the sort of broad, unscientific generalization that Boas objected to in the works of the Darwinists. One can't help noticing, however, that it provided a justification for the promotion of anthropological studies. Boas imbued his students with an urgent sense of mission. They must make haste to travel to the most remote parts of the globe and document threatened cultures in the hope of discovering "promising" solutions to the social problems that continued to vex Europeans and Americans.

Cultural relativism—the premise that standards of good and evil vary from one culture to the next—is to some degree a truism. Whether Franz Boas was also a moral relativist is debatable. A Neo-Kantian, Boas was educated in a tradition that upheld the existence of natural law, and he believed that human beings possessed a moral faculty called *Herzensbildung*, or structure of the heart, which gave them an innate awareness of right and wrong. Presumably, therefore, right and wrong existed as ideals, independent of culture.[4]

However, as a matter of opinion, if not necessarily theory, Boas found some cultures more sympathetic than others. Although he could enter into the minds of Baffin Island Eskimos and Kwakiutl Indians, he seemed utterly incapable of empathizing with the culture of his adopted homeland. A socialist, an atheist and a pacifist, he was against almost everything his native-born colleagues held sacred, and he wasn't slow to take issue with the prevailing wisdom. He explained in one article that America's acquisition of colonies during the Spanish-American War had permanently soured him on the American dream. He publicly opposed the entry of the United States into World War I, and his ensuing battle with the president of Columbia University led to his decision to teach his undergraduate courses at the women's college, Barnard, instead of at Columbia College.

The evolutionists had a tendency to see race as the explanation for everything that had happened in history. Boas often took the opposite position, identifying the "racial snobbery" of Anglo-Americans as the root cause of social conflict—for instance, the conflict over immigration. In reality, this debate probably had less to do with arguments over the size of the Central European brain than with the use of imported labor to drive wages down and keep workers from organizing. Immigrants were filling low-wage jobs that might otherwise have gone to native-born workers, including blacks. Such economic and social considerations, however, rarely intruded on Boas's thoughts.

Boas was perhaps the first to promote black studies as a means to improving race relations. In a letter to Andrew Carnegie, he suggested creating an "African Institute" that would showcase the accomplishments of African civilization. Addressing the all-black 1906 graduating class of Atlanta University, he deprecated the strategies of education and self-help, telling the graduates that it was useless to court the approval of their "white neighbors," which would never be forthcoming. Instead, they should look for inspiration in the glories of the African past. His evocative description of the "old Negro kingdoms" of West Africa made a deep impression on one of his listeners, W. E. B. Du Bois, who later wrote, "I was too astonished to speak. All of this I had never heard."[5]

The dueling scar on Boas's cheek, a souvenir of his student days in Germany, testified to his combative nature. He thought of himself as a perennial outsider, the victim of both anti-German and anti-Jewish prejudice. In fact, he was rather well connected. His uncle, Dr. Jacobi, had married a daughter of publisher George Putnam, and as a result Boas was related by marriage to the influential director of Harvard's Peabody Museum. Adept at academic politics, Boas succeeded in placing his students in influential positions in universities and professional organizations. Many of his clashes with colleagues had less to do with theory than with battles over academic turf. Others were the result of his famous temper. Boas was one of those humanitarians who always seem to be angry at somebody. After World War I, when a young graduate student, Ralph Linton, made the mistake of appearing in uniform to apply for a job, Boas treated him so rudely that Linton never forgave him. In 1918, Boas wrote to the *Nation* announcing that he planned to vote Socialist as a protest against the Espionage Act, which, he complained, had destroyed freedom of speech and created a climate of fear. A year later, in a letter to the same publication, he denounced four American anthropologists as spies and called for them to be drummed out of the profession because they had, allegedly, shared information about conditions in Mexico with the U.S. government.

Boas sounded very much like a cultural relativist when he publicly decried the "intolerant attitude" of Americans who failed to understand that the individual liberties they enjoyed might not be appropriate for other nations. The American, he wrote, "claims that the form of his own Government is the best, not only for himself but for all of mankind.... I have always been of the opinion that we have no right to impose our ideals on other nations, no matter how strange it may seem to us that they enjoy the kind of life they lead." However, such sentiments did not stop Boas from finding some forms of government more attuned to his universalist principles. In his later years, he signed so many pro-Soviet petitions that columnist Walter Winchell nicknamed him "Columbia's number one Commie."[6]

Margaret Mead and Ruth Benedict weren't necessarily Boas's most important pupils from the point of view of academic anthropology, but over the years they did the yeoman's work of popularizing his views, in the process adding a few psychosexual twists of their own.

A woman who planned to become famous even before she had decided on a profession, Margaret Mead became a public figure who for decades personified anthropology in the minds of most Americans. In her later years Mead transformed herself into a Druid-priestess figure who invariably wore earth-toned dresses, a flowing cape and Hobbit-like shoes. As an all-purpose expert, she held forth in the pages of the *Ladies' Home Journal* and other popular magazines on childrearing and sexuality, but also on UFOs (suggesting that aliens are keeping watch over us to make sure we don't set off a nuclear chain reaction) as well as astrology and telepathic communication with houseplants.

Mead understood very well that a scholar has influence in the public sphere only insofar as she is provocative and entertaining. When I heard her speak at Swarthmore College in the mid-1960s, she created a stir by suggesting that placing cameras on street corners and in public buildings would be an effective way to reduce crime; Samoan villagers didn't object to having their neighbors know their business, so why should

we? Video surveillance was a novel idea at the time and it was impossible to tell whether Mead actually favored the plan, but she had certainly
sized up her audience and knew that it would get their attention. During the informal discussion that followed, Mead perched on a sofa in the
Commons Room, as serene as visiting royalty, while overexcited students
huffed and puffed over their objections.

Ruth Fulton Benedict, by contrast, was a reclusive woman who
saved her private thoughts for her journals. Born in 1887, Benedict claimed
that her earliest memory was of being lifted up to view her dead father
lying in his coffin. She was just twenty-one months old, and her father,
Dr. Frederick Fulton, a homeopathic physician, had succumbed to a mysterious fever contracted during the course of his medical studies. His
widow, Bertrice, was left the sole support of Ruth and her younger sister,
Margery. While bringing up her daughters, Bertrice worked as a schoolteacher in St. Louis, the principal of a private academy in Minnesota, and
a librarian in Buffalo, New York. According to Ruth, her mother never
got over the loss of her husband and gave herself over to a "cult of grief."
Whether or not this was so, Ruth herself was certainly preoccupied with
death. In an autobiographical essay written in middle age, she describes
her lifelong awareness of the contrast between her mother's reality of everyday cares and sadness on the one hand, and "the world of my father, which
was the world of death and which was beautiful."[7]

A withdrawn child, Ruth spent her free time with an imaginary
playmate in a fantasy realm she called the Delicious Mountains. When
she started school, her teachers recognized that she was partially deaf,
perhaps as a result of contracting measles as an infant. In spite of her
hearing impairment, Ruth excelled in the classroom. At home, however,
she was subject to fearsome tantrums. Screaming and kicking at anything that got in her way, she would rage on until she was overcome by
the urge to vomit, or until she wore herself out and cried herself to sleep.
One day when she was eleven, her frantic mother forced her to swear on
a Bible that she would never lose her temper again. Amazingly, the spells
ended, though Ruth remained subject to mood swings and migraine
headaches.

A gift from a generous alumna enabled Ruth and Margery to attend
Vassar College, where their course of study included Latin, German, history, English, astronomy, philosophy and ethics. The student body at
the time was divided between a large number of young women who saw

college as a prelude to marriage and a much smaller group who planned to continue their studies and have a career, usually in teaching. Ruth had ambition, but no plans. Graduating third in her class, one place behind Margery, she departed on a tour of Europe, paid for by another benefactor, then tried social work for a while. Eventually, at twenty-four, she found herself teaching English at Miss Orton's School for Girls in Pasadena, California.

In the journal she was keeping around this time, Ruth protested against talk of the importance of character. To her, character was just another name for the mask that she wore to hide from the world: "What was my character anyway? My real *me* was a creature I dared not look upon—it was terrorized by loneliness, frozen by a sense of futility, obsessed by a longing to *stop*. No one had ever heard of that Me."[8]

Tall, awkward and difficult to get to know, Ruth dreaded ending up as an old maid. "It really isn't a joke at all. It's quite tragically serious," she wrote. "There were three of them on the faculty. They retold all their twenty-year-old conversations with men—conversations that of course *might* have developed into love affairs *if* they'd allowed the liberty—so that you might be led to realize they were not old maids by necessity." Benedict dreamed of finding a "great love" that would motivate her to commit herself fully to marriage and motherhood. "To me it seems a very terrible thing to be a woman," she wrote. "There is one crown which perhaps is worth it all—a great love, a quiet home and children. We all know that is all that is worth while, and yet we must peg away, showing off our wares on the market, if we have money, or manufacturing careers for ourselves if we haven't."[9]

For a time Ruth managed to persuade herself that she had found her great love in Stanley Benedict, a researcher at Cornell Medical School and the brother of a Vassar classmate. The couple married in 1914 and moved to Long Island. Within four months of the wedding Ruth was once again tormented by her "blue devils" of rage, boredom and suicidal impulses. She longed for a baby, in the hope that motherhood would give her life a purpose, but she was unable to become pregnant. Meanwhile, she wrote poetry, which she eventually would begin to publish under the pseudonym Ann Singleton, but her other efforts to make a career as a writer were unfocused. She tried her hand at detective stories, drawing on her husband's knowledge of chemistry for inspiration, but her fiction was lifeless and unconvincing. Next, she began a biographical study of three independent women from different eras: feminist Mary Wollstonecraft, transcendentalist Margaret Fuller, and the South African novelist Olive Schreiner. Unfortunately, Benedict fell prey to the occupational disease of the biographer—projecting her own conflicts onto her subjects; and since those conflicts were never resolved, the work couldn't be finished either. Judith Modell, a close student of Benedict's work, comments that her treatment of Wollstonecraft's love for Gilbert Imlay reflected her own fear of the destructive power of passion: "The idea that sexuality, especially heterosexuality, undid the 'whole self' persisted in Benedict's writings."[10]

By 1918, Stanley was beginning to lose patience with Ruth's moodiness, and she was discouraged about making a career as a writer. Deciding that the time had come to resume her education, she studied educational philosophy with John Dewey and took a course called Sexual Ethnology taught by the colorfully eccentric Elsie Clews Parsons, who had done extensive fieldwork among the Pueblo Indians. Eventually, she found her way to the anthropology department at Columbia, where Franz Boas recognized her ability and designed a program that made it possible for her to finish her doctoral degree in a year and a half, with minimal fieldwork.

Benedict became Boas's teaching assistant in 1922, at a time when the old lion, "Papa Franz," was past sixty and beset by family tragedies. His son was killed in a train accident, his daughter succumbed to polio, and his wife fell ill, dying in 1930. Benedict gradually made herself indispensable, taking over Boas's heavy administrative duties, teaching his graduate seminars and supervising his students' plans for fieldwork. As a married woman in her mid-thirties, however, she didn't fit into Boas's long-term plans for his department. He passed over her to appoint another woman to a tenure-track position, while she held only an unpaid lectureship, surviving on outside research grants and financial support from Stanley, whom she now saw only on weekends.

In spite of her uncertain status, Benedict was fiercely loyal to her mentor and, at times, more of a Boasian than he was. In 1924, she took over the editorship of the *Journal of American Folklore* and promptly banished "white folklore" from its pages. Her policy led to a rebellion by sponsors and contributors that kept the publication in a state of crisis. In 1939, when Boas was near death, she would dutifully take up the task of writing a book that summarized his ideas about race for a general audience.

The book is credited with popularizing the term "racism," unfamiliar to most readers at the time. It also took the now commonplace position that racial prejudice could be eliminated only by an activist government committed to ending poverty and guaranteeing material security for all.

As Benedict saw it, the mission of Boasian anthropology was to make the world safe for difference. While Papa Franz was concerned with orphan cultures, she was more interested in individual misfits or, as she called them, "deviants." Benedict counted herself in this category. For one thing, she was attracted to other women, though it is far from clear when she first acted on her desires. From today's perspective, it's tempting to think that Benedict's homosexuality, a secret she did not discuss explicitly even in her journal, explains her perception of herself as an outsider. It would seem, however, that Benedict was at least as concerned with her sense of herself as a spiritual misfit. Like most depressives, she felt distanced from other people, from daily experience and from her own emotions. Her passions found expression only in the interior monologue of the "Real Me," which she translated into poetry filled with over-ripe adjectives and strangled metaphors.

Her biographer Hilary Lapsley observes that Benedict took a maternal interest in female students and Jews, who could expect to face prejudice in the job market. More specifically, she was attracted to students who were, in some sense, spiritual "deviants" like herself. "She struggled to find them jobs in the unfavorable economic climate," writes Lapsley, "lent them money, books, even her car on occasions; she listened to their woes, engaged them to take risks, wrote them letters in the field, drank with them, and made them coffee."[11]

Benedict's students were rarely neutral on her merits. Those not part of the favored group often found her lectures vague and her manner almost eerily distant. Deafness made listening a chore for her, and this may explain why she habitually tuned out people she deemed unworthy of the effort. Frequently, the students Benedict found uninteresting were white male gentiles, a group she referred to as "the boys." But anyone who threatened the interests of Boasian social science could quickly become a bore in her eyes.

The most notorious example of this phenomenon is Henrietta Schmerler, who was murdered while doing fieldwork on the White Mountain Apache reservation in eastern Arizona in July 1931. The verdict of the local authorities was that Schmerler had violated Apache mores by behaving provocatively, asking questions about sexual practices and accepting an invitation to go riding with a young man. In the wake of the murder, Schmerler's family and the press demanded to know why Franz Boas had dispatched a student into a dangerous area without a proper research plan or support system. In fact, the decision to approve Schmerler's project had been Benedict's, and was made despite a mild demurral from Boas, who wondered if the reservation wasn't rather an untamed area. As the trial of Schmerler's killer approached, Benedict was horrified by the thought that she, or even Boas himself, might be called to testify. In a letter to Margaret Mead she fretted over the prospect: "Papa Franz as the butt of an Arizona murder trial that has carte blanche to play up the motifs of sex and race!" On learning that the trial would not require her presence, Benedict celebrated by holding an impromptu party in her apartment, opening a bottle of Cointreau to toast the good news.

Ultimately, of course, the Schmerler case was not about "motifs of sex and race"; it was about murder. It never seemed to occur to Benedict that it was the department's responsibility to seek justice on behalf of a woman who could no longer speak for herself. Her and Mead's lack of concern for the victim shocks even their very sympathetic biographer Hilary Lapsley. "In Ruth's and Margaret's eyes, it seems, anyone who violated the mores of a culture was fully to blame for the consequences," she comments. Benedict's chilly attitude also infuriated the Schmerlers, and as recently as the early 1990s one member of the family was still researching the incident, hoping to find new evidence that would restore his great-aunt's reputation.

When Ruth began her doctoral work at Columbia she rented a furnished room near the campus. Over the years, she continued to spend weekends at the home that she and Stanley maintained in Bedford Hills, New York, and the couple even vacationed together in New Hampshire. But Stanley longed for a home that would be a respite from his long hours in the laboratory. Seeing his wife's growing independence as a signal that she might be ready to release him from his marriage vows, he hinted that she might want to file for divorce. (It would have been thought ungentlemanly for him to divorce an unwilling wife, and under New York law at the time, such a thing was impossible without proof of adultery.) Ruth, however, was devastated by Stanley's sexual rejection and clung to the skeleton of her marriage. In 1930, when Stanley had fallen in love with another woman and insisted on getting a place of his own, Ruth even took over the task of decorating his new apartment. One day in 1936, Benedict picked up a newspaper and learned that her husband, just fifty-two years old, had died of a heart attack. After a court fight with Stanley's sisters, she inherited his estate.

Meanwhile, Benedict had been pursuing other relationships. Beginning in 1922, she began to rely on fellow anthropologist Edward Sapir for emotional support. One of Boas's most brilliant pupils and, like Ruth, a gifted part-time poet, Sapir worked for the Canadian Geographical Survey and was struggling with a domestic tragedy. His young wife, Florence, suffered from mental illness as well as a cascading series of unattractive physical maladies. When Sapir brought Florence to New York for treatment, Ruth babysat for their children, and during periods when he was at home in Ottawa, he and Ruth exchanged batches of poems. Many intimate subjects, including Ruth's suicidal impulses, were touched upon in their letters but always delicately, in the guise of critiquing one another's poetry.

Almost simultaneously, Ruth was developing a romantic attachment to her favorite pupil, Margaret Mead. In contrast to Benedict, who was haunted by the depressive's sense of being stuck on the fringes of life, Margaret's days were packed with melodrama. She got to know Ruth shortly after the suicide of a Barnard friend, Marie Bloomfield. Margaret had planned to look after the emotionally fragile Marie, recently released from the hospital after a six-week stay, but her good intentions were thwarted when another friend was stricken with hysterical blindness after a difficult physics exam. By the time Margaret got around to visiting Bloomfield, she was dead from a self-administered dose of cyanide. Ruth wrote Mead a letter of consolation, and the two women found common ground in venting their anger against the "adult world of doctors and deans" who insisted that Bloomfield's suicide was evidence that she was not in her right mind. Ruth "was the one person who understood that suicide might be a noble and conscious choice," Mead would recall.[12]

Born in 1901, Mead was the first child of parents with advanced ideas. Her mother, Emily Fogg Mead, was a passionate social reformer who had studied for a doctorate in sociology. Edward Mead pursued affairs but doted on his little girl, whom he nicknamed "the Punk." Margaret originally planned to become a psychologist. She chattered glibly about the Oedipus complex and repression, but found the brand of psychology taught in her courses at Barnard stodgy and mired in social conservatism.

Benedict was fifteen years Mead's senior and not the sort of person one would expect a romantic like Margaret to find attractive. A lanky woman with potentially striking features, Ruth seemed to go out of her way to make herself invisible. Her style was not masculine but mousy and rather spinsterish, and one dowdy blue dress of hers that had been seen on many occasions was the subject of a running joke among her students. But Benedict did know how to make anthropology alluring. Her vision of the field's future was imbued with a sense of moral urgency. The wisdom of primitive cultures had to be gleaned now, before it was corrupted by contact with European civilization. Of course, anthropology also involved opportunities for travel to exotic destinations—far preferable to spending years doing statistical analysis of psychological test scores.

Mead later wrote that in all the schools she attended as a girl, "I felt as if I were in some way taking part in a theatrical performance in which I had a role to play and had to find actors to take the other parts." So, too, as an adult she went about brusquely casting supporting players in the drama of her life.[13]

She had been engaged since she was sixteen to Luther Cressman, who was studying to be an Episcopalian minister. The wedding was planned for September 1923, a few months after Margaret graduated from Barnard. During the course of the summer, Margaret and Ruth began a clandestine love affair. Even before this development, it was obvious to everyone except Cressman himself that Margaret was not in love with him. Edward Mead offered his daughter a trip around the world if she would cancel the wedding, and when this bribe attempt failed, he refused to pay her graduate school tuition. Ruth managed to scrounge up $300 to pay the bill, and Margaret went through with the wedding. On her honeymoon, once the formalities were taken care of, she moved to a separate bedroom, informing Luther that she had a book review to finish and needed privacy so she could think.

But while Margaret could be amazingly self-centered, at this time in her life she was far from in control. She was a young woman with two possibly incompatible goals. She wanted very much to be married, with a companionable husband and a family of her own. But she also dreamed of an important career in anthropology. Luther, who took pride in his enlightened ideas, did not object to having a wife who planned to go off alone to the South Pacific to do fieldwork among the Samoan islanders. Such a man could not easily be replaced. Marriage to Luther also established Margaret's heterosexual credentials. Her view was that same-sex liaisons didn't really matter so long as they did not interfere with one's adjustment to heterosexuality later on. Perhaps she also wanted to set some boundaries on her relationship with Benedict. Ruth had been a lonely woman for a long time, and one suspects that she thought of her secret connection with Margaret as something more than a tender interlude.

Margaret Mead met Edward Sapir at a conference in Toronto, a few months after his wife died. They were immediately attracted to each other. A romantic attachment developed over the course of the following year, and in July 1925 they agreed to meet in New York City and check into a hotel together. The tryst proved anticlimactic in every respect. Edward was too overcome by guilt to enjoy sex with a married woman, and he began pressing Margaret to divorce Luther and cancel her planned fieldwork in Samoa. Margaret, it seems, had seen herself as the personification of the New Woman, courageous and even noble in her willingness to give herself sexually to an older man without asking anything in return. It hadn't occurred to her that Edward would take their dalliance so seriously. Recently widowed, he imagined that he had found a new life partner and a stepmother for his orphaned children.

In retrospect, it's hard to think of Margaret Mead as frail, but she was a petite, emotionally intense young woman who had been recently diagnosed by her doctor as suffering from nervous fatigue. For Sapir, who had watched his wife's mental stability deteriorate along with her physical health, the doctor's warning had an ominous ring. Knowing nothing of Margaret and Ruth's affair, he turned to Benedict for help, begging her to help him talk Boas into canceling Margaret's imminent departure for Samoa.

Margaret found this interference irrational and peculiar. "After all, men were not told to give up field work to stay home and have children!" she huffed. Busy with last-minute preparations for her departure, she decided that she had no time to see Edward and let him down gently. Meanwhile, it fell to Ruth to advise Boas by letter that Sapir's worries about Margaret's health were overstated.

In the midst of this tempest, Ruth returned from her summer vacation to spend a long-planned day in New York with Edward. He could talk about nothing but how wonderful Margaret was and how much he loved her. Moreover, he confided, Margaret was in love with him. Ruth would call this the "worst day of her life." But, of course, she knew a few things that Edward could never, in his wildest imagination, have suspected. That very evening, Margaret would take leave of her husband and board a train for San Francisco, the first leg of her journey to the South Pacific. Ruth, departing from New York, would already be on board the same train. Traveling west together, the two women had scheduled time for a quick trip to the Grand Canyon before Ruth headed for the Zuni pueblo, where she was to spend the summer collecting material for a study of Zuni myths. While taking in the idyllic scenery, the two women agreed on a plan for discouraging Edward Sapir. Margaret would write him a letter telling him candidly that she didn't believe in exclusive relationships.[14]

Ironically, the assignment Franz Boas had given Mead for her Samoan fieldwork involved the question of whether free love could make people happy. Mead had hoped to study child development, but Boas instructed her to investigate the sex lives of teenage girls: Was the emotional turmoil of adolescence inevitable? Or was it caused by the repressive customs of white civilization?

The sexual habits of primitive peoples was a novel area of research and a formidable subject for a novice who had been given virtually no instruction in fieldwork methodology. All Mead had going for her was youth and an abundance of self-confidence; to Boas she must have seemed little more than an adolescent herself. Mead, on her part, was fortified by her belief that the culture of the Samoans was "simple," and therefore capable of being "covered" in a brief period of time. After a stop in Hawaii, where she was briefed by the curator of the Bishop Museum, Mead arrived in Pago Pago, the capital of American Samoa. She moved into the rundown hotel made famous by Somerset Maugham's play *Rain,* and found a Samoan nurse, Miss Pepe, who was willing to give her a one-hour language lesson every afternoon.

In November 1925, she sailed on a U.S. Navy minesweeper to the fourteen-square-mile island of Ta'ū, where she occupied a room in the naval dispensary. The girls who gathered on her porch in the evenings were hardly untouched by "white culture." They happened to be students at a school run by the London Missionary Society and most of them lived in the household of the local Samoan pastor, who made sure that they were closely chaperoned. Mead, moreover, was hampered by distractions, including a hurricane and side trips to nearby islands. She originally planned to do detailed interviews with 66 girls, but by March 14, 1926, she had fragmentary notes on just 25. Still, she wrote to Boas announcing, "My problem is practically completed." "Because I feel absolutely safe in generalizing from the material I have," she went on, she planned to cut short her fieldwork and omit detailed statistical studies. Mead left Ta'ū in April, and on May 10 she departed Pago Pago on a ship bound for Australia. Her plan was to return home via Europe, where Luther had been studying on a one-year fellowship.[15]

The romantic misalliances of the Boasians continued to be more exotic than anything going on in Samoa. On the ship taking her to Europe, Margaret met a New Zealander named Reo Fortune. A brooding Heathcliff type, he was tall and lacking in social polish but fiercely intellectual. A psychologist by training, Fortune had studied the interpretation of dreams, a subject of abiding interest to Mead. Inevitably, romance blossomed as the ship made its leisurely way from Ceylon to Aden to Sicily, and by the time it reached Marseilles, where Luther was waiting on the dock, Fortune was prepared to change the course of his life. Margaret and Reo were so engrossed in arguing about his demand that she come to England with him immediately that they were the last passengers to disembark.

In Reo Fortune, Margaret had found a potential husband who could also become her professional partner. Together, they would be able to work in remote parts of the world where it would be difficult if not impossible for a woman to conduct research alone. Still, she had not quite made up her mind about her new lover. Reo did not want children. Also, he was prone to fits of jealousy, a trait that did not recommend him as a mate for Margaret Mead.

Once Luther Cressman got over the initial shock of seeing his wife disembark with a glowering stranger in tow, he accepted the situation fatalistically. Fortune was more of a problem. He wanted Margaret to file for a divorce at once, but his impatience only made her nervous. She liked to be the one making the decisions. Luther, proud of himself as usual for refusing to give in to base emotions, resigned himself to waiting for Margaret to make up her mind.

During Margaret's absence, Ruth Benedict had been faithfully sending her packages, dealing with the embittered Edward Sapir, and waiting anxiously for letters from Samoa. Now she arrived in Europe, having made plans to spend time with Margaret in Paris and again in Rome, where they were to attend the Congress of Americanists. Once again, Ruth found herself in the position of acting as a sounding board for Margaret's confusion over men. According to the Mead-Benedict theory of relationships, it would have been wrong for Ruth to impose constraints on Margaret's selfhood. Their unconventional love was supposed to be immune to base emotions like jealousy, which were nothing more than cultural artifacts. Still, Margaret found her friend "deeply depressed"— so much so that her hair had begun to turn white. Ruth's comment on seeing the Cathedral of Notre Dame was "Isn't it unbearable that this is all about nothing?" And in her journal she wrote, "Passion is a turn-coat, but death will endure always."

Ruth confided to an alarmed Margaret that she'd dreamed about committing suicide. Her journal shows that she eventually rejected self-destruction on the grounds that it was the easy way out: "It's a cheap way of attaining death, and death at least need not come cheap." Their painful reunion continued in Rome, where the two women made a pilgrimage to Keats' grave and accidentally got locked inside the Protestant cemetery when it closed for the night.

On her return to New York, Mead visited a gynecologist, who told her that she had a tipped uterus and would never be able to have children—a piece of misinformation which tilted the scales definitively in Reo Fortune's favor. She also turned in her field report and waited nervously for Boas's verdict. The dutiful graduate student had returned with findings that dramatically upheld her mentor's belief that sexual mores were culturally determined. As she had written to Boas before leaving Samoa, her conclusion was that "The neuroses accompanying sex in American civilization are practically absent, such as frigidity, impotence and pronounced perversions." Moreover, since the Samoans made no attempt to curb adolescent sexuality, "there is no conflict at all between the adolescent and the community."[16]

Still, her data was sketchy, to say the least. Revealingly, when Boas summoned her and Ruth to his office for a conference, Margaret's first thought was "I have betrayed him, like everyone else." In the event, Boas requested only one change. "You haven't made clear the distinction between romantic and passionate love," he told her. It's hard to say why Boas was not more critical. Perhaps Mead wondered this herself, because she comments in her autobiography, *Blackberry Winter,* that Papa Franz had been a stern taskmaster to his first-generation disciples, anthropologists like Alfred Kroeber, Robert Lowie and Edward Sapir, whereas he treated her and Benedict "rather like grandchildren."[17]

Ruth had by now recovered from the depths of depression and volunteered to advise Margaret on how to turn her field report into a manuscript suitable for trade publication. The result was an instant bestseller, an anthropological study that read like escapist fantasy. *Coming of Age in Samoa* begins with a vision of young lovers enjoying midnight "trysts beneath the palm trees" to the soothing accompaniment of "the mellow thunder of the reef." Mead describes an island paradise where every girl's goal is to enjoy "as many years of casual lovemaking as possible." Adolescent angst and, indeed, "strong passions" are unknown because society "never exerts sufficient repression to call forth a significant rebellion from the individual." Homosexual activity is for the most part "simply play, neither frowned upon nor given much consideration." Because young people are thoroughly experienced by the time their parents arrange a marriage for them, sexual problems are rare and "intercourse only once in a night is counted as senility."

The key to this beguiling way of life, according to Mead, is Samoan childcare. The Samoan infant is reared by an extended family and "owes no emotional allegiance to its father and mother." In place of strong bonds with their mothers, island children enjoy the easy affection of "a group of adults all of whom have their interests somewhat but not too importantly at heart." In other words, it takes a village....

One doesn't have to be a psychoanalyst to see that Mead had transformed Ta'ū into her own personal Fantasy Island, a place where it was possible to experiment sexually without becoming entangled in the social and emotional repercussions that were making her own life so complicated.

Nor does it take a trained anthropologist to see that there are major problems with Mead's conclusions. For one thing, in her Samoa, premarital sexual intercourse does not lead to pregnancy. Asked about this anomaly in later years, Mead speculated that Samoan girls are so closely in touch with the rhythms of their menstrual cycles that they instinctively know when to avoid intercourse.

Furthermore, Mead's own data belies her claim that adolescence in Samoa is "easy." Four girls out of the twenty-five in her core sample exhibited serious behavior problems, including stealing and habitual lying. Another was expelled from the mission school for sexual misconduct. One had been involved in an incestuous relationship with her uncle.

Nevertheless, on its publication in 1928 *Coming of Age in Samoa* included an introduction by Franz Boas, attesting to the author's "painstaking" research. With additional boosts from Ruth Benedict, who praised her lover's work in the pages of the *Journal of Philosophy* and the *New Republic, Coming of Age* was immediately accepted as authoritative. Its conclusions were incorporated into the 1930 edition of the *Encyclopedia of the Social Sciences* and dutifully summarized in college textbooks. As late as the 1960s, moreover, copies of the 35-cent Mentor paperback could be found on drugstore bookracks, one of a handful of nonfiction titles shelved among the pulp novels and astrology guides. Every literate American could rest assured that "science" had proven that teenage sexuality could be wholesome and beautiful, if only parents and "society" would stop interfering.

One of the few dissents to Mead's vision of a sexual utopia came from Edward Sapir, who offered his by no means neutral perspective in an article on the subject of changing sexual mores. The revolt against Puritanism, he warned, was giving rise to an equally extreme "religion of promiscuity." Feminists were encouraging women to make a "sacrifice of love" on the altar of an "ambition that is essentially insatiable." As a result, emotional security and true intimacy between men and women were threatened and "compensation in the form of homosexuality" was becoming more common. "The cult of the 'naturalness' of homosexuality fools no one but those who need a rationalization of their own problems." In a letter to Ruth Benedict, Sapir assured her that his comments were by no means an attack on *her.* As for Margaret, he added, she had become "hardly a person to me at all," just "a symbol of everything I detest in American culture."[18]

The glistening generalizations of *Coming of Age in Samoa* made it a tempting target for debunkers. But, amazingly enough, a full-scale refutation did not appear until 1983, five years after Margaret Mead's death. In the interim, many individuals had their doubts about the soundness of her work, but to take on both Mead and the reputation of Papa Franz, who had endorsed her book, would have been the academic equivalent of a double regicide. When the attack did come it was launched by a New Zealander, Derek Freeman, an anthropologist who had spent four decades studying the culture that Mead covered in a few months. In *Margaret Mead and Samoa*, the first of his two books on the subject, Freeman methodically dismantled Mead's free-love fantasy. Far from being the land of free and easy sex, Samoa in the 1920s was a society that prized female virginity. In fact, Mead, who never did tell her Samoan hosts that she was married, was herself thrice honored in rituals proclaiming her a "ceremonial virgin." The dark side of this obsession with virginity was a custom known as *moetotolo*, or "sleep crawling": sneaking into a girl's hut after nightfall to manually deflower her and thus claim her as a prize. Mead was aware of this "abnormal" practice, but dismissed it as little more than a prank.

Almost everyone who did not have a professional stake in the survival of Boasian theory recognized at once that Freeman's critique was essentially correct. Still, Mead's admirers reacted by herding their wagons into a circle. A discussion of Freeman's claims was held during the American Anthropological Association's annual convention in Chicago, but Freeman himself was not invited to take part. The meeting degenerated into a frenzy of denunciations, and before the convention ended the delegates passed a formal resolution condemning Freeman—presumably to eternal darkness. Further attacks on Freeman followed a familiar pattern. His basic argument being incontrovertible, he was charged with sloppiness about details. Then his motives for addressing the subject were questioned and, finally, all else having failed, Freeman was accused of making a bore of himself by reiterating what everyone already knew.

The often astute Hilary Lapsley, whose joint biography of Mead and Benedict is written from a feminist perspective, goes all to pieces on the subject of her countryman, accusing him of demonstrating "undeniable malice" against Mead by suggesting that her "private life colored her view of Samoa." Simultaneously, she complains that Freeman is too naïve to grasp the postmodernist critique of social science—"the suggestion that anthropology says as much about anthropologists as it does about the cultures they study would not be a startling claim; it is more a truism than a slur." Moreover, she ventures, "There is a strong argument to be made that rather than Mead's having produced 'bad science,' it is the critics who have misunderstood the nature of Mead's fieldwork and the process by which she turned her material into a critique of American society."[19] Putting postmodernist quotation marks around "bad science," however, doesn't change the fact that *Coming of Age in Samoa* was not presented to the public as Mead's personal critique of American society, but as a work of scholarship.

Freeman, far from harboring malice against Mead, painstakingly showed how she could have been misled by a combination of her own preconceptions and a few mischief-making informants, who had no scruples against telling the visiting American what she clearly wanted to hear. "A Boasian ideologue she may have been; a deliberate cheat about major anthropological issues, she was not," he concludes. If there is malice in Freeman's work it is directed against the community of scholars that allowed her work to escape detailed scrutiny for so long. As he notes, in the absence of critical inquiry, social science theory has a way of hardening into myth, and once that happens, researchers find only what massages their own prejudices. "A set of beliefs, once implanted," he writes, "impels even highly educated individuals to cling fervently to doctrines which have been shown to have no scholarly or scientific basis."[20]

Although Ruth Benedict no longer thought in terms of finding a "great love" and the subterranean emotional fires that once found expression in her poetry had been damped down, she had made an accommodation of sorts. In 1926, while Margaret was in Samoa, Ruth had met twenty-one-year-old Natalie Raymond, the woman who would eventually become her live-in lover. Nat, who had previously dated physicist J. Robert Oppenheimer, was a chemist, like Stanley Benedict. Within a few years she and Ruth would take an apartment together on Central Park West, but apart from the pet dogs they both doted on, the two women seemed to have little in common. Eighteen years Ruth's junior, Nat loved fast cars, brisk hikes and an active social life. Ruth, now in her forties, did not travel well and was prone to fainting spells and migraines.

Despite much talk about Nat finishing her degree in chemistry, she drifted from one job to another, typing manuscripts and working as a clerk in a bookstore. After a few years of uneventful domesticity, she also began to socialize with friends closer to her own age, going out to parties and pursuing infatuations with young women. Once again, Ruth graduated from her role as lover to that of confidante and mother figure.[21]

Ruth seems to have played a similar role with her friends, a circle of highly educated women whose flightier members were constantly in a tizzy over their *faux*-adolescent crushes, melodramatic scenes, petty gossip and dizzying changes of sexual preference—from women to men and back to women again. Margaret Mead's friend, the writer Leonie Adams, nicknamed these drama queens the "Oh-What-a-Pain Girls." As the exasperated biographer Hilary Lapsley observes at one point, "The attractions, affairs and heartbreaks, both heterosexual and homosexual, that the supposedly New Women confided to Ruth provided her with a continuing source of entertainment."[22]

Judith Modell notes that one adjective Benedict's friends invariably used to describe her was "civilized." This may have been in part a tribute to Ruth's literary accomplishments but it was mainly a comment on her reserved personality. Ruth didn't believe that human beings should let their behavior be controlled by base emotions like jealousy and anger, and she tried to rise above them in her dealings with others. But from another perspective, this effort at spiritual discipline reflected the depressive's horror of open confrontation. Benedict dealt with people who irritated her by refusing converse with them at all, deflecting their attempts at engagement with a serene smile. As a frustrated graduate student once put it, trying to communicate with Mrs. Benedict was "like dealing with plasma." And, unfortunately, the base emotions that Benedict refused to acknowledge often turned against her, transforming themselves into the "blue devils" of despair and psychosomatic illness.[23]

In 1936 the seventy-eight-year-old Franz Boas finally retired, and Benedict hoped to be named his successor. Although she was only an assistant professor, her published work had made her one of the best-known anthropologists in the United States, and she believed that her sex was the only consideration against her. In fact, Benedict did not have the support of her colleagues, including the more prominent women in anthropology. Elsie Clews Parsons, her onetime mentor, opposed her appointment, and even Margaret Mead, who loved Ruth, considered her psychologically unsuited for the job. In the end, the post went to Ralph Linton, the very man Boas had insulted years earlier because he dared to show up for an interview in the uniform of an American soldier.

Linton arrived at Columbia to find that Boas, though officially retired, was still ensconced in the chairman's office, with Ruth next door. Boas was openly antagonistic, but Linton found Benedict's chilly hauteur far more unnerving. While Linton tried to get a grip on his job, she gradually retreated from active participation in the department's affairs, and meanwhile conducted a sniping war against him through her correspondence, accusing him of anti-Semitism, paranoia and generally being a "swine." This demonstration of the higher morality in action should have been enough to give anyone pause.

Benedict lived, of necessity, a highly compartmentalized existence. Many of her colleagues at Columbia neither met nor heard of Natalie, and the nature of her relationship with Mead, though suspected by quite a few, remained secret until after both women's deaths, when it was acknowledged by Mead's daughter, Mary Catherine Bateson. In 1934, however, Benedict felt confident enough to take up the subject of homosexuality in an academic paper entitled "Anthropology and the Abnormal." Instead of simply arguing in favor of greater candor and social acceptance for homosexuals, Benedict took on the concept of normality. Many behaviors such as homosexual conduct, sadism and running amok have been considered normal in other cultures, she observed. If homosexuals in America tended to be neurotic or antisocial, it was only because the stress of trying to conform to culturally determined sex roles and moral codes made them into deviants.[24]

Benedict would expand on this theme in *Patterns of Culture,* published that same year. Although it lacked the sex appeal of *Coming of Age in Samoa,* Benedict's book became a perennial bestseller, with more than one million copies printed in the Mentor paperback edition alone. A staple of college reading lists and surely the most widely read anthropology book of all time, it defined the social outlook of cultural relativity.

Benedict begins *Patterns* by observing that Western civilization, which she also calls "white civilization," has spread around the globe through a set of "fortuitous" (meaning accidental) historical circumstances. In the past, we Westerners have been unable to appreciate the virtues of other cultures because we were blinded by our belief in the "Divine Truth" of our Judeo-Christian tradition. Now, however, "we have thrown off that particular absurdity" and need only to set aside our "Anglo-Saxon intolerance" and racist prejudices in order to study other cultures objectively and learn from them.

She then offers for our consideration sketches of three cultures, each with its own distinct "personality": First, the materialistic, self-glorifying Kwakiutl Indians of the Pacific Northwest, who squander their wealth on useless gifts which they exchange in potlatch ceremonies. Second, the superstitious Dobuans of Papua New Guinea, who are obsessed by the fear that their enemies will cast magic spells against them. And third—Benedict's model of the "good society"—the Zunis of the southwestern United States.

According to Benedict, the Zunis are antiauthoritarian and anticompetitive. Their culture is restrained, or "Apollonian," and "takes no delight in any situation in which an individual stands alone." Their religion is "folkloric," and their ceremonies are lacking in "sex symbolism" (i.e. gender neutral). Economic matters are "comparatively unimportant" for them and goods are shared widely, not distributed through the "funnel system" of trickle-down capitalism. Drunkenness is considered "repulsive" and suicide is unknown: "It is simply too violent an act ... to contemplate." Jealousy is an aberration. The Zuni language, moreover, makes no distinctions between a man who has many love affairs and one who has many friends. Husbands readily forgive unfaithful wives and changing husbands is "a really tolerable procedure." For the Zunis, asserts Benedict, "sex is just an incident in a happy life."

Many readers have recognized *Patterns of Culture* as a work that asks to be read as satire, the anthropological equivalent of *Gulliver's Travels*. The insanely acquisitive Kwakiutl, continually swapping gifts that will never be used, resemble the stock market speculators of the 1920s. The credulous Dobuans, blaming their misfortunes on scapegoats, are a parody of religious fundamentalists or, perhaps, the Knights of the Ku Klux Klan. The Apollonian Zunis represent agrarian socialists whose communitarian values enable them to live in harmony with one another.

Moreover, as Marvin Harris observes in *The Rise of Anthropological Theory*, many anthropologists had severe reservations about Benedict's book for a variety of reasons. Their objections were rarely aired openly, however, since *Patterns of Culture* served as a wonderful advertisement for their field. "Because of its great popularity, it has served as the most important single source of recruitment for anthropology as a profession," writes Harris. Therefore, "there are anthropologists who regard criticism of Benedict's *Patterns of Culture* as a kind of sacrilege." Nevertheless, he continues, *Patterns* is filled with "extravagant assertions ... [that] cannot be dismissed as a mere peccadillo."[25]

Benedict's portrait of the Dobuans was the first to come under fire. Her description of this obscure and highly unpleasant tribe was based entirely on the reports of a single observer—none other than Reo Fortune, who spent six months studying them while Margaret Mead was in

New York finishing her first book and preparing to join him in New Guinea. Fortune arrived on Dobu knowing not a word of the local language, and since he had paranoid tendencies himself, it has often been suspected that he projected his own fears onto the people he was observing.

By contrast, when it came to writing about the Kwakiutl, Benedict was able to draw on what she described as "tons" of raw data compiled by Boas, who made more than thirteen trips to the Pacific Northwest and received regular supplemental reports from an associate. The problem, as pointed out by anthropologists Verne Ray and Victor Barnouw, is that Benedict made sweeping generalizations about an entire people based on rituals like the potlatch, a ceremony practiced by Kwakiutl chiefs during a period when the tribe was coping with a flood of trade goods. This would be roughly the equivalent of judging American culture by the fundraising rituals of the Clinton White House.

But it is Benedict's profile of the Zunis that has drawn the most criticism. The Zunis are a fascinating and widely studied people whose unique characteristics have inspired many imaginative hypotheses over the years. (Most recently, anthropologist Nancy Yaw Davis has theorized that the tribe is descended from Japanese sailors shipwrecked on the coast of California in the thirteenth century.) Still, mysterious as they may be, real-life Zunis are scarcely recognizable in Benedict's Apollonian stick figures, so eerily lifeless that they might as well be denizens of the "bright world of death" that she associated with her deceased father.

Benedict did fieldwork among the Zunis for a total of about four months during the summers of 1924 and 1925. She never lived with a Zuni family, but shared a rented house outside the pueblo with Ruth Bunzel, who was studying Zuni pottery. Moreover, Benedict never mastered the Zuni language and she spoke very little Spanish. Most of her months in the field were spent taking notes on myths narrated for her benefit by a single paid informant named Nick Tumaka. Hardly a typical Zuni, Tumaka was well known to visiting anthropologists. Alfred Kroeber described him as "the outstanding intellectual among the Zunis," and Tumaka had become especially close to Ruth Bunzel, once even proposing marriage to her.

Benedict saw Nick Tumaka as an example of a creative individual who pushed the boundaries of his people's definition of the normal. In *Patterns of Culture* she writes that Tumaka (who is never mentioned by name) was a misfit because of his "personal magnetism," occasional violent outbursts, and "scornful and aloof" manner. He had been accused of such indiscretions as peering into someone's window and boasting while drunk. In fact, Tumaka was also accused of witchcraft and shunned because of his cooperation with visiting anthropologists. The Zunis regarded their history and lore as the property of the tribe, not to be shared with outsiders. Later, during the period when he was close to Ruth Bunzel, Tumaka dreamed that his association with a white woman had caused the tribe's guardian spirits to withdraw their protection from him, a dream he interpreted as an omen of approaching death. When he died shortly afterward, his relatives held Bunzel responsible.

Benedict had another run-in with the Zuni attitude toward outsiders before a 1927 visit to New Mexico, when she wrote to the linguist Jaime de Angulo asking him for help in locating additional informants. De Angulo was horrified. "Do you realize that this is just the sort of thing that kills the Indians?" he wrote back. According to Judith Modell, Benedict met de Angulo a few years later and, over a few rounds of whiskey and soda, she "persuaded him of her good intentions."[26]

It's curious that a woman whose whole life was devoted to scholarship would be so attracted to a culture in which intellectual curiosity could be equated with witchcraft, but Benedict's writings make it abundantly clear that she identified with mystics and people given to falling into trances. Her sense of herself as a social "deviant" had at least as much to do with her mystical leanings as with her lesbian inclinations. Perhaps the feeling that she had some intuitive link to the Zuni mind accounted for her failure to mount a more general defense of the claims of scholarship. In the long run, however, good intentions are not a sufficient justification for doing things that offend people, and Benedict's lame response to de Angulo prefigured a time when anthropologists would gradually come to accept the idea that asking questions is not only insensitive—which it often is—but also a form of cultural exploitation. Today, anthropologists and other social scientists, not excluding historians and professors of journalism, are often hemmed in by bureaucratic restrictions, including the requirement that they obtain advance permission to conduct interviews.

As for Benedict's views on the Zunis in general, even anthropologists who worked with Nick Tumaka didn't necessarily agree with them, and later scholars would not hesitate to find fault with her portrait of a people steeped in Apollonian serenity. It simply was not true that there were no documented cases of suicide among the Zunis, or that Zuni husbands didn't get jealous. Drunkenness could be a serious problem, especially during festivals, and the critic Edmund Wilson describes how the local authorities set up roadblocks to search tourists' cars for smuggled bottles of whiskey. Far from being placid and cooperative, moreover, the Zunis have a history of partisan in-fighting, including what anthropologist Li An-Che characterizes as "strife of immense magnitude" between Protestant and Catholic factions. Summarizing these discrepancies, Marvin Harris also takes note of reports that Zuni medicine society rites, which are closed to outsiders, include such un-Apollonian activities as sword swallowing and walking barefoot over hot coals.

In the final chapters of *Patterns,* Benedict zeroes in on her main concern: the problem of "abnormals," those men and women who are out of sync with the dominant values of their cultures. Once again, she argues that abnormality must be seen as completely arbitrary. For example, "The individual in Dobu who was thoroughly disoriented was the man who was naturally friendly." Western civilization, she goes on, "tends to regard even mild homosexuality as abnormal." By contrast, most North American Indians recognized the phenomenon of the *berdache,* the man who chooses to wear women's clothes and practice womanly occupations. The *berdache* had a recognized place in the social order, even though he was sometimes regarded with "a certain embarrassment." Benedict fails to mention that in Western civilization, too, male homosexuals have often excelled at tasks typically performed by women and been well rewarded for it. The difference is that in Western culture, individuals are increasingly unwilling to be consigned to narrow social niches based on their sexuality. Hence, there's a much greater preoccupation with what is normal and what is neurotic.

Benedict's crowning argument is that the true abnormals in any society are those individuals who most fully exemplify its core values. Since "society supports them in their furthest aberrations," such people have "a license which they fully exploit" to engage in "psychopathic" behavior. This is her cue to unleash a tirade on the subject of competitive, authoritarian white males:

> Arrogant and unbridled egoists as family men, as officers of the law, and in business, have been again and again portrayed by novelists and dramatists, and they are familiar in every community. Like the behavior of Puritan divines, their courses of action are often more asocial than those of the inmates of penitentiaries. In terms of the suffering and frustration

they spread about them there is probably no comparison. There is very possibly at least as great a degree of mental warping. Yet they are entrusted with positions of great influence and importance and are as a rule fathers of families.[27]

This screed gives the lie to the notion that cultural relativists are prepared to judge every culture by its own standards. The Zunis, the Dobuans and the Kwakiutl were interesting to Benedict mainly as a catalogue of cultural options that she could mine in her effort to reimagine Western culture along utopian lines, an enterprise she increasingly referred to as "humanistic" social science. This remaking of the culture was supposed to come about through the process of redefining what is normal: "No society has yet attempted a self-conscious direction of the process by which new normalities are produced in the next generation," she writes, serenely oblivious to the lessons of the French and Bolshevik revolutions. But "[John] Dewey has pointed out how possible and yet how drastic such social operations would be." (Though Benedict doesn't elaborate, Dewey proposed that morality should be based not on codes of personal behavior, but on the pursuit of progressive social goals.)

The message of *Patterns of Culture* is that intelligent, educated people will have no trouble agreeing on the outline of a "rational social order." As Benedict wrote in her earlier essay "Anthropology and the Abnormal," there are no "universal normalities" but there are "universal sanities." It never seemed to occur to her that reasonable people might disagree about the merits of competition, for example, not to mention standards of morality or the existence of God. Benedict's complacency was supported by her confidence that anyone who disagreed with her on such issues would be reacting emotionally. Still, she assured her readers that after an initial period of confusion and pessimism, the "new opinion" would come to be "embraced as customary belief" and a "bulwark of the good life."[28] In a time of economic depression at home and intimations of war abroad, this vision may have been reassuring, at least to those who weren't overly sensitive to the project's totalitarian implications. The difference between Benedict's vision and the new social orders envisioned by Nazism and communism is that she saw the transformation as essentially nonpolitical, a social revolution that would be spearheaded by psychologists, sociologists and anthropologists, all reasonable and enlightened people like herself.

Chapter 2

Fully Human

When Ruth Benedict called for redefining normality in a single generation, the chances of such a thing happening seemed remote at best. Within a few years, however, her friend and sometime student Abraham Maslow would lay the groundwork for a new theory of personality that would do just that. Maslow made short work of the challenge by adopting Benedict herself as his model of the "good human being." In a breathtaking reversal, she was transformed from a woman who considered herself a "deviant" to an example of ideal psychological health—in fact, one of those rare human beings who had managed to become more "fully human" than the rest of us.

Benedict's sense of herself as an outsider had deep appeal for Maslow. Like her, he had been a hypersensitive and deeply lonely child who found solace in the world of books. Born in Brooklyn in 1908, he read his way through the neighborhood branch of the public library. Unfortunately, reaching this after-school haven meant venturing onto streets dominated by Italian and Irish toughs who delighted in tormenting the undersize, timid Abe. For self-protection he tried making friends with the Jewish boys on his block, only to discover that their favorite pastimes were torturing cats and pitching stones at girls. He had no stomach for either activity, even though the girls, at least, seemed to enjoy the attention.

Abe's parents, Sam and Rose, were immigrants who had met in New York and married despite being first cousins. Sam was the passive type who dealt with the tension at home by working long hours to build up his cooperage business and disappearing periodically on lengthy "business trips." Rose, on the other hand, was emotionally volatile, and rejection of his mother would become the driving theme of Abe's life. As an adult, he would pass up few opportunities to denounce her as a "horrible woman," ruled by superstition and peasant prejudices, who punctuated her lectures with shrieks of "God will strike you dead!" Rose, he would recall, was so stingy that she kept a lock on the refrigerator door and so vicious that once, when he rescued a litter of starving kittens from the streets, she bashed their skulls against the basement wall while he looked on in horror. As if that weren't enough, Maslow would charge his mother with "sloppiness and dirtiness," "lack of family feeling," and exhibiting "a primitive animal-like care for her body and her body alone." He also called her "schizophrenogenic," meaning that she was the sort of person who literally drove others crazy. On occasion, he blamed her for neglecting his sister, who died of pneumonia at the age of four, and for causing his lifelong back problems by failing to give him orange juice when he was a baby. "The whole thrust of my life philosophy and all my research and theorizing," he once wrote, ". . . has its roots in a hatred for and a revulsion against everything she stood for."[1]

Rose's other children would find this description hurtful and, for the most part, unrecognizable. No one denied that Rose was a difficult woman with a bad temper, and her oldest son's refusal to fight back, a tactic so like Sam's, probably drove her to distraction. But Rose, after all, had been just a teenager, one year away from a Ukrainian shtetl, when Abe was born. Six more babies soon followed. Still, she and her husband were determined to give the children the cultural advantages that had been denied to them. Even with a new baby coming almost every year, Rose somehow managed to attend night school. Though it took her ten years, she became literate in English and earned a high school diploma. Moreover, even when money was short, the Maslow home was always provided with books, classical records and a piano. Rose and Sam saw to it that all six surviving children received a good education. Abe, marked early on as the family scholar, would be supported by his parents through graduate school.

Though not highly religious, the Maslows belonged to a Conservative temple and Rose kept a kosher home. When the time approached for his bar mitzvah, Abe was expected to attend Hebrew school where, much to his dismay, he was given a speech filled with platitudes to memorize. On the day of the ceremony, he got as far as the section where he was supposed to express his gratitude to his dear mother when he choked on the words and fled the podium in disgust. "See how he loves me!" Rose said later, "He can't even express the words." With hindsight, this sounds like the reaction of a woman who hoped to cover her own embarrassment and deflect criticism from her son, a possibility that would never occur to Abe. "My mother loved it and thought this was very sentimental and that I was overcome with great feelings," he would recall.[2]

By the time he entered high school, Abe had begun to emulate his father by avoiding home as much as possible. When not staying with relatives, he left the apartment before breakfast and returned home after dinner, surviving on the 15-cent lunches covered by his allowance. Six feet tall, he weighed at one point barely 112 pounds. In an effort to put some muscle on his spindly frame, he joined Will Maslow, his cousin and only real friend, in games of handball and tennis. Otherwise, he spent his free time in the reading room of the New York Public Library at 42nd Street.

Maslow attended Boys High, a well-regarded public school that set many sons of Jewish immigrants on the path to success. One of his teachers introduced him to the novels of Upton Sinclair, which inspired him to attend lectures at socialist institutions like the Labor Temple and the Rand School, where he heard the historian Will Durant and Socialist Party leader Norman Thomas. But despite all his hours of solitary reading and study, Maslow's grades were mediocre and his academic career would be a series of false starts. As a freshman at City College, he failed trigonometry and earned a series of C's that landed him on academic probation. To please his father he enrolled in an undergraduate program at Brooklyn Law School, but left after a few weeks, dismayed at having to read so many cases that were nothing more than the record of the doings of "evil men" and the myriad "sins of mankind." Next, he joined his cousin Will at Cornell, but while Will was thriving in the collegiate atmosphere, Abe felt homesick and out of place. He loathed his part-time job as a waiter in a fraternity dining room, where the frat boys, he complained, never spoke to him or made eye contact. After one unhappy semester, he reenrolled at City College.

Abe desperately envied the "all-American boys," by which he meant Jewish boys who were more assimilated than he was, and he was deeply ashamed of his timidity and social isolation. "Oh yes, I was all alone in the world," he told an interviewer in 1963. "I felt peculiar. This was really in my blood, a very profound feeling that somehow I was wrong. Never any feelings that I was superior that I can remember. Just one big aching inferiority complex."[3]

The only bright spot in his life was his cousin Bertha Goodman, who had arrived in the United States in 1922 when she was thirteen. Abe developed a crush on Bertha, traveled all the way to her parents' apartment in the Bronx to tutor her in English, and mooned over her so pathetically that one day in 1927 Bertha's older sister became exasperated and pushed the young couple into one another's arms, instructing Abe, "For the love of Pete, kiss her, will ya'!" For Abe, this was the moment that transformed an ugly, morose boy into a man.[4]

Six months later, in the spring of 1928, Abe decided to transfer yet again, this time to the University of Wisconsin. After one semester he couldn't bear the separation from Bertha any longer, and he wrote her a letter instructing her to scrape together bus fare and come out to Madison, where they would be married. Both sets of parents were horrified. Given Sam and Rose's blood relationship, arguments against the marriage of first cousins were destined to fail. But Bertha, at nineteen, was still a few courses short of earning her high school diploma, and without help from his family Abe would never be able to support a wife.

Abe may have been insecure on the inside, but in his letters to Bertha he was very much the young scholar-princeling, very sure of his superior intelligence and disdainful of anyone who tried to thwart him. When Bertha refused to come, explaining that she did not want to lose her father's respect by eloping, Abe wrote back, calling her "dumb," an "ass" and a "baby," among other things, for being too spineless to escape from the "smothering" embrace of her family. Obviously, he added, Bertha's father loved her too much to "let her starve," and once they were married, both families would accept the match and help them out financially. Much to his amazement, Bertha took offense at being called stupid and still refused the summons to Madison. In his next letter, Abe railed at her for being unable to follow his "logical" arguments and threatened that he would end the relationship rather than return to the Bronx to fetch her. Bertha still didn't come, and in December Abe showed up in New York, where the young couple was married. They promptly returned to Wisconsin, and Abe set about playing Pygmalion. He tutored Bertha for her high school exams, arranged for her to enter the university as a special student, and started her on a reading list that he had compiled for her benefit.[5]

Luckily for Maslow, he had married a very patient woman. A letter he wrote to Bertha in 1935 finds him registering his discovery that she had "depths" whose existence he had not hitherto suspected. After six years of marriage he was beginning to recognize that his wife was not just a pretty doll who needed the benefit of his superior reasoning powers, but a true partner with whom he could share his ideas and dreams. Wisely, he added that his ability to see this was probably a sign that he was "growing up and becoming more manly."

Intellectually, too, Maslow was beginning to come into his own. He had decided to major in psychology, a discipline that seemed to offer a scientific approach to the big social and philosophical questions that intrigued him. In 1932 he became the first research assistant to Dr. Harry Harlow, then a newly minted Ph.D., just beginning his groundbreaking studies of primate behavior. Maslow got along well with Harlow, whose corrosive wit put many people off, and was fascinated by his observations of monkeys at the local zoo, where Harlow was doing his research at the time. Maslow noticed, for example, that both male and female monkeys engaged in a great deal of sexual behavior unrelated to procreation. These heterosexual and homosexual couplings appeared to be a way for high-dominance—or, in today's term for it, high self-esteem— animals to establish their place in the group pecking order. As he happened to be reading Freud at the time, Maslow couldn't help but notice that this behavior appeared to contradict Freud's belief that sexually promiscuous women were maladjusted. Among monkeys, it seemed, the females with status were also the most sexually voracious.

Maslow might well have continued his work as a specialist in animal behavior, but he was twice turned down for a National Research Council grant to study with Robert Yerkes at his primate research center near Jacksonville, Florida. He attributed these rejections to anti-Semitism, probably correctly. Nearly finished with his doctorate, he had to face the dismal truth that there were very few Jews in the field of academic psychology, and at the height of the Great Depression, colleges and universities could afford to discriminate. Harry Harlow, a Protestant, had changed his last name from "Israel," lest anyone get the wrong impression; but when Maslow considered a similar dodge, Bertha threatened to file for divorce. Reasoning that an M.D. degree might help him land a job in research, he entered medical school, but he couldn't stand to see patients in pain and left after a few months.

He was near despair when he was awarded a Carnegie Fellowship to work under Edward L. Thorndike at Columbia University Teachers College. Thorndike is best remembered for experiments supposedly proving that children derive no general benefits from studying subjects like Latin and algebra, thus bolstering progressive educators' arguments for vocational training. A great believer in IQ tests, Thorndike administered them to all of his research assistants, and when Maslow scored a phenomenal 192, Thorndike decided to give him the freedom to follow his own interests.

What Maslow was interested in was sex. Like many educated people of his generation, he had no doubt that puritanical sexual mores were responsible for much of the world's misery, even though he himself lived by a standard that would have passed muster with Cotton Mather. Not only had he married the first girl he ever kissed, but he once wrote that he had never seen an erect penis other than his own. While at Columbia he managed to recruit almost a hundred female subjects for in-depth personal interviews that covered such topics as masturbation, sexual fantasies and homosexual experiences. The interviews supported his hypothesis that women who scored high in self-esteem were also more likely to be sexually active and much more open to experimentation. The study was unprecedented and considered shocking by some; his supervisor, Dr. Thorndike, couldn't even bring himself to read the interviews. It was also a daringly original piece of work that many researchers would have mined for the rest of their careers. Maslow, however, grew disillusioned with the project. He had found that women with low self-esteem—in other words, those who were shy or just modest—were extremely reluctant to answer his questions, while more dominant women were at times a bit too eager to cooperate. He was even more suspicious of the responses of the small number of male subjects he had interviewed; most of them, he thought, exaggerated to make themselves seem more experienced than they actually were.

By 1935, when Maslow joined Thorndike's lab, New York City had become the new capital of psychoanalytic thought, a mecca for refugee analysts in flight from Nazism. Maslow attached himself for a while to Alfred Adler, got to know Karen Horney and Erich Fromm, and audited courses at the New School given by Gestalt psychologist Max Wertheimer, who emphasized the importance of inspiration—the "aha!" moment. It was a heady time, and Maslow began to think that it might indeed be possible for him to synthesize an important new theory of personality. Research-oriented behavioral psychology increasingly struck him as too narrow, focusing on the most routine aspects of human behavior while neglecting the ideas and emotions that made people interesting. Freudian psychoanalysis, on the other hand, was preoccupied with the abnormal, the pathological. The question Maslow wanted to pose was: "What is the nature of psychological health?"

Defining health as anything other than the absence of disease is always tricky. Defining psychological health is even more challenging. Before we can say what qualities make up the healthy personality, we must make assumptions about the meaning and purpose of life. Despite the revolutionary impact of his ideas, Freud basically accepted the social mores of his time. Masturbation, homosexuality and female promiscuity were all maladjusted behavior in his eyes. And while repressing our unacceptable desires may make us neurotic, repression is the price we pay for civilization. Maslow's theory of personality would be a protest against the idea that there is a necessary conflict between the individual's pursuit of happiness and the good of society as a whole. If conforming to the rules of civilization made people feel stifled and unhappy, then there was something wrong with the rules. Looking back on his work in 1968, Maslow acknowledged, "My concerns were socialistic, with American socialism. . . . There is the Jewish tradition of the utopian and the ethical and I was pretty definitely looking for the improvement of mankind."[6]

The search for utopian alternatives led Maslow to Columbia's Department of Anthropology. He had become fascinated by Boasian anthropology back in Wisconsin when Bertha took a course taught by Ralph Linton. Now, in New York, he began attending lectures at the department and even wrote papers that he presented at meetings of the

American Anthropological Association. Abe's volatile mix of ambition and insecurity made him one of Ruth Benedict's favorites. She took him out to lunch, encouraged him to broaden his cultural horizons, and counseled him to be less driven and more "Eastern" in his outlook. In Maslow's eyes, she became almost a surrogate parent—the calm, supportive, cultivated mother he never had.

Maslow was so smitten with Benedict that he gave his first child, Ann, the middle name Ruth in her honor. Meanwhile, his own younger sister Ruth decided to become an anthropologist, as did her fiancé, Oscar Lewis, later the author of the classic *The Children of Sanchez*. During the summer of 1937, Lewis and Maslow were part of a group of students who received grants to do fieldwork among the Blackfoot and Blood Indians in Montana and the Canadian province of Alberta. Benedict never coped well with the stress of managing researchers in the field, and this expedition got off to a bad start when, on the second day, one of her charges had an automobile accident that killed his Indian passenger. Complaining of migraine headaches, Benedict retreated to her tent, where she remained for the duration.

Maslow and two other anthropologists, Lucian Hanks and Jane Richardson, had been posted to the Northern Blackfoot reservation in Canada, where they were largely unaware of the tense situation in Montana. Maslow's projected study of dominance behavior required him to spend most of his days interviewing young men at the pool hall in town. It was the closest thing to male bonding he had ever experienced, and as a result, his view of Blackfoot culture took on a roseate glow. He soon learned that tribal traditions of communal property discouraged individual initiative. His chief informant, a half-Chinese Blackfoot named Teddy Yellow Fly, owned the only car on the reservation, and custom required him to lend it to anyone who asked; so Teddy, observed Maslow, had all the expense of maintaining the vehicle but rarely the use of it. This charmed Maslow, who pronounced the Blackfoot an almost perfect example of Benedict's concept of "ego security," products of a culture that promoted individuals who were "happy, spontaneous, outgoing, loving, friendly, cooperative, happy, unfrustrated, and with little anxiety or conflict."[7]

At the same time, his fieldwork led Maslow to question the principle of cultural relativism. Allowing for their different customs, the tribe still produced a "range of personalities" similar to what he would have expected to find in New York. For that matter, he surmised—no doubt correctly—that Ruth Benedict didn't really believe in relativism either. In their private conversations, Benedict dropped her pretense of non-judgmentalism and chatted freely about "nice" and "nasty" societies. In more formal contexts, of course, she used less loaded terms. Maslow was especially taken by a lecture Benedict gave at Bryn Mawr in which she contrasted "high synergy" and "low synergy" cultures. The Zunis, for example, were an example of a high-synergy culture, one in which what is good for the individual is also good for the group. The capitalist United States of America would be classified as a low-synergy culture, in which individuals succeed at the expense of the group. Maslow didn't bother to ask himself why, with all this synergy going for them, the Zunis were few and poor while low-synergy Western civilization was expanding its reach around the globe. His concern was less with the way things were than with the way they ought to be.[8]

On his return from Canada, Maslow took up a full-time teaching job at Brooklyn College, a newly established branch of New York City's public university system that was beginning its first year at its permanent campus in the Flatbush section of the borough. Maslow's position, which carried the lowly title of "psychology tutor," was much less than a researcher with his academic background might have hoped for, but in many respects he had found an ideal situation. Much like Maslow himself, the typical Brooklyn College student was the child of Jewish immigrants, the first in his family to attend college. And for many students, Maslow's introductory psychology course would serve as a bridge to a world of new ideas, at once challenging and anxiety-provoking.

The youth who had been ashamed of his looks and too sensitive to make friends had matured into a rather glamorous figure. Female students found Abe's homely features appealingly rugged, and, in what surely was an overstatement, nicknamed him "the Frank Sinatra of Brooklyn College." One Brooklyn alumnus who served as president of the Psychology Club during his student years retains a vivid image of Maslow's physical presence: "[he] walked with charismatic ease and grace. He spoke in beautiful mellifluous tones.... And he was flattering. What he said was very reassuring." As he moved around campus, Maslow was often surrounded by his "coterie," a small group of students who looked up to him as their mentor. The group often met at Maslow's home, where he encouraged them to discuss their goals and personal problems, including sexual problems. His advice, on the rare occasions he offered it, was restrained by today's standards, but the very notion that such matters could be openly discussed at all was a revelation.

Safely on the track to tenure, Maslow was now free to concentrate on developing his ideas, some of which he tried out on his students in a course he called "The Normal Personality." He adopted the term "self-actualization" to describe the state of ideal psychological health achieved by only a small percentage of men and women. And he chose two of his own mentors, Max Wertheimer and Ruth Benedict, as models of the self-actualized personality. The choice of Wertheimer appeared to provoke little discussion, but analyzing the elusive Ruth Benedict was almost a parlor game among her friends. Maslow had become quite close to Margaret Mead—"one of the smartest people in the world," he called her—and to Mead's friend Jane Belo, who was married to the writer Colin McPhee. When the three friends got together, "the Benedictine enigma" was often the chief topic of conversation. In 1939, they were abuzz because Benedict kept extending her sabbatical visit to California, even though her absence was creating an opportunity for Ralph Linton to solidify his control of the anthropology department, eliminating the jobs of some of Benedict's friends. As it turned out, the solution to this particular mystery was entirely personal. Benedict had begun a liaison with a woman named Ruth Valentine, and the two of them were delaying their move back East until Ruth's New York lover, Natalie Raymond, figured out that their long but troubled affair was over.[9]

Benedict was undoubtedly a worthy subject for study. After all, she had managed to carve out a successful and rewarding career despite her lifelong struggle with depression. But only a man in the throes of hero worship could have considered her a model of mental health. The best-informed objection would come from Margaret Mead in a letter written after Benedict's death: "Maslow's theories about her work I have always regarded as major misapprehensions," Mead wrote. "He speaks of her as a fully actualized person. Actually she was a very deeply troubled one and her achievements were the fruits of tragedy rather than actualization in this sense." Erich Fromm, another friend of Benedict's, agreed that she was a woman who was "very deeply alone" and who, in the latter part of her life, had simply given up and "stopped fighting loneliness."[10]

In 1943 Maslow published the first in a series of articles that would outline his theory of motivation. Based on his knowledge of animal behavior studies, he believed that the higher primates—chimpanzees and gorillas—had evolved to the point where they no longer exhibited aggression except in reaction to a threat. This assumption, later shown to be incorrect, justified his belief that human infants come into this world with no evolutionary imperative to succeed at the expense of others. An inborn "instinctoid drive" will lead them to grow into loving, unselfish adults *provided* they are first able to satisfy four basic levels of needs: 1) physiological needs, such as food and shelter; 2) security needs; 3) belonging needs, for love and acceptance; and 4) self-esteem, which implies both actual accomplishment and recognition from others. Only after these "deficiency needs" have been satisfied are human beings free to begin the process of self-actualization and the maximization of creative potential—"to become everything one is capable of becoming." Of that group, he estimated that perhaps 2 percent of the population achieve the ultimate goal and become fully self-actualized—or, as he sometimes preferred to put it, "fully human." Though Maslow never expressed it in quite these terms, fully actualized men and women were the living equivalent of religious scripture. They represented the closest humanity had come so far to embodying absolute good.

Maslow understood early on that the most problematic part of his theory was his notion that a self-actualized elite was living among us right now. Who *were* these people? Moving beyond his original pair of role models proved tricky. When he approached likely candidates for interviews, most of the subjects were either horrified or embarrassed. Maslow asked his students to write essays on "the most self-actualized person I know." He administered batteries of tests to his classes, including a Social Personality Inventory of his own devising, which one former student remembers as being "largely self-verifying." The results of these tests, nevertheless, were not encouraging. The students who scored highest in ego security often turned out to be vain, manipulative and shallow in person. Maslow speculated that self-actualization was a lengthy process and it made little sense to try to identify candidates too early in life. As a result, the list of names in his "Good Human Beings" notebook was confined mainly to historical figures, along with a few contemporaries who were so famous that they could hardly object to the designation on privacy grounds: Thomas Jefferson. Abraham Lincoln. Benedict Spinoza.

William James. Jane Addams. Albert Schweitzer. Albert Einstein. Eleanor Roosevelt. Candidates who did not quite make his final cut but seemed close enough for study purposes included Frederick Douglass, Eugene V. Debs, Robert Benchley(!), Peter Kropotkin, John Muir and Walt Whitman.

Everyone on the list was highly accomplished, and the one quality Maslow could single out without hesitation was that all self-actualizers showed an "almost priestly" dedication to their work. But this, surely, was not enough. People who put all their energies into their work are generally not considered psychologically healthy. Indeed, most people would be inclined to agree with William Butler Yeats' poem "The Choice":

> The intellect of man is forced to choose
> Perfection of the life, or of the work,
> And if it take the second must refuse
> A heavenly mansion, raging in the dark.

Maslow was well aware of this objection. He also accepted that some people find themselves trapped in routine, unrewarding work through no fault of their own. Not everyone can be an artist or a statesman. Does that mean the average person has no hope of achieving his or her full potential?

In his efforts to sketch a more generalized portrait of self-actualizers, Maslow emphasized their tendency to be highly inner-directed. Much of what he wrote on this subject is so vague that it could apply equally well to saints or monsters. Still, from the mists of self-contradiction, a rather chilling portrait of the new paradigm of "health" begins to emerge. Self-actualizers are capable of loving more deeply and intensely than other human beings, and their love is never needy or possessive, but they can also be quite ruthless in cutting themselves off from unhealthy relationships. They may exhibit "a certain remoteness," which others misinterpret as coldness. Self-actualizers experience sex more deeply and have better orgasms than the average person, but at the same time, sex "does not play any central role in the philosophy of life." The self-actualized man respects women as human beings, but cares little for the "so called signs of respect for ladies that are hangovers from an unrespecting past." Similarly, self-actualized women are suspicious of men who display formal good manners, realizing that these customs are really signs of contempt.

Self-actualizers, moreover, "tend to be good animals," at home with the earthier sides of their natures. They are spontaneous and relatively free from anxiety or guilt. "Very few of them are religious." They can make an effort to follow conventional rules of behavior when necessary, but when they are absorbed in what they are doing, these rules are likely to be dispensed with. As highly evolved individuals living in an imperfect society, self-actualizers "resist enculturation and maintain a certain inner detachment from the culture in which they are immersed." Indeed, "the unthinking observer might sometimes believe them to be unethical, since they can break down not only conventions but laws when the situation seems to demand it. But the very opposite is the case. They are the most ethical of people even though their ethics are not necessarily the same as those of the people around them."[11]

One can't help but notice that Maslow's list of "good human beings" tilts heavily to the left side of the political spectrum. This was no accident. Maslow had nothing but contempt for Communists, having run afoul of the very active Stalinist faction on the Brooklyn College campus on a few occasions. Indeed, he felt a certain distaste for any politics that involved an open clash of ideas. Nevertheless, he believed that a progressive social agenda was necessary if the majority of humanity was ever to fulfill unsatisfied deficiency needs. It was the function of government to create good human beings, and as a Roosevelt Democrat, Maslow took it for granted that only the national government could or would undertake this mission. In the meantime, of course, the "fully human" 2 percent would be free to continue with their loftier mission according to the dictates of their own situational ethics.

During the 1950s Maslow accepted Adlai Stevenson as a probable candidate for his list of self-actualized human beings, but when a colleague nominated Dwight D. Eisenhower and Harry S. Truman, he couldn't quite stomach the idea of including them. As he later explained, Ike was a "nice" man, but he and Truman were, at best, "merely healthy," as opposed to ideally healthy, since "they like the culture, and they find it quite good, and they work within it, and they improve within it."[12] Thus, an unsuccessful politician who made speeches about world government ranked above a United States President who in his role as general had merely organized the defeat of Adolf Hitler.

Personally, Maslow's worst faults were the egotism born of ambition, a habit of impatience and his enduring grudge against his mother—

this last, a problem he would eventually address in psychotherapy. He had few social vices, and well into middle age he exhibited that special variety of naïveté found only in academia. Like many psychologists at the time, he gave little thought to drugs or the problem of addiction in general. Nor did he show much awareness of how avidly many quite normal people pursue sex, money and power, not to mention thrills. Maslow's files contain articles on astronauts and nudists, but one suspects that he could have vastly expanded his understanding of human personality through visits to the Aqueduct racetrack, Gold's gym or his neighborhood bar.

In 1945, returning to his earlier interest in human sexuality, Maslow agreed to help Alfred Kinsey recruit subjects on the Brooklyn College campus. Kinsey took his fellow sex researcher on a walking tour through Times Square, pointing out the pimps and prostitutes plying their trade—an eye-opening experience for Maslow, who confessed that he had walked the same blocks many times without recognizing the obvious signs of sex for sale.

Maslow kept his promise to help Kinsey find subjects. Among those he approached was the president of the Psychology Club, who agreed to talk members of his House Plan, a sort of residential social club, into signing up. Later, however, Maslow checked Kinsey's data against the psychological tests he administered to all his classes and sent Kinsey a note warning him that his sample was skewed. Just as had happened at Columbia, the students who were willing to talk about their sexual experiences tended to be those who had a lot of them, or claimed to. Kinsey ignored the warning and retaliated by cutting all references to Maslow's research from his bibliographies. In 1952 Maslow published a note in the *Journal of Abnormal and Social Psychology* questioning the validity of Kinsey's statistics, but like other attacks on Kinsey's methodology, the note made no impression on nonspecialists, who accepted Kinsey's highly dubious data as accurate.[13]

While his experience with Kinsey contributed to his growing disenchantment with research, Maslow was continuing to revise his profile of the self-actualized individual. While not religious, a number of his subjects had spoken of quasi-mystical experiences that led to lasting creative insights. These "peak experiences," as Maslow called them, were moments when the individual felt himself to be at one with the universe, egoless and yet wholly himself. They occurred when a dancer lost herself in the dance, a writer was transformed by the act of writing, a mother felt a mystical sense of union with her child. Maslow considered that he himself had enjoyed a peak experience when he kissed Bertha for the first time. Initially, he assumed that peak experiences were rare and came only to self-actualizers. He was somewhat surprised when he described the phenomenon to his classes, and found that virtually all of his students claimed to have had peaks, too. (On the other hand, when he interviewed Eleanor Roosevelt a few years later, she declared brusquely that she had no idea what he was talking about.)

Although there was nothing explicitly religious about peak experiences, they could only be understood in the context of the psychology of religion. This was dangerous territory for a man who believed that religion was mere superstition as well as a major force for evil in the world. (To be precise, it was *Western* religion that Maslow abhorred. He had become at least mildly interested in Taoism on the recommendations of Max Wertheimer and Ruth Benedict.) The very idea of immersing himself in the literature of religious experience and consulting scholars who specialized in this unfashionable area of psychology was repugnant.

The first mention of peak experiences appears in Maslow's papers in January 1946. Coincidentally or not, around the same time Maslow's health began to fail. Exhausted and complaining of a long list of seemingly unrelated symptoms, he was soon too weak to continue teaching. The doctors he consulted were baffled. Maslow's three younger brothers had relocated the family cooperage business to California, where it served the state's growing wine industry, and they invited him to take a leave from Brooklyn College and resettle his family near them. For two years Maslow was on their payroll, working whenever he felt able and trying to recover his strength.

The illness, which sounds in retrospect like depression, cleared up as mysteriously as it began. Maslow gradually went back to reading and writing, and in the fall of 1949 he began teaching classes at Brooklyn College again, apparently reconciled to the unconventional direction his research was taking. A year later he published his first description of self-actualized individuals in a small journal edited by his friend, the depth psychologist Werner Wolff. These speculations seemed unlikely to do anything for his career, which so far had hardly been stellar. After more than a decade at Brooklyn College, Abe was still only an associate professor with a heavy teaching load. Popular as he was with undergraduates, he did not always get along well with colleagues. Nor was he a success when it came to mentoring graduate students. Maslow excelled at poking holes in the design of research projects, but he was often less helpful when it came to suggesting ways to make improvements. Ph.D. candidates who chose him as a mentor sometimes gave up in frustration without ever finishing their degrees.

Maslow's career took a sudden turn for the better in 1951 when the founders of Brandeis University invited him to organize psychology studies for the new school. In addition to his popularity with Jewish students in Brooklyn, Maslow had been an early supporter of Israel and he was distantly related by marriage to David Ben Gurion. His optimistic, holistic and vaguely leftish approach to his discipline also recommended him to Brandeis, where he joined such luminaries as Leonard Bernstein, nuclear physicist Leo Szilard, political journalist Max Lerner, sociologist Philip Rieff, and the Marxist theorist Herbert Marcuse.

The prestige and intellectual cachet of his new position gave Maslow a degree of professional visibility he had never enjoyed during his years at Brooklyn, and the appearance in 1954 of *Motivation and Personality*, a compilation of his articles on self-actualization, was a career-making event. Maslow's view of motivation had immense appeal for students of education, social work, management and other branches of applied psychology. It released them from the burden of having to defend traditional moral codes that they personally considered outdated or overly harsh and imbued them with a sense of mission. An army of counselors, therapists, trainers and enlightened teachers would be needed to satisfy the deficiency needs of America's young and not-so-young, lifting them to the level at which they would be able to take charge of their own personal growth.

From a broader perspective, Maslow's theory offered an apparently nonpolitical justification for what has come to be known as the nanny state. If his ideas were correct, childhood poverty was not just a hardship to be overcome, it could inflict psychic damage that might well be permanent. Adults, too, were in need of emotional support. In an early paper, for example, Maslow had argued that unemployment insurance was necessary to bolster the self-esteem of workers, reassuring them that layoffs were not a reflection on their worth as persons.

In the long run, the hierarchy of needs supported what one commentator called the "Officer Krupke Defense"—"I'm depraved on account'a I'm deprived." Maslow utterly failed to anticipate this. *Motivation and Personality* is infused with a spirit of optimism. Infants, according to Maslow, are born perfect, and if allowed to satisfy their needs in a loving and non-coercive atmosphere, they will grow up to be good people. "From the point of view, then, of fostering self-actualization, a good environment (in theory) is one that offers all the necessary raw materials and then gets out of the way and stands aside."[14] Maslow even alluded briefly to his utopian vision of Eupsychia, an ideal community of one thousand psychologically healthy families. The organization of such a community would be basically "anarchistic," he predicted, since its inhabitants would feel no need to impose their opinions, religious beliefs or personal tastes on others. The ruling spirit would be "Taoistic but loving" and everyone, young people included, would enjoy "a good deal more free choice than we are used to."

Maslow also devoted a few pages of his book to describing an informal survey he had conducted on "peak experiences." He had asked "many" people to describe "the most wonderful, most ecstatic experiences of their lives." Some people talked about passionate lovemaking, some about the act of creating a work of art or writing their most inspired paper. Others had "peaked" while communing with nature, and one woman said her most ecstatic moment had been the act of giving birth. Although the triggering experiences differed, Maslow noted, the language people used was remarkably similar and paralleled descriptions of peak experiences found in the works of such students of the mystic experience as Bucke, Suzuki and Huxley.

Although Maslow didn't elaborate, his mention of Richard Bucke shed light on the direction of his thinking. Bucke's 1901 book, *Cosmic Consciousness,* argued that about six hundred thousand years ago the human race made a giant evolutionary leap from simple animal consciousness to self-consciousness. According to Bucke, *Homo sapiens* was on the brink of another such transformation, a giant leap forward to the stage of "cosmic consciousness." Since such important evolutionary changes don't take place all at once, a few exceptional individuals had already moved to the next level, among them Jesus Christ, Buddha, St. Paul and Mohammed. In all such cases, added Bucke, their transformations were associated with a life-changing mystical experience that occurred around the age of thirty.

Maslow didn't promise a leap up the evolutionary ladder, but he certainly made peak experiences sound alluring. As he explained it, the process of adjusting our behavior to social norms inevitably creates anxieties. In repressing unacceptable desires, man "protects himself from the hell within himself, [but] he also cuts himself off from the heaven within." Peak experiences dissolve our anxieties and defenses and make us whole again. "The civil war within is neither won nor lost but transcended."[15]

Analyzing an expanded version of a paper that Maslow delivered at a 1956 meeting of the American Psychological Association, psychologist Richard Lowry has pointed out a glaring flaw in his logic. Maslow had asked people to tell him about "wonderful" experiences, and they had happily obliged; then, based on their responses, he concluded that all peak experiences were positive. In a follow-up report, citing a data base of just 190 college students, Maslow concluded: "The peak experience is only good and desirable, and is never experienced as bad or undesirable."[16]

When Maslow was invited to speak at a prestigious symposium at the University of Nebraska in 1955, he used the occasion to share his conviction that the pursuit of "pure cold truth for its own sake" was no longer enough. He aspired to find ways to use his knowledge for the improvement of humanity, showing people how to be "brotherly, peaceful, courageous and just," and he opined, "I sometimes think the world will be saved by psychologists—in the very broadest sense—or it will not be saved at all."[17]

The Nebraska speech sowed the seeds of the movement that came to be known as humanistic psychology or, somewhat more broadly, as the Third Force—third, because it was neither behaviorist nor Freudian. A year or so earlier, Maslow had begun organizing a circle of correspondents made up of like-minded psychologists, including Gordon Allport, Carl Rogers and Erich Fromm, as well as sociologists, liberal theologians and writers, among them Lewis Mumford, Paul Goodman and Jacques Barzun. The circle eventually grew to about 125 members, united in their concern that mainstream psychology—or, as Maslow once referred to it, "low ceiling psychology"—was too focused on the problems of individuals, to the exclusion of social issues like racism and nuclear disarmament. Frustrated by their inability to get articles on such subjects accepted by the leading journals, members of the group began sharing their unpublished manuscripts. In 1961, with Maslow's approval and support, Anthony Sutich launched the *Journal of Humanistic Psychology* and two years later the Association of Humanistic Psychology held its first conference in Philadelphia. During the socially conscious decade that followed, the AHP grew in size and influence.[18]

Existentialism was much in vogue at the time, and humanistic psychologists were sometimes described as American existentialists. This wasn't quite accurate, though there were definite similarities between the two movements. Both movements grew out of Nietzsche's proclamation that God is dead. (However, Maslow would add wryly, "Marx also is dead.") Both emphasized alienation from values based on the authority of received religion and a need for the individual to derive meaning through his search for identity and authenticity. Perhaps the most striking difference between humanistic psychology and European existentialism was their contrasting moods. Maslow had no use for what he called the "high IQ whining" of Sartre, Camus and Heidegger, who nattered on endlessly about angst, dread and nothingness. He was more sympathetic to the religious existentialists like Sören Kierkegaard and Martin Buber, whose concepts of God were sufficiently abstract that even an enemy of organized religion like himself could feel comfortable with them.

After two world wars and the Holocaust, some might concede that Europeans were entitled to feel gloomy, but Maslow saw their negativity as just the morning-after blues of people who had once believed in God and then lost their faith. When European intellectuals got over this "phase," they would realize the wonderful possibilities of constructing a new secular value system based on progressive ideals. Maslow's writing during this period, collected under the title *Toward a Psychology of Being,* would focus on his theory that certain values, which he called "Being-values," were inborn in every person and found their fullest expression through self-actualization. Rather than follow the dictates of scriptures or obsolete codes of morality, human beings could realize their inborn potential for good by studying the lives of the self-actualized few as well as through personal peak experiences and the search for authenticity.

Maslow had almost nothing to say about the traditional concerns of moral education. Violent behavior, thievery and sexual exploitation would presumably disappear once their root causes—unmet deficiency needs—were addressed. Psychologically healthy people would be capable of regulating their private behavior. Social controls merely created unnecessary conflicts and stifled human creativity. A more relaxed or "Taoistic" approach to governing human nature, one that was content to let people be truly themselves, would result in a tremendous outpouring of positive energy.

Surprisingly, Maslow's ideas would find their most successful application in the field of management. The early 1950s had been the era of the Organization Man, when corporations sought to apply the principles of the assembly line to human resources. The Soviet Union's launching of Sputnik, the first earth-orbiting satellite, in 1957 led to a wave of soul searching among educators and executives who wondered if American technology had lost touch with the iconoclastic spirit of inventors like Thomas Edison. Somewhat to his surprise, Maslow began to find himself in demand as a creativity consultant. Among his first clients was Cal Tech, which hired him to suggest ways to broaden the intellectual horizons of engineering majors. Maslow found the students overly competitive. He suggested adding more liberal arts courses to the curriculum and moving the families of resident advisors into the dorms to temper the hyper-masculine atmosphere.[19]

In 1962 Andy Kay, the president and founder of Non-Linear Systems, invited Maslow to spend a summer as a scholar-in-residence at his factory in Del Mar, California. The producer of the first commercial digital voltmeter, Kay was a man of many enthusiasms. A great believer in vocabulary expansion, he had concluded that people who knew many words were insulated against paranoia. Inspired by Maslow's idea that healthy people were self-motivating, Kay had junked his factory's time clocks and replaced his assembly line with production teams. He made no demands on Maslow, who used his time in California to read up on industrial psychology and keep a journal, originally published in 1965 under the title *Eupsychian Management.*

Maslow started from the assumption that no one wants to be bored. Given opportunities to learn and use their initiative, employees will work harder and identify with the goals of the company. His radical advice to managers was: "Assume everyone is to be trusted." Moreover, one person's success need not come at the expense of another's. Enlightened institutions work synergistically: "What is good for General Motors is then good for the U.S., what is good for the U.S., is then good for the world, what is good for me is then good for everyone else, etc." The factory was just a microcosm of Eupsychia, the community of self-actualized individuals, and "the definition of a good society is one in which virtue pays."[20]

Eupsychian management seemed hopelessly eccentric in the context of how most large corporations operate, with decision making concentrated at the top of the organization chart and armies of middle-management types assigned to control production workers. But Maslow's ideas were attractive to entrepreneurs, especially in the technology startups that were beginning to transform American industry. *Eupsychian Management* also proved popular in Japan, where the team approach to production was widely adopted. Maslow influenced (and was influenced by) theorists like Peter Drucker and Douglas McGregor, and helped set the tone for the era of garage startups and the home-away-from-home office. By 1968 he had begun to talk about "Theory Z," which correctly anticipated a major shift in the way Americans view work. Instead of selling their time and services to a company in exchange for wages and fringe benefits, managers and technical people would begin to think of their careers the way artists and intellectuals do—as a life-long process of personal growth. Instead of opting for lifetime security, such workers would change jobs to take advantage of opportunities to improve their skills and learn new ones. Workers who thought this way would prove far more prepared to survive in the era of industrial reorganization that began during the 1980s.

With hindsight, it's ironic that Maslow's utopian vision of human nature found its most successful application in industrial psychology. Of course, this happened because the business environment is paved with reality checks. Even if workers are told they're not in competition with one another, they tend to suspect that they really are. Take away the time clock and ambitious people work more hours, not fewer. If one executive keeps in touch with the office while on vacation, others feel pressured to do the same. Employees who abuse their freedom are not popular with co-workers and they tend to be let go.

Moreover, while the economy as a whole may be synergistic, individual corporations are still subject to the tyranny of the balance sheet. Andy Kay's experience proved to be a case in point. Kay moved on from the digital voltmeter to develop the Kaypro computer. One of the first practical desktop computers, the Kaypro was especially popular with writers, reporters and other nontechnical types who used their machines primarily for word processing. By 1984 Kay's company was booming, with sales of $120 million. Within a few years, however, Kaypro would be in bankruptcy. Many of Kaypro's problems were the typical challenges of expansion, including lining up new financing and meeting increasingly stiff price competition. But Andy Kay's enthusiasm for eupsychian management did exact a price. Out of loyalty to longtime employees, he resisted turning over direction of his booming company to an outside management team and moving some production overseas. So in Kay's case, the moral seemed to be that virtue pays, except when it doesn't.[21]

Even as his national reputation grew, Maslow was becoming increasingly frustrated with the situation at Brandeis. In an effort to build the strongest possible department, he had avoided filling slots with people personally loyal to him. Now, as his outside commitments multiplied, he missed having junior colleagues and graduate students who were willing to take over the routine tasks that filled his schedule. He confessed in his journal to feeling "a little Nietzschian" on this subject. Surely, he mused, people with IQs of over 180 were in a class by themselves; given all that they had to contribute, they deserved support. But this thought immediately caused him pangs of guilt. After all, *he* was the one telling people that they had a duty to pursue self-actualization. How, then, could he secretly believe that his work was more important than theirs? It was a conundrum.[22]

Still more disappointing to Maslow, the rapport that he had enjoyed with Jewish students at Brooklyn College failed to carry over to his new post. Brandeis students tended to be the doted-upon children of lawyers, doctors, businessmen and professors. They weren't caught between two cultures like the ambitious Brooklyn College kid who had to cope with a Yiddish-speaking mother and a father who hoped he would take over the family dry cleaning business. The typical Brandeis freshman took it for granted that his opinions deserved to be taken seriously, and he wasn't particularly flattered or surprised by Dr. Maslow's avuncular interest in his personal welfare. In Brooklyn, Maslow had introduced many a bright but unsophisticated student to a more challenging and liberal intellectual environment, one where it was possible to ask the big philosophical questions and come up with answers different from the ones dictated by tradition and family. At Brandeis, which had its share of red diaper babies and radical activists, Maslow was more likely to be perceived as a fuzzy-minded liberal. Though a supporter of big-government programs, he did not hate capitalism and—heretically, from the New Left point of view—he accepted consulting fees from corporations and even the United States Army. The most radical thing he ever did was announce to freshmen in his introductory psychology course that it was okay to use words like *fuck* because obscenity was an artificial concept, the product of our repressed, conformist society. For the programmatic radicals, it was hard to see how using bad language in class could have any political impact.

Maslow, on his part, found Brandeis students overindulged, complacent and strangely oblivious to considerations of morality. In a memorable passage in his journal, he complained, "they seem never to admit to guilt, and are usually astonished by punishment."[23]

Still, there were some students who were profoundly touched by Maslow. Among them was Abbot Hoffman, the son of a medical supplies salesman who grew up in a working-class section of Worcester, Massachusetts. Abbie Hoffman had survived in Worcester by disguising his bookishness behind a ducktail haircut, pegged pants and a Marlon Brando slouch. At Brandeis, he found he was still a misfit, though for different reasons. He hung out with a bohemian crowd but refused to give up the affectations of the small-town hood, and his new friends didn't quite know what to make of his passions for playing the horses and driving powerful American-made cars.

Unlike his more affluent classmates, Hoffman understood Maslow perfectly. He saw self-actualization theory as setting out a sort of "moral ladder," challenging people to ratchet up their standards of social responsibility, undoubtedly what Maslow had in mind. He also grasped the theory's special appeal for outsiders—Jews, racial minorities, and working-class kids who were the first in their families to attend college. Counselors in the 1950s continually emphasized the need to adjust to the values of the group. But kids like Abbie Hoffman had already made a break with the values of their parents just by deciding to go away to college, and they didn't necessarily feel comfortable aping the manners of either the genteel middle class or the lefty bohemians they met on campus. Embarrassed by their families at times, they were also bitterly resentful of professors and fellow students who looked down on them.

For young people caught between two worlds, Maslow's vision of creating an authentic personality through self-actualization offered an attractive alternative. His writings emphasized the virtue of creative rebellion. You could challenge authority, pick and choose your values, do what felt good inside, and create a new identity that was uniquely your own.

Hoffman latched on to Maslow like an eager puppy. He switched his major to psychology, signed up for every course Maslow gave and became part of the circle of students who got invited to the professor's home for dinner and discussion. He even dated Maslow's younger daughter, Ellen, a few times and developed a close friendship with her that would survive long after he graduated. Hardly a man given to hero worship, Hoffman would include an effusive tribute to Maslow in his 1980 autobiography, *Soon to Be a Major Motion Picture.* "Most of all, I loved Abe Maslow . . . ," he would write in part. "Maslovian theory laid a solid foundation for launching the optimism of the sixties. Existential, altruistic, and up-beat, his teachings became my personal code."[24]

Chapter 3

Mushroom People

One day in the spring of 1962, Harvard psychologist Timothy Leary drove to Logan Airport to pick up two houseguests who were arriving on the shuttle from New York. Salinas, the girlfriend of Jack Kerouac's road buddy Neal Cassady, was a striking brunette in skin-tight jeans and a skimpy top that showed off her lithe figure. Her flashier companion, Flora Lu Ferguson, wife of the jazz trumpeter Maynard Ferguson, had begun decking herself out in multicolored oriental silks and heavy ethnic jewelry long before they became fashionable. As he was about to pull out of the airport, Leary spotted Abe Maslow waiting at the taxi stand, his stooped shoulders the picture of depression. The contrast between the somber professor with his bulging briefcase and woebegone expression and Leary's happy group was almost painful, but Leary recovered his composure in time to offer Maslow a lift, introducing him to his guests as the man who had coined the term "peak experience."

"That's what we're going to have tonight," said Salinas, inviting Abe to join the party.

Maslow refused with a shake of his head. "Those who theorize about it are often the last to do it," he intoned. "Freud taught us that."[1]

It wasn't literally true that Abe Maslow had never had a peak experience. Still, at fifty-four he found that the transcendent moments of his life were few and far between. Despite what was supposed to happen

according to the theory of self-actualization, his emotional life was growing more constricted. Burdened with professional duties, he had even
given up favorite pastimes like bird watching and nature walks.

By contrast, Tim Leary, just twelve years younger, was self-actualizing
like mad. After only three years at Harvard, he was the star of his department, spending more time jetting off to international conferences and
meeting celebrities than he did on analyzing data or writing papers. Leary
was one of a small group of researchers in the Cambridge area working
with psilocybin, a synthesized version of the active ingredient found in
Psilocybe mexicana, the sacred mushroom of the ancient Aztecs. The buzz
around town was that Leary and his associates were having remarkable
success using the drug in therapy sessions with prisoners at Concord State
Penitentiary. Early reports had it that even hard-core recidivists like the
locally notorious safecracker Jimmy Berrigan were having religious epipha-
nies and vowing to turn their lives around.

Just a few years earlier, Maslow's interest in the psychology of mystical experiences had been professionally embarrassing. His Brandeis colleagues, all atheists, chided him. Prestigious journals refused to publish
his papers. Now the mood had shifted, and the nature of consciousness
was a hot topic. At radical Brandeis, the student newspaper ran articles
on Zen Buddhism. MIT had awarded a visiting professorship to Aldous
Huxley, whose account of his experimentation with mescaline was fast
becoming an underground classic. On the West Coast, psychiatrists were
said to be administering a far more powerful "creativity drug," called
LSD, that enabled subjects to achieve peak experiences lasting up to
twelve hours at a stretch. One enthusiast, Dr. Sidney Cohen, had given
the new drug to scores of mental health professionals as well as policy
analysts from the Rand Corporation think tank, including Dr. Herman
Kahn, the father of the H-bomb.

Around Cambridge, psilocybin—nicknamed "mushrooms"—was
at this point better known than LSD. Mushrooms were a Truth-and-
Love drug. Once you took them, your anxieties and prejudices fell away
and you lost all interest in power, money and the hypocritical games of
our screwed-up society. Lisa Bieberman, a student who began using mushrooms as part of Leary's group at Harvard, would recall:

> There was a whole new world in the mushroom, so we said—the key to
> a stronger, richer human life soon to be made available to every man. We
> were full of the happy excitement of sharing a soon-to-be-public secret

that was going to save the world. . . . To my younger, naiver eyes, the mush-room people were as brave as Christian martyrs, and full of wisdom. They were an indissoluble family, destined to go forward, hand in hand, to win souls and bring in the Kingdom.[2]

Abe Maslow's relationship to this development was an uneasy one. According to his biographer Edward Hoffman, Maslow and Leary "had become quite friendly and spent many hours discussing their mutual interests in creativity, superior mental functioning and peak experiences." Beginning shortly after Leary's arrival in Cambridge in the fall of 1959, the two men had fallen into the habit of getting together for lunch once a week or so. Maslow invited Leary to lecture at Brandeis psychology colloquia on more than one occasion, and two members of the Brandeis faculty, Ricardo Morant and Harry Rand, became interested in working with consciousness-expanding drugs themselves. Maslow's daughter Ellen even went to work for Leary as one of his office assistants for a time.

The relationship between Maslow and Leary was undoubtedly an example of Abe's favorite concept, synergy. The theory of peak experiences provided the context that gave Leary's work intellectual credibility, while Leary in turn was generating exciting results and a groundswell of publicity that made Maslow's theory of uncommon interest to people who otherwise would never have heard of him. Still, Maslow refused to try the new drug, even once. Fascinated as he was, the notion that a person could attain transcendence through drugs made him profoundly uneasy. Peak experiences were supposed to be rare and precious. They were supposed to be *earned.* One of his students, Debby Tanzer, was doing her thesis on natural childbirth as a trigger for peaks. Now *there* was an example of an earned peak experience! Leary listened to Maslow's concerns and dismissed them as the quibbles of an old man resistant to technological change. Travel by train, automobile and airplane used to be rare and special, too. Now distant, exotic destinations were within everyone's reach. What was so wrong about that?[3]

Maslow's inability to answer this question reflected the shortcomings of his theory. Like the "aha!" moment described by his mentor Max Wertheimer, the peak experience presumably represented the mind's spontaneous reorganization of perceptions and emotions into a new pattern, a "gestalt" that was entirely original. But Maslow had invested the concept with so much moral weight that it was difficult to describe peak experiences objectively, much less compare them with other forms of learning or states of emotional excitation. Debby Tanzer had made a game effort in that direction, though many women who have given birth by Caesarean section would contest the notion that their experience of motherhood was any less spiritual than that of mothers who go through natural childbirth. Since peak experiences were both intensely private and, by definition, good, it was hard to get beyond describing them in vague, quasi-mystical terms.

There was another factor that would soon contribute to Maslow's unease, even if he didn't specifically acknowledge it. The excitement over consciousness-raising drugs was making him famous and financially secure for the first time in his life. His book *Toward a Pyschology of Being*, a collection of papers including two on the subject of peak experiences, was brought out by the academic publisher Van Nostrand in the spring of 1962 with a first printing of 2,000 copies. Six months later it had already sold 7,000 copies and was on its way to sales of 200,000 over the next six years—and that just a prelude to trade and paperback editions. Even Maslow's earlier works were suddenly selling well. His spring 1963 royalty check from Harper's, which had published a book called *New Knowledge in Human Values,* was unexpectedly large. Even *Motivation and Personality* had sold more copies than in any other six-month period since its appearance.

Since Maslow's essays were never easy reading, how could one account for the popularity of *Toward a Psychology of Being?* The answer is that young people were reading the book as an endorsement of seeking self-realization through drugs. In one chapter, entitled "Peak-Experiences As Acute Identity Experiences," Maslow explained that peaks enabled the individual to come close to experiencing his "unique self." In peaks, "the individual is most here-now, most free of the past and of the future in various senses, most 'all there' in the experience." Peaks made people better listeners, freed them from the burden of habit and expectations, and placed them "beyond desire." Moreover, "the person now becomes more a pure psyche and less a thing-of-the-world living under the laws of the world." As they said in the sixties, this was *heavy*.[4]

In fairness to Maslow, drugs were probably the last thing on his mind when he wrote those words. At the beginning of the 1960s it was still quite possible for a prominent psychologist to have given very little thought to the problems of alcoholism, drug abuse or addictive behavior in general. Nor, like most writers of academic tomes, had Maslow imagined that his words would be read and taken literally by the general public. Now he was caught by surprise. The evolutionary change in consciousness that he had called for was actually happening! As the decade unfolded, Maslow would vacillate between hopeful excitement and deep depression over the unexpected repercussions of this development.

As for Timothy Leary, he was by no means the first to experiment with consciousness-raising drugs at Harvard. He wasn't even the first to give LSD to students. The study of mind-altering substances at the university had an impressive lineage going back to William James, the founder and guiding spirit of Harvard psychology studies. When he was in his late twenties James had fallen into a deep depression, which he would later identify as a crisis of self-feeling, or self-esteem. Every morning he awoke to find his stomach in knots, his thoughts paralyzed by an overwhelming sense of dread. Suicide seemed the only way out. On April 30, 1870, he reached the point where he knew he had to make a choice if he expected to survive. He recognized that he *needed* to believe in the existence of free will, and hence in the existence of a Supreme Being.

Therefore, James decided, he would *choose* faith. Part of him, he confessed in his diary, still wondered if the exercise of free will was possible. But, he wrote, "I will assume for the present—at least until next year—that it is not an illusion." When negative thoughts intruded, he would banish them by forcing himself to concentrate on phrases such as "the eternal God is my refuge" and "I know that my Redeemer liveth."[5]

William James' self-cure remains controversial. Psychiatrist Howard M. Feinstein argues in a recent biography that James' decision to believe was not a turning point but "just another episode following the same pattern of moralizing self-constriction that James had pursued since 1861." Feinstein is certain that nothing of lasting importance could come from a method of "rational, willful self-treatment" that ignored underlying issues, such as James' conflict with his father.[6]

The definition of a cure lies, it seems, in the eye of the beholder. It is quite true that the crisis of 1870 was not James' first bout with depression, nor would it be his last. James never claimed that the "gospel of habit" was a miracle cure or that it enabled anyone to resolve all his personal problems. As a philosopher, he found it slightly embarrassing to be extolling something so simple-minded as the power of habit. Never-theless, experience had taught him that we become what we do. Thus he advised a friend who was worried about his academic progress, "How-ever discouraging the work of the day may seem, stick at it long enough, and you'll wake up one morning—a physiologist—just as the man who takes a daily drink finds himself unexpectedly a drunkard."

Unlike his father, who underwent his own religious crisis in 1844, William James never established what he called "a living sense of com-merce with a God." He was a modern man, alienated from a personal relationship with God by his inability to believe that the Scriptures—or anything else—represent the "eternal edition" of Truth. Faith on any level was a struggle for him. But he concluded that it was also a useful adap-tation. The habit of belief helps us to anchor our personalities against the terrors of doubt and serves us well as a defense against *Unheimlichkeit,* psychological homelessness.

Even though he attended church regularly, James still found it impossible to pray. His search for a more immediate religious experience eventually led him to the study of mysticism, and to an experiment with nitrous oxide. The inhalation of nitrous was being advocated at the time by a self-educated promoter named Benjamin Paul Blood, who called it "the anesthetic revelation"—a wonderful, if unintentional, oxymoron. James breathed deeply of laughing gas and was transported to another plane of consciousness. Euphoric, he picked up his pen and began tak-ing notes, which read in part:

> What's mistake but a kind of take?
> What is nausea but a kind of -ausea?
> Sober, drunk, *-unk,* astonishment....
> Agreement—disagreement!!
> Emotion—motion!!!
> Reconciliation of opposites, sober, drunk, all the same!
> Good and evil reconciled in a laugh!
> It escapes, it escapes!
> But—
> What escapes, WHAT escapes?[7]

When the high had passed, James reread his notes and pronounced them "the veriest nonsense." Ironically, the average reader today proba-bly finds them easier to comprehend than James' wordier paraphrase in

The Varieties of Religious Experience. At any rate, there was no question in James' mind that he had just had an experience of "some metaphysical significance." He was persuaded that "our normal waking consciousness" is just one of many "potential" forms of consciousness that exist somewhere beyond out reach, separated from the waking mind by "the filmiest of screens." The nature of the mystical revelation had something to do with contradictions being resolved in Oneness. Unfortunately, its essence was private, nonverbal and fleeting. The problem with the mystical experience was that it lacked any authority to communicate itself to others.

James was less successful when he attempted to get in touch with the infinite via peyote. His personal physician, the prominent neurologist S. Weir Mitchell, was among the first to take an interest in Native American peyote cults, which had begun to spread northward from Mexico some time after the Civil War. Mitchell also sent samples of peyote to the poet William Butler Yeats and the British sex researcher Havelock Ellis. James found that the dried cactus buds were bitter, turdlike lumps, too nauseating to keep down.

On the eve of World War I, peyote would be "discovered" all over again by socialite Mabel Dodge, who happened to be a former school friend of Ruth Benedict's. A hostess who cultivated D. H. Lawrence and other famous writers, Dodge had established a home in Taos, New Mexico, where she married one of the local Indians, Tony Luhan. Obtaining some of the sacred cactus buds, she brought them back to New York, and for a time peyote parties were the rage among Greenwich Village bohemians. Dodge substituted an electric light bulb covered with a red cloth for the traditional campfire, and her guests gathered around it reciting chants, said to be based on authentic Kiowa rituals.

Getting high on peyote was always a race between psychic enlightenment and gastric rebellion. Not surprisingly, the peyote fad soon died out, and interest in mind-altering experiences became the province of a small band of botanists, pharmacologists and intellectuals with a penchant for the esoteric. The poet Robert Graves became curious about mind-altering plants when he was researching his novel *I, Claudius* and found himself wondering what sort of poison Agrippina might have used on the emperor. Gerald Heard, a onetime science reporter for the BBC and the author of thrillers like *The President of the United States, Detective,* transformed himself into a walking, talking—especially talking—

encyclopedia of arcane information on ancient mystery texts and vision-inducing substances. Heard was responsible for converting his friend, novelist Aldous Huxley, to the practice of Hindu meditation.

The religions of the Far East are, of course, serious business, major world faiths with millions of followers. But for Huxley, Heard and their friends, their appeal was largely antinomian. Studying the Vedanta enabled them to delve into theology without bothering about inconvenient moral duties imposed by their own culture. Spiritual tourists, they could pick and choose those aspects of any given religion that appealed to them at the moment. Appropriately enough, during the early 1940s, when not touring the United States advocating pacifism, Huxley and Heard studied meditation at the feet of the Swami Prabavananda, whose Los Angeles ashram was built in the shape of the Taj Mahal, a building that has as much to do with Hinduism as the Cathedral of Notre Dame. In the course of the spiritual exploration, Huxley and Heard would become interested in many of the same books on the mystical experience that would later attract Abe Maslow, especially Richard Bucke's *Cosmic Consciousness.*

Boasian anthropologists also took an interest in the mystical experience. In *Patterns of Culture,* Ruth Benedict observed that cataleptic seizures were regarded by twentieth-century Americans as "blots on the family escutcheon and as evidence of dreaded disease," whereas among many Native American tribes the tendency to fall into trances was the mark of a shaman, a revered authority figure. Anthropologists' interest in drug-induced trances would increase as the result of the scientific spadework of ethnobotanists like Richard Evans Schultes, long the director of Harvard's Botanical Museum.

Perhaps the most intriguing of these amateur sleuths was R. Gordon Wasson, a onetime public relations vice president with the J. P. Morgan bank. Wasson's Russian-born wife, Valentina Guercken Wasson, was a pediatrician by training and an avid amateur mycologist who set out to write a cookbook, compiling recipes for the wild fungi that she and her husband collected on their walks through the woods. The cookbook project mushroomed, so to speak, into a decades-long quest that took both Wassons on field expeditions to remote parts of the globe and eventually required the assistance of hired consultants, including specialists in Sanskrit etymology. In 1957 the Wassons published *Mushrooms, Russia and History,* tracing the spread of mushroom cults through Scandinavia and Siberia. Valentina Wasson died in 1959, but Gordon went on to write *Soma: Divine Mushroom of Immortality*, which identified *Amanita muscaria* as the main ingredient in soma, the mysterious "divine drink" of immortality mentioned in ancient Vedic texts.

Gordon Wasson's idea that religion began with the ingestion of "entheogens"—a word he much preferred to hallucinogens or psychedelics—is debatable, to say the least. It is true, however, that psychoactive plants of one type or another have played a role in religious rites in many parts of the world, including Europe. The oracle of Delphi may have breathed the fumes of burning seeds, possibly henbane, to induce a trance state. Even the image of witches riding on broomsticks was no mere fantasy of the medieval mind. Pagan cults, which survived in Europe long after the arrival of Christianity, made use of a salve containing *Atropa belladonna*, aconite and other substances, which female devotees rubbed on their inner thighs and introduced into their vaginas by means of a stick. The salve acted as an aphrodisiac and, in high doses, gave the sensation of flying.[8]

Advocates of vision-inducing drugs tended to assume that the suppression of drug cults by Christianity was a plot on the part of the ruling classes to solidify their power by cutting off individuals' direct access to God. Rarely did it occur to them that shamans and witches were not always wise and benevolent, or that the advent of monotheism and the religion of the Word was a step forward, assuring that there was one truth and one law for everyone. There were exceptions, however. Gordon Wasson speculated that the ancient soma cult was suppressed because it had become corrupt, and he saw no place for drug cults in the modern world. Wasson devoted decades of his life to the study of mushrooms and two Mesoamerican varieties were named in his honor; but during all his years of fieldwork, he actually consumed vision-inducing mushrooms on about thirty occasions. Nor did the Wassons court publicity. *Mushrooms, Russia and History*, was published in a limited edition of just 512 copies. *Soma*, self-published on handmade paper by the Stamperia Valdonega press in Verona, Italy, had an edition of 680 copies. For many years both books were more talked about than read, and it was only after Gordon Wasson's death in 1986 that economical reprints became available.

During the early 1950s, the Wassons received a letter from Eunice Pike, a missionary for the Wycliffe Bible Translators, who reported that Mazatec folk healers near Huautla de Jimenez in the Mexican state of

Oaxaca still conducted vision-rituals, called *veladas,* that involved the consumption of mushrooms. In 1955, on his third visit to the area, Wasson was introduced to a *curandera* (folk healer) named Dona Maria Sabina, who agreed to perform a *velada* for him and a traveling companion, photographer Allan Richardson. A few days later, the ritual was repeated. This time, Richardson abstained from using the drug and took photos instead. Solicited by an editor from *Life,* Wasson agreed to let the magazine do a picture essay featuring the Richardson photos. Valentina Wasson also agreed to write an article for *This Week* magazine. The appearance of the *Life* photo spread, in particular, in the May 13, 1957, issue caused a sensation. Hundreds of Americans descended on Dona Maria's remote mountain village, scouring the ground for samples of the sacred mushroom. A disgusted Wasson thought the Mexican *federales* were quite within their rights to arrest them.

As long as hallucinogenic substances were hard to find (and harder to digest), they were likely to be of lasting interest only to a select few. The accidental discovery of the properties of LSD-25 on April 19, 1943, raised the ante dramatically. Albert Hofmann, a researcher for Sandoz pharmaceuticals in Basel, Switzerland, had been looking for a drug that would control bleeding during childbirth. Instead, he stumbled across the first hard evidence that the symptoms of psychosis could be produced by biochemical changes in the brain. Sandoz classed LSD-25 as a psychotomimetic and made it available to researchers who wanted to study mental illness under controlled conditions. This was how Robert Hyde, also associated with the Massachusetts Mental Health Center, became the first to do LSD studies at Harvard in the early 1950s. After testing the drug on himself, Hyde used student volunteers, including undergraduates, who took LSD in a hospital setting on the understanding that they would see what it was like to be insane for a day. A few of the graduate assistants on the project noticed that the drug had certain recreational possibilities—there was at least one incident involving spiked punch at a party. Still, Hyde's research, which later turned out to have been surreptitiously funded by the CIA, came and went without generating controversy.

All drugs are wonder drugs at the beginning, and within a few years medical researchers who began studying LSD for its power to mimic psychosis were touting its usefulness for everything from treating alcoholism to allaying depression in terminally ill cancer patients. The late Oscar

Janiger, a Beverly Hills psychiatrist, gave the drug to a number of his patients including the writer Anaïs Nin and a group of bohemian painters from Malibu. Dr. Sidney Cohen, affiliated with the Los Angeles Neuropsychiatric Hospital, a Veterans Administration facility, reported that his hospital patients had "powerful integrative experiences" on LSD, though he also cautioned that the effects often didn't last. This warning made less of an impression than the amazing experiences that Cohen's colleagues had when they took LSD as his test subjects. By 1960 Cohen had a database of 25,000 trips taken by 5,000 individuals. He reported only 1.8 psychotic episodes and 1.2 attempted suicides per 1,000 doses and pronounced the drug "astonishingly safe." Around the same time, psychiatrist Arthur Chandler began offering LSD therapy to Hollywood actors, directors and producers for $100 a session.[9]

The advent of LSD gave rise to a strange web of alliances. Psychiatrists soon learned that it didn't pay to put subjects in brightly lit hospital rooms and ask them to complete batteries of standard psychological tests. In order to understand the nature of the drug, they had to ask unconventional questions, and some turned to writers, artists and students of the mystical experience, who seemed more capable of describing the drug's effects. Even the CIA got into the mix. Curious about LSD's potential for interrogation and brainwashing, the agency indirectly funded some of the earliest research. Meanwhile, through its own MK-ULTRA project, the agency was administering LSD to civilians. For a time the CIA operated a brothel on Telegraph Avenue in San Francisco where unsuspecting johns were given drinks spiked with the hallucinogen, just to see how they would react. This was not the agency's finest hour. However, considering the very real concern that the KGB was doing research along similar lines, the CIA's interest was legitimate. Nor was its loosey-goosey approach to work with human subjects unusual for the times.

Today we know that LSD is chemically similar to serotonin, a substance thought to be related to mood regulation and self-esteem. The popular antidepressant Prozac, sometimes referred to as a "mood brightener," also affects the levels of serotonin in the brain, but through a different process. Our growing understanding of the relationship between brain chemistry and conscious thought poses profound questions for our understanding of the self. Dr. Peter D. Kramer, the author of *Listening to Prozac,* cites research showing that monkeys with increased levels of serotonin score higher in dominance behavior. Human patients on Prozac often report enhanced levels of self-esteem. Shy people become more confident and less sensitive to rejection. "Self-esteem is not primarily a set of thoughts about the self," Kramer concludes, "it is an aid or an impediment to locating the self, and a lens through which one's history is viewed."[10] LSD wasn't just a brightener, it packed enough wattage to light a Hollywood movie set. Far more intense than an antidepressant, even if temporary, the drug's effects enabled users to experience a severance of the connection between self-concept and external reality. How people reacted to this phenomenon seemed to depend a great deal on their intellectual preconceptions.

In 1956 Roger Heim, a world-famous botanist on the staff of France's National Museum of Natural History, accompanied Gordon Wasson on a trip to Mexico and later sent a sample of the "god's flesh" mushroom to Albert Hofmann at Sandoz, who used it to produce the synthetic analog, psilocybin. Hofmann tried out his creation and found his mind flooded with Aztec imagery. In 1963 he made a pilgrimage to Oaxaca, where Maria Sabina tried Hofmann's product and declared its effects authentic: "Millions of things I saw and I knew. I knew and saw God: a vast clock that ticks, the spheres that go slowly around, and inside the stars the earth, the entire universe, the day and the night, the cry and the smile, the happiness and the pain."[11]

Meanwhile, Dr. Humphrey Osmond, who was doing research with schizophrenics at a veterans' hospital in Saskatchewan, had begun a correspondence with Aldous Huxley. When Osmond came to Los Angeles for a professional conference in 1953, he gave his new acquaintance a sample of mescaline, the synthetic form of peyote. Closer chemically to epinephrine, mescaline is a much less powerful substance than LSD or even psilocybin, though it produces some of the same effects. Even so, the mescaline trip that Huxley described in his famous essay *The Doors of Perception* has to have been one of the dullest on record. The melancholy Brit contemplated the spines of the books on his library shelves and the folds of his gray flannel trousers. The highlight of his afternoon was a trip to Schwab's Drugstore in Hollywood, where the wares on the shelves appeared VERY bright and colorful. Huxley's drug-induced visions were far less exciting than his sober ruminations on Henri Bergson's theory that the mind is a sort of reducing valve, whose job is not to receive sensory data but to filter out the flood of sensations that serve no useful evolutionary purpose. For those of us who read Huxley and discussed the reducing-valve theory over endless cups of bad coffee in college snack bars, the very notion that it might be possible to manipulate our consciousness was novel and exciting to an extent that seems unimaginable today.

By the end of the decade, all the elements that would support the LSD craze were in place. Humphrey Osmond and his Canadian associates had concluded that LSD made traditional psychotherapy passé; increasingly, they gave patients massive doses of the drug one day and sent them home the next. The Canadians had also coined the term "psychedelic," or mind-manifesting, to describe the new miracle drugs. In Los Angeles in 1959, Arthur Chandler's patient Cary Grant confided to a startled interviewer for *Photoplay* that more than sixty LSD trips had transformed him from a "horrendous" human being who "hurt every woman I ever loved" into a new man: "I have been born again," he announced. Several books extolling the transformative power of LSD were in the works, one of them by Adelle Davis, otherwise known as the author of bestsellers on health and nutrition. Interestingly, most of the early enthusiasts for psychedelics were middle-aged, and often they were veterans of years of ineffective psychotherapy. There were rumors that LSD was becoming a feature of the Los Angeles party scene, but no one except Huxley seems to have given much thought to the possibility that psychedelics would have special appeal for young people. To a large degree this was because the youth culture scarcely existed except as a market for rock-and-roll records. Timothy Leary would change all that when he took up psychedelics, touting them as the ideal weapon in his personal war against middle-class values.

Dazzling intellect, twinkling blue eyes and abundant Irish charm opened many doors for Timothy Francis Leary over the course of his lifetime. No sooner were those doors flung open than he would launch a campaign of sabotage from within. Leary was essentially a secretive man, and it is often hard to separate the myths he created about his own life from the facts, much less to know what fueled his personal campaign against authority. Still, there can be no question that he was a consummate con man, and like all good cons he did not so much tell lies as give people permission to believe in their own fantasies. For this reason, many people who were victimized by Leary would remain under his spell. They couldn't dislike the man without repudiating a part of themselves.

Leary was born in Springfield, Massachusetts, in 1920 to a well-to-do Irish Catholic family. The original Timothy Leary, Tim's grandfather, had been the chief medical examiner for Boston and a professor at Tufts University. His father, known as Tote, was at one time the post dentist at West Point. Tote and his eight siblings specialized in Jazz Age dissipation, calculated to shock the devout Catholics of Springfield. One Leary aunt married an Episcopalian, then sailed for Paris and there obtained a divorce. Tote practiced dentistry in a desultory fashion but spent most of his time gambling, drinking and waiting for his father to die so that he could inherit the family fortune. He was the kind of drunk who when in his cups would declaim long swaths of Shakespeare and Coleridge.

Young Tim often delighted in tormenting his drunken father. In his autobiography, *Flashbacks,* he tells of rigging a string to his bedroom door so that he could make it mysteriously swing open every time the drunken Tote tried to pull it closed. In 1934, however, an event occurred that would transform Tote into a mythical figure in his son's eyes. Grandfather Leary died and the reading of his will disclosed that the family wealth was gone, dissipated by the 1929 stock market crash and years of unpaid loans to Tote and his irresponsible siblings. Tote handed his only son a hundred-dollar bill from his meager inheritance and disappeared from his life. Years later, family friends of the Learys would recognize the once debonair Tote as the steward who served them martinis aboard a trans-Atlantic liner.

Leary could forgive his absent father, but not his harried mother, who struggled to maintain a semblance of respectability and normality. (This theme, of course, is a familiar one. Ruth Benedict idolized her dead father but resented her widowed mother for being sad and preoccupied with making ends meet. Abe Maslow, as an adult, was able to forgive his father, who had been a distant figure during his teenage years, but he remained so bitter toward his mother that he refused to have anything to do with her.) Abigail Leary's family, the Ferrises, must have been people of some culture; Leary would recall a house filled with reproductions of Giotto, Raphael and Titian. They must also have doted on Tim, since they helped pay for his private school education, which was beyond Abigail's means. In Tim's eyes, however, the Ferrises were pious, phobic about sex and dull. One of their failings was that they had no use for Tote. Not surprisingly, since they had repeatedly taken in Abigail and her son when Tote was drunk and abusive, they regarded his disappearance as good riddance. Nevertheless, Tim romanticized his father as the Wild Irishman, a poet soul who could not be confined by mere domesticity and middle-class routine. By contrast, his strongest memory of his mother was of seeing her on her knees in the garden, sobbing over a plant that had been destroyed by the family's pet German shepherd. Leary "sensed something self-indulgent" in his mother's tears.[12] One can't help thinking that he blamed his mother for giving in to the feelings that he was working so hard to suppress.

Abigail sent her son to Classical High School in Springfield, whose motto was borrowed from Immanuel Kant: "No one has the right to do that which if everyone did would destroy society." Leary credited his first sexual experience, at age sixteen, with giving him the courage to be a nonconformist, and soon he contributed an editorial to the school newspaper denouncing Kant's categorical imperative as "totalitarian" and a rationale for the welfare state.

Moving on to the College of the Holy Cross, Tim spent two years taking his classmates' bets on sporting events until his high score in a competitive exam won him a congressional nomination to the United States Military Academy. Although he loved the physical education courses, he soon found West Point's academic offerings an insult to his intelligence. As for the academy's rules and regulations, they were an irresistible challenge to his ingenuity. Within days of his arrival, he was sneaking into nearby Newburgh, New York, to forage for booze and fast girls. In November of his plebe year an incident occurred that would lead to his being "silenced"—in other words, ostracized by his fellow cadets.

Leary's accounts of his silencing give the impression that he inadvertently ran afoul of West Point's antiquated honor code. That isn't quite what happened. Returning from an excursion to Philadelphia for the Army-Navy game, Leary smuggled four pints of whiskey onto the troop train, which he shared with a plebe buddy as well as two first-classmen who were having their own party in the cramped toilet facility. The older cadets had every reason to think their celebration would pass unnoticed. But Leary, even though he was already an experienced drinker and adept at getting away with hi-jinks when he really wanted to, behaved in a manner that drew attention to himself and made a full-scale investigation inevitable. As the cadets marched back to their dorms that evening, he insolently smoked a cigarette while in formation. The next morning, he slept through reveille, a major infraction.

When Leary was found in his room, in the throes of a major hangover, the obvious explanation was that he was the victim of a hazing incident. The first-classmen must have lured, or perhaps ordered, a naïve plebe to drink beyond his capacity. The company commander soon discovered that, on the contrary, Leary had supplied the whiskey, and he was furious with Tim for not volunteering this information immediately. Since the incident occurred on the first day when demerits would officially count on his permanent record, one can't help suspecting that consciously or otherwise, Leary had provoked it, not caring if he took a few other cadets down with him. At any rate, the cadet honor committee that voted to silence Leary was certainly correct in its judgment that he was untrustworthy and unfit to be an officer.

Leary, however, drew a different moral. In a letter to his mother, he wrote that he had learned an important lesson: "As long as I can keep from taking myself too seriously, then no matter what happens I shall be happy. The silencing is the best thing that has ever happened to me.... It has made me broad-minded so that I can laugh at the foolish, thoughtless, childish stupidity & the blind cruelty of the immature minds that bother me."[13] Although he hated West Point, he now made up his mind to stay on, glorying in his role as a victim. He survived a court-martial and returned to the Point for a second year, doing his best to undermine the impact of his silencing by making friends with members of the incoming class during "beast barracks," the period before the official beginning of the academic year when the newcomers weren't yet required to ostracize him. Worried that Leary was becoming a sympathetic figure, the academy became eager to get rid of him, and Leary agreed to a negotiated departure, leaving with a statement from the Honor Court that it accepted the not-guilty verdict of the court-martial. This was a hollow victory at best. The West Point honor code would long survive Timothy Leary. But forty years later, Leary still saw himself as a victim. In *Flashbacks* he compares himself to the first African-American cadets at the Point, who were also subjected to silencing. He even calls himself a "white nigger," as if getting drunk, and doing it sloppily, were the equivalent of being persecuted for breaking the color bar.

Leary next entered the University of Alabama at Tuscaloosa. Alabama was known as a party school, but what fascinated Leary was his discovery of a powerful, though of course never publicly acknowledged, "gay infrastructure." Though heterosexual, Leary saw the advantage of allying with gays—or, at least, with those who combined impeccable insider credentials with a subversive attitude. He became the "surrogate son" of a psychology professor whom he identifies in *Flashbacks* by the pseudonym "Dr. Dee." His mentor couldn't save him when he was caught spending the night in a women's dormitory and expelled for it, but later on, during World War II, Dr. Dee would come to Leary's rescue. Days before Leary was scheduled to be shipped off to a paratrooper support unit in the South Pacific, the former professor, now a medical officer in the U.S. Army, arranged for Tim to be reassigned to the staff of a veterans' hospital in Butler, Pennsylvania.

After the war, Leary appeared to be on track for success. He married Marianne Busch, a vivacious brunette who as an audio technician at the veterans' hospital had correctly diagnosed a hearing impairment, a problem somehow never recognized by his family. Marianne was from Oregon City, Oregon, where her father owned a furniture store. She and Tim moved to the Pacific Northwest and enrolled together at Washington State University, where Tim received his master's degree. Moving on to Berkeley to finish his doctorate, he was appointed to a prestigious position as the research director of the Kaiser Permanente clinic in Oakland. He specialized in the interpretation of psychological tests, and made a name for himself by questioning the usual demarcation between normal and abnormal, arguing that at the margins, extreme normality and abnormality met. Leary was also hired as a consultant by the Lutheran Church, advising its seminaries on which applicants were psychologically suited to the ministry.

Success did not agree with Leary, who felt that he was being sucked into another "gray bureaucracy," no different from West Point. He no longer had much faith in conventional psychotherapy. A study he worked on at the Kaiser clinic found that patients on the waiting list for therapy did about as well as those who actually received it. Discouraged as well as bored, Leary found himself wishing for a "psychlotron," some new technology that could split the psyche into its component parts for study purposes just as the cyclotron split atoms. For a time, he thought he might have found such a technique in encounter group work, a movement then in its infancy. Sponsored by the Unitarian Church, he led some experimental groups. But Leary, for all his garrulous charm, wasn't comfortable talking about his own feelings, nor was he particularly good at getting others to talk about theirs.

At the Leary home in the Berkeley hills, there was more drama in a single day than the dull Ferris family of Springfield had mustered over the course of decades. Tim complained that the arrival of their first child, Susan, in 1947 transformed his wife into "a duplicate of her mother" and him into "an industrious father robot." Marianne apparently suffered from postpartum depression, a problem that recurred after the arrival of a son, James Busch Leary, two years later. Tim, on his part, gave his wife plenty to be depressed about. In addition to a long-running affair with his research assistant, conducted in a rented Telegraph Avenue apartment, he had sex with his female patients. He and Marianne, meanwhile, had a relationship based on drinking together in good times and bad, a pattern that continued throughout her treatment for depression. As Leary himself later acknowledged, he was an alcoholic and had reached the stage in which it only took a drink or two to bring out his mean streak. The situation resolved itself when Marianne chose to celebrate her husband's thirty-fifth birthday by asphyxiating herself in the garage. Leary later told a colleague that Marianne left a note saying, "I can't live without your love."

As would invariably happen when his bad behavior provoked a reaction, Leary was shocked and emotionally devastated. Nevertheless, in *Flashbacks* he pins the blame for his wife's death on alcohol: "If only Marianne and I could have sat in front of the fire discussing our marital problems while smoking giggly marijuana instead of downing pitchers of stupefying martinis," he writes. He also assigns some of the responsibility to his wife's parents, who just prior to Marianne's suicide had refused to finance her plan to take the children to the Alps for "a few months" of skiing and recuperation.

In the wake of Marianne's death, Leary resigned from the Kaiser clinic and took off for Europe, where he held a series of guest lectureships and left a trail of bounced checks. Frank Barron, a close friend and Berkeley colleague, caught up with him in Florence and gave him a recommendation to Dr. David McClelland of the Harvard Center for Personality Research, who happened to be in Italy on sabbatical. Leary explained to McClelland that he was no longer interested in the diagnostic work that had made his reputation. In his next book, he would advocate a new approach to therapy that he called existential-transactionalism. The existentialist approach to therapy, just then becoming popular, aimed to break down the separation between therapist and patient. Instead of expecting patients to conform to *their* reality, therapists must encounter patients on their own terms and, in Rollo May's phrase, "be willing to catch what the patient is communicating on many levels." The term "transactional" referred to the proposition that life is a series of transactions, or games. In order to transform themselves from losers into winners, patients needed to figure out the rules others were playing by and master them.

Leary explained to McClelland that the key to his new method was that the psychologist must be willing to change "as much or more than the subjects being studied." According to his account, McClelland was intrigued and delighted. Leary's brand of existentialism was moving in the direction of the humanistic psychology of Maslow, Rogers and Allport, whose radical, antiauthoritarian ideas were the latest trend. "You're just what we need to shake things up at Harvard," the dean said.[14]

Not everyone bought Leary's line, however. Social psychologist Herb Kelman recalls that Timothy Leary's arrival at Harvard in the fall of 1959 was the cause of some excitement. At a relatively young age, he was a name in his field: "People talked about Leary wheels"—a reference to the circular charts Leary used to illustrate his diagnostic theory, which described normality and abnormality as a continuum, rather than polar opposites. Many colleagues were disappointed to learn that Leary had dropped this promising line of research. Instead, he talked tiresomely about playing "the professor game," "the Harvard game," and even "the Timothy Leary game." Kelman happened one day to hear Leary ranting against the psychology establishment. Kelman's own politics were on the left and he was hardly a defender of the status quo, but the tone of Leary's diatribe was disturbing. He began to question Leary about existentialism and discovered that "he knew nothing. He hadn't read the basic texts."[15]

Jay Stevens, in his book *Storming Heaven,* relates a story told by another psychology instructor, Charles Slack, who frequently had drinks with Leary during his first year on the faculty. One day they were grousing about the overuse of the term "psychopath" when Leary turned to Slack and said, "You know I really am a psychopath." Slack laughed, but

Leary volunteered that he had violated every rule in the American Psychological Association's code of ethics "except the ones about money." In fact, he confessed, he had violated the prohibition against sex with patients "many times."[16]

Leary kept telling people that he was on a mission to destroy academic psychology, but only a few people took him seriously. In part this was because others at the time were saying similar things, and it was widely agreed that the field was in need of a radical shake-up. Psychology studies at Harvard were divided between the research-oriented behaviorists, who were rich in grant money, and the Center for Personality Research, which attracted large numbers of students. Young people majored in psychology because they wanted to understand that eternally fascinating topic, themselves, and learn what makes others tick. Graduate study in clinical psychology was also subsidized by the government, on the theory that trained personnel were needed to work in mental hospitals. In the event, however, few people with master's degrees or doctorates were eager to spend their careers laboring in institutions for the clinically insane. The pay was low and the work mostly unrewarding. Grad students at the Center typically hoped to do outpatient therapy in some form and/or train others to be therapists. Unfortunately, recent studies like the one Leary had done at the Kaiser clinic raised doubts about the efficacy of talk therapy. Insurance companies and the government weren't likely to extend coverage for treatment that could not demonstrate practical results.

Humanistic and existential psychology promised to open new vistas for psychologists who might otherwise find themselves underemployed. Instead of trying to cure the mentally ill, they could focus on promoting healthy individuals and healthy social institutions. The humanistic psychologists' desire for a more socially aware, value-conscious psychology may have been driven by their personal idealism, but viewed in colder, harder light it was also a power play. Once psychologists became the arbiters of social values, they would take over many of the functions formerly assigned to professionals trained in the humanities—ministers and teachers, and perhaps even policymakers and businessmen.

Leary was a prophet of this new order. He had no reverence at all for Freud and even less for psychiatrists who treated all human problems from a medical perspective. From his point of view, civilization was just a series of games, and some people had a head start because they got to make up the rules. He encouraged his students to get out of hospital clinics, look at programs in prisons and community centers, and begin thinking in terms of changing society.

Leary's radicalism appealed to Richard Alpert, an assistant professor at the Center who was having severe doubts about his choice of a profession. A pleasantly nerdy guy who sported a crew cut and horn-rimmed glasses, Dick Alpert had all the accouterments of the good life that Leary lacked: a very wealthy and indulgent father, social-register friends, an antique-filled apartment where he hosted "very charming" dinner parties, a Mercedes-Benz sedan, an MG sports car, a 500 CC Triumph motorcycle and a sailboat, and he was soon to acquire his own Cessna 172 airplane. But Alpert was also insecure and in the closet. Even his father, a philanthropist and one of the founders of Brandeis University, had been unable to get him into Harvard as an undergraduate, but by dint of hard work, he had climbed the academic ladder and gotten himself hired by the university that once rejected him. So successful was Alpert that he held no fewer than five separate appointments, including one in the school of education, where he taught child development. Still, despite a $26,000 investment in psychoanalysis, he got diarrhea every time he had to deliver a lecture. Not only did he feel that *he* was a fake, he was beginning to suspect that psychology was fake, too, and that on some level his colleagues knew it. He suspected that his therapy patients weren't improving in any meaningful way. All they really did was pick up "subtle reinforcement clues" and learn to say what was expected of them. Psychology texts treated human beings as agglomerations of "ambulatory variables," while human fulfillment remained as elusive as ever.[17]

Leary and Alpert became friends almost immediately. They started as drinking buddies, consuming martinis and Irish whiskey, and soon planned to teach a course together. In the spring of 1960, Leary began to talk about summering in Cuernavaca, where his friend Frank Barron had sampled the magic Aztec mushrooms the previous summer, and he invited Alpert to fly down to Mexico. Eager to impress his charismatic friend, Alpert hadn't mentioned that he was only a novice pilot, not yet qualified to fly solo. While working as a consultant at Stanford during the early part of the summer, he squeezed in as many lessons as he could, qualified for his license, and took off for Cuernavaca the next day. After all this, he arrived too late to take part in the great adventure. Anthropologist Gerhart Braun, another of Leary's friends, had obtained some of the elusive mushrooms from a *curandera* near Toluca, and the guests at Leary's rented villa were in no mood to wait. Leary swallowed seven of the black, moldy fungi and was off on a four-hour "brain tour" that took him from Hindu temples and "Babylonian boudoirs" all the way back to the beginnings of life on earth. He had found his psychlotron. A dazzled Leary drove ten miles to the home where David McClelland was vacationing and talked the skeptical dean into approving his plan to start a psilocybin research program at Harvard.

On his return to Cambridge, Leary had no trouble recruiting some of the Center's most promising graduate students as research assistants: George Litwin and Michael Kahn had already tried mescaline and knew the literature better than Leary did. Gunther Weil had been a Fulbright scholar. Ralph Metzner had a first-class degree from Oxford and was interested in psychopharmacology. Dick Alpert wasn't around for the launching of the Harvard psilocybin project; he was spending the semester in Berkeley as part of a swap that had brought Frank Barron to Cambridge. The project's work with prisoners at Concord State Penitentiary would get under way some months later, but it was never more than the visible top layer of the group's activities. In the meantime, Frank Barron, who shared Maslow's interest in the nature of the creative impulse, suggested giving psilocybin to a variety of gifted people to see if it would stimulate their talents.

This in itself was nothing new. Oscar Janiger, the Beverly Hills psychiatrist, had taken this free-form approach in his experiments. What set Leary's program apart was his allegiance to the existential principle that the researcher must change as much as—if not more than—his subjects. The Harvard project was never a case of naïve scholars led astray by a powerful drug. Its anti-intellectual agenda was in place before the supply of pink pills from Sandoz arrived in the mail. Leary planned to deconstruct scholarship by first deconstructing the minds of scholars and cultural taste-makers. And he was quite prepared to begin with himself. When the shipment of psilocybin was delivered, he wasted no time, swallowing twice the maximum dosage indicated in published studies and washing it down with Scotch.

Arthur Koestler, the author of *Darkness at Noon* and propagator of unconventional theories about evolutionary biology, became one of Leary's first experimental subjects. Koestler had tried psilocybin before, an encounter that brought on flashbacks of being tortured during his time as a political prisoner. He had a better experience at Leary's house, but he was still not a convert. In an article for the London *Sunday Telegraph* he described listening to classical music while on the drug as a descent into "cosmic schmaltz."

Beat poet Allen Ginsberg and his lover Peter Orlovsky showed up at Leary's house in December 1960, chattering about their recent trip to Peru in pursuit of the vine-induced highs enjoyed by the ancient Incas. After swallowing their pink pills, they got naked, dialed the White House and explained to the operator their plan to set up a summit conference where JFK, Khrushchev and Norman Mailer could get high together.

Leary gave psilocybin to Bill Wilson, the founder of Alcoholics Anonymous; to the poet Robert Lowell, who had a history of manic-depression; and to Beat icon Neal Cassady, who pronounced it "more mellow and cozy than heroin." Jack Kerouac, a confirmed alcoholic, was another guinea pig. Leary asked all his subjects to write up a report of their experiences, and Kerouac was one of those who complied. After taking the drug in a group that included Ginsberg and Orlovsky, Kerouac reported, he had managed to keep his high going for five days by sipping Christian Brothers port on the rocks. The author of *On the Road* recalled that he'd had a good long talk with his mother and loved her more than ever. At times, he had believed he was the Holy Spirit incarnate and the Master of Trust in the Universe. There were, however, some negative side effects to the experience, including a stiffening of the joints, "anxiety about breathing itself," and disturbing hallucinations that his friends were following him everywhere, even on his trips to the bathroom. Also, he'd seen "communists all around us"—not necessarily a delusion, considering the company. All in all, Kerouac concluded, "Walking on water wasn't built in a day."[18]

Despite his claim to be interested in the psychology of health, Leary was in awe of the Beats, who embraced drugs precisely because they were degraded. The Beats' philosophy—some might say their pose—was that insanity and degradation were the logical responses to mass culture and the decay of Western civilization. Ginsberg, the Holy Idiot of the group, actually did get mellower after discovering mushrooms. But Leary, in line with his "existential" principles, was already beginning to resemble the people he was supposed to be studying. Significantly, Cassady's ready comparison of psilocybin to heroin did not strike him as ominous. And in the summer of 1961 he and Allen Ginsberg made a special trip to

Tangier to roust the junkie author William Burroughs out of his darkened quarters and persuade him to come to America and speak at a symposium held during the American Psychological Association's annual conference. Billed as an expert on drugs, Burroughs delivered his largely inaudible talk to a packed room.

Burroughs also visited Leary in Cambridge, where he proved to be a less than satisfactory houseguest. The Leary group's talk of "love engineering" with psychedelics made Burroughs cranky, and he shocked the Harvard men by extolling the delights of buggering twelve-year-old boys. After leaving Cambridge, he circulated a letter accusing the Harvard scientists of cheating him out of a fee for his speech and dispensing "love in slop buckets." Leary was impressed. Like so many addictive personalities he had a tendency to confuse a boundless capacity for inebriation with greatness of soul. Leary eventually patched up the disagreement and became Burroughs' friend, and in his memoirs he expresses shame that he and his colleagues allowed "obtuse game playing" to interfere with their appreciation of this "genius-shaman-poet guide"[19]

Even while he courted the dissolute Beats, Leary was presiding over another circle of drug experimenters recruited from the area's seminaries. His link to this group was Aldous Huxley, whose gaunt frame and grayish complexion made Leary's thirteen-year-old daughter Susan think of Gandalf, the wizard in *Lord of the Rings*. Huxley gave Leary's phone number to Huston Smith, an authority on world religions who was teaching at MIT. Smith had been introduced to meditation by Gerald Heard, but after practicing for twenty years he still hadn't achieved enlightenment and he feared that a "direct experience of religion" would always elude him. On New Year's Day, 1961, Smith and his wife took mescaline at Leary's house in the company of Leary, Frank Barron and psychiatrist George Alexander. The experience was so powerful, he would recall, that for several years afterward psychedelic drugs became "the center of my reflective and social life."

Smith helped form a group of devotees who met regularly to use psychedelics in a "sacramental" context, complete with ad hoc rituals and informal testifying in the style of a Quaker meeting. Alan Watts, a former Anglican priest as well as a leading authority on Zen Buddhism, was writing a book on LSD, and during this period he was a frequent visitor to Leary's home and office, where he sat around consuming gallons of gin while discoursing on the nature of the Over-Mind. On Easter

Sunday, 1961, he presided over an LSD mass, dispensing the drug in solution from a chalice and combining Bible readings with Zen koans. Susan and Jack Leary served as acolytes.

Other members of the religion circle included Walter Huston Clark, the dean of Andover-Newton, an interdenominational Protestant seminary, and Paul Lee, who was Paul Tillich's teaching assistant. Overall, the group played the role of fellow travelers in Leary's growing movement. Although they often severely disapproved of things Leary did, they still saw him as a hero or, in the words of the late Dr. Clark, "a saint . . . conned, robbed, and imposed on by thousands."[20]

In February 1961, Dick Alpert returned to Harvard from his semester in Berkeley and joined Leary as co-instructor of clinical practices, a required course for students enrolled in the Ph.D. program at the Center for Personality Research. Leary and Alpert had renamed the course "Existential Transactional Behavioral Change," and while they didn't exactly order their students to take psilocybin, they strongly implied that anyone who wasn't at least curious about this new frontier of psychology probably didn't belong at Harvard. Students who worried that drugs might interfere with their ability to meet deadlines for class assignments or finish their degrees on time were accused of letting their middle-class inhibitions interfere with a unique opportunity to do their own "neurological fieldwork." Alpert, in particular, offered the kind of testimony guaranteed to appeal to idealistic young people: All his life he had been a reflexive liberal, mouthing slogans about racial equality; then he took psilocybin with Dr. Madison Presnell, the "Negro" psychologist who was in charge of mental health services at Concord State, and realized they were the "same person" under the skin. Among other miracles, psychedelics offered an instant release from white guilt.

Herb Kelman happened to be on sabbatical in Oslo that spring, and he began receiving letters from students saying, "You wouldn't believe what's going on here in Cambridge!" Kelman had a chance to see for himself when he attended the Congress for Applied Psychology in Copenhagen in August and heard Leary, Alpert and Huxley take part in a panel discussion on the topic of "New Directions." Huxley's presentation struck Kelman as reasonably objective—surprisingly so, coming from a nonacademic. Alpert's talk was a combination of first-person testifying and scholarship, but he at least tried to separate the two. Leary's contribution, however, was a rambling monologue studded with the most fantastic claims. He recommended psychedelic drugs as the best way to "clear the cortex" of the "game structure" of Western civilization, and promised that under optimal conditions it was possible to achieve *satori* (enlightenment) in three hours.

On his return to Harvard in the fall, Kelman discovered that only one clinical practices student, a former Brandeis radical, had adamantly refused to try psilocybin. Other doctoral candidates found Leary and Alpert's message alarming, and they worried that their reluctance to join the love-and-brotherhood brigade would affect their grades. Few dared complain publicly, since they assumed that the two men must have the support of the administration. Kelman began to feel that the Center at least owed its graduate students a clarification on this point. A number of junior faculty agreed that something had to be done, but they ran into opposition from senior members of the department. David McClelland was fond of Dick Alpert, who had stood as godfather to his children, and the charismatic, witty Leary was receiving international attention for his work. Above all, there was the usual reluctance to start a fight that would split the department and attract unfavorable publicity. The showdown was tabled for the time being.

While the mills of academic politics ground away at their usual leisurely pace, an eccentric Englishman named Michael Hollingshead arrived in Cambridge toting a sixteen-ounce mayonnaise jar filled with LSD-laced powdered-sugar icing. Hollingshead had been living in New York, doing fundraising for Huntington Hartford's British-American Cultural Foundation, when he discovered that it was possible to buy small quantities of psilocybin and LSD at a store near his LaGuardia Place apartment. Both drugs were quite legal at the time, and Hollingshead sensed an opportunity. He and a pediatrician friend, John Beresford, wrote up a proposal for a nonexistent research project and submitted it to Sandoz, which duly shipped out a gram of LSD with a bill for $285. In the course of cutting the pure LSD with powdered sugar, Hollingshead accidentally treated himself to a massive dose. He was never quite the same again. "The reality on which I had consciously tried to build my personality had dissolved into Maya, the hallucinatory façade.... I was lost, exhausted, ambushed by stagnation and depression."[21]

Hollingshead wrote to Aldous Huxley for advice, and Huxley suggested that he consult Professor Timothy Leary at Harvard. During their first meeting, Hollingshead, an inveterate name-dropper, claimed to bring

Leary greetings from the British philosopher G. E. Moore (who had died in 1958), and he entertained Leary by narrating the story of his great unwritten novel about a man who suddenly develops the power of levitation during the act of sexual intercourse. A day later, he followed up the conversation by calling Leary at his office and threatening to commit suicide. Hollingshead was broke as well as distraught, and Leary offered to let him stay in a furnished room on the third floor of his house. Hollingshead's wife and child showed up, then abruptly departed, the wife complaining that Michael was trying to pressure her into cashing in a bond portfolio she had inherited from her father. Friends from New York warned that Hollingshead was a con artist who had scammed his way across Europe. More unpleasant than ever following his heavyweight bout with LSD, he had also worn out his welcome in New York. But none of these bad omens could overcome the allure of that mayonnaise jar, its contents good for roughly five thousand trips to the far side of consciousness.

By November 1961, Timothy Leary had swallowed psilocybin perhaps two hundred times. Still, according to his own account in *High Priest,* his first taste of LSD took him to a new plateau. Since that experience, he wrote, "I have never been able to take myself, my mind, and the social world around me as seriously." This, of course, echoes what he had already "learned" years earlier from his troubles at West Point, but now he went much farther. Reality wasn't just a game, it was a figment of his imagination: "I have been acutely aware of the fact that everything I perceive, everything within and around me is a creation of my own consciousness. . . . I am an actor and that everyone and everything around me is a stage prop and setting for the comic drama I am creating. LSD can be a profoundly asocial experience."

For the first time since he discovered psilocybin, Leary had allowed another individual to play the role of guide, directing the journey to the center of his own mind. In the process, Leary suspected, Hollingshead had managed to instill an element of "mind manipulation paranoia" that he couldn't shake off. From that day forward, he was never quite sure that he was in control. Yes, he was just a "cosmic buffoon," but he was no longer even in control of the script. The question he kept asking himself was, "who's the sponsor of the show?"[22]

Hollingshead took LSD every day, often while watching soap operas and babysitting for Leary's children. He loved to play mind games on other stoned people, telling them things that weren't true and generally trying to manipulate them. This worried Leary's associates because it wasn't supposed to be possible. Psychedelics were peace-and-love drugs— at least, so they had concluded. Unfortunately, they didn't worry enough. By the time spring came, LSD had replaced psilocybin as the group's drug of choice, and Hollingshead had joined the payroll of the psilocybin project. He was assigned to teach a weekly two-hour course preparing Harvard graduate students for their psilocybin sessions.

While all this was going on, Leary's professional reputation continued to grow. According to anecdotal reports, prisoners at Concord who took psilocybin were undergoing dramatic personality changes that caused them to lose all interest in deceptive or aggressive behavior. If these results could be substantiated, Leary had discovered an important new tool for rehabilitation, with sweeping implications for changing all sorts of negative behavior patterns. As a result of his involvement in a hot research area, he had his pick of invitations to international conferences and his future publications were eagerly awaited. Under the circumstances, it was easy to dismiss complaints from the junior faculty as jealousy.

Even so, David McClelland had forebodings of trouble as early as October 1961. At that time he noted in a memo that Leary and his associates appeared to have lost interest in their academic responsibilities and were exhibiting a "blandness or superiority, or feeling of being above and beyond the normal world." More troubling still, the documentation on the Concord project was months in arrears. This was puzzling since only thirty-six prisoners were involved in the program while Leary had forty research assistants on his staff. Dick Alpert and Michael Kahn responded to McClelland's memo by trying to clean up the paperwork, but it wasn't easy to translate visions of nirvana into acceptable academic prose and data. For one thing, Leary hadn't bothered to set up a control group, so there would never be a reliable yardstick by which to measure the prisoners' progress.

Herb Kelman kept on pressing for an opportunity to air his concerns about the psilocybin project, and McClelland finally agreed to schedule the discussion for the March 16 staff meeting. Kelman arrived expecting a collegial debate and was amazed to find the room packed with spectators, including students and a reporter from the Harvard

Crimson. Undeterred, he had his say, charging Leary with fostering an anti-intellectual atmosphere within the graduate program. Another of the younger professors, Brendan A. Maher, backed Kelman up, reading aloud from papers in psychiatric journals which recommended that psilocybin be used only in a hospital setting.

Leary appeared taken aback by the intensity of their attack. He tried to dismiss the articles as a power play on the part of medically trained psychiatrists. By defining consciousness expansion as a medical procedure, they were trying to wrest control of a powerful new therapeutic tool away from clinical psychologists. "I take anything said by a psychiatrist with a grain of salt," he quipped. Dick Alpert then rose to defend the project. Starting out calmly, he gradually worked himself into a tirade, denouncing the meeting as an ambush organized by colleagues who were jealous of his and Tim's success. The meeting ended in the usual academic fashion with the appointment of a committee to look into the matter further. Pending the committee's report, however, Leary and Alpert agreed to entrust their supply of little pink pills to Dr. Dana Farnsworth, the director of the student health center, who would dole out the medication only as needed for the work with prisoners. This was a major defeat and it left Leary's critics with the impression that the psilocybin project had been reined in, at least for the rest of the semester.[23]

In fact, nothing said at the meeting had made any real impression on the Learyites. From their colleagues' point of view, they appeared to be suffering from some kind of mass depression. The signs included the bland affect noticed by Dean McClelland, as well as their lack of interest in normal personal, professional and social activities. But the Leary group found such suggestions hilarious. Life had never been more exciting! Strange and magical things were happening every day! They had seen the aurora borealis up close, felt the breath of God whispering in their ears, shared belly laughs over the cosmic in-joke that is the universe! Obviously, it was "straights" like David McClelland and Herb Kelman who were depressed, wasting their days on trivial projects and mind-deadening routines. The staff meeting had only emphasized the immense gulf between people who had been turned on to consciousness expansion and those who hadn't yet crossed over. If you were among those in the know, communication with the straights was futile.

At this point, Leary claimed to have given psilocybin to over three hundred subjects and had not one negative reaction. This assurance, of course, was coming from a man who, according to his own 1968 memoir, no longer believed that the world was real and lived in the shadow of what he called "a recurring science fiction paranoia." It all depended on your definition of "negative," and Leary had made the transition to a new dimension of consciousness where such things were fungible.

On the most practical level, however, Leary was quite sane. Undoubtedly he knew from the outset that the Concord prison project would never pass scientific muster. He also didn't care. Tripping on psychedelics with writers and assorted celebrities was a lot more fun than drawing pie charts and fooling around with standard deviations. He had played the professor game so astutely that soon he would be too big for Harvard, and ready to move on to the next act in the drama.

Chapter 4

Miracles

Academic psychology was losing patience with Tim Leary, but the theologians would prove much more tolerant. During a two-year period, the Harvard psilocybin project had succeeded in turning on sixty-nine men of the cloth—Protestant ministers, rabbis and at least two Jesuit priests. Huston Smith, meanwhile, was running drug sessions at MIT for students enrolled in his history of religion course. And in the spring of 1962, even as administrators at the Center for Personality Studies were clamping down on the psilocybin project, or thought they were, Leary was running a psychedelic seminar for divinity students, so heavily subscribed that it was necessary to divide the group into two sections. This was an amazing development considering that Leary was an atheist who loathed Christianity with the laser-like concentration that only a lapsed Roman Catholic can muster.

Leary made at best a pro forma effort to hide his true feelings, disguising them behind a line of Buddhist/Taoist/pantheist patter that he had picked up from acquaintances like Aldous Huxley, Gerald Heard, Alan Watts and a Hindu monk named Fred Swain, who had invited him to conduct a psilocybin session at Boston's Vedanta ashram. The students and ordained ministers who signed up to hear Leary's "preaching," as he called it, tended to approach their faith in a highly intellectual way. They were the sort of believers who would find a Pentecostal service or a pilgrimage to Lourdes embarrassing, but Leary's blend of cutting-edge pharmacology and Eastern religion was aesthetically acceptable.

Not everyone was fooled, however. During the course of an afternoon session, one tripping minister accosted Leary and demanded that he "look into the eyes of Jesus." And Leary couldn't do it. He turned away, causing another man of the cloth to exult, "The master of games has met his match in the eyes of Jesus."

"I was amused and irritated because I saw the 2000 years of Christian moral-one-upmanship and missionary coercion and holy sadomasochism," Leary would write of the incident.[1]

Leary was past caring about the holy grail of scientific respectability, but the religious community was not, and they had found their Sir Galahad in the person of Walter Pahnke, a motorcycle-riding Lutheran from the Midwest who was a candidate for a Harvard doctorate in religion. Pahnke already had his M.D., and he was doing his dissertation on the physiology of the mystical experience. Under the guidance of an advisory committee that included fourteen ministers of the Gospel and experts on the history of religion, Pahnke had designed a classic double-blind experiment: At noon on Good Friday, twenty divinity students from Walter Clark's seminary would gather in the basement sanctuary of Boston University's Marsh Chapel, where loudspeakers would allow them to listen in on the three-hour service being conducted by the university chaplain, Rev. Howard Thurman, in the main sanctuary upstairs. Ten of the students, chosen at random, would be given psilocybin, the other ten a placebo dose of nicotinic acid. Five proctors, or guides, would be present to supervise the students and record their reactions. To make the test a true double blind, both the psilocybin and the placebo were ground up and transferred to identical gelatin capsules. The proctors, unaware of which students had been randomly assigned to get the drug, would be present and taking notes. Another panel of neutral observers would evaluate questionnaires filled out by the subjects after the fact.

Apparently it hadn't occurred to any of Pahnke's distinguished advisors that scheduling such an experiment in the chapel during the most solemn three hours of the Christian calendar might be considered sacrilegious. Dana Farnsworth did think of it, however, and on Thursday of Holy Week, he refused to authorize release of the necessary drugs. Farnsworth and the Harvard administration knew nothing of Leary's mayonnaise jar full of LSD, and they also didn't realize that Leary had taken the precaution of doling out some of his supply of psilocybin to researchers not connected with the university. Within twenty-four hours Leary was able to reclaim enough little pink pills to allow the experiment to go forward. In exchange for his help, he insisted over Pahnke's objections that half of the guides be allowed to take the drug along with the experimental subjects. Moreover, one of the five guides was to be that "expert" on drugs, Michael Hollingshead.

Thirty minutes after the students swallowed their pills, it became abundantly clear who had gotten the real thing. The ten students in the control group sat huddled together in one pew. Meanwhile, a normally shy seminarian began tearing the buttons off his shirt, proclaiming, "I am a fish!" Another student got down on the floor and writhed like a snake, a third played weird chords on the organ, and a fourth was stretched out on a pew, "stiff as a board" according to Hollingshead.

This last individual may have been Michael Young, in training to become a Unitarian minister. Before the pills were handed out he had prayed, "Please God, let me get the real thing." His prayers were answered and he soon felt himself trapped in the center of a giant mandala. Each band of color was another path he could choose to follow in life, but he felt himself inert, paralyzed, and he realized that before he could begin his journey he would have to experience the death of his ego, a horrifying prospect. He scribbled a note to himself: "No one should have to go through this, ever!"

In the confusion, no one noticed when another subject left the sanctuary and strode out into the traffic of Commonwealth Avenue. Huston Smith and Walter Pahnke belatedly gave chase and caught up in time to see the young man rip a package from the arms of a startled mail carrier and enter the headquarters of BU's School of Theology, headed for the dean's office. The young man said later that he felt empowered to proclaim the arrival of the Messiah and he thought the dean of the theology school ought to be the first to know. Pahnke eventually had to subdue him with a shot of Thorazine.[2]

By the end of the afternoon, the other nine subjects had worked through the negative portions of their trips and were feeling euphoric. So, too, was Leary. Although he had scorned Pahnke's project as naïve, he now realized that the experiment would likely be approved by his advisors after all. Pahnke had done what Leary hadn't quite managed to get around to in two years of psilocybin "research": complete a minimally respectable experiment that could be the basis for a publishable paper. In his excitement, Leary jumped to the conclusion that the religious community would be as enthralled by the day's work as his own little group. Here, after all, was scientific evidence that psychedelics were the key to an instant mystical experience, recognizable even by the conventionally pious. Every minister, priest and rabbi in the country would have to take notice, and soon God-fearing people from coast to coast would be clamoring for the drug.

In Leary's mind, at least, it was clear that this development would eventually destroy organized religion as it then existed. Drug-induced mysticism was inevitably pantheistic and antinomian, substituting doctrine with personal truth. By the time the conventionally religious caught on to this, however, it would be too late.

The so-called "Miracle of Marsh Chapel" became the talk of Cambridge and was written up in *Time* magazine, but the reaction was not at all what Leary expected. Pahnke did get his Harvard Ph.D., but Walter Clark narrowly escaped being fired by the trustees of the Andover-Newton seminary. The publicity also energized investigators from the state Board of Narcotics and the FDA, who had already been alerted to the existence of the psilocybin project by news accounts of the faculty debate in March. By the summer of 1962, prior FDA approval would be required for all research involving psychedelics, and therapists around the country who had been quietly administering psilocybin, LSD or mescaline to their patients for years received visits from federal agents, who ordered them to hand over their supplies and terminate the treatment at once.

Four decades later, the Miracle of Marsh Chapel remains an iconic event for the small but beleaguered minority who still see psychoactive drugs as a path to religious truth. (Represented by organizations like the Council on Spiritual Practices, this group disdains the term "psychedelic" for its unfortunate associations with the hedonism of the 1960s; they much prefer Gordon Wasson's neologism "entheogen," which means "the God within.") The events that took place that Good Friday are one of the best-documented drug experiments of the era, and a unique opportunity to examine the proposition that "peak experiences" generally are a path to spiritual growth.

Much of our information about the Marsh Chapel incident comes via Rick Doblin, the president of a group called the Multidisciplinary Association for Psychedelic Studies, which is dedicated to ending the war on drugs and promoting the "cultural reintegration" of drugs like MDMA (ecstasy), the psychedelics and marijuana. Doblin's follow-up study of the experiment, done in the late 1980s, was published in the *Journal of Transpersonal Psychology.* Walter Pahnke had died in a scuba diving accident in 1971, and the documentation for his thesis had been lost, but Doblin was able to locate sixteen of the original twenty subjects, including seven of the ten men who received psilocybin. Of the three subjects not interviewed, one was deceased and one couldn't be identified. The third, the young man who was subdued with Thorazine, wanted no part of the study and threatened to sue if his name was revealed.

According to Doblin, all of the seven Marsh Chapel veterans recalled that Good Friday vividly as "one of the highpoints of their spiritual life." Most had never used psychedelic drugs again, though they claimed to have had other mystical experiences. All seven felt that taking part in the experiment had brought about lasting positive changes in their lives; however, defining these changes proved more difficult. Several mentioned feeling more joyful, closer to nature, and more committed to the ministry than before. But any actual differences in their behavior would seem to have been more political than spiritual. In Doblin's summary, "Feelings of unity led many of the subjects to identify with and feel compassion for minorities, women and the environment. The feelings of timelessness and eternity reduced their fear of death and empowered the subjects to take more risks in their lives and participate more fully in political struggles."[3]

Whether these thoughts were inherent in the drug experience, or just a reflection of the seminary students' social milieu at the time, could be debated. Interestingly, the only one of the seven subjects who said that the "miracle" had a direct beneficial impact on his "personal growth" reported that the nature of that benefit was that he became motivated to take more psychedelic drugs "at the earliest opportunity."

The most dismaying part of Doblin's article is his revelation that Walter Pahnke's thesis failed to mention that he found it necessary to administer Thorazine to the student who had a bad reaction. Furthermore, this subject's own description of his experience as a "psychotic episode" was buried in the fine print of the footnotes. Pahnke also seems to have minimized the difficulties of another subject, identified in Doblin's study as L.R. An ordained minister when Doblin located him, L.R. recalled that he had been in a state of anxiety when he volunteered for the experiment. After taking the psilocybin, he had "a very strong para-noid reaction" and felt that the chapel was a prison. He, too, fled the building but was brought back inside by a proctor. Doblin speculates that Pahnke was fearful of giving "ammunition" to the opponents of fur-ther psychedelic research. No doubt. But if a well-respected theology stu-dent and M.D. was able to rationalize fudging his results, it would seem that all research that claims benefits from the use of such drugs must be viewed with extreme skepticism.

Huston Smith returned to the subject of the Marsh Chapel Mira-cle in a 1996 interview, recently republished in his book *Cleansing the Doors of Perception.* In the introduction to this volume, Smith writes that the phrase "Nostalgia for the Infinite," the title of a Chirico painting, sums up his life's journey. The child of Protestant missionaries who toiled in rural China, he was converted to philosophy as a graduate student at the University of Chicago, where, he recalls, "John Dewey was the 'Jesus' of naturalism, and Alfred North Whitehead was its 'Saint Paul.'" Not long before he was due to receive his Ph.D., Smith picked up a book on mysticism and, in an instant, lost his faith in his "Jesus" (Dewey). His allegiance to the naturalistic worldview had "collapsed like a house of cards."

Smith went on to a long and distinguished career as an expert on world religions. His work is the subject of a five-part series hosted by Bill Moyers that debuted on PBS in 1996. But except for the period of his involvement with Tim Leary, the "direct experience of God" proved elu-sive. Although it has been many years since the now elderly Dr. Smith used entheogens, he remains fascinated by the subject. Smith under-stands well that drugs are basically antinomian. His continuing belief that they may have some place in spiritual life grows out of his pessimism about the future of organized religion. In what he sees as an inexorable process, the advance of scientific knowledge undermines belief in reli-gious revelation. Moreover, he observes, churches today are buffeted by social controversies and increasingly powerless in the grip of "cross cur-rents of innumerable sorts."[4] Smith may be correct, though one won-ders if the conflict between science and religion might not turn out to be just a temporary dilemma faced by intellectuals in the modern and

postmodern eras. As for the church, it has been buffeted by "cross cur-
rents" in the past, yet it still survives and many people manage to feel
the presence of God without resort to powerful drugs.

The Reverend Michael Young is no doubt more typical of those
who had a brush with psychedelics in the Sixties. Just twenty-three when
he took part in the Marsh Chapel experiment, he found that despite the
terrifying moments he endured, long-term effects were positive. "Religious ideas that were interesting intellectually before, took on a whole
different dimension. Now they were connected to something much deeper
than belief and theory," he said in a 1994 newspaper interview. Young
went on to become an ordained Unitarian minister. He also spent years
working as a probation officer and designed rehabilitation programs for
drug offenders. With his wife, Nancy, he had two biological children,
adopted a third, and helped rear twenty-one foster children.

Young never made a secret of his participation in the Marsh Chapel
incident. He spoke about it in sermons, and volunteered to help Rick
Doblin locate other volunteers who took part. Almost wistfully, Young
expressed the wish that someone could find a way to use entheogens for
a good purpose, but he also doubted that society was wise enough to
allow such a thing. In the meantime, he saw no contradiction between
his positive feelings about the experiment and his efforts to warn his own
and other people's children about the dangers of drugs. As he put it, "a
hatchet is a very useful tool, but you don't use it for parting your hair."

Rick Doblin, on his part, judged the long-term effects of the Marsh
Chapel Miracle as "overwhelmingly positive." Many readers will disagree.
There can be little doubt that the participants had genuine mystical experiences, even though in most cases they weren't specifically Christian
experiences. On the other hand, one self-described "psychotic" episode
and one mixed result following the administration of a single dose to ten
carefully screened subjects can hardly be considered a good outcome. No
clinical drug would pass muster with a similar safety record, especially
one whose benefits were entirely subjective.

Entheogen advocates cite the peyote rituals of the Native American Church or the use of psychoactive plants by certain tribes in the
Amazon basin as evidence that the ingestion of drugs for religious purposes can be benign; but the use of more potent drugs like psilocybin is
more comparable to the handling of serpents as practiced in remote corners of Appalachia. One can make a case for tolerating such practices on

libertarian grounds—in a free society people may be permitted to do many things that are harmful to themselves—but most people find something chilling about pursuing spiritual enlightenment by a method that is known to take casualties.

A larger question is whether the pursuit of mystical revelations through psychedelics—call them what you will—can coexist with Judeo-Christian values. Tim Leary certainly hoped that they could not. Like Maslow, he saw peak experiences as an alternative to organized religion, which, he imagined, would quickly fade away once people discovered psilocybin and LSD. The backlash against the Marsh Chapel experiment opened his eyes. "It became clear to me that religion played a larger part in American society than I had realized," he writes in *High Priest*. Suddenly he noticed, apparently for the first time, that what he called "Judeo-Calvinist" values underlay every institution in American society, from General Motors to Harvard. Moreover, the people in charge of these institutions were not quite as ignorant as he had thought, and they were determined to use their power to resist his efforts to popularize the psychedelic sacrament. A longer-term effort would be required to undermine traditional values by attacking "the part of your mind that is attached to the current social taboos." In the near term, he concluded, he and his friends would have to resort to "the classic solutions of the new religious cult."

The Leary cult began to coalesce that summer in Zihuatenejo, Mexico, where he and thirty-eight followers, mainly male graduate students and their wives, as well as nine children, lived communally in a dilapidated beachside hotel, the Catalina. The idea was to replicate Pala, the utopian community described in Aldous Huxley's latest novel, *Island.*

Island was a disappointment to many admirers of Huxley's antiutopian novel, *Brave New World,* and it received tepid reviews at best, but in its misguided way it is a weirdly prophetic book. Huxley describes an ideal society that has achieved the elimination of two-thirds of the world's suffering by doing away with heavy industry, using birth control to limit the population, and employing chemicals to subdue the aggressive impulses of the young as well as assorted social misfits. ("A year in jail won't cure Peter Pan of his endocrine disbalance or help the ex–Peter Pan to get rid of its psychological consequences ... what you need is early diagnosis and three pink capsules a day before meals.") Children on Pala grow up bombarded by uncritical love and acceptance. Ecology is the foundation of the school curriculum. And, of course, everyone enjoys "sacramental" experiences thanks to the ingestion of moksha, an LSD-like drug.

Pala, in short, was a blissed-out version of Eupsychia. Maslow didn't much care for this representation, though he liked Huxley very much. Moreover, there were times when he questioned the very existence of "peaks." As early as October 1961, he had fretted in his journal that he feared his theory was about to "blow up in my face." The question he had asked himself was: "Are peak-experiences real, or are they mostly just feeling good inside & having nice fantasies about the world?"[5] This moment of self-doubt passed, but Maslow was increasingly unhappy about the way others interpreted peak experiences. He envisioned them as promoting social consciousness and feelings of attachment to others, not a retreat into the self.

Leary had no such reservations. His version of Pala called for dividing his followers into three groups. On any given day, one group would take LSD while the second watched over them and the third would rest up, go to the beach and drink cocktails at the hotel bar. But, somehow, the stoned serenity of Pala eluded the transplanted academics. Most of them were still absorbing the very real probability that their prospects for advancement at Harvard had been permanently derailed by the fall-out from the Marsh Chapel experiment. Leary, for his part, had become entranced by the *Tibetan Book of the Dead,* a favorite text of Huxley's that traced the soul's journey through death to reincarnation. Leary continually emphasized the dangers of trying to impose one's conscious will on the mind-manifesting experience. You had to let the drugs take you where they would, and be prepared to experience even the soul's extinction in order to be reborn on a higher plane. Although his followers still talked about "love drugs," Leary's message was increasingly about death.

Returning to Massachusetts for the autumn 1962 semester, the Learyites moved into a pair of rented houses in Newton Center. The spiritual nexus of the commune was a meditation room—actually a converted closet in Leary's house, reachable only by climbing a ladder from the basement. Residents of the block complained of multiple stereos simultaneously blasting different styles of music at top volume and disreputable-looking strangers who came and went at all hours. Leary's dog, meanwhile, roamed freely and, reportedly, bit seven people. Angry neighbors tried to get the communards evicted on the grounds that the block was zoned for single-family houses, but their effort was thwarted by George Alpert, Dick's attorney father, who won a landmark ruling establishing that the definition of "family" could not be limited to individuals related by blood.

Leary's group dismissed the locals as narrow-minded working-class types, alarmed by the sight of visitors with long hair and beards. In reality, Leary family values were more bizarre than the neighbors' most feverish imaginings. In an effort to push themselves to the next level of consciousness, members of the commune had begun staging confrontational trips, during which everyone focused on the shortcomings of one individual. At other times they listened to language instruction records while high, hoping that the liberated cortex could learn to speak in foreign tongues, and they experimented with nonpsychedelics like DMT. Leary no longer made even a pretext of playing "the professor game." Though he planned to collect his salary until his contract was up at the end of the academic year, he was making no effort to remain in the good graces of the Harvard administration.

This development threw Dick Alpert into tailspin. Unlike Tim, he cared about his family, his colleagues and his classes. But he also felt ashamed of being the kind of guy who "always seemed able to skirt the line: to keep it together." This had been his operational mode for most of his life, and it was still the role he was playing as Sancho Panza to Tim's Don Quixote. Leary, on occasion, would refer to Alpert as his "wife" because it had become Dick's job to look after Susan and Jack, manage the house, and see to a thousand tasks too petty for Tim to bother with. Emotionally torn and convinced that "I didn't ever DO anything quite crazy enough," Alpert began consuming mega-doses of LSD in an effort to avoid "the extraordinary kind of depression" he felt when he came down and thought, "Oh, here I am again—Richard Alpert—what a drag!"[6]

In his overwrought state, Alpert seduced a married graduate student who was living in the commune with his wife and baby. The young man had a history of psychiatric problems, and the homosexual encounter pushed him to the verge of another breakdown. He was so panicked that at one point he threatened to burn down the house. Instead of seeking psychiatric help, the housemates tried to resolve the problem by holding tribal meetings.

In November, Leary and his associates announced the formation of the Institute for Intellectual Freedom, an organization dedicated to the fight for "the fifth freedom—freedom of consciousness." The New Left was just beginning to coalesce in the Boston area. The big issues of the day were not the Vietnam War or even racial justice, but nuclear disarmament and JFK's policy toward Cuba. Protest politics consisted of attending SANE rallies, where one could listen to speeches by psychologist Erich Fromm and comedian Steve Allen. In this milieu, Leary's foundation was years ahead of its time, having boiled down the emerging agenda of Sixties radicalism into the ultimate in identity politics: the right to choose one's own level of reality.

The IFIF's statement of purpose, issued in January 1963, noted: "Some accept prevailing institutions as God-given and inviolable. Others see them as conventions which can block freedom, stifle creativity and stunt lives. . . . For the past two and a half years a group of Harvard University research psychologists have been studying these issues." These psychologists had concluded that "the politics of the nervous system—psychophysical processes involving censoring, alerting, discriminating, selecting, and evaluating"—were responsible for human beings' failure to use more than about 10 percent of their brain's capacity. The IFIF therefore urged people to form ad hoc "research groups" to explore the use of "indole substances" like LSD and psilocybin to release their untapped mental power.[7]

The new organization sent out a mailing to solicit funds, and distributed leaflets in Harvard dorms warning that the great evil facing America was CONFORMITY and encouraging young people to opt for ECSTASY and ENLIGHTENMENT instead. Meanwhile, its newsletter, the *Psychedelic Review,* devoted columns to rebutting rumors of bad trips, invariably dismissing them as urban legends or blaming them on bad street drugs purchased in New York.

According to *High Priest,* the IFIF's goal was to have four million Americans turned on to LSD by 1969, a number that Leary figured would be the "critical figure for blowing the mind of the American society." In the event, they would reach this benchmark by 1967 because, as Leary explained, "we failed to anticipate the use of LSD by high school kids." With hindsight, he would blame the spread of psychedelics to schoolchildren on America's "sick, static society," which had failed to provide its own sacred vision ritual for teenagers.[8]

Other LSD researchers were livid with outrage over the IFIF's creation. Many still had hopes that the FDA would approve at least some investigation into the use of LSD under supervised conditions, but Leary's gambit made a public outcry against the drug inevitable. Aldous Huxley, meanwhile, was frustrated with Leary because he had tried in vain to get him to issue a public warning against swallowing something called "green LSD," a liquid of unknown origin that was being sold on the streets of Cambridge. Leary wasn't interested. He was dismissive of students who ran to the health center, telling "flamboyant stories" about their bad trips to doctors who naïvely pronounced them psychotic.

Huxley was still the best-known advocate of psychedelic drugs in America. Nevertheless, according to his biographer Sybille Bedford, he actually ingested mescaline, psilocybin or LSD no more than a dozen times during the course of his lifetime. He couldn't imagine that anyone would *want* to take these drugs more than once a year, or once every six months at most, and he relied on the assurances of Humphrey Osmond and other researchers that they were not addictive or subject to abuse. Huxley simply couldn't grasp the extent of Leary's drug use or the changes it had made in his thinking. In a letter to Osmond written in December 1962, he reported that he and Tim had recently spent an evening together, and Tim had talked so irrationally "that I became quite concerned." But Huxley dismissed the thought that Leary might be insane, concluding, "this nonsense-talking is just another device for annoying people in authority ... the reaction of a mischievous Irish boy to the headmaster of his school. One of these days the headmaster will lose patience."[9]

The headmaster, in the person of David McClelland, had indeed lost patience. Dana Farnsworth reported that students were coming into the Harvard health center suffering from the aftermath of bad trips and several had required psychiatric hospitalization. It may well have been true, as the *Psychedelic Review* kept insisting, that these cases represented only a small fraction of the Harvard students using mind-expanding drugs, but somehow Farnsworth didn't find this comforting. In an editorial for the *Journal of the American Medical Association (JAMA),* he speculated that "people who are attracted to the hallucinogenic drugs are often those most likely to be harmed by them." Sidney Cohen, who had pronounced LSD safe in 1960, was also having second thoughts. In the May 1963 issue of the *Archives of General Psychiatry,* Cohen reported on nine adverse reactions among health professionals. The alarming thing about these cases was that they were so unpredictable. One psychologist developed paranoid delusions after using LSD only three times, and had threatened to stage a raid on Sandoz's Swiss headquarters to liberate its supply of the drug.[10]

By the spring semester the Harvard community was in turmoil. As Leary himself put it, Harvard Yard was "seething with drug consciousness." The alumni and parents were up in arms, and several writers were preparing articles for major national magazines. David McClelland was contemplating his next move when he was approached by Andrew Weil, a reporter for the Harvard *Crimson*. The student newspaper wanted to do an exposé of Leary's clique, and it offered to share information with the administration. Weil was hardly anti-drug. Two years earlier, writing a paper on social attitudes toward drugs for David Reisman's course in American society, Weil had approached Leary and volunteered as a research subject, only to be turned down because he was an undergraduate. Rejected, he and seven other students placed an order for mescaline with a chemical supply company and did some ad hoc experimenting of their own.

At this point, it seems, the students closest to the campus drug scene were often the ones most appalled by Leary's activities. Since he and Alpert had specifically promised not to involve undergraduates in the psilocybin project, finding evidence to the contrary became the focus of Weil's investigation. Eventually Weil was able to give McClelland the names of twelve undergraduates who had received the drug, though only one was willing to admit as much to the dean.

In the event, it wasn't necessary to use the information against Leary. With the IFIF under investigation by Massachusetts authorities, Tim decamped to Mexico, taking with him the proceeds from a recent fundraising campaign. Harvard then canceled his contract on the grounds that he had abandoned his duties. This left Dick Alpert to enjoy the solitary distinction of being fired by Harvard for giving LSD to an undergraduate.

In later years Leary would come up with the colorful explanation that he and Alpert were the targets of a plot by the CIA, which wanted to prevent the American people from gaining access to the benefits of consciousness-altering substances. Since the agency's surreptitious funding of drug experiments had done much to popularize psychedelic drugs in the first place, such an effort might have been called for, but no such plot existed. Leary's favorite excuse for the ouster at the time was that it was motivated by homosexual jealousy, a notion he brought up again in *Flashbacks:* "Dick ... got caught in the middle of a love triangle involving an editor on the Harvard *Crimson* staff."[11]

But the real reason for Harvard's action, as explained by Brendan Maher in a report to the Massachusetts Psychological Association, was that Leary and Alpert had turned against reason itself, promoting their own brand of "mystic anti-intellectualism": "Not only were students being indoctrinated in the belief that communicable knowledge was the end-product of some kind of pointless 'game,' but ... the drug experience was being held out to them as a kind of redemption from the rigors of rationality."[12]

Ironically, Andrew Weil went on to build a career as a drug researcher and promoter of cosmic consciousness. After medical school, thanks in part to his reputation as the man who had enabled Harvard to fire Timothy Leary, Weil was approved to do a study of the effects of marijuana under the auspices of the National Institute of Mental Health. In 1972 he made the transition to best-selling author by publishing *The Natural Mind,* in which he predicted that America was in the midst of "a revolution in consciousness that will transform human society ... a shift from straight to stoned thinking on a grand scale.... Stoned consciousness is spreading through the population like a chain reaction. And at some point, most of us will be experiencing our perceptions in a stoned way all of the time. What will happen to external reality at that point is anybody's guess."[13]

The summer of 1963 found Leary in Mexico, busily completing the transformation of the Catalina Hotel into his version of Pala. He planned to call the place Freedom House and operate it as a "transpersonative community" where paying guests would learn to escape "the game of YOU" and be trained as LSD guides for IFIF drug exploration circles—conductors, if you will, for the psychedelic underground railroad. The dream ended abruptly when a Mexican psychologist who had heard Leary deliver a semicoherent speech at a professional conference tipped off the authorities. Summarily deported, Leary received an invitation from a Rastafarian-style cult leader to join him on the island of Dominica, but the cultist turned out to have ties to rebels allied with Fidel Castro and the police suspected Leary of being part of an arms smuggling operation. Summarily kicked off the island, Leary and his followers decamped for Antigua, where the local government proved similarly unwelcoming.

Homeless, unemployed and, worse, temporarily out of LSD, the Learyites straggled back to Cambridge. By this time, some members of the group were ready to move on. Gunther Weil, on the recommendation of Abe Maslow, would find a post at Brandeis. Oddly enough, another sometime member of the Leary circle who landed on his feet was Michael Hollingshead, who wound up on the staff of the Agora Science Foundation in Manhattan. According to Hollingshead, Agora had a patron with influence at the Office of Naval Research, and this connection explained why it was able to obtain supplies of LSD after other researchers had been cut off.

Agora's best-known researcher was Jean Houston, an associate professor at the New School who was billed as the smartest woman in America. Houston was an exception among drug investigators in that she didn't indulge in psychedelics herself but administered them to others in the hope of eliciting visions that would confirm the validity of Jungian archetypes. As Hollingshead describes her work, she "was interested in advancing the intellectual capabilities of the modern American—to meet and solve the problems not of today or tomorrow—but of the day after tomorrow. And by means of a process that you might call traveling in the ANTECEDENT FUTURE—that is inducing the ego to scan the cognitive parts of the cortex in order to develop the ability to bring into the present what is already in the memory." Thirty years later, Houston would employ this technique, *sans* drugs, in her effort to persuade Hillary Clinton to get in tune with the spirit of Eleanor Roosevelt.

By autumn, Leary and his remaining band had found refuge at Millbrook, a Dutchess County, New York, estate owned by the family of Dick Alpert's friend Peggy Hitchcock and her twin brothers, Billy and Tommy. Grandchildren of Judge Thomas Mellon and heirs to the Gulf Oil fortune, the Hitchcocks found Leary and Alpert amusing and let them take over the property's main residence, Die Alte Haus, a sixty-four-room gingerbread mansion with a sweeping front porch, miscellaneous turrets and its own bowling alley—but no functioning central heating. Millbrook was no Pala, but it did happen to be conveniently close to New York City, and in short order its weekend parties became a mecca for denizens of the underground art scene, writers, jazz musicians, trust fund babies, leggy fashion models and assorted glitterati.

No one ever accused Tim Leary of lacking a sense of style. He was always trying out new images, like dressing up as a cowboy and driving around the grounds in a covered wagon pulled by a pair of horses painted Day-Glo pink and Day-Glo green. Other innovations that he and his friends tried at the big house were quickly copied by his artist guests. During one LSD session, the residents decided that sitting upright was too much effort, so they cut the legs off the tables and moved the chairs and sofas into storage. Soon, hip young people across America were living at floor level, exchanging their furniture for paisley-covered cushions. The commune members replaced the old house's French bronzes and landscape paintings with mandalas and tantric statues, and it was only a matter of time until head shop owners everywhere were peddling cheap knockoffs of these items. Tim developed a passion for the German Nobel Prize winner Hermann Hesse, and before long Hesse's novels were on the bestseller lists.

But by far Leary's most influential teaching was that reading itself was passé. As he predicted in 1965, "The future is not going to be what book you read, but which chemical you use to accelerate your mind." Difficult as it is to picture now, in the 1950s middle-class people considered it attractive, even sexy, to be literate. *Playboy* carried advice on how to impress women by faking an understanding of existentialism. The ability to drop references to Wittgenstein and Sartre into everyday conversation was that decade's equivalent of sporting six-pack abs. Very much a middle-class academic himself, for all his disdain for the role, Leary was slow to catch on that he was engineering his own obsolescence. When the parties ended at Millbrook, his little coterie of unemployed psychologists treated themselves to marathon acid sessions, then labored to produce scripts intended for use by IFIF-trained guides who would lead others on the journey to the land of stoned consciousness. Leary and Ralph Metzner's first venture along these lines was *The Psychedelic Experience,* a bowdlerized version of the *Bardo Thikol,* the "Tibetan Book of the Dead."

Out on the Left Coast, Ken Kesey discovered LSD in 1957 while a volunteer subject in a drug study done at a veterans' hospital in Menlo Park, California. By the time Leary was settling in at Millbrook, he and his friends had already figured out that it wasn't necessary to listen to Bach, read German novels, or follow obscure ancient texts. Kids whose minds were utterly innocent of intellectual furniture could drop acid, turn up the volume on the hi-fi, and party down. The effect, in the memorable phrase of the Grateful Dead's Bob Weir, was often "like pouring rocket fuel into a lawnmower." But so be it. When Kesey and his Merry Pranksters showed up at Millbrook during their 1964 cross-country bus tour, Leary was incommunicado, enjoying a three-day sex-and-drugs retreat with a new girlfriend, and so he was able to remain in happy ignorance a little while longer.

Leary and his followers talked endlessly about the importance of "set and setting." By this they meant that the quality of the psychedelic experience was a function of the mindset of the person taking a drug as well as his physical surroundings. While there was some basis for this, the "set and setting" mantra served as a mechanism of denial. The truth was that the Learyites couldn't even control their own set and setting, much less advise other people how to manage theirs. Quite inadvertently, Millbrook became exhibit A of what happens when educated middle-class people decide to scuttle their "Judeo-Calvinist" belief systems. Artie Kleps, a former school psychologist from Long Island, gives a vivid description of the disintegration process in his memoir, *Millbrook*.

Arriving in late 1963, Kleps fell in love with Millbrook at first sight. In those days you could run into Charlie Mingus practicing his trumpet on the lawn, or find Alan Watts delivering an impromptu lecture in the living room. Playing with the nature of reality was fun. One morning Ralph Metzner got creative with food dye, serving up a breakfast of green eggs and black milk to make the point that peoples' expectations that certain things will always be certain colors was just another "mental hang-up." Peggy Hitchcock and her socialite friends would drop by decked out in designer gowns "crawling with ermine." Dick Alpert always had the newest toys, like "psychedelic spectacles" fitted with tiny strobes. "Life as it was lived was livelier, more meaningful, funnier, happier. It was an adventure just to hang out," Kleps enthused. Granted, the Millbrook regulars were crazy, but in the amusing and nonthreatening ways that people with high IQs and advanced degrees tend to be crazy.

Gradually, all that changed. Dick Alpert's boyfriend, a Harvard student and heir to a major American fortune, was replaced by men Alpert had met on his forays into Greenwich Village, an assortment of rough-trade types and street hustlers, at least one of whom carried a knife. A band of eco-egalitarians set up a teepee encampment on the grounds. Runaway high school kids found their way to the estate and slept wherever they could find shelter, usually in the long-abandoned chicken coops. For a time, a rock group named Aluminum Dreams took over the third floor of the house, practicing at all hours. One day a female guest confided to Kleps that she had burned Haitian dictator "Baby Doc" Duvalier in a deal for orange sunshine acid and was terrified that the Tontons Macoutes were going to raid the estate in retaliation. This might have been a fantasy, but who could be sure? He advised her to purchase a semi-automatic rifle and keep it under her bed. And she did.[14]

In the beginning the psychologists' wives took responsibility for keeping house and even Leary pitched in with the gardening chores. Dick Alpert took care of paying the bills, occasionally flying off in his Cessna to score drugs in Canada or hit up wealthy acquaintances for donations. But Alpert got tired of his role as Tim's gofer, and the wives either left Millbrook or lost interest in doing housework for a pack of strangers. In December 1964 Tim married Swedish model Nena von Schlegrugge (later the mother of Uma Thurman), and the newlyweds departed on an extended honeymoon in India, where Ralph Metzner had already gone to study Hinduism. In their absence, the residents of the mansion split into factions, quarreling so bitterly that fistfights broke out. With tensions mounting, the premises fell into neglect. Dishes piled up unwashed. Dogs ran free in the house and no one bothered to clean up the messes they made. An artist who had taken up residence covered the walls with psychedelic murals.

Leary's second marriage did not long survive the honeymoon, and neither did his partnership with Dick Alpert. Doubtless Alpert had much to complain about. Millbrook's finances were a shambles, and Leary seemed unconcerned. Alpert gave lectures to raise money and even tried a stint as a standup comedian in a Greenwich Village club. According to Leary, however, the break came after Alpert complained that Leary had never fully accepted his homosexuality. After Alpert had departed for the West Coast, Leary tried to raise cash by organizing drug-free weekend seminars for paying guests, featuring yoga classes and lectures on tantric Buddhism. The "straights" showed up, but they irritated the Millbrook regulars by playing the "cocktail party game." In other words, they introduced themselves to one another, made small talk and formed friendships. Michael Hollingshead, back on the scene and decked out in a kilt, red cape and fez, figured out that he could inhibit this behavior by forcing the guests to exchange their street clothes for robes made out of sheets and proclaiming a rule of silence. Saturday dinners, complete with Hollingshead's improvised rituals and guests dressed in white sheets, reminded Art Kleps of a Klan meeting.

Leary's friends inevitably assured skeptical strangers that Susan and Jack Leary were normal kids despite their bizarre environment. This actually seemed true of Jack, who had inherited his father's good looks and ready wit. Jack dropped out of school for a while, but by 1967 he was a sophomore at Millbrook High, where he overcame the notoriety of his name and became one of the most popular boys in his class. Susan Leary, on the other hand, was basically a shy girl who was looking for a father figure in all the wrong ways. In his memoir, Kleps refers to Susan as "the house Lolita." On one occasion she greeted her Uncle Art by sticking her tongue into his mouth, then sulked and refused to speak to him because he failed to reciprocate.

In 1967 two high-school-age reporters from *Ovum,* an underground magazine published in Poughkeepsie, New York, paid an unannounced visit to Millbrook and got into a conversation with a nine-year-old boy, the son of a female resident, who told them that the children of Millbrook went on LSD picnics in the woods, taking liquid acid mixed with apple cider under the supervision of an adult guide. The nine-year-old said he had been on five trips so far. This information was confirmed by the boy's older brother and by Jack Leary, who dutifully echoed his father's line by denying that LSD caused hallucinations. (Hallucinations are by definition not real, and since reality *is* whatever you think it is at the moment, there can be no such thing as a hallucination.)[15]

At first, Leary had banned marijuana and hashish from the house because both substances were clearly illegal, unlike psychedelics, whose status was still unclear. Even by the standards of the times, however, Leary was a prodigious drinker. So, too, was Kleps, who assured his welcome when he moved in by buying a case of Hennessy's as a housewarming gift. Alcohol diminished the effects of LSD, so it was odd that many of the residents drank even as they talked endlessly about the need to break through to a higher level of consciousness. Dropping LSD too often also greatly diminished the drug's potency. Some of the housemates simply refused to accept this, and made an effort to trip continuously, renewing their high several times a day. Others paced themselves, but needed something to fill in the gray days in between. In 1964, while Dick Alpert was off trying to replenish the house supply of acid, someone decided that it was possible to get a buzz from morning glory seeds, if only you could keep enough of them down. Grass and hashish showed up, despite Leary's ban, as did miscellaneous other drugs including cocaine, DMT and something called JB 318. When in New York, Leary also took amphetamine shots from Dr. Max Jacobsen, the notorious "Dr. Feelgood," whose celebrity client list had included President Kennedy.

Art Kleps' "breakthrough" to the other world occurred after he absent-mindedly swigged what he thought was brandy from a glass he found next to Leary's bed. Kleps swore that whatever he had swallowed rendered him temporarily invisible. Susan Metzner, Ralph's wife, told him later, "I was not stoned in any way. But you turned every color of the rainbow and disappeared in front of my eyes." Hooking up with Leary had cost Kleps his job, and he was on his way to losing his wife as well. Now he began to see "winkles"—blobs of light that flew across his field of vision at inopportune moments. But he had attained enlightenment. "I just see the meaning in everything," he told Dick Alpert. "No matter what happens, I see it as a message to me, to me personally."

A confirmed atheist, Kleps often wondered about Leary's infatuation with Eastern religion. Was he sincere? It was hard to tell, though Leary did appear mightily impressed by the words of an Indian guru who had told him that everything that happened in the world for the last five hundred years had been preparing the way for Timothy Leary and his proclamation of Freedom of Consciousness. Kleps particularly despised the death-obsessed rhetoric of *The Psychedelic Experience,* Leary's version of Tibetan-style reincarnation. One day, after they had made a trip to the post office in Poughkeepsie, Leary opened an envelope containing a $1600 royalty check, smirking as he waved it under Kleps' nose. It occurred to Kleps that the *Tibetan Book of the Dead* was Leary's "cash cow." Or, worse: "It was as if he deliberately and with malice aforethought polluted the Psychedelian cultural stream at its source."[16]

In protest, Kleps decided to found his own antireligion, the Neo-American Church. The Native American Church had just won a court case establishing its right to use peyote in its rituals. Why, Kleps wondered, shouldn't white people have the same rights? The Neo-American Church's sacraments were drugs. Its priests were known as Boo-Hoos, or if female, Bee-Hees. ("Boo" was an old slang term for marijuana.) The church's only doctrine was "solipsistic nihilism," which, Kleps had detected, was also the essence of Leary's belief system. *Life is a dream, so never mind.*

Up in Cambridge, Lisa Bieberman had been running the IFIF office and publishing the *Psychedelic Review.* Bieberman was the ultimate responsible entheogen user. A highly spiritual person, she took drugs only as an aid to meditation. The Millbrook crowd considered her boring, and Art Kleps complained that she could spend an hour and a half staring at a tadpole. Bieberman, on her part, was appalled by Millbrook and found Leary's Joycean monologues and rhetoric about reality-as-a-construct perplexing. Her own ventures into the mystical realm had more in common with the Judeo-Christian heritage than with Eastern religious traditions. As she saw it, the message of LSD consisted of "simple things that everyone knows." The drug merely enabled her to know them with "blinding certainty." These things included:

> The world is real;
> the God who created it is alive,
> and will stay that way;
> Life has meaning.
> There is a difference between
> good and evil.[17]

In 1965, after an unpleasant weekend visit to Millbrook, the religious fellow travelers decided that the time had come to break their ties with Leary. For Walter Houston Clark the separation never quite took psychologically. Bieberman was more determined. She resigned from Leary's foundation to form her own Psychedelic Information Center. Still, when Art Kleps got into a drunken brawl with his wife on a train platform in Florida and was arrested on an old warrant, Bieberman scraped together $1,000 to cover his bail. Kleps repaid her by skipping his court date; the bail bond was forfeited and he never repaid her. Then a college freshman in Kansas who had joined Kleps' mail-order church was arrested after two undercover agents infiltrated his "congregation." Kleps cheered the young man on in his newsletter, but when the friends who were preparing his legal defense tried to contact Kleps to find out if the government informants had signed membership cards, they ran into a blank wall. The woman who answered the phone number given in Kleps' literature claimed not to be sure who he was. Bieberman got in touch with Leary, who sent his love, but no money or information. Eventually, the Episcopalian Church paid for the student's defense.

By the fall of 1965, even Leary recognized that the guru game had reached a dead end. He had lectured at Cooper Union, done his own turn in a Greenwich Village nightclub, and staged a psychedelic light show at a midtown theater rented for him by Billy Hitchcock. But the center of the psychedelic movement had shifted to the West Coast, where Ken Kesey was running his famous Acid Tests. The Millbrook inner circle was breaking up, its members moving on to other things. Dick Alpert had left for San Francisco, a way station on his journey to becoming a Hindu sage. Ralph Metzner was writing a book on the nature of consciousness. Michael Hollingshead was about to return to England. Leary had received a $10,000 advance for his autobiography and acquired a new girlfriend, an irreverent thirty-year-old redhead named Rosemary Woodruff. Rosemary couldn't keep a straight face when Tim went into his guru spiel. She wanted a real home, and she and Tim talked about the possibility of his starting a new career. Perhaps he could write science fiction or find a college adventurous enough to give him an appointment.

Just when he was about to be re-domesticated, Tim decided to take Rosemary and his children on a family vacation in Mexico. The government of Mexico had deported Leary in 1963, one of a series of actions that made its hostility to psychedelic drugs abundantly clear. Nevertheless, Leary wrote to the Department of Tourism outlining his itinerary, and received a letter that he interpreted as giving him permission to enter the country. Tim, Rosemary, Jack, Susan and a boy named Rene, a friend of the children's, piled into a rented station wagon and headed south. Arriving on schedule at the Nuevo Laredo border crossing, Leary was shocked—*shocked*—to see the same federal policeman who had interviewed him at the time of his deportation two years earlier. It was after 5 P.M., and the officer told the travelers to return the next morning so that he could check with his superiors in Mexico City before issuing them a tourist card.

According to Woodruff's account, as the station wagon headed back across the International Bridge, she suddenly remembered a small silver box of marijuana that was packed with their luggage. She crawled into the back and dug it out, but the rear window was blocked by the luggage and so she tried handing off the box to Rene, motioning frantically for him to toss it out of the passenger side window. But Rene was immobilized by fear and Tim, who wasn't wearing his hearing aid that day, was oblivious to the excitement. At the last minute, Susan grabbed the box and hid it under her clothing. Not surprisingly, U.S. customs decided that Timothy Leary and his party were candidates for a thorough search. The silver box found on Susan's person contained a small amount of marijuana. (Also in the box were capsules identified as detroamphetamine sulfate, which for some reason never figured in the charges.) Told that drugs had been found on the person of his eighteen-year-old daughter, Leary said, "I'll take responsibility for the marijuana."[18]

At first, Leary didn't seem worried. Immediately on his return to Millbrook, he circulated fliers advertising a $400 summer school session that would teach students how to have a psychedelic experience in fourteen days. This was the last straw for the Dutchess County assistant DA, G. Gordon Liddy, who staged a nighttime raid on the house but found nothing indictable, just a bunch of zonked-out hippies watching a film loop of an endless waterfall. Leary was able to spin the story of the raid in his favor, portraying it as evidence of just how clueless law enforcement was when it came to understanding the benign folkways of the psychedelic adepts.

But the authorities were fast losing patience. By 1966 LSD was no longer limited to enclaves like Cambridge and Berkeley, and parents across the country were starting to see it as a threat to their children. Sid Cohen, once the drug's most vocal advocate, echoed the fears of the older generation when he told a Senate subcommittee that the greatest hazard of LSD was its potential to cause young people to retreat into solipsism and negativity. "We have seen something ... more alarming than death in a way. And that is the loss of all cultural values, the loss of feeling of right and wrong, of good and bad."

Even as Congress and the states rushed to make LSD possession a felony, the U.S. Justice Department was ready to plea-bargain with Timothy Leary. He could avoid a long jail sentence, but only if he would publicly warn young people about the dangers of drug abuse. Leary would have none of it. He decided to go to trial in March 1966, basing his defense on a claim of freedom of religion. Citing recent court decisions favorable to the Native American Church, his attorney asserted that Leary had converted to Hinduism during his trip to India and used marijuana during meditation to lift himself to the third level of consciousness. Fred Swain, a/k/a/ Sri Kalidas, the Hindu monk from the Cambridge ashram, appeared as a witness in Leary's defense. Under questioning by prosecutors, however, Swain said that he personally never smoked marijuana in the United States.

The jury didn't buy the Hinduism defense. Leary also managed to enrage the sentencing judge by explaining that he had reared his children "the old fashioned way," making sure they were exposed to his beliefs about drugs and religion. "From the very beginning of this work, I felt that it was a natural, personal, if you will, sacred experience that was not to be a secret or behind doors. I couldn't bring—I had to have this—my children to be open to this, to see what was going on."[19]

The judge sentenced Leary to thirty years in prison. Eighteen-year-old Susan, who had waived a jury trial, got three years of unsupervised parole.

Leary's arrest was almost a replay of his run-in with the cadet honor committee at West Point. Newspaper stories inevitably gave the impression that Leary had gallantly taken responsibility for his daughter's reckless act. In reality, the situation was the reverse: Susan had been holding the drugs in an attempt to protect her dad and Rosemary. In fact, Leary's behavior throughout had been so imprudent that one can't help but suspect he was tempting fate. What kind of man would take his family on vacation to a country that regards him as a menace, inform the authorities in advance of his arrival, and then show up at the border with drugs in his luggage? It seems that Leary intended to provoke an incident—perhaps another deportation—that would land him back in the spotlight. Susan, who adored her father, was devastated to find that his misinformed admirers blamed her for getting him into trouble. An often-reproduced photograph taken at the time of the trial shows Tim seated against a white background in such a way that he appears to be levitating. Susan, looking much younger than her years, is curled up at her father's side in a fetal position, her expression a heartbreaking mixture of hero-worship and wounded trust.

As usual when his bluff was called, Leary seemed genuinely stunned, like a child who can scarcely believe that sticking his fingers in the fire actually resulted in their getting burned. Shortly after his conviction, he appeared with Art Kleps before a Senate subcommittee, where, much to the outrage of Kleps, he abandoned his freedom-of-religion argument and called for a government program to license LSD and marijuana users. A pot-smoking license should be relatively easy to obtain, like a driver's license, he suggested, but an LSD license would require more extensive training. Leary suggested that laboratory courses in LSD consumption could become a feature of the college curriculum. Senator Edward Kennedy, in one of his wittier moments, worried sarcastically that children who didn't get into college would be left behind.

Settling down with Rosemary was now out of the question. Free on bond pending his appeals, Leary had moved on to a new stage in his life, playing the Celebrity Martyr game. The usual celebrities—Steve Allen, Peter Fonda, Norman Mailer et al.—signed a petition expressing outrage over his sentence, and *Playboy* paid a hefty fee for an interview. In addition to repeating his call for government licensing, Leary told *Playboy*'s readers that a woman could have hundreds of orgasms in a single LSD session—a "fact" he later acknowledged making up on the spot. He also proclaimed LSD a "specific cure" for homosexuality and stated that if he had young children he would rather see them on heroin than enrolled in the first grade of an American school.[20]

That June, Leary's old friend Frank Barron organized a conference in San Francisco, inviting critics like Sid Cohen as well as the now dwindling group of researchers who still thought LSD had therapeutic promise. The *Playboy* interview had not yet appeared, and Leary, who had seemed chastened since his conviction, was invited to deliver a paper. This proved to be a mistake, since he stole the headlines by telling reporters that he wasn't a bit worried by Sandoz's decision to halt the manufacture of LSD. Acid was now being cooked up in underground labs, he assured the press, and the Golden State would soon be flooded with two billion doses.[21]

By September, even as his *Playboy* interview hit the newsstands, Leary was back on the religion track, calling a press conference to announce that he was establishing his own psychedelic church, to be called the League for Spiritual Discovery. Its message was "Turn on, tune in and drop out"—admittedly a catchier slogan than "solipsistic nihilism." People who cared about consistency had reason to be confused. Was getting high a form of religious expression? Or was it an activity that the government could regulate, like drinking alcohol? Of course, very few heads cared about consistency. Nor, certainly, did Leary.

In *Flashbacks,* he describes his role at this time as "cheerleader for change." But Leary's cheerful nihilism flummoxed even his most sympathetic contemporaries. In February 1967, the *San Francisco Oracle,* a newly established underground newspaper, devoted its seventh issue to the transcript of a "summit meeting" held aboard Alan Watts' Sausalito houseboat, featuring Leary and Watts in conversation with Beat poets Gary Snyder and Allen Ginsberg. Leary stole the show by urging young people to turn their backs on "the fake-television-set American society." They should just drop out, move perhaps to places like Haight-Ashbury where they could begin to build their own tribal societies. The American educational system, he declared, is a "narcotic and we should have NOTHING to do with it. Drop out of school. Drop out of college. Don't be an activist."

Leary's insistent mantra made Watts and company sound like old fogies by comparison. "But you've got to do *something*," protested Watts. "Where are you going to learn engineering, or astronomy, or things like that?" sputtered an indignant Ginsberg. Gary Snyder observed sourly that in *his* day, just ten years earlier, dropping out meant that you were willing to pick strawberries, work in construction, do any kind of job you could find to support yourself. He himself had spent three years as a grad student at Berkeley, eating horsemeat from the pet store and vegetables he scrounged from supermarket dumpsters. But Leary, Buddha-like, prattled on about the fall of Rome and tribal structures until a frustrated Ginsberg all but called him a hypocrite, pointing out that while Leary may have dropped out of Harvard, he still had his legal defense team, his lecture fees, and so on. Surely, Ginsberg continued, Leary didn't mean to "cultivate a lot of freak-out hippies goofing around and throwing bottles through windows when they freak out." He passed on the suggestion of a kid who had said that Leary's slogan should be rearranged to "Drop out, turn on and tune in."

"Sounds like bullshitting," retorted Leary, unmoved.[22]

Leary had caught the current of the Zeitgeist for sure. He and Rosemary had been befriended by John Griggs, the leader of the band of legendary drug smugglers known as the Brotherhood of Eternal Love. Griggs provided them with a picturesque cabin in the San Jacinto hills. But the tribal idyll didn't last long. Griggs dropped dead, apparently from an overdose of psilocybin, and Leary's legal problems mounted. The authorities in Poughkeepsie staged another raid on Millbrook. Once again, their information was faulty and they missed Leary, who was in the East but not on the estate on the day the raid went down. Still, he and others in the Millbrook inner circle were indicted on multiple charges, including keeping a disorderly house. In California, Leary endured multiple arrests for possession of small amounts of marijuana, some no doubt setups. The Supreme Court overturned his federal conviction, but even this victory turned out to be Pyrrhic, as the Justice Department promptly reindicted him on an amended charge.

None of this was at all surprising considering that Leary was making a career out of corrupting the youth of America. Leary, however, preferred to see himself as the victim of a personal vendetta on the part of the CIA's Cord Meyer. Back in the Fifties, when Leary was still living in Berkeley, he and Meyer had been active in different factions of the American Veterans Committee. Meyer's group was out to rid the AVC of a Communist-led caucus, but Leary had sided with a third faction headed by Michael Straight, the publisher of the *New Republic* and, as later revealed, a onetime KGB agent. While he was at Harvard, Leary had supplied LSD to Meyer's ex-wife, Mary Pinchot Meyer, who, he intimates, may have turned on her lover, President Kennedy. Mary Meyer was later murdered in her Washington, D.C., neighborhood, and Leary hinted darkly that the CIA was behind her death, presumably as part of a plot aimed at him. This was not even remotely plausible, but it became one of the urban legends of the New Left.

By 1967, veteran "mushroom people" like Lisa Bieberman were in despair. Explaining her decision to dissolve the Psychedelic Information Center in the pages of the *New Republic,* Bieberman wrote sorrowfully that the many hopeful initiatives she had reported on in her newsletter had turned out to be "a catalogue of frauds and failures." Day after day, she had sat in the center's office, fielding inquiries from teenagers with dead eyes who dropped by looking for news of rock concerts and drug busts. Timothy Leary had long ago turned his back on the message of peace and love that he proclaimed in 1962. But for some reason he kept attracting new followers, even though, as Bieberman noted, "Of the group that started [at Millbrook] none remain except Leary and his daughter and son. In the mad scramble to be In, nobody asks what became of the people who were In last year. . . . How long can this farce be played out? Apparently indefinitely. . . ."[23]

Apparently so. Some months after these words were written, Art Kleps visited Tim in Berkeley and found his house filled with "White Panthers" who made small talk about blowing up buildings. Revolution was now In, and Leary was trying to find a place for himself on the New

Left, without much success. Paul Krassner, publisher of the *Realist,* had tried repeatedly to forge an alliance between Tim and Abbie Hoffman. But Tim thought Abbie was mired in old-fashioned leftist negativity, and Abbie's attitude was that Leary was turning the youth of America into "blissed-out pansies" who would be easy targets for elimination by the establishment. On the eve of the 1968 Democratic convention in Chicago, Leary offered to organize a series of nude love-ins, but the plan got nowhere. Leary's goal was to defuse potential violence and help Hubert Humphrey win. He cared nothing about the war in Vietnam, but he was terrified of Republicans and of Richard Nixon in particular. Nixon understood him, and was determined to see him behind bars. Electing Humphrey was, of course, the last thing on the minds of the demonstration organizers. They wanted to "bring the war home" by provoking a confrontation that would discredit conventional politics as practiced by both major parties.

Leary's next big idea was to run for governor of California. He promised to make marijuana available in state stores and subcontract the running of the state to another politician. John Lennon wrote the beginnings of a campaign song, later released as "Come Together," but Leary was too preoccupied to campaign. His plan was to film a pseudo-documentary that showed him winning the election. California voters would have a chance to see the film before they went to the polls and, presumably, be inspired to make their reality coincide with his. Later, the movie could be shown internationally and earn millions.

In January 1970, Leary's political career was cut short when he was ordered to stand trial on an earlier arrest for possession of two joints of marijuana. The jury began deliberating on the same day that Captain Jeffrey McDonald, an army doctor in North Carolina, reported that his wife and daughters had been murdered by home invaders chanting, "Acid is Groovy. Kill the Pigs!" Leary was found guilty and sentenced to ten years. Adding ten years on the pending charge in Texas and a potential twelve years stemming from the Millbrook situation, Leary was looking at the possibility of spending the rest of his life in prison. Realistically, this wasn't likely, but with Nixon in the White House and Ronald Reagan in Sacramento, the political winds of the moment were not favorable and Leary was in a state of panic. He accepted an offer from the

Weather Underground to facilitate his escape from the minimum-security facility in San Luis Obispo, where he spent his afternoons playing hand-ball to get in shape for the breakout.

If Leary's account in *Flashbacks* can be believed, he and the get-away drivers supplied by the Weathermen rendezvoused with Bernadine Dohrn, Jeff Jones and "Bob Ayers" (actually Bill Ayers) in the moun-tains of northern California and they all drove to Seattle, where the Weathermen provided Tim and Rosemary with fake IDs. With his head shaved and carrying a false passport, Leary boarded a commercial jet bound for Paris. Rosemary was on the same plane, also traveling under an alias. The two of them passed up an opportunity to go underground in Switzerland and instead flew to Algiers to live under the protection of Eldridge Cleaver, the Black Panther leader-in-exile. For a time, Leary issued statements advocating a violent uprising in the United States: "Arm yourselves and shoot to kill" and "To shoot a genocidal robot police-man in the defense of life is a sacred act." But the Revolution Game quickly grew stale as Tim and Rosemary found themselves being ordered to do maid's work by the very surly Cleaver and his teenage Algerian mis-tress. Retrieving their passports on the pretext of picking up a large money order—Cleaver very much needed cash—they made their escape.

Eventually, Leary and Woodruff were able to fly to Switzerland, where Tim was jailed in Lausanne while his lawyer successfully fought an attempt to extradite him to the United States. Rosemary bailed out, unable to take any more chaos, and Tim soon hooked up with a new girlfriend, a twenty-six-year-old adventuress named Joanna Harcourt-Smith, the niece of physicist Stan Ulam and political scientist Adam Ulam. Then Susan Leary, now called Susan Martino, showed up with her husband and baby daughter as well as a brother-in-law and his wife and their baby. None of the adults had jobs or money. Leary was broke and complained of being exploited by a shady arms dealer who had offered him sanctuary. Nevertheless, during this period he found time to exper-iment with heroin, a drug he had avoided in the past, and when he col-lected $40,000 from a book advance, he used the money to buy a gold Porsche.

His life had become a paranoiac's dream. The CIA may not have been after him in 1962, but it certainly was now. He was an interna-tional fugitive who'd had contacts with major-league drug smugglers, terrorists and arms dealers on three continents. U.S. authorities were determined to bring him back home to face justice one way or another. Shopping for a country that might offer him sanctuary, Leary passed on Austria and Switzerland and settled, improbably, on Afghanistan. He was arrested at the airport minutes after he and Joanna deplaned. Leary's friends would inevitably refer to his capture as an "illegal kidnapping," a characterization that only exposed their naïveté. The absence of an extradition treaty between the United States and Afghanistan was not a Get out of Jail Free Card, and the country, then a monarchy, was under no obligation to shelter any fugitive who managed to make his way to Kabul.

Back in California, Leary was remanded to Folsom Penitentiary, where the prisoner in the next cell, Charlie Manson, sent him gifts of tea and honey and asked, wonderingly, "How did you blow it?" Put on trial for his prison escape, Leary was mainly concerned to rebut the rumors being circulated by Eldridge Cleaver that he was "brain-fried." Michael Kahn, his former Harvard student, administered a battery of psychological tests and appeared in court to swear to Leary's genius-level IQ. This testimony only provided more ammunition for prosecutors who had charged Leary with nineteen counts of drug distribution, alleging that he was part of a ring operated by the Brotherhood of Eternal Love. A defense that he was just a celebrity pawn, exploited by the real bad guys, might have done Leary some good. But if he was such a genius, then he obviously knew what was going on.

Leary liked to joke that he'd get out of prison when the Democrats returned to office. In the event, that's what happened. Facing a total of ninety-five years, he decided to turn federal witness. In a statement later released by the FBI, Leary eagerly told interrogators that his cooperation was part of a "longer range plan" to get out of jail because "I intend to be extremely active in this country in the next few years." Leary's information about the Weather Underground didn't result in any indictments, possibly because of the lack of corroborating evidence. He did, however, throw in a bonus by snitching on his own attorney, Georges Chula, who had smuggled cocaine to him in prison. Joanna Harcourt-Smith helped set up Chula, and he eventually served three months. Leary also arranged a raid on the home of Michael Horowitz, the father of his godchild Winona Ryder and a staunch friend who had preserved Leary's personal papers during his years on the lam. Although he actually began cooperating a year and a half earlier, Leary was released only in 1976, after Jerry Brown became governor of California.

For Jack Leary, his father's decision to give evidence against friends was the final disappointment. All his life, Jack had watched his dad party on, with a twinkle in his eye and a beautiful woman on his arm, while he himself was reduced to the role of bit player in the picaresque comedy of "Tim Leary's Excellent Adventure." Tim seemed to genuinely love his children when he happened to think of them, but their interests had never come first. At a press conference called by ex-Yippie leader Jerry Rubin and *Berkeley Barb* editor Ken Kelley, an embittered Jack rose to denounce his father's actions. In those years many a child of famous parents was going public with grievances that were trivial by comparison, but Jack got little sympathy. The popular slogan "never trust anyone over thirty" apparently didn't apply in this case. Paul Krassner rose to scold Jack for disloyalty, and he was heckled by another of Tim's supporters, who had arrived dressed in a kangaroo suit.

It was understandable that Leary's supporters thought him ill-used. A satirist like Krassner had to cringe at the thought that a man could be branded a public enemy and prosecuted to the limits of the law for making irresponsible statements in public. But the rush to find scapegoats was less attractive. Joanna Harcourt-Smith, who admittedly had helped to set up Georges Chula, became the remaining Learyites' favorite target, variously described as a DEA informant and a CIA asset. Responding to accusations leveled by Krassner in a 1999 article that appeared in the journal *Tikkun,* Harcourt-Smith wrote, "I was fascinated and infatuated with [Tim] to the point of indeed committing many dishonorable acts . . . and deeply regret the harm I have done to others."[24]

This was more of an apology than anyone would ever get from Leary. With the possible exception of Bill Clinton, it is hard to think of a public figure who capitalized so successfully on a reputation for irresponsibility. By living totally in the here and now, Leary relieved all of us of the need to consult our consciences. After his release from prison he made an effortless transition into a cult nostalgia figure, his twinkling blue eyes seemingly fixed on a painless if blurry vision of the past. Leary continued to publish books and went on the lecture circuit with his onetime nemesis G. Gordon Liddy, but his most reliable source of income came as an actor. He appeared, for example, in the closing episode of the hit TV series *Moonlighting,* presiding over the wedding of Cybill Shepherd and Bruce Willis's characters.

Assessing the impact of LSD on American culture isn't easy, even today. It is no secret that many middle-aged Americans still remember their youthful encounters with the drug as essentially positive, and the present author happens to be one of them. For years I felt certain that LSD had changed my life in some significant but indefinable way. Like Lisa Bieberman, I still believed the things I had believed before, but with a blinding certainty. As the years go by, however, it becomes harder to be sure that LSD was responsible even for this. Perhaps, after all, it was just the spiritual equivalent of skydiving, a thrilling but risky pastime.

When veteran LSD researchers gathered in Switzerland in 1993 for a symposium commemorating the fiftieth anniversary of the drug's synthesis, they left no doubt that they held Timothy Leary personally responsible for transforming an interesting and potentially useful discovery into a social disaster. But Leary didn't operate in a vacuum. The call to pursue peak experiences and utopian values was issued before Leary ever arrived on the scene. Moreover, the contributors to Robert Forte's memorial anthology for Leary make the point again and again that what they loved about him was that he gave them permission to indulge their antisocial fantasies and live in Neverland outside the authority of science, religion or morality. Ram Dass, the former Richard Alpert, asserts that Leary's mission was political; he preached the need for "freedom from being controlled by others, by a social system." Forte himself sums up Leary's influence by saying that it was his goal "to induce chaos into an excessively ordered culture." Philip Slater, formerly of the Brandeis sociology department, writes approvingly of the power of psychedelic drugs to undermine people's faith in everything from Republicans and militarism to the idea that there are biological differences between the sexes—this last a belief that Slater rejects because "it's not optimism." Another contributor, the late Terence McKenna, born in 1946, celebrates psychedelics for democratizing consciousness and liberating us all from "analytical European thinking." Before his death in 2000, McKenna had liberated himself to such a degree that he came to see psilocybin as a "megaphone used by an alien, intergalactic order to communicate with mankind." He also predicted, with the help of the I Ching, the end of the world on December 22, 2012.[25]

One also finds in this anthology Dr. Andrew Weil, the man whose youthful journalistic fact-finding set the stage for Harvard's repudiation of Leary. No longer prophesying the triumph of stoned consciousness, Weil is best known today as a promoter of health food supplements and holistic medicine. Although Weil invariably insists that he is neither for nor against drugs, he downplays the risks of psychedelics, describing them as much less dangerous than cigarettes and alcohol, and agrees with Robert Forte that the opposition to LSD is "so irrational that the only way you can explain it is that it is deeply threatening on some unconscious level." Weil also takes issue with the rumors that Leary had "fried his brain" through overindulgence, saying, "I have seen Leary over the years and he always looked to me very physically and mentally healthy." This, of course, presupposes a very narrow definition of health.

As for the charge that the opposition to LSD is irrational, one can only point out that Weil has no problem with irrationality in other contexts. For example, he favors teaching holistic techniques like "energy healing" in medical schools. Western science, he insists, needs to learn that "external reality can be changed by changing internal reality." During a 1997 panel discussion on "The Psychedelic Vision at the Turn of the Millennium," held at the Asilomar Conference Center in Monterey, Weil gave the following example: When he was younger, he had very fair skin and was subject to "endless" blistering sunburns. In 1970, however, he decided, "this is something that has got to change." And "with psychedelics, for the first time I lay naked in the sun and exposed my whole body to the sun, and lo and behold, my skin got tan for the first time in my life and it has ever since."[26] *Earth calling Dr. Weil:* If some people feel threatened by LSD, perhaps it is because they aren't wild about the prospect of placing their health in the hands of doctors who think that being stoned confers immunity to ultraviolet rays.

Perhaps the most plausible claim made for LSD by its remaining enthusiasts is that it unleashed a wave of creativity. Advocates of this view invariably invoke the cliché that American culture before 1962 was dull and conformist—as if Abstract Expressionism, the Beat poets and bebop, not to mention Little Richard and Elvis Presley, never existed. The psychedelic revolution did supply a jolt of creative energy for a while. Rock music, especially, had a good run. But the fun didn't last. As Jay Stevens writes in *Storming Heaven: LSD and the American Dream,* "What at first was a stimulus, a supercharging, became over time a dulling: the visions caused by these drugs were so wondrous that they rendered everything else petty and slight." Psychedelic art became notable for its crass excesses.

The essence of the psychedelic experience being nonverbal and nonlinear, it was especially inhibiting for writers. Stevens makes the point that Ken Kesey's embrace of LSD diminished him as a novelist. One might add that Allen Ginsberg became less interested in actually writing poetry than in personifying a certain kind of poet-guru. The best writing produced during the heyday of LSD was journalism, and the literary classic of the era is *The Electric Kool-Aid Acid Test,* the work of a conservative satirist, Tom Wolfe.

But it was in the moral realm that psychedelics had their greatest impact. In one of his moments of lucidity, Art Kleps pointed out that the reality-is-but-an-illusion mantra provided "a philosophic justification for making fraudulence and mendacity one's guiding stars in life." As he put it, "If as it seems, it is all an illusion, then it's all a fraud, which means that you are a fraud and I am a fraud, so let's all freely lie to one another, each in his own charlatanic fashion, and may the best pretender prevail."

Kleps was thinking of Leary when he wrote these words, though they could just as well have applied to him. After doing time in Massachusetts for possession of the "sacraments," Kleps moved to Amsterdam with his second wife. Within a few years, he managed to run afoul of the tolerant Dutch by denying that the Holocaust ever occurred. The "holohoax," he called it. It hardly seems an accident that Kleps managed to commit the one thought crime that the Netherlands refuses to countenance. Kleps returned to the United States, where he remained perpetually indignant that his denunciations of the "heebocratic" media were interpreted as evidence of pro-Nazi leanings. He died in July 1999, but the Neo-American Church lives on, with his widow taking over as chief Bee-Hee. Of all the organizations formed in the name of consciousness expansion, the church of solipsistic nihilism has proved to be one of the few survivors.

Chapter 5

Good Boy
No More

During the 1930s, while Abe Maslow was auditing courses at the New School and debating over coffee with famous mentors like Alfred Adler, Karen Horney and Ruth Benedict, Carl Rowan Rogers was on the front lines of therapy, counseling troubled and abused children as a staff psychologist for the Rochester, New York, branch of the Society for the Prevention of Cruelty to Children. Of all the founders of the humanistic psychology movement, Rogers was the last who could be accused of being an ivory tower intellectual. And yet, in many ways he was the most radical. Peter D. Kramer, the author of *Listening to Prozac,* credits Rogers with an "extensive contribution to contemporary culture, to our sense of who we are." As to the nature of that contribution, Kramer sums it up nicely: "For Rogers, the cardinal sin in therapy, or in teaching or family life, is the imposition of authority."[1]

Born in Oak Park, Illinois, in 1902, Rogers was the fourth of sixth children. He attended an elite private elementary school whose students included Ernest Hemingway and the children of Frank Lloyd Wright. But when Carl was twelve years old his family moved to a farm so that his father, who had made a fortune in construction, could indulge his interest in scientific agriculture. The younger Rogers boys tended the stock and managed their own egg business, not out of economic necessity but because their parents thought that farm work was wholesome and educational.

The young Carl was shy and bookish. He would grow up with bitter memories of being the inevitable butt of his brothers' jokes, even as he was starved of joy by his mother, Julia, a devout Congregationalist who disapproved of drinking, dancing, card playing and every other form of entertainment that might appeal to a growing boy. Even a sip of soda pop, he would recall, was accompanied by "a slight feeling of wickedness." Carl's brother Walter, like the siblings of Abe Maslow, painted a happier picture of their mother. When interviewed by Rogers' authorized biographer, Howard Kirschenbaum, Walter recalled only the usual childhood horseplay and defended his mother as a fair and reasonable woman. Carl, he pointed out, won the argument with her about dancing, and Julia Rogers then paid for the children to take lessons on the grounds that if they were going to dance they ought to do it well.[2]

Rogers planned to become a Congregationalist minister, and at the age of twenty, while a student at the University of Wisconsin, he was chosen to attend a YMCA conference in Beijing, then known as Peking. The journey to China, with stops in the Philippines, Korea and Japan, exposed him to depths of human misery he had never imagined possible and brought him into contact with social gospel clergymen who doubted the divinity of Jesus and defined the mission of modern Christianity as one of service to humanity.

During his college years Rogers also renewed his acquaintance with Helen Elliott, who had been one of his second-grade classmates in Oak Park. Helen planned to become a commercial artist and had trouble seeing herself as a minister's wife. She transferred to the Chicago Academy of Fine Arts, but Rogers courted her with ardent and touchingly sincere letters, 169 of them. The couple married in 1924, and Rogers entered the liberal Union Theological Seminary in New York City, where he was "emancipated," as he put it, from what remained of his faith. In one paper, on the subject of church history, he concluded, "there is no such thing as the religion of Christianity—the term is simply a name with which we cover a multitude of religions."[3] From this it was only a short step to the conclusion that belief in an "eternal verity" was inconsistent with modern science, Rogers transferred to Columbia Teachers College, where he studied with William Heard Kilpatrick, a disciple of John Dewey, and Edward L. Thorndike. Like Maslow some years later, Rogers got a top score on the IQ tests that Thorndike gave to all his students and research assistants.

In 1928, when Rogers went to work in Rochester, very few Ph.D. psychologists were doing therapy. Most were teaching, doing research or administering tests. Those who were involved with individual clients typically worked for social agencies. Neither Freudian analysts nor medical doctors, they were more inclined to see dysfunctional behavior as a reflection of the ills of society as a whole. Practically speaking, they often had minimal training in methodology and were under pressure to make quick diagnoses. During his twelve years in Rochester, Rogers came to realize that many counselors he worked with were poor listeners, quick to interrupt their patients and make snap judgments. Over time, he concluded that patients not only understood their own problems better than therapists, they were uniquely capable of solving them. The proper role of the therapist was to be a sensitive facilitator, providing the client—a term he came to prefer to "patient"—with a therapeutic environment of unqualified support and approval.

Rogers' 1939 book, *The Clinical Treatment of the Problem Child,* offered much-needed guidance to practitioners in a growing field. On the strength of its success, he became a full professor at Ohio State University in 1940, where students sometimes referred to Rogers' text as "the Bible." In December of that same year he gave a speech at the University of Minnesota in which he suggested that the goal of therapy was not to solve particular problems but to "assist the individual to *grow.*" The concept of therapy as nurturing the "growth experience"—helping clients to achieve their full potential as human beings—would lead Rogers to a concept of self-actualization that was similar, though by no means the same, as Abe Maslow's. It won him a devoted following that included social workers and pastoral counselors as well as therapists. But it also alienated many psychologists and psychotherapists who recognized the worrisome implications of Rogers' approach, especially his emphasis on "feelings" over intellectual analysis. Always more popular with students than with his peers, who often found him arrogant and irritating, Rogers was happy to leave Ohio State in 1945. He moved on to the University of Chicago, where he established and directed the university's Family Counseling Center.

There can be no doubt that Rogers was an effective therapist in his own right, though perhaps not always for the reasons he thought. During the 1940s many people saw doctors as almost priestly figures, and one can be sure that many of the patients he treated in Chicago didn't see any particular significance in the fact that his diploma was a Ph.D., not an M.D. Rogers, moreover, exuded a quiet self-assurance. Like Robert Young's character in *Father Knows Best,* he didn't have to raise his voice or issue orders to be an authority figure. That such an important personage had faith in their ability to help themselves must have made a powerful impression on patients.

Rogers, however, came to believe that patients must direct their own therapy, to the point of deciding how many sessions they needed and when they were "cured." The joke inevitably told about the nondirective Rogerian method concerns the patient who tells his therapist, "I sometimes feel my life is worthless."

"You say you feel your life is worthless," the therapist echoes.

"That's right. In fact, I feel like jumping out of the window," the patient replies.

"You say you feel like jumping out of the window," the therapist says.

The patient doesn't answer because by this time he has negotiated the windowsill and is on his way to a fatal encounter with the pavement below.

This was an exaggeration, though perhaps not by much. In his own therapeutic work, Rogers was more subtle than his writings imply; he once told an interviewer that an important component of his treatment strategy was "stealth." Rogers could communicate more with a simple "uh-huh" than many counselors managed to get across in weeks of pontificating. Still, his method took for granted a degree of risk. Increasingly convinced that all power relationships were harmful, Rogers ran the Chicago clinic by choosing talented therapists and graduate students and allowing them extraordinary freedom. Staff members were taught that it was the task of the therapist to make himself "real" to the client and achieve "congruence" with his fears and hopes. On occasion, this meant refusing to intervene and hospitalize individuals who expressed suicidal or even homicidal thoughts. Turning a patient over to the psychiatrists, who would stick him with a label like "schizophrenic" or just plain "psychotic," was an admission of defeat.

In the case of one female schizophrenic, practicing "congruence" led Rogers himself to the brink of nervous collapse. This woman, whom he had treated during his years at Ohio State, showed up one day in Chicago, telling Rogers that she needed to resume intensive therapy. Two or three sessions a week weren't enough for her. She began to appear on his doorstep in the mornings, demanding ever more "realness" and "warmth," and turning hostile whenever Rogers showed signs of failing to live up to his own standard of unqualified acceptance. Eventually, Rogers would recall, "I recognized that many of her insights were sounder than mine, and this destroyed my confidence in myself, and I got to the point where I could not separate my 'self' from hers."

One day, facing a dreaded afternoon appointment, Rogers realized that he had reached his breaking point. Turning over the woman's treatment to a colleague, he rushed home and told Helen to throw some belongings in a suitcase. Within an hour they were on the road, headed for Seneca Lake in upstate New York, where they owned a small cabin. Rogers remained in semi-seclusion for six months, recovering his composure with the patient assistance of his wife. He himself would call this his "runaway year."

On his return to Chicago, Rogers entered therapy with Nathaniel Raskin, a colleague at the Family Counseling Center. During these sessions he became aware of his own deeply rooted insecurity, "a feeling that no one could ever love *me,* even though they might like what I did." In July 1951, summarizing the results of two years of therapy, he concluded that he had become "much less fearful of giving and receiving love.... I think that I see in myself now more freedom in developing into deep emotional relationships with clients, less rigidity, more ability to stand by them in their deepest emotional crises."

As Rogers saw it, human loneliness is caused by the fear that our deepest selves are unacceptable to others. The key to overcoming loneliness is to take the risk of stripping away our defenses and presenting ourselves to the world "without armor." Of course, the problem of the schizophrenic patient was that her deepest self *was* unacceptable—needy, hostile, obsessive and ultimately psychotic. The challenge Rogers faced as a therapist was to reorient his personality so that he could tolerate the intolerable.

In 1946, somewhat to his own surprise, Rogers was elected president of the American Psychological Association. Previously, he had been regarded by academic psychologists as something of a maverick, a man whose theory was a bit squishy even though he did good work with patients. The APA presidency was in part a reward for his tireless organizational work on behalf of therapists, who represented a growing segment of the organization's membership, as well as his overall reputation for fairness. But it was also a product of increased public attention to teenage crime, known in those days as juvenile delinquency.

During the early 1940s the problem had been the subject of a major study known as the Cambridge-Sommerville Delinquency Project, involving six hundred at-risk boys, some of whom received Rogerian-style nondirective therapy. Other boys received more traditional therapy, were sent to summer camp and given tutoring, or were assigned to a control group that got no special help. A report issued in 1948, three years after the study ended, showed that the boys who got therapy, of whatever variety, were no less likely to get into trouble with the law. (For that matter, a thirty-year follow-up study, released in 1978, found that the subjects who had undergone therapy were *more* likely to have been convicted of multiple crimes, possibly because they had learned to rationalize their behavior.) As sometimes happens, however, the buzz surrounding this study made more of an impression than the anticlimactic outcome. The media and the general public were beginning to see juvenile delinquency as a problem with psychological roots.[4]

Moreover, as veterans returned home from World War II, clinical psychologists based in veterans' hospitals were designing programs to treat battle trauma. Therapy was no longer just for rich neurotics. It was increasingly accepted as the enlightened way to address the problems of segments of the population who formerly would have been dismissed as criminals, misfits or, in the case of veterans, victims of shell shock.

Rogers' reputation was enhanced during this period as the result of his ongoing debates with B. F. Skinner, the leading spokesman for behaviorism. The dialogue reached its high point when the two men faced off during the APA's 1956 convention, the same year that Rogers received the organization's lifetime achievement award. Just two years younger than Rogers, Burrhuis Frederic Skinner was a towering figure in academia. His theory of operant conditioning was the centerpiece of introductory psych courses, and many a grad student had been assigned to demonstrate its validity by running rats through mazes. Skinner was brilliant, but his personality wasn't exactly calculated to reassure the general public or bolster psychology's image as a helping profession. He had published an article in the *Ladies' Home Journal* describing how he managed to "mechanize" the care of his infant daughter by raising her in a germ-free, temperature-controlled, plastic-sided enclosure, which he called an AirCrib. To his surprise, a plan to market this invention failed for lack of demand. Skinner was also the author of a novel, *Walden Two*, about a utopian community of one thousand in which private property had been eradicated, children were reared communally, and democracy was abolished as obsolete. Walden Two's ruler, a social engineer named Frazier, made labor assignments based on the principle that the people who did the most unpleasant jobs worked the fewest hours.

To those who questioned whether it was possible to be happy without freedom, Skinner replied that "choice" is an illusion. We've been living in a behaviorist world all along, he insisted, whether we recognize it or not. Each individual is the sum of his past experiences. Parents, teachers, employers and the government know this very well, and use both positive and negative reinforcement to influence behavior. *Walden Two* simply proposed to replace negative reinforcements, like prison and poverty, with a community based on positive reinforcement alone.

More than one generation of undergraduates would have a go at dissecting the assumptions behind *Walden Two*. Rogers addressed the more practical question of whether it was ethical for psychologists employed by third parties to manipulate people's behavior in ways that were not necessarily of their own choosing, or even in their best interests. Stories about the brainwashing of American prisoners of war in Korea made such concerns pertinent. At home, meanwhile, advertisers, marketers, pollsters and the mass media were using techniques developed by psychologists to gauge and influence public opinion. Colleges and private employers judged applicants on the basis of required psychological tests. It was all too easy to stigmatize an overly demanding student as having a problem with authority figures, Rogers pointed out. How many faculty members would care to have their complaints handled the same way? "We can choose to utilize our scientific knowledge to make men happy, well behaved, and productive, as Skinner earlier suggested," Rogers said, "Or at the other end of the spectrum of choice we can choose to use the behavioral sciences in ways which will free, not control, which will develop creativity, not contentment; which will facilitate each person in the process of becoming." Rhetorically, at least, Rogers had much the better of the argument.

J ust a year after this debate, Rogers was lured back to the University of Wisconsin. His old alma mater offered him a double professorship, with appointments in psychology *and* psychiatry. Often accused of poaching on the rightful territory of the psychiatrists, Rogers now dreamed of creating a joint training program for M.D. and Ph.D. candidates. Moreover, despite his troubling experience with the woman from Ohio, Rogers believed that nondirective talk therapy could work for schizophrenics. He had lined up more than half a million dollars in grants, a small fortune at the time, and planned an ambitious research project that would compare the progress of patients at Mendota State Hospital with normal subjects of similar ages and backgrounds. He and Helen bought an attractive home five minutes from the Madison campus. The Rogers' son, David, and daughter, Natalie, were both married by this time, and they believed the house's lakeside setting would be perfect for entertaining grandchildren.

Almost immediately, there were problems. The University of Chicago Family Counseling Center had been Rogers' creation and, for all his disdain for authority structures, he had presided as a benign patriarch. In Madison, Carl Rogers was just one among many. His high salary made him a target of resentment on the part of some colleagues, especially since he was absent from the campus for months at a time, taking up visiting professorships on other campuses. Rogers' ambitious plan to reorganize the highly competitive graduate education program, eliminating rigorous requirements and allowing nearly all students admitted to graduate with Ph.D.s, met with stiff resistance. No diplomat, Rogers fired off peremptory memos that only stiffened his colleagues' resistance.

Meanwhile, the Psychotherapy Research Group, known to insiders as the "schiz project," was also having its problems. Many of the Mendota State patients were simply too ill to benefit from talk therapy. For that matter, some of the paid volunteers in the control group of "normals" rebelled when they realized they were expected to discuss deeply personal issues with therapists. Worst of all, Dr. Charles B. Truax, the associate responsible for managing project records, was having mental problems of his own. Increasingly paranoid, Truax refused to allow other staff members to see the data and eventually reported to the police that the records had been stolen from his home. They were never recovered, and ultimately Truax committed suicide. During this crisis, Rogers was on the West Coast, spending the academic year 1962–63 as a visiting fellow at Stanford. His biographer Howard Kirschenbaum cautions that Rogers' failure to assert control over the troubled project should not be interpreted as a refutation of his "optimistic view of human nature." However, in this instance, the belief that people spared the heavy hand of authority would work out their problems on their own proved to be false.

It may be that Rogers was already losing interest. During his 1960 summer vacation, he had pulled together a collection of articles for a book that turned out to be a breakout bestseller and made him one of the first celebrities of the nascent human potential movement. *On Becoming a Person* outlined Rogers' version of self-actualization. Where Maslow emphasized dedication to creative work and "peak experiences," Rogers outlined a process of self-exploration by which the individual strips away the "false fronts" that he has used to present himself to the world and becomes "the self which one truly is." Anticipating the day when nonfiction would be dominated by personal narratives, he began with a chapter entitled "This Is Me." The remainder of the volume equated "personhood" with the discovery of one's inner, presocialized "me." The search for truth, Rogers wrote, must begin and end with identifying one's true feelings. "Neither the Bible nor the prophets—neither Freud nor research—neither the revelations of God nor man—can take precedence over my own direct experience."

Rogers' autobiographical account of his lifetime "learnings," however, describes an enviably serene and ordered existence compared with the torment endured by some of the clients described in later chapters of *On Becoming a Person*. One client Rogers writes about feared that after stripping away his masks he would find "nothing" underneath, but instead found "a dam holding back violent, churning waters of emotion." Then the dam broke, and he was awash in "utter self pity, then hate, then love." At last, the tides of feeling receded and he emerged, unsteady but still alive. "I don't know what I was searching for or where I was going but I felt then ... that I was moving forward."

Only the promise of locating a "true self" purged of doubts and anxieties could make such a perilous interior journey worthwhile. The appeal of Rogers' book lay in his calm reassurances that his readers need have no fears about calling up and unleashing their hidden desires. The lion is often depicted as a "ravening beast," he observed, but in reality he only kills when hungry and "keeps his handsome figure better than some of us." Just so, the animal nature of the human being is less fearsome than we've been taught to believe. Of course, accepting ourselves means that we must also accept the unleashing of other people's innermost desires. Here, Rogers quotes Maslow, who wrote, "As the child looks out upon the world with wide, uncritical and innocent eyes, simply noting and observing what is the case, without either arguing the matter or demanding that it be otherwise, so does the self-actualizing person look upon human nature both in himself and in others." Among the practical consequences of adopting this nonjudgmental outlook, Rogers notes in passing, is that we would no longer be so fearful of communism, "a view of life different from our own."[5]

Returning to Madison after his California sabbatical, Rogers found the strains between himself and his colleagues too much to overcome. Two former students, Richard Farson and Thomas Gordon, had established the Western Behavioral Sciences Institute in La Jolla, California, for the purpose of doing humanistically oriented research. Rogers had served on the board of directors since the institute's founding in 1959, and Farson and Gordon were eager to have him come to La Jolla as a senior fellow-in-residence, with the freedom to pursue his own interests. Compared with the discouraging trend of the Mendota State research, the situation in California was tempting.

The WBSI, as it was called, was involved in the hot new field of encounter groups, then known as T-groups, which was creating quite a stir in California. Originated by Gestalt psychologist Kurt Lewin, T-groups had been developed as a tool for training and the study of group dynamics. Group work made leaders more "sensitive" to the feelings of underlings and encouraged them to redefine goals and group norms so that no one was left out. During the 1950s the National Training Labs, affiliated with the NEA and funded by the Carnegie Corporation, ran popular summer T-group sessions in Bethel, Maine. Rogers and his staff also did some pioneering group work in Chicago, training staff for VA hospital rehabilitation programs. But it was only at the beginning of the 1960s that enthusiasm began building for T-groups based on their potential for producing dramatic personality changes in a short period of time. Gestalt psychologist Fritz Perls took up residence at the Esalen center, on Big Sur, where he experimented with groups emphasizing nonverbal "trust" exercises. The WBSI was more focused on group interaction within institutions. It had major contracts with the Office of Naval Intelligence and the Joint Chiefs of Staff, and would eventually do work with consumer groups and welfare clients.

Perhaps the most striking development was the popularity of T-groups with young people who had no obvious reason to seek therapy. So many intellectuals and artists of the older generation had undergone Freudian analysis that seeing a shrink had become a status symbol; anyone who needed to hire an expert to plumb his psyche at top hourly rates was obviously deep and intriguing. But men and women in their twenties seldom had either the bank balances or, in many cases, the patience for psychoanalysis. T-groups were a self-service alternative, affordable and a lot less forbidding.

While on leave from Brandeis in 1962, Abe Maslow observed T-groups run for the employees of Andy Kay's company, Non-Linear Systems, and visited the WBSI, where he became caught up in the euphoric spirit of the moment. Enthused, he began to talk about a movement that would create a world filled with "Olympians," men and women who had carried self-actualization to the point where they could set aside negativity and unleash their full creative potential. He wrote in his journal:

> Let's roar off the face of the earth for awhile. Let's play total acceptance. . . .
> As in therapy, where I guess this just happens, —we learn to open up, not
> fear being laughed at, scolded, punished. We learn to be naked and show
> the secret scars we've been hiding all along. We discover from the true
> friend, or from the accepting therapist, that we can jump and we posi-
> tively will not be hurt.[6]

Back in Wisconsin, when Rogers suggested that he might move to California and focus his efforts on therapy for "normals," his staff was incredulous at first.

"You're going to California to find normals!" one amused aide exclaimed.

But Rogers did go. Also making the move to California was his research assistant, William R. Coulson. As a candidate for a doctorate in philosophy at Notre Dame, Coulson had chosen to write his thesis on Carl Rogers' theory of human nature. Rogers not only cooperated, he had found a place for Coulson on his staff, and the Roman Catholic philosophy student had become so enthusiastic about Rogers' work that he changed fields. In California, Coulson would earn a Ph.D. in counseling at Berkeley and become an enthusiastic promoter of group work.

With the possible exception of Fritz Perls, Carl Rogers would become more closely identified with encounter groups than any other individual. In fact, he was something of a latecomer, becoming immersed in the movement only gradually after his move to La Jolla. What he brought to encounter work, however, was a reassuring measure of professional credibility, combined with an approach that had radical political implications. Rogers preferred to call group leaders "facilitators," implying that they functioned like nondirective therapists, allowing the members of the group to set their own agenda. While many of the facilitators he personally trained in workshops sponsored by the WBSI actually were practicing psychologists, therapy had been democratized. Since the self was, in theory, the ultimate arbiter of truth, neither professional expertise nor, indeed, an objective referee was necessary. In practice, it rarely worked this way. No matter how "nondirective" his manner, the facilitator usually influenced a group's agenda through the force of his personality.

Rogers saw early on the potential of encounter groups to shake up institutions and challenge the legitimacy of authority. In 1965 he began to search for an institution, preferably a school system, willing to commit itself to an intensive course of group work. An article that he published in the journal *Educational Leadership* came to the attention of the Los Angeles–based Sisters of the Immaculate Heart of Mary through a relative of one of the nuns, who happened to have been one of Rogers' associates at the University of Wisconsin. At the time, the Los Angeles congregation of the order had 560 teaching sisters. In addition to providing staff for several Catholic elementary schools, the order operated its own college and high school. Maureen Reagan was among the IHM high school's famous graduates, and its best-known member was Sister Corita (later known as Frances Kent), an artist whose silk-screen prints featuring bold graphics and politically inspired slogans were influenced by her friend Ben Shahn.

In April 1967, Bill Coulson addressed a packed meeting held in the gymnasium of the IHM high school in Hollywood. Most of the sisters were enthusiastic. The reluctant minority was reassured to find that

Coulson, who would serve as project coordinator, was a devout Catholic. The IHM agreed to take part in an intensive two-year experiment that would involve the entire religious community, students and lay teachers as well as nuns, and require a staff of sixty facilitators. Dubbed the Education Innovation Project, the program was financed by grants, primarily from the Mary Reynolds Babcock Foundation.

What could the good sisters have been thinking? Why would a Roman Catholic order place itself in the hands of a psychologist who believed that there was no truth beyond the self?

The IHM sisters were hardly naïve. Some of them had already participated in encounter groups led by Father Adrian Van Kaam of Duquesne University and social worker Charles Maes. At least one IHM sister, later known as Midge Turk, wrote a book called *The Buried Life,* describing how role playing with Maes helped her to get in touch with a wellspring of buried anger. Once tapped, the anger was so powerful that she resigned from the order and moved to Pittsburgh for further therapy with Maes.

Leaders of the IHM order, moreover, were well versed in contemporary theology and philosophical trends like existentialism. Perhaps this was part of the problem, since even after a close reading it was often difficult to separate thinkers who wanted to redefine faith from those who were happily defining it out of existence. Catholic intellectuals at the time were deeply attracted to Third Force (humanistic) psychology because it offered an alternative to the sex-obsessed view of human nature they found in Freud and to the amorality of Skinner. Rogers, Maslow and other leaders of the humanistic movement often quoted freely from religious existentialists like Sören Kierkegaard.

Even Abe Maslow, who made no secret of his desire to replace organized churches and synagogues with some form of "religion surrogate," was enthusiastically received by Catholic audiences in the early 1960s. During Holy Week in 1962, for example, he gave a talk on self-actualization at Sacred Heart College in Newton, Massachusetts. One nun in the audience, a Mother Gorman, was suspicious of his message and questioned him sharply, but the rest of the audience responded to his talk with loud applause. The evening's work left Maslow feeling drained. In his journal he noted: "They shouldn't applaud me—they should attack. If they were fully aware of what I was doing, they would."[7]

Rogers lacked this element of self-awareness. So, too, did Coulson, who assured the IHM sisters that "when people do what they deeply want to do it isn't immoral." For the Notre Dame–trained philosopher, Rogers' message was life-affirming. "We have human potential and it's glorious because we are the children of a Loving Creator who has something marvelous in mind for every one of us."[8]

Rogers' program appealed to an order that hoped to be in the forefront of the revolutionary changes that were taking place in the wake of the Second Vatican Council, which ended in 1965. Priests, nuns and even laypersons had been invited to take part in discussions that would lead to sweeping changes in long-established practices. At that time there were 183,000 nuns in the United States, and the mood among progressive Catholics was one of great optimism. They confidently expected that once the church had shrugged off its medieval trappings, significant numbers of idealistic Baby Boomers—the same sort of young people who had volunteered for the Peace Corps—would be drawn to the religious life.

The public baring of one's innermost feelings is so taken for granted today that it's difficult to imagine the sense of unease that pervaded the initial IHM encounter sessions. Told that the group was a protected environment where they could bring up anything that might be on their minds, participants hardly knew where to begin. At first they talked about organizational matters, as if they were at a staff meeting. But before long the discussion turned personal, often with electrifying results. One older nun acknowledged in a tremulous voice that she was so locked into her role as a teacher and caregiver that she had never been able to admit her own need for emotional support. With a little prodding from the facilitator, one student in the group approached the sister and enfolded her in a supportive hug. This, of course, was something unheard of. A male student hugging a nun! It was, well, almost a miracle. The sister left the room to compose herself, and when she returned, she was still so flustered that she sat on the dinner tray that had been left on her chair during her absence.

Acknowledging one's vulnerability was learned behavior—all too quickly learned, as it turned out. IHM sisters reported proudly that they had begun to share their feelings of insecurity with their classes. To promote closeness, they encouraged students to call them by their first names, dispensed with tests and grades and taught only material that their classes found "meaningful." The students caught on quickly, and in record time the curriculum itself had became a vehicle for personal transformation.

The president of the IHM college complained that trying to control the students' enthusiasm for the encounter experience was "like trying to control dating, only in this case the students have fallen in love with themselves."[9]

Not everyone relished the heady atmosphere. Quite a few sisters and students had doubts, and some complained of being used as guinea pigs. One student remarked,

> I am in a literature course which I can honestly say has become a suffering class. Every single novel we read is not explicated in the old way— symbols, style, the author's intention—but we delve in identification between the character as a person with *feeling* and we try to find a point of identification between that person and ourselves. There is a human pushing, pushing all the time. Sometimes I come out of there, and I feel like I really want to cry.

Of course, the people who expressed such reservations tended to be the ones who were reluctant to take part in the groups, so Rogers and his staff found it easy to dismiss them. There would always be some individuals who resisted the process of "opening up." Just as LSD seemed to appeal most strongly to brainy loners, the Rogerian gospel of the self had a way of capturing those who were the most sincere and committed. Touchingly eager to make their mission relevant to the needs of contemporary society, they were willing to embrace teachings that were precisely the opposite of those that had drawn them to the Church in the first place.

In September 1966, Pope Paul VI gave his approval to the decree known as *Perfectae Caritatis,* empowering religious orders to begin "wide-ranging experimentation." The IHM moved speedily to take advantage of the papal directive. Novices still in their teens were moved from the serenity of the motherhouse in Montecito, near Santa Barbara, to an overcrowded convent on Second Street in downtown Los Angeles, a skid row neighborhood. Sisters nearing retirement age were told that they could no longer count on the community to support them. Suddenly, there were no more Latin prayers or Gregorian chants at Mass. Novices heard their religion teachers "reinterpreting" doctrine in startling ways. Many sisters reverted to their birth names, and plans to retire the order's traditional blue and black habit were in the works. In one of the most disconcerting changes, members of the order were no longer required to follow a regular schedule, beginning with attendance at 6:30 A.M. mass. A spiritual discipline developed by Catholic orders over the centuries was scuttled overnight because, as Carl Rogers advised, rules and regulations were artificial. Better to liberate the spirit and allow people to express their inner holiness spontaneously.

Feeling abandoned by their superiors, sisters began turning to each other for comfort. Many a tearful conversation begun during an encounter group was resumed in the convent, or on occasion even in the parking lot. Often, the shared intimacies progressed quickly toward sex.

While prayer was now optional, exploring one's sexuality had become virtually a requirement for anyone committed to the encounter experience. Group work meant stripping away social masks—everything that makes us civilized, thinking beings—in order to explore the bundle of murky impulses underneath that constitute the "real me." If one accepted this model, it was impossible for anyone to make a considered decision to practice chastity in order to be free to develop his or her spiritual potential. Such a choice was not only unnecessary, it was contrary to human nature. There was no such thing as sublimation, only repression—a symptom of unresolved conflict. Indeed, according to Rogers, every man and woman has a duty to explore what he called the "increasingly strange and unknown and dangerous feelings in oneself." Only by becoming comfortable with the dark side of the self could the individual hope to find his true identity and become "real" in his relations with others.

At a time when culture as a whole was celebrating free love and the open expression of sexuality, it was inevitable that some in religious communities would reassess their vows. Instead of offering context and guidance, the order had turned its members over to psychologists who advised the sisters to follow their "feelings," which of course were in turmoil thanks to months of encounter work. Not surprisingly, quite a few sisters rushed headlong into relationships. One nun, a woman in her late thirties, made sexual overtures to Father Ellwood "Bud" Kieser, a tall, strapping man who combined his calling as a parish priest in the Westwood section of Los Angeles with a successful career as an independent producer. Kieser was tempted, but declined. The Education Innovation Project then referred the sister to a humanistic psychologist, who diagnosed her problem as repression—though it would seem that she hadn't been too repressed to proposition a priest. The psychologist prescribed a series of sexual role-playing games. Soon, he and the sister were seeing one another outside of therapy, and the psychologist demanded a divorce from his wife so that he would be free to marry again.

The sister, now well on her way to being an ex-nun, continued to seek out Father Kieser for counseling, telling him that she wasn't sure she would ever be able to overcome the burden of guilt she carried over breaking up the marriage. In his 1991 autobiography, *Hollywood Priest,* Kieser tells how he was torn by a mixture of righteous indignation at the psychologist's behavior and raw jealousy. He thought about killing the therapist, but managed to restrain himself. The ex-nun and her psychologist, once married, became co-facilitators of marathon encounter sessions.

Amid the outpouring of empathy, self-expression and liberated sexuality, the dominant emotions seemed to be anger and partisanship. Jeanne Cordova, nineteen at the time, would write, "I saw lots of not going to Mass, lots of particular friendships, a whole sub-culture of in-group and out-group, who they were and how they did it and how you could just lie your way out of anything. To a lonely postulant in a miserable friendless world, it was an absurd outrage. I fell out of love with Jesus and the IHM's who betrayed and mocked my innocence." Such anger was almost inevitably interpreted as righteous wrath and directed at the Church and "society," which were obviously responsible for stigmatizing and suppressing the free expression of sexuality.[10]

Cordova's story appears in a 1986 volume entitled *Lesbian Nuns: Breaking the Silence,* which recounts the experiences of forty-nine sisters and (mainly) ex-sisters, including veterans of the IHM experiment. A few of these tales are heartrending, like the story of an emotionally fragile young woman identified only as Coriander. While attending a sensitivity training group in 1966, Coriander, then an IHM sister and fourth-grade teacher, began an affair with another nun, Eva, who introduced her to radical politics. "I had so much stored up virtue, I was a veritable arsenal of rage," Coriander writes. "I threw rocks at windows, rolled flaming trash cans into the street, learned to shout 'Fuck you!'" After a year of practicing this "new religion," Coriander found herself denounced by Eva, who then walked out on her. There followed sessions with a psychic, belly dancing lessons, living as a squatter, a stint in guerrilla theater, affairs with men and women including a female called "Gnome," and conversion to goddess worship.

Lesbian Nuns is intended as a celebration, but the road to sexual freedom has been anything but smooth. Former nuns for the most part exchanged their commitment to a universal church for the particularist struggles of lesbian rights and feminism. Still, one woman confesses wistfully that in decades of activism she has never found a community of women that functioned as successfully as the old IHM. Another woman, from a different order, remembers the serenity of her early days in the convent as the best time in her life. Very few of the love affairs that led these women to leave the convent lasted more than a couple of years, and Mary Mendola, ex-Maryknoll, even puts in a good word for the constrained particular friendships of pre-Vatican II days. While emphasizing that she is not "advocating celibacy," Mendola muses about the days when nuns "lived their religious lives together, some even retiring together and growing old as life-long lovers. I would never assume anything sexual in these relationships. The whole orientation of these women was a traditional approach to celibacy. Funny isn't it? But our sexually-oriented society might learn a lot about loving from just such homophile relationships."[11]

Traditionally, religious orders functioned as refuges for men and women who for one reason or another—not necessarily a homosexual orientation—did not wish to marry, start a family and become part of the "real" world. The creators of these orders believed that sex outside of marriage was a destructive force, a view that Carl Rogers was given to dismissing as Victorian. Ironically, the IHM experiment almost seemed designed to show just how wrong he was. Less than two years after the Education Innovation Project was begun, the IHM order was in chaos. By 1968 some three hundred sisters had declared their intentions to leave the order entirely and the remaining sisters were split into two quarreling factions. As a summary report of the project, prepared by IHM administrators, observes, "The psychological stripping represented by encounter group work proved to be a balm for some. But . . . suspicions were bred, and most damaging of all, intolerance for opposing views."

Parents had begun withdrawing their children from IHM schools, and Cardinal James McIntyre, the archbishop of Los Angeles, alarmed by growing defections from the order, refused to approve its sweeping modernization plan. Rather than submit to the cardinal's authority, one faction of sisters declared their independence from the hierarchy. Calling themselves the Immaculate Heart Community, the sisters took their fight against McIntyre to the newspapers, meanwhile waging a legal battle against a loyal faction for control of the order's property. Students continued to flee, and the IHM college was closed. Several years later, Cardinal McIntyre having retired, relations between the community and the hierarchy softened a bit, and IHM sisters were once again permitted to teach in Catholic schools; but the order never recovered. Today only a few dozen sisters remain.

The fate of the IHM sisterhood was just an extreme example of the impact of encounter groups on Catholic orders in the 1960s. Carl Rogers alone ran programs for the Sisters of Mercy, the Sisters of Charity of Providence, the Jesuits and the Franciscans. The Jesuits at the time were discussing something called the "third way," a path somewhere between the vow of celibacy and marriage. Bill Coulson recalls discussing this proposal with a group of Jesuits at a 1967 conference in Santa Clara, California. When he wondered aloud how a "third way" could possibly work in practice, one priest quipped, "It means you don't have to marry the girl."[12]

A year after this conference, Rogers was approached by St. Anthony's Franciscan Seminary in Santa Barbara, California, which like the IHM was concerned with bringing the order up to date. As usual, Rogers advised that the strict discipline governing the conduct of friars was infantalizing. Unlike the IHM sisters, St. Anthony's avoided a direct confrontation with the hierarchy. Some regulations were eliminated outright; others—including, apparently, a rule that forbade students from the seminary's boarding school to visit the friars' rooms—were simply no longer enforced. The friars, meanwhile, responded enthusiastically to encounter work. Some time later, the WBSI received a letter from one participant, a friar who was also a college professor, saying, "I am behaving like mad, with true self blossoming all over the place. Killing me." The last comment was assumed to be in jest.[13]

Twenty-five years later, in 1993, St. Anthony's was revealed to be the location of what the London *Guardian* called the "most widespread and scandalous" pedophilia ring in the history of the Roman Catholic Church in America, involving a minimum of thirty-four victims, one just seven years old, who reported being molested by at least eleven friars. Although the first allegation dated back to 1964, before the friars discovered encounter groups, the abuse rate exploded after the order relaxed its regulations. According to newspaper accounts, of eleven known offenders—fully one-third of the seminary teaching staff—one friar was subjected to criminal prosecution and another later committed suicide.

The names of the other offenders were never made public, and they were referred to a Church-run clinic for treatment.

Newspaper stories that appeared at the time quoted Father Stephen Rosetti, a clinical psychologist employed by St. Luke's, a Catholic clinic for abuser-priests in Suitland, Maryland, who blamed the abuse scandal on the church's "blanket repression of sexuality ... [which] resulted in halting the abusers' development, freezing them as perennial teenagers." The *Guardian,* in its account, goes on to suggest that part of the problem may be that religious orders attract people with "low self-esteem."[14]

Only a fool would suggest that priests never misbehaved before Carl Rogers. Still, it's amazing that even a priest-psychologist like Father Rosetti, who is surely familiar with the history of the order, sees no connection between the friars' behavior and Rogerian teachings. On the contrary, Rosetti accepts Rogers' view that repression makes priests into child molesters, and his treatment for the problem is more of the same style of therapy. His priest-patients keep a daily "sex log," recording in detail all their "fantasies, inclinations and awakenings" in order to bring their sexual impulses into the open. They also take part in dramatized reconstructions of their offenses, undergo Rolfing (deep massage) therapy to help them locate the physical seat of their anger, and attend meetings of Emotions Anonymous. The only novel element in the treatment mix is that the patients are also required to take Depoprovera, a drug that dampens their sex drive. Of course, mature adults don't normally write down all their passing sexual fantasies or spend hours each day dissecting their own emotions. If anything, this routine seems calculated to insure that the errant priests will remain "perennial teenagers." Take away the Depoprovera, and what's left is a group of highly sexualized, self-absorbed men who've been taught that the Church's "blanket repression" is the cause of their problems.

If the humanistic psychology movement had its own sacrament, it would have been the group hug. When Abe Maslow began acting as a consultant to Saga, a food service corporation managed along Eupsychian lines, he quite seriously advised the senior executives that managers must feel free to hug one another. Carl Rogers worried that he was inhibited when it came to expressing physical affection for clients, and William Coulson would begin his 1970 book on encounter groups by confessing that he started out life as a nonhugger: "As I got older, I didn't hug my father or kiss him, and I found it difficult even to hug my sisters." On becoming a facilitator, Coulson worried that any attempt to put a hand on a participant would be misinterpreted, and when he finally overcame his reticence, he was pleasantly surprised to discover that "the sexual part of my feeling was not all that great."[15]

The humanistic movement has made us a nation of huggers. Today, parishioners exchange hugs during church services. Even major-league baseball players hug. And yet, somehow, utopia eludes us. In truth, hugging is a social custom and not an accurate measure of how deeply individuals feel. But for the humanistic psychologists the hug symbolized an attempt to overcome our existential loneliness by giving and receiving unqualified acceptance of one another. The possibility that a hug might be sexual evoked both anxiety and hope because, in an ideal world at least, sex would be just a better way of breaching the loneliness barrier.

Eupsychian Management, the journal that Abe Maslow kept during his visiting fellowship at Andy Kay's factory, includes his musings about a study he had read about the habits of "lower-class Negroes" in Cleveland, Ohio:

> Among those Negroes the sexual life began at puberty. It was the custom for an older brother to get a friend in his own age grade to break his little sister in sexually when she came of a suitable age. And the same thing was done on the girl's side. A girl who had a younger brother coming into puberty would seek among her own girl friends for one who would take on the job of initiating the brother into sex in a nice way. This seems extremely sensible and wise and could also serve therapeutic purposes in various other ways as well. I remember talking with Alfred Adler about this in a kind of joking way, but then we both got quite serious about it, and Adler thought that this sexual therapy at various ages was certainly a very fine thing.

One can understand why Maslow's heirs chose to excise this passage from the book's recent second edition. But as embarrassing as it may be today, it reflects the view of a contemporary of Margaret Mead who had read and believed her *Coming of Age in Samoa.* Like Samoans, poor African-Americans were supposedly spared the repressive influences of white culture. Even their children could enjoy sex "in a nice way," without hang-ups.

Maslow could be equally naïve about politics. He once suggested making the T-group the basic unit of democracy, and he wrote in his journal that lying to the public about important matters ought to be a crime. It didn't trouble him that someone would have to be given the arbitrary power to separate lies from truth. Still, even Maslow was aghast at Carl Rogers' radically simplistic view of human nature. As early as 1962 he groused in his private journal about the deficiencies of his colleague's theory:

> Not enough sociology, history, politics, economics, etc. Social determinants not important for him. No ethnology. No notion of society as itself necessarily, intrinsically bringing power, problems, evil, dominance, into intrapsychic situations ... Where is anti-Semitism, anti-Negroism in Rogers' theory? Where is murder? Death? Destruction? Why do people go insane? Neurotic?[16]

This was quite a bill of complaint from a man who himself wrestled with his inability to explain why good people do bad things. Presciently, Maslow also wondered whether Rogers wasn't encouraging people to confuse the real self with their "inner child." But Rogers' tendency to oversimplify, which so worried Maslow, was also the source of his growing popularity. Despite the rhetoric about facilitators being nondirective, groups were powerful learning experiences, and almost inevitably followed Rogers' teaching that emotions were the seat of truth. The message, to repeat Coulson's formulation, that *"when people do what they deeply want to do, it isn't immoral"* was electrifying. Even among the trainers who worked at the WBSI, it sparked personal dramas that made professional objectivity an afterthought.

Hunter College psychologist Donald H. Clark spent time at the institute while on a fellowship from the Carnegie Corporation during the1968–69 academic year. Although married with two children, Clark was homosexual, and like other closeted gay psychologists of the era, he had spent years of his life, and thousands of dollars, in analysis. Freud believed that homosexuality, like masturbation or female promiscuity, was a mental illness, but as liberal psychologists and religious leaders became more accepting of sexuality in general, gays and lesbians felt increasingly singled out and stigmatized. When he began attending encounter groups, Clark came to the conclusion that there was nothing wrong with homosexuality in itself. The problem was the socially instilled prejudice against homosexuality, which functioned exactly like racial prejudice.

During the summer of 1969, Clark immersed himself in the literature of black liberation, mentally substituting the word "gay" for "black," and by the time he arrived at the Association of Humanistic Psychology's annual convention, the comments on homosexuality he heard during a "leaderless" encounter group were enough to put him in a white-hot fury. Clark resigned from his academic post, closed his practice and moved to San Francisco. He also told his wife about his homosexuality for the first time, and she agreed to stand by him as his "companion in exploration and growth." (The marriage would dissolve a few years later, after Clark declared his love for a male friend.) In 1971, while speaking as one of a panel of gay psychologists at a convention of the Western Psychological Association in San Francisco, Clark became one of the first psychologists to say openly that analysis didn't—and, more to the point, shouldn't—change anyone's sexual orientation. In a moment of "inspired and unexpected rage," he challenged any gay therapist in the audience to "put his or her right hand on the crotch of the person of the same gender seated nearest, leave it there for five minutes, and see if you still feel complacent." He received a standing ovation.

Clark's courage in coming out was applauded by Rogers and his staff, and they added his name to the WBSI's list of recommended speakers. However, Clark had leaped from the Freudian frying pan into the humanistic fire. Freud taught that the very condition of having homosexual desires was a sickness. Rogers said that anything a person deeply desired must be moral, and if one's fellow human beings thought otherwise, they were enemies, or at the very least, candidates for re-education. Substituting for Carl Rogers at a conference of South Dakota schoolteachers, Clark delivered a talk entitled "Humanistic Teaching—A Vote for Deviance." Discussing the talk in his 1977 book, *Loving Someone Gay,* Clark shows no understanding of why his speech was received in silence. Rather, he writes that the audience's chilly response "punished" him for being who he was.[17]

Meanwhile, Clark had submitted a manuscript, *Humanistic Teaching,* for publication as part of a series of books on person-centered psychology, co-edited by Rogers and Coulson. Bill Coulson was taken aback by one passage in particular:

> Signs of change are in the air.... Today's under-thirties, far more than in previous generations, accept many forms of deviance or individuality, and they will soon set the standard for our culture.... You cannot buck the

cultural taboo no matter how enlightened you are, by permitting or encouraging wholesale physical expression among boys, but you can permit or encourage what the traffic will comfortably bear.... Little children with arms around each other can be going to Funsville, and older youngsters can be blindfolded and try to identify classmates by feeling their hands and faces.[18]

The manuscript also included a section of encounter games to help both boys and girls get over their inhibitions against physical contact, advising, "Frequently, you will find girls do not like to be touched and might hold back at least in the beginning. A boy in our experimental group noted that when he confronted one girl she was almost trembling."

Clark's book was published in 1970, but Coulson began to reconsider his attitude toward touching exercises, which were becoming ever more popular. Why should a little girl have to get used to being touched if she didn't want? Why should an adult? Touching was supposed to express an intimacy that already existed. Now, more and more, it was the prelude to intimacy. Observing a student-led encounter group at a local college, Coulson was amazed to hear one young man suggest a backrub as a way to "get to know" a female member of the group. Far from freeing people to be themselves, the group had set up an alternate set of norms, one that reversed the usual order of making a new acquaintance. "First you could touch a total stranger, *then*, because of the touch, feel close to him, then maybe even want to talk," Coulson reflected. From there it was a short step to the approach of the "militant" who says, "Hold still, man, I'm going to touch you. Then we'll get along better."[19]

Donald Clark was fully prepared to revolutionize education, break down children's sense of modesty about their own bodies, and celebrate "deviance." But the 1977 edition of *Loving Someone Gay* demonstrates that he hadn't yet thought through the most immediate consequences of coming out. Clark counseled homosexuals to take their time about revealing their true sexual orientations to their wives and husbands. His advice was just to "act Gay," and leave it up to the spouse to ask the right questions. This method would supposedly be "less traumatic." (But for whom?) The wife or husband who walked out after guessing the truth was, according to Clark, acting out of "anti-Gay training or homophobia." But, he assured his readers, many marriages would survive the revelation. "Sharing the other person is easier if you remember that the more one loves, the more capable of loving one becomes." Clark assured straight spouses that while marriage to a partner who is also having homosexual relationships might be difficult at times, "think whether you would change places with the silent bored couples you see in restaurants."

Addressing gay couples, Clark advised that the rules developed for heterosexuals wouldn't work for them, and brief sexual "excursions" could enrich even the most loving partnership. Recreational sex in gay bathhouses or parks was presented as an option, though one that involved "some risks." A better approach might be to have sex with one's friends. No one need be left out of the revolution. Even the preference of gay men for certain physical types (good-looking ones), Clark wrote, is the result of society's "programming" and could be changed. This reassuring, humanistically oriented advice was delivered just a few years before the AIDS epidemic was recognized. But readers who heeded Clark's advice were forewarned that he wouldn't take the blame for any adverse consequences. In discussing venereal diseases, Clark blamed their existence on our "hypocritically righteous" society. If it weren't for widespread prejudice against sexual freedom, "we undoubtedly would have developed vaccines long ago."[20]

Another eager disciple of Rogers was Dr. Hal Lyon. A prominent educator who served as deputy assistant commissioner of education during the Carter administration, he was the Department of Education's liaison to *Sesame Street* and responsible for programs for gifted students. Lyon incorporated Rogers' ideas into federal education programs, and at one point he received a grant from the Ford Foundation to run an encounter group for congressional staffers. He also produced an autobiography with the ultra-humanistic title *It's Me and I'm Here! From West Point to Esalen: The Struggles of an Overachiever to Rebuild His Life through the Human Potential Movement.* Lyon claimed to have discovered "a religion of the self.... Really a worship of the inner self." By 1981, he had worshipped himself into a criminal charge for distribution of pornography. Public humiliation and a stint in prison caused him to rethink his enthusiasm for self-actualization. He emerged a changed man and spent the next two decades patiently rebuilding his reputation and reconstructing his career in a different area of specialization.[21]

Bill Coulson's wife, Jeanne, had heard so much about the benefits of group work that she decided to begin holding family encounters for their seven children. At first the young Coulsons were delighted to have a chance to speak up about whatever was on their minds. They looked forward to family meetings and resented any interruptions. Bill and Jeanne were reluctant to discuss their own personal issues in front of the children, but then several of the children began to talk about how much they missed their dad when he worked long hours and traveled on business. A response seemed to be in order, so Coulson decided to share his own ambivalent feelings about balancing work and family. Unfortunately, it was one thing to discuss such problems and another to resolve them. There always seemed to be more hurts and conflicts than there were solutions, and the children began to complain that the meetings were too intense. One day, Bill and Jeanne concluded that if they didn't take dramatic action, their family was in danger of splitting apart. Bill requested a year's leave, and he and his wife rented a farm in rural Maine, where the entire family spent their time working together and rebuilding trust.

Later, Coulson, a former professional trombone player, came up with an idea for a "family success project." With help from Dixieland cornetist Lu Waters, a family friend, he created the Coulson Family Band, which made its debut on *The Gong Show* and eventually became good enough to play a few professional gigs, including one at Disneyland. Before the children moved on to other interests, the group cut a 45 rpm record and wrote and illustrated a book about the experience.

Coulson hadn't set out to prove a hypothesis, but these experiences made him skeptical about educational theory, Rogers' in particular. "Child rearing didn't used to be anything people knew about," he would write. "They just did it. They worked the land for a living. Everybody pitched in. Some of those people were children. In the process they grew up. It was a pretty effective system."

Although Coulson continued to co-edit a series of books with Rogers until 1977, he would grow increasingly appalled by the social impact of the encounter group movement. Eventually, he concluded that humanistic psychology wasn't solving anything. In fact, it was creating new pathologies that hadn't existed before: "The therapy was the disease."[22] By the 1990s he would be devoting most of his time to criticizing Rogerian psychology from a Catholic perspective.

According to Coulson, Carl Rogers at times expressed doubts about the direction his revolution was taking, and on occasion he even became "depressed" over the human casualties. It is hard to see this, however, in Rogers' published writings. In his 1970 book on encounter groups, Rogers dismisses the charge that encounter work is a form of brainwashing. In fact, he equates all criticism of the movement with the paranoid ravings of the "far right," a segment of the population filled with "authoritarian personalities."

Carl Rogers on Encounter Groups makes it clear that unconditional acceptance of other people's "true selves" is no longer just a therapeutic strategy but a social duty imposed on all of us. Rising affluence and the growth of large, impersonal institutions, Rogers writes, account for the fact that people "nowadays are probably more aware of their inner loneliness than has ever been true before in history." Overcoming that loneliness by tearing away the "masks" of virtue and civility might be a gamble, but it is a necessary one.

While adults were quick to catch on to the rules of encounter work, leaders occasionally faced resistance from teenagers who objected to the nonauthoritarian approach. Rogers writes of one rebellious group that shouted at a facilitator who refused to eject two misbehaving boys, "Throw 'em out! You've just got to make us behave!" The leader, of course, knew better than to give the teens what they wanted. Rogers goes on to give an example of a more successful group of "institutionalized adolescents," in which a boy named George volunteers a startling confession:

"Well, I raped my sister. That's the only problem I have at home. I've overcome that, I think."

"Ooh, that's weird," says a girl named Freda.

At this point, another group member, Mary, chimes in. "People have problems, Freda, I mean ya know ..."

"Yeah, I know, but yeOUW!!!" Freda exclaims.

The recalcitrant in this group is Freda, who thinks it's weird to rape one's own sister and then describe the act as "the only problem I have at home." According to Rogers, Freda "is completely shutting [George] out psychologically." Mary's reaction is admirable because she shows "deep acceptance." As for George, he has learned that he needs to get over his embarrassment about discussing his crime in front of a mixed group of his peers. As he says, "It hurts to talk about it. But I've got to so I won't be guilt-ridden the rest of my life."[23]

As existentialist theory dictated, the facilitator had a duty to make himself a part of the process, changing at least as much as the other members of the group. And so Carl Rogers, in his early sixties, embarked on his own quest to become more "real," more "fully a person." Therapy had led him to the conclusion that he lacked a gift for intimacy and spontaneity. He considered himself too inhibited physically and too slow to express his anger—though some of his colleagues at Wisconsin would have disagreed about the latter observation. Ironically, his problem—his reserved personality—also happened to be the key to his years of success as a therapist. Maslow, who saw this, aptly described Rogers as playing the role of the "motherly father." But times had changed, and the feelings revolution now required him to get in touch with his true—if undoubtedly less functional—self.

Rogers' problem was that he came from a remarkably stable and comfortable background. His career had been a string of successes and his personal life blessed with good fortune. It wasn't easy to match the personal stories of men and women who had been marginalized for being black, gay, female, or, simply, unloved as children. Nonetheless, he concluded that his parents were the problem. They had brought him up to be a "good boy" and done such a thorough job of it that he internalized their lessons without much effort. "One of the fascinating things about my parents' control was that it was so subtle that it did not seem oppressive," he told fellow humanistic psychologist Warren Bennis. "I was a good boy, but that seemed to be the way I should be. It didn't seem as though I had to be this way against my will."

"Yeah, that's neat," commented Bennis. "Marx said that the sign of a truly oppressed person is when they don't know they're oppressed."[24]

Of course, Rogers' parents were able to live with their Calvinist consciences because they were Calvinists. They had God to back them up. As a nonbeliever, Rogers had all the responsibility on his own shoulders. Playing God-as-all-forgiving-therapist must have been lonely at times. And, perhaps, at long last he had concluded that he deserved a little of the unqualified acceptance he'd spent a lifetime dispensing to others.

At his age, Rogers didn't find it easy to change, and many of his efforts to overcome his "good boy" programming were inconsequential except to the people directly inconvenienced. He missed some deadlines and showed up late for meetings. By 1968, he had also become embroiled in a quarrel with the new head of the WBSI, over the latter's plan to hire a business manager and impose a semblance of corporate discipline.

Denouncing these changes as "reactionary" and "Hitlerian," he resigned, taking twenty-five staff members with him to form a "non-organization" that he called the Center for Studies of the Person.[25]

Rogers also made an effort to overcome his shyness about physical contact, becoming a prodigious hugger. Center training films show him embracing, and on one occasion exchanging tearful "I love you's," with much younger and often very fetching female clients. Rogers acknowledged that he felt some sexual attraction to these women but insisted that he was demonstrating that physical contact in the group setting was constructive for both parties.

It isn't clear whether Rogers pursued other relationships in his private life. In his book *Becoming Partners,* he mentions vaguely "one real attachment" that upset his wife. But his discovery when in his sixties of what he called "the sensuous side of my life" made some observers uncomfortable and sent a powerful message of permissiveness to other facilitators and therapists, some of whom were having sex with clients on a regular basis. A panel at the 1971 convention of the Association of Humanist Psychology openly debated the pros and cons of sexual relations with patients, and as late as 1977 Rogers wrote of his decision to share an effusive hug with a female patient named Michele as "a major learning for the whole community" that "intimacy is safe."[26]

Rogers' ideas about marriage had come a long way. When he wrote *On Becoming a Person* in 1960, he doubted that it was possible for most people to overcome jealousy. His 1977 book, *Carl Rogers on Personal Power,* however, reprints excerpts from the letters of "Fred" and "Trish," described as a couple in a successful open relationship. In the beginning, writes Fred in a letter to Rogers, Trish had trouble accepting his affairs with other women. Then she met Chip, who became her lover and a part of their little family along with Fred's married lover, Janet. Fred is pleased with Trish's progress. "Every day she is exhibiting more of the qualities of the person she has the potential to be," he reports. Trish's letter confirms that she is basically happy with the situation, although she mentions that maintaining two serious relationships sometimes leaves her pressed for time.

But as the correspondence continues, we learn that other aspects of Fred's life aren't proceeding as smoothly as his open marriage. The stress of his Ph.D. exams leaves him fearful that he will never finish his thesis and get a good job. He begins to feel like a "fraud." Overcome by depression, he takes an overdose of drugs and is in a coma for seven days, hooked up to machines in an intensive care ward. A letter from Trish supplies the additional information that Fred's suicide attempt followed a "manic" episode, and he is being treated with lithium.

"I cannot arrive at any solid conclusions from the story of Fred and Trish," comments Rogers. Perhaps, he suggests, Fred's illness has a chemical basis, but the trouble cannot possibly have anything to do with Fred and Trish's marital arrangements, which Rogers sees as courageous. All things considered, he suspects that Fred's problem is that his standards are too high: "Setting yourself up to be an achiever or *someone who is always together* is a dangerous proposition." In all areas of his life Fred has put too high a premium on thinking of himself as a "together" person. He needs to get in touch with his "horrible feelings" and learn to share them with others. Rogers recommends that Fred work with a therapist who subscribes to "person-centered" views.[27] It would be interesting to know how this advice turned out.

Rogers, meanwhile, had begun to "open up" during group sessions at the WBSI by volunteering information about his own marital frustrations. In the eyes of his students and admirers, Carl Rogers' marriage had always been one of the most attractive things about him. More outgoing and practical than her sometimes prickly husband, Helen Elliott Rogers had been an active faculty wife whose social skills undoubtedly furthered her husband's career. Over the years, she had opened her home to countless graduate students and junior associates, who sometimes thought of her, with affection, as "Big Mama" because she seemed so much more competent and down-to-earth than her often distracted husband. In addition to bringing up two children, Helen was a dedicated volunteer for Planned Parenthood and an accomplished amateur painter. She was quite well read, and kept up with developments in her husband's field. She enjoyed traveling and looked forward to her and Carl's extended vacations in the Caribbean, Mexico and the Philippines.

As the Rogerses entered their sixties, they presented a model of how a couple could take on new creative challenges even in their senior years. Despite Carl's growing fame and substantial book royalties, he and Helen continued to live simply, generously supporting their favorite causes. They both had hobbies that they pursued with considerable success— he constructed mobiles and did photography, and Helen continued her volunteer work with Planned Parenthood. In her seventies, however,

Helen became incapacitated by arthritis. Her mobility restricted, she urged her husband to cut back on his professional commitments and spend more time at home with her. Still in vigorous health, Rogers was in no mood to pass up the honors and travel opportunities that were the rewards of a lifetime of hard work.

Coping with a chronically ill spouse is never easy, but Rogers' situation was complicated by his belief that truth consists of whatever happens to be going on now, in the moment. As he wrote at the age of seventy-five, "In my experience, I have found that one of the hardest things for me is to care for a person for whatever he or she *is*, at that time, in the relationship. It is so much easier to care for others for what I *think* they are, or wish they *would* be, or think they *should* be." In the larger context, Helen Rogers was the girl he had ardently courted five decades earlier, the wife who had borne him two children, and the woman who had stood by him selflessly during the emotional crisis of his "runaway year," a time when, by his own account, he been unable to perform sexually or professionally. But, of course, these memories were just "thoughts," abstractions. In the here and now, Helen Rogers was an ill, aging woman making inconvenient demands, and he began to insist on his need for more independence.[28]

Instead of discussing his unhappiness with close friends or in private therapy sessions, Rogers used it as raw material for his facilitator training sessions. In 1976, for example, during an encounter group taped for his archives, he launched into a lengthy monologue about how his wife's love for him had been transformed "into a clinging love." As he put it: "If I give up my life or my personhood to take care of her, then I'm going to become bitter. I'm going to become angry inside at what I've given up. I'm not going to want to be with her—it would be out of a sense of duty—and that isn't the kind of relationship I want. It isn't the kind of relationship she would appreciate either, though she might think now that she would."[29]

Such speeches were awkward for the trainees, some of whom knew Helen Rogers personally. They also offered a dramatic demonstration of the power of the group to trump outside loyalties. Helen did not take part in encounter groups herself; she had attended a few sessions shortly after the move to California and concluded that the participants would never be able see her as anything other than the Great Man's Wife. Yet she could hardly avoid knowing that her needs were the subject of open discussion in WBSI training sessions, and Carl's discovery of his need "to live a life of my own" left her "baffled" and "often deeply hurt." Her husband, however, wrote approvingly in 1980 that "she is giving up the old model of being the supportive wife. This change brings her in touch with her anger at me and at society for giving her that socially approved role."[30]

Helen was also having to cope with recriminations from her daughter, Natalie, who writes in her autobiography that her mother had sent a message through her behavior that taught her, "Children and husband come first, my own needs come last." By being a model of self-sacrifice and maternal devotion, Helen, it seems, had incurred responsibility for her only daughter's troubled life.

Born in 1928, Natalie Rogers had been reared according to principles that were permissive by the standards of the times. Helen did not believe in rigid feeding schedules, and Natalie and her brother, two years older, were allowed to run around the house naked. A meticulous man, Carl Rogers expected the children to be neat and careful of their belongings, but the rules in the Rogers home were mostly implicit. Carl rarely lost his temper or even raised his voice. Helen was a little freer with her emotions and opinions, but still a calm presence. Natalie attended the progressive Harley School in Rochester where, she would recall, the students were encouraged to dance with colored scarves and tambourines while their teacher played passages from operas like *Hansel and Gretel* and *Siegfried* on the piano. "Both our school and home environments gave the message that to be a conformist was a deadly path. We were encouraged to think for ourselves, to be our own authorities," Natalie writes in an essay entitled "The Creative Journey."[31]

As a ninth grader, Natalie wrote a paper on traditional versus progressive education that many a graduate student would have been proud to claim, and while studying psychology at DePauw University she published two research papers in professional journals. Nevertheless, like many women in the postwar era, she felt pressured to make a choice between marriage and a serious academic career. Passing up graduate school, she went to work for the United World Federalists in New York, and in 1950 she married Lawrence Fuchs, a political scientist. Fuchs joined the faculty of Brandeis, and over a seven-year period the couple had three daughters. By her thirtieth birthday Natalie was eager for a new challenge. Abe Maslow, who was a friend of the family as well as a colleague of her husband's, encouraged her to resume her study of psychology. By 1960 she had earned her master's degree from Brandeis and published another academic paper, "Play Therapy at Home."

But behind the façade of a successful marriage, according to her account, something was drastically wrong. Shortly before their wedding, Natalie had written Lawrence a letter telling him that she was looking forward to "living through you"—not a sentiment one would expect from a woman of her uncommon background, even in 1950. A decade later, she was seriously depressed, alternating between childish dependency on her husband and barely suppressed rage. She felt lonely in the midst of her family, and entertained fantasies of running away, even of self-destruction.

In her self-published memoir *Emerging Woman*, Natalie attributes her unhappiness to the prevailing model of marriage, which made it difficult for a woman to establish an independent identity. Her husband's work was always assumed to be more important than hers. She felt apologetic about asking him to look after the children so she could attend classes, and he, indeed, acted as if he were doing her a favor. Obviously, there is some validity to her complaint, though the immediate problem was not so much the errors of society as Natalie Rogers' internalized sense of helplessness.

Aware of her daughter's unhappiness, Helen Rogers volunteered to look after the children so that Natalie could attend a weeklong "Workshop on Human Relations" that Carl was conducting at Sonoma State College in California during the summer of 1964. The workshop's purpose, according to fliers handed out at the time, was "an attempt to meet and assuage the loneliness which is felt by most individuals in this modern age." As Natalie later wrote in her journal, the week at Sonoma State was a revelation. "People were relating to me—not as a wife, not as a mother, but just plain me."[32]

Natalie returned home to Massachusetts determined to assert her "personhood." She had learned from the workshop that overcoming loneliness meant taking emotional risks, but Lawrence seemed unwilling to change the ground rules of their partnership—or, possibly, he was just bewildered and ultimately wearied by his wife's unpredictable moods. After failed attempts at family therapy and a bitter, extended separation, Natalie found herself divorced after nineteen years of marriage. She soon decided to sell the house and move to San Francisco. ("I was tired of fighting for my own identity. In a new town I could just form it.") In California she dropped the surname Fuchs, became a humanistic therapist and often joined her father in conducting workshops. In 1985, in partnership with her daughter Frances, she founded the Person-Centered Expressive Therapy Institute, which offers Rogerian therapy primarily for women.

As its title suggests, *Emerging Woman,* is intended as an inspiring story of her discovery of feminism and rise to personhood. Many women who went through similar experiences during the late 1960s and 1970s will see much of themselves in Rogers' story. (I myself had similar misadventures, and can empathize with her inner turmoil.) Nevertheless, since Rogers writes as a therapist who is showing the way for other women, it is legitimate to ask certain questions. Is it really possible that the people she met in encounter groups at the Sonoma State conference were unaware of who she was? Were they reacting to "just plain" Natalie or to the daughter of the occasion's organizer? How is it that she couldn't find an independent identity in Massachusetts as Mrs. Lawrence Fuchs but *could* find it in California as Natalie Rogers, therapist, the daughter of the great Carl Rogers himself? There is, of course, nothing wrong with a daughter carrying on her father's work, but it's hard to see this as a blow to the patriarchal structure of society.

Most important, did following her father's advice to make herself vulnerable and take more risks really contribute to Natalie Rogers' cure? Judging by her own account, it seems only to have exposed her to an endless cycle of humiliation and pain. Risk-taking can be rewarding, but in the absence of a code of morality, a healthy sense of self-protection or a perspective on the needs of others, it becomes almost a form of masochism.

Writing of the day she left her house in Massachusetts, Rogers tells how she finished the last of the packing and slipped into the bathtub to "nurture my soul" with a leisurely soak while waiting for the movers. Just as she settled into the tub, the long-distance van pulled up outside. Instead of getting dressed to greet the moving crew, Natalie called out the window, asking the men to wait on the lawn for ten minutes while she finished her bath. Being on the clock, they ignored her, entered the house and got to work. In an hour, the house was empty. "The movers walked in even when I had asked for my time alone," she writes. "(It was a new and courageous step for me just to ask.)" Years later, recounting the incident still causes Natalie to contemplate "the violation inherent in this scene." The movers' need to keep to their schedule symbolizes the refusal of our male-dominated society to allow more sensitive souls like Natalie Rogers to take time to "integrate and center ourselves."[33]

After resettling in California, Rogers continued her identity-formation project. Giving her "emerging self" the nickname Solo, she tried art therapy, dance therapy, Rolfing, Jungian therapy and window-pane acid. At forty-six, she took part in a three-day Native American–style fast and vision quest in Death Valley. She also worked at overcoming her sexual prudery. Stifling her initial embarrassment, she devoured books like Betty Dodson's *Liberating Masturbation* and began to incorporate vaginal and labial forms in her artwork.

Meanwhile, serial affairs helped Natalie overcome the "programming in my head" that caused her to expect fidelity and commitment from the people she cared about. One married man told her that he had an open marriage but would never divorce his wife. Shortly after Natalie ended their five-year relationship, the man did file for divorce, only to reject Natalie's suggestion that they resume dating. Another affair with a married man took a bad turn after Natalie and her lover "wondered how jealous we would feel if another sexual partner came into the picture." She decided to find out by taking a second lover. Both relationships soon ended. Later she pursued a male co-worker until he was cornered into admitting that he was gay, and then took another lover twenty-two years her junior, whom she credits with helping her to overcome "ageism." None of these men emerge as individuals from the pages of Rogers' memoir. It's difficult to tell one from another, much less figure out whether Rogers loved them, and if so why.

Even though she was in her early fifties when she came to write *Emerging Woman,* Rogers never stops to consider that there might be other paths to personal growth beyond just going with one's impulses of the moment. She is as much a prisoner of her moods as any toddler and, for a therapist, strangely oblivious to other people's feelings. (Confronted by the wife of one of her lovers, who accuses her of being emotionally needy and a husband stealer, Rogers indignantly reminds the woman that by having sex with her husband she has put herself "in a very vulnerable position.... Why should I not act on my own feelings? I am open to hearing yours, and relating to you, also." She seems not to notice that the wife has just expressed her feelings, quite clearly.)

According to Rogers, her book failed to find a commercial publisher because editors who read the manuscript didn't want to be seen as advocating a sexually liberated lifestyle. But surely, in the late 1970s plenty of books were published that depicted liberated lifestyles. No doubt the real

reason editors had qualms is that Rogers shows no awareness of how pun-
ishing her behavior is to others, and most of all to herself. Her story is supposed to inspire hope, but she seems depressed and desperate throughout.

What makes *Emerging Woman* worth attention is that Natalie Rogers
is honest. Because she declines to make up stories to justify her sense of
victimization, her narrative illustrates all too clearly how the search for
the "true self" gives rise to an unquenchable rage against any and all who
continue to be guided by the old value system. A good deal of Rogers'
anger is free-floating. She scorns "society for creating such an unequal
world" and men for their selfishness. Overhearing one man in a supermarket invite another to a dinner party where one of the guests will be
a divorcee who is "hot to trot," Rogers is outraged. "So that's how these
upper-class Yankee townsmen feel about the newly single woman!" she
huffs. The men's offense is that they think dating is fun and, well, sexy.
Rogers, by her own account, was sexually avid, even aggressive, but for
her it's a deadly serious business.

But Rogers' chief target is her mother. Unlike Carl Rogers, who
practiced what he preached and refrained from overt judgments about
his grown children's behavior, Helen Rogers occasionally offered suggestions and even expressed disapproval. Moreover, she invariably put
her family's welfare first. When her husband and young children needed
her, Helen had set aside her painting for months at a time. "Art was considered a luxury she did after everything else was completed," Natalie
writes. "Unfortunately, I adopted this attitude and have found it very
difficult to shake. It is particularly difficult because our culture does not
reward the artist. Our Western Culture prefers to reward computer pro-
grammers, baseball players and movie stars."[34] Of course, it isn't really
true that our culture does not reward artists, but why miss a chance to
take a swipe at Western civilization?

Born at the dawn of the twentieth century, Helen Rogers could hardly
be blamed for thinking homemaking an honorable and sufficient career.
Natalie recognized this intellectually, and in 1977, during a period of relative calm in their stormy relationship, she wrote a poem in honor of her
mother, which she read aloud at a women's discussion group held during
the annual convention of the Association of Humanistic Psychology, celebrating Helen as a symbol "of the many unsung women in the world."

Helen Rogers' reply, which she also delivered before the audience
of eighty women in the discussion group, shows that she is well aware

of her failure to live up to the Rogerian ideal. As her daughter tells it, Helen begins by offering "a few thoughts of my own which will show that I am also very human. There have been times when I have not listened to you [Natalie] in an empathic way. There have been times when I have been too authoritative." But after listing her shortcomings in a public act of confession, Helen also protests that she has never thought of herself as an "unsung woman": "I feel that all of my life I have done what I wanted to do. I had choices and, for me, my choices have been rewarding in themselves."

The truce declared on this occasion does not last long. Five months later Helen is hospitalized with a diagnosis of leukemia, and Natalie writes her a frantic letter, filling four closely spaced pages. She says in part: "Mother, I see you as having held in your resentments and anger for years! ... I see those resentments oozing into your sore joints, your aching body. The scars on your milky white torso, the swelling of your joints, the bone marrow that won't manufacture red cells.... I have been angry at you for not allowing me to be angry at you. You seem to create an environment around you which says, 'Thou shall not get angry.'... I live my life, in part, to change the karma of the you in me."[35]

Fortunately, Natalie had the compassion not to deliver this letter; yet she published the text in full in *Emerging Woman,* where it serves as a caution to any reader who might be tempted to sacrifice her own interests for the sake of her husband and family.

One can't help noticing that Helen Rogers was criticized for being unable to express her anger but also for being too judgmental and, when ill, too demanding and "clinging." She was wrong when she expressed her feelings, and also wrong when she didn't. Her real crime was that she was prepared to live with the consequences of her choices. By upholding the old, pre-Rogerian, standards of behavior she made everyone else feel guilty. And this was unforgivable.

During her final illness, Helen became preoccupied with the possible existence of an afterlife. God was still unthinkable to the enlightened Rogerses, but she and Carl did visit a medium who made "contact" with Helen's deceased sister by tapping out messages on a tabletop. Carl found these messages "extraordinarily convincing" and "certainly nonfraudulent." As a result, he was now "open" to all sorts of paranormal phenomena, including "precognition, thought transference, clairvoyance, Kirilian photography, even out-of-the-body experiences."[36]

The couple's emotional estrangement had grown over their last decade together, as Carl continued to assert his need not to feel stifled by Helen's demands. He had reached the point where he would be able to write, shortly after his wife's death, "I wanted to care for her but I was not at all sure that I loved her." One day, however, while his wife lay in the hospital—where she had begun to talk of visions of a white light, à la Elisabeth Kübler-Ross—Carl felt himself emotionally overcome. Describing that evening, he tells of rushing to his wife's bedside where he poured out a declaration of love, thanking Helen for her many "positive initiatives" during the course of their fifty-five years together. At the end of this heart-felt speech, Rogers told his wife "she should not feel obligated to live." Her family was doing well without her, and the decision between life and death was one that she must make on her own. "I also told her that I hoped the white light would come again that night," he adds.[37]

It did come. After he left the hospital, Helen summoned her nurses, thanked them for taking care of her, and told them that she planned to die. By the following morning, she was in a coma from which she never awoke. Carl later had another consultation with the "nonfraudulent" medium, who assured him that his wife's passing had been "very peaceful."

Carl Rogers remained active almost until his death at the age of eighty-seven. He made numerous international trips and continued to write and expand his influence. Natalie and her daughter Frances, meanwhile, were giving feminist workshops for mothers and their adult (over sixteen) daughters. Natalie describes with approval the words of a mother who took part in one such session. Responding to her daughter's demand for a role model this woman replied, "Go find out who you are and what you want, with my blessings. Stop asking *me* to be what you want for *yourself.*"

Natalie Rogers insists that the human potential movement made women into a "revolutionary force." But has it? Certainly, "stop asking *me*" is not a very powerful message.

Chapter 6

Revolutionary Science

For Abe Maslow, the most outrageous development of 1963 wasn't the mess that Tim Leary had made at Harvard. Rather it was the protests by "intellectual primitives" who objected to the Supreme Court's ruling banning prayer from the public schools. Maslow had persuaded himself that the only way to save modern culture from "the chaos of relativism" was to purge religion from public life and go about the business of creating a new system of values based on "naturalistic" principles.

Maslow outlined his plan in a small book entitled *Religion, Values and Peak Experiences,* which appeared in 1964. Much of his essay was a diatribe against organized religion, which he dismissed as an attempt to communicate spiritual truth to the "non-peakers" of the world. At best, this was a futile project; at worst, it became "an actual *support* of daily evil." In the future, he wrote, each individual must learn to cultivate his own peak experiences, which will put him in touch with inborn "B-values" (Being Values) such as Wholeness, Dichotomy-Transcendence, Necessity, Aliveness, Justice and Order. Ultimately, each of us will develop his or her own "private religion," complete with "private revelations" and "private myths and symbols, rituals and ceremonies, which may be of the profoundest meaning to him individually and yet completely idiosyncratic."

Prayer and worship didn't make Maslow's list of activities that may trigger peak experiences, though sexual intercourse and natural childbirth did. And for "the right people and under the right circumstances," LSD and psilocybin might make it possible to experience peaks at will, without waiting for them to occur spontaneously. Maslow added helpfully that just one peak experience—"a single glimpse of heaven"—might be enough to inoculate an individual for life against suicide.

Once people agreed on the same basic B-values, Maslow thought, the job of translating them into specific policies could be left to "scientists," meaning, of course, social scientists. There was no telling what this emerging Eupsychian social system would look like, though Maslow assumed it would mean the elimination of "idiocies" like the four-year college degree and required courses. The one imperative was that it must help "every single human person (not only an elite)" to achieve "his full humanness." Inclusiveness was to be the first and only commandment of the emerging eupsychian society. There had to be room for each and every individual to flourish, but also room for every individual's "idiosyncratic" interpretation of religious truth.[1]

Maslow's published views reflected a missionary zeal—or, more accurately, an antimissionary zeal—at odds with his private reflections. His calendar had never been busier. He was deluged with requests for speaking engagements, and his books were selling briskly. Many of his utopian fantasies were being realized beyond his wildest dreams. But he had also begun to fear that the social ferment was getting dangerously out of hand. Listening to his friends on the Brandeis faculty discuss the war in Vietnam, he was stunned by their reflexive anti-Americanism. More and more often, he groused in his journal, he felt as if he were taking part in one of his friend Solomon Asch's social psychology experiments, the naïve subject in a room full of ringers who were deliberately saying crazy things just to see how long he would go along for the sake of keeping the peace.

Still in his fifties, Maslow was plagued by an assortment of physical ailments, from stomach problems and suspected heart disease to chronic insomnia and low-grade depression. He wrote of the need to be "patient and Taoistic" with students, but more often, he was irritable. At one workshop, Maslow launched into a denunciation of prosperous suburban Jews, calling them "fat slobs" and stupid. ("That's a new phenomenon, stupid Jews.") He was, of course, denouncing the very people who loyally supported Brandeis, the Democratic Party and the state of Israel, all causes dear to his heart. His problem with suburban Jews, apparently, was that they were enjoying middle-class prosperity in a time of revolutionary change.

Such outbursts did not endear Maslow to his colleagues in the Brandeis psychology department, though people close to him were more understanding. "Abe was a kvetcher, a great Jewish trait," recalls Gunther Weil, who saw Maslow as "a little bit of a father figure for me." Protected by his mentor Gordon Allport, who had helped his parents emigrate from Germany years earlier, Weil had managed to hang on at Harvard for another year after the departure of the rest of the Leary group. Maslow then got him a job at Brandeis, pushing the appointment through over the objections of his colleagues.

Weil had trouble achieving re-entry to conventional academic life. Departmental politics and routine committee work struck him as petty and irrelevant. "I wanted to go and join Tim and change the world," he recalls. In 1965 he left Brandeis with Maslow's blessing and moved to Millbrook, but within a few months he concluded that Leary's stoned commune was no place for a man with a wife and two small children. Weil took various research-related jobs in the private sector and eventually developed his own practice, specializing in individual consulting and seminars for businessmen. Meanwhile, he spent twelve years studying the philosophy of Gurdjieff, and later became a disciple of the Taoist teacher Mantak Chia.[2]

This was a fairly typical path. The pursuit of peak experiences through drugs was too chaotic to sustain for very long, but it was hard to go back to waiting for "peaks" to occur spontaneously, and so many humanistic psychologists went from studying mysticism to practicing it in some form. Intellectuals in America had long been interested in the philosophy of Lao-Tse, and related Taoist disciplines, like Tai Chi, were attractive because they stressed the connection between mental and physical well-being. But New Age spirituality and the scientific method were an uneasy mix, and when the two clashed, science was often the loser. The National Qigong Association, which Weil helped found, operates a Taoist Healing Academy that gives instruction in both Tai Chi Chuan and Feng Shui. Recent academy literature boasts that the academy also permits its students to earn M.A.s and Ph.D.s in "topics as arcane as Taoist Inner Alchemy!"

Maslow, meanwhile, remained of two minds about the significance of mind-expanding drugs. As Weil puts it, the older man was "fascinated" but also "nervous," all without ever having any personal experience of the drugs' effects. Moreover, while Maslow was in a position to know a great deal about Leary's activities, he managed to remain more than a little oblivious. As late as 1965, he groused in his journal that Leary had appeared to deliver a lecture at Cooper Union in New York dressed in blue jeans instead of a suit and tie—surely the least of Leary's offenses against middle-class values. Leary, Maslow wrote with exasperation, insisted upon talking to "stage 3" people in "stage 5 terms." This was "like talking French before people who don't speak French," and it could only delay the arrival of Eupsychia.[3]

The American Psychological Association's Committee on Ethics took a far dimmer view. In July 1965 its agenda included a motion to censure Leary and Alpert for abandoning scientific methodology and making exaggerated and sensational claims for their work. As a member of the committee who knew both men well, Maslow was in a position to play the decisive role in the deliberations. His first impulse was to skip the meeting, using a recent bout with a summer virus as an excuse. But Dick Alpert was desperate to avoid being censured, and his father, George Alpert, made a personal plea to Maslow, who left his sickbed and flew to Washington for the meeting.

While listening to other committee members debate Leary and Alpert's fate, Maslow found himself wondering how Jung would have fared in a similar proceeding. Probably not very well, he thought. While his APA colleagues might not care to admit it, much of psychology could not be backed up by hard scientific evidence. Moreover, since humanistic psychology had a mission to transform society, perhaps it was unfair to hobble it with a code of ethics designed with "normal" science in mind. The code, for example, called for "modesty, caution & due regard for the limits of scientific knowledge." But perhaps, he mused, in the case of revolutionary science, timidity itself should be unethical.[4]

Without support from Maslow, the censure motion fizzled. The direct consequences were not great since Leary and Alpert had chosen other paths, but the APA had missed its opportunity to take an ethical stand and warn the public about the risks of putting themselves in the hands of therapists who would use them as guinea pigs in their "revolutionary science" experiments.

Around this time, Maslow's daughter Ellen moved to New York, where she was running the office of the Poor People's Corporation, a cooperative set up by the Student Nonviolent Coordinating Committee to sell handicrafts made by poor blacks in Mississippi. Maslow loved his daughter dearly and respected her idealism, but he was distraught over the Che Guevara poster on her wall and her pessimism about the future of democracy. On his visits to New York, he found himself drawn into political arguments with her friend Abbie Hoffman, who also worked for the Poor People's Corporation for a time. Maslow was appalled by Hoffman's "clownishness" and his rabid pursuit of media attention. But whether Maslow chose to see it or not, Hoffman was engaged in the very project he had outlined in his essay on peak experiences—cultivating his own idiosyncratic vision as part of the process of sweeping away old values to make room for the new. Hoffman's Yippies—a party that sometimes claimed to be a put-on, and vice versa—engaged in virtual politics, with the goal of persuading young Americans that the Establishment was a bad dream, which would vanish the moment a critical mass of people no longer believed in it. As Hoffman wrote, "Reality is a subjective experience. It exists in the head. I am the Revolution."[5]

As far as Hoffman was concerned, the saying "America is a Free Country" meant "You don't have to pay for anything." He scored a publicity bonanza by founding the Free Store, which mocked capitalism by giving away used clothing and household goods. In actuality, the Free Store was regularly plundered by second-hand dealers and became a favorite hang-out for street toughs who vandalized the premises and raped the volunteer clerks. None of this appeared to trouble Hoffman, who was more interested in the *idea* of the store than the reality of its day-to-day operations.

Although the Yippies and the prophets of psychedelic change agreed that reality was whatever one *thinks* it is, their subjective realities were too far apart to make a practical alliance possible. One attempt to forge a detente, organized by a faction called the Jade Companions, came to grief when Dick Alpert dismissed the war in Vietnam as an illusion, and suggested that instead of protesting the war, activists needed to do something about the anger inside of them. This was going one step too far for Hoffman. He could be coy about whether the Yippies existed, but he was certain that the war was real.[6]

It was, however, no accident that Hoffman's brand of humanist/existentialist theory increasingly came to resemble Timothy Leary's. According to his biographer Marty Jezer, Hoffman was introduced to LSD in the fall of 1965 by his former Brandeis roommate. The two friends took their first trip in the company of a Catholic priest whom Hoffman had met through his work for a Catholic-run community center called The Phoenix, in Worcester, Massachusetts. Around the same time, in November 1965, Hoffman presented a program at The Phoenix based on Maslow's ideas, entitled "Morality for the Non-Religious."

By 1973, when Hoffman's passion shifted to cocaine, he boasted that he had taken about three hundred acid trips. But drugs weren't Hoffman's only problem. In 1980 he was officially diagnosed with bipolar disorder, commonly known as manic-depressive psychosis; however, as Jezer notes, Hoffman had suffered from hypomania, a less severe form of the disorder, for most of his adult life.

If Maslow remained somewhat indulgent toward Leary, he was repulsed by what Hoffman had become. In his journal he calls Hoffman a "psychopathic personality," not a characterization he used lightly. Perhaps he even had Hoffman in mind when he began to question whether peak experiences were necessarily healthy. In an essay written in 1966 but not published until thirty years later, Maslow acknowledged "the present impossibility of distinguishing between a healthy peak experience and a manic attack.... Until we have better techniques of phenomenology and personality assessment, this issue remains one of the weak spots of the entire system of humanistic psychology."[7]

To call this a "weak spot" was an understatement. If the emerging values of Eupsychia were being formulated by delusional manic-depressives, surely this was a fundamental problem. Even if better techniques of "personality assessment" could be devised, this meant that only trained psychologists would be capable of separating the self-actualized elite from the crazies. Ultimately, then, it would be the psychologists, not the self-actualizers, who dictated values to the rest of the population. And if those psychologists happened to be practicing "revolutionary science," then they probably weren't terribly interested in developing better assessment tools anyway. The circularity of this reasoning was not lost on Maslow. Judging by his voluminous journals, there were days when he was almost messianic about the potential of humanistic psychology and other days when he was bitterly dismissive of what he now called "this SA stuff," meaning self-actualization.

But after devoting decades of his life to his theory, Maslow could hardly tell his followers, "Never mind." His journals reflect the interior struggle of a man who knew his ideas were deeply flawed but couldn't quite think his way out of the quandary. In entry after entry, he kept coming back to the problem of evil. Frank Manuel, his best friend on the Brandeis faculty, had warned Maslow as early as 1960 that his inability to account for the presence of evil in the world was a potentially fatal flaw in his attempt to construct a "religion of human nature." If human beings were born good, then how could one account for the state of what Maslow liked to call "our cockeyed society"?

At first, Maslow dismissed this question as an annoying quibble. He didn't deny that evil existed. He was even prepared to accept that a few people came into the world with biological defects that rendered them in some sense morally disabled. Still, it seemed obvious to him that most bad behavior must be a response to the environment. People wanted to do the right thing. If they didn't, either their basic needs hadn't been met or they hadn't been given enough information to make good decisions. The problem was that this contradicted his belief in free will. Unless people had the freedom to choose evil, then goodness wasn't a real choice at all. Suggesting that the choice of good was inevitable given the correct input came perilously close to an endorsement of behaviorism, which was anathema to the personal growth movement.

In one journal entry in 1969, Maslow characterized bad behavior as a "flick-back reaction," an instinctive response to a perceived threat to the self. This reduced evil to a behavioral tic or momentary misdirection of the survival instinct. "If we understand it this way, then we can be above it," Maslow wrote, "transcend it in a kind of Olympian, godlike, noblesse-oblige indulgence—as of an adult among children."[8]

Who were the "we" who understood evil from such Olympian heights? Presumably, psychologists—or, perhaps, all intellectuals of the humanistic persuasion. Since there was no God, *someone* had to be on the mountaintop, surveying the follies of humankind with detachment and compassion.

Unfortunately, Maslow couldn't even understand his own motives. One morning, just a few months before he wrote the lines quoted above, he was eating breakfast with Bertha when a chance remark she made prompted a revelation: His lifelong quest for utopia was a reflection of his unresolved anger toward his mother! Feeling deprived of mother-love, he had compensated by imagining a nurturing society, where peace and universal love prevailed.

This was as good an explanation as any for Maslow's idealization of human nature. Unfortunately, the more he refused to judge humanity in general, the more frustrated he became with people in particular. In 1960, Maslow had concluded that as much as 50 percent of the population was too emotionally stunted to be candidates for self-actualization. By the mid-Sixties he had raised his estimate to 90 percent, concluding that in order to rescue future generations, society would have to undertake a massive early-intervention effort that would guarantee every child his "right to be loved."

During his messianic phases, Maslow saw the encounter movement as offering the best hope of jump-starting the process of self-actualization for the masses. In 1968, when he was interviewed by Jane Howard, who was writing a major article for *Life* magazine, Maslow said, "Face-to-face therapy is a luxury. It's too slow, and too expensive. It's not the right answer if you think, as I shamelessly do, in terms of changing the whole world."[9]

Unfortunately, ideas that sounded liberating when Maslow proposed them often turned out to be less inviting in practice. At one point, he became curious about nudist camps, accumulated a file of literature on nudism and suggested to colleagues that it would be interesting to run encounter groups in the nude. Soon California psychologist Paul Bindrum was doing just that, staging his weekend-long sessions in borrowed suburban houses to evade the attention of the police. Howard attended one of Bindrum's groups and observed such exercises as "crotch eyeballing": A naked woman lay on the floor as Bindrum raised and spread her legs, while asking her a series of questions including, "Who in this room would you least like to have know about this area of yourself?"

Howard was almost as disturbed by her visit to the stodgy National Training Labs, where she heard a group leader talk earnestly about the need to create networks of families who would "monitor" one another's psychological health. With hindsight, the most interesting aspect of *Please Touch,* the hardcover version of Howard's odyssey through Encounterland, was her acceptance of the principle that she needed to get over what she called her "free-floating Protestant guilt." Howard was a respected writer—she later produced an excellent biography of Margaret Mead—but encounter groups instantly reduced her to the status of the quiet girl in thick-rimmed glasses, as vulnerable as any junior high school wallflower to the charge that she was too inhibited to be much fun. Despite her skeptical tone, Howard's book probably left most readers with the impression that encounter groups offered an opportunity to get involved in titillating situations without lasting consequences, and might actually do them some good in the bargain. On the downside, however, Howard mentioned that she had acquired a penetrating stare that made some of her old friends uncomfortable.

Howard had caught Maslow on a good day. While he usually refrained from criticizing the encounter movement in public, he had begun to question his belief that affluence and emotional nurturing freed people to concentrate on higher values. Carl Rogers' methods clearly didn't work for everyone. Some people, offered unqualified acceptance, just became more self-absorbed and childish. As for Esalen, Michael Murphy's growth center on Big Sur, it was fast developing into a spa for people whose main goal was to get high and share a hot tub with naked strangers. Esalen was suffering from the overweening influence of its therapist-in-residence, Fritz Perls, a man with a big reputation and a bigger ego. Well into his sixties, Perls avidly pursued female guests and cultivated an anti-intellectual atmosphere at Esalen, often to the frustration of Murphy. In January 1966 Maslow was invited by Murphy to lead a weekend workshop on his theory of B-values. During his Friday night talk, Maslow found himself being heckled by Perls, who objected to the academic tone of the presentation, complaining, "This is just like school." During the Saturday night session, Perls acted out his dismay, first rolling around on the floor imitating a crying baby and then crawling over to Maslow and clinging to his legs. By Sunday afternoon, Maslow had composed himself enough to deliver a scathing rebuttal, denouncing staff and guests alike for their smug anti-intellectualism. The brain, he reminded them, was also a part of the human body: "If you don't use your brain, you're not fulfilling your potential."[10]

Concerned that the "Dionysian" impulse was getting out of control, Maslow began to talk about the need for "aggridants." The aggridant was a sort of Nietzschean superman, a highly self-actualized individual who could take the place of traditional authority figures and exercise leadership in the spirit of "loving dominance."

One example of an aggridant was Chuck Dederich. A former alcoholic who broke with AA over its principle of belief in a higher power, Dederich founded his own drug and alcohol rehabilitation program, Synanon, in 1958, treating addiction with a tough-love version of the encounter group. Sessions of "The Game," as it was called, could go on for many hours and featured "haircuts," in which the entire group would focus on one participant, breaking down his defenses with a torrent of verbal abuse.

In 1965 Maslow made an overnight visit to Daytop Village, a program on New York's Staten Island that used the Synanon approach. Maslow credited the experience with causing "a revolution in my thinking." The bullying tactics practiced at Daytop Village were the opposite of the gentle utopia of Maslow's dreams, but he concluded that a tough-love approach might be necessary to reach addicts and others struggling with unmet deficiency needs. The community experience simulated the strict but loving family that addicts presumably never had. In a thank-you letter to his hosts, he suggested creating a network of "experiential workers" who could run a similar program "parallel to the present educational system," and talked of unionizing "experiential professionals" who would create degree programs and a system of certification. Although he acknowledged in his journal that he had "no real 'knowledge'" of the program, Maslow went on to write favorably about Synanon-style techniques in his book *The Psychology of Science,* published in 1966.[11]

As it turned out, however, the founder of Daytop Village was not on good terms with Charles Dederich, who had anathematized the former as a "splitee" after the two men disagreed on a minor doctrinal issue, and both men objected to Maslow's suggestion that their programs were essentially the same. Dederich, who had learned of Maslow's interest from Richard Farson of the WBSI, sent him a fan letter, declaring his debt to Maslow's early work and inviting him to inspect Synanon's facilities on the West Coast. Maslow accepted, visiting Synanon's center in Santa Monica during the same California trip that took him to Esalen. Fortified by his reading of a very favorable new book by Lewis Yablonsky (*Synanon: The Tunnel Back*), Maslow even agreed to testify on Synanon's behalf as an expert witness in a court case.

Maslow's personal impressions of Dederich were mixed, to say the least. He found him a powerful personality and certainly a "great man," in the sense that Napoleon, Charles de Gaulle and Lyndon Johnson were "great." All the same, he didn't much like him. Dederich was domineering, a loud talker who brooked no opposition to his opinions even though, Maslow suspected, he was probably not very bright. The visit left Maslow feeling that he had been "finagled and shanghaied" into appearing in the court proceeding. Later, Dederich presented him with a Synanon Club lapel pin, and Maslow felt as if he were being branded with a "badge of ownership." Nevertheless, he wrote of Dederich in his journal, "I'll back him up whenever I can." Such was the price of solidarity when you were part of a revolutionary movement.[12]

Maslow's instincts about Dederich were on track, and it's unfortunate that he didn't place more trust in them. A man of erratic moods, Chuck Dederich had a history of conflict with community groups, and by the late 1960s there were already rumors that the generous donations that local merchants made to Synanon were wrung out of them by threats and shakedowns. Ironically, however, the most ominous aspect of the Synanon program was what Maslow found appealing. Very few rehabilitated addicts ever emerged from the program to rejoin society. The great majority stayed on, contributing their labor to the group's expanding mission. Synanon had begun to acquire real estate holdings in San Francisco, Oakland and Marin County, and in 1968 Dederich announced plans to welcome nonaddicts, called "lifestylers," to the program. All would live together in Synanon City, a self-contained community with its own school, library and art center. Like him or not, it appeared to Maslow that Dederich was creating an alternative social order based on evolving values, a real-life Eupsychia.

A few months after his trip to California, Maslow learned that he had been elected president of the American Psychological Association, an honor that added to his already heavy load of teaching and professional responsibilities. On occasion, he continued to defend his vision of revolutionary science in public. In April 1967, for example, he spoke in favor of psychedelic research at a conference in Cambridge, Massachusetts, commending colleagues' plans to build a major personal growth center in the Boston area. He was also interested the new humanistically oriented educational theories of writers like John Holt and James Herndon, and planned to write his own book on education. But a sabbatical financed by a Ford Foundation fellowship and recuperation from a heart attack that he suffered in late 1967 kept Maslow out of the classroom for some time, and when he returned to Brandeis in the fall of 1968, he found the campus in the throes of a student rebellion. A black militant group was occupying one of the buildings on campus and library collections had been vandalized.

Students in Maslow's seminar on Experiential Approaches to Education immediately demonstrated their mastery of Rogerian theory by declaring their intention to cancel the class in favor of a leaderless encounter group.
When Maslow, sitting in on one session of the group, ventured to correct a
misstatement about humanistic psychology, one student challenged him,
saying rhetorically, "Who are you to tell us what's correct and what isn't?"
The student couldn't understand why Maslow burst out laughing.

On another occasion, Maslow told a group of rebellious students,
"When you get older, you'll be nice people. But right now you're immature jerks!"[13]

Disheartened and exhausted, Maslow was relieved to be able to
take early retirement and move to Menlo Park, California, accepting a
fellowship created for his benefit by businessman William P. Laughlin,
an admirer of his work in management studies. A generous patron, Laughlin even presented him with a new Mercedes-Benz. Maslow no longer
had the energy to keep up a full schedule. When he did accept invitations to speak in public, he sometimes made an effort to qualify his earlier enthusiasms. But it was too late to stuff the genie of revolutionary
science back into its bottle. Either Maslow's second thoughts were
expressed in terms too mild to attract much notice, or they prompted
vigorous protests. At a conference held in Iowa in April 1970, for example, Maslow tried to take back some of the claims he had made for peak
experiences, suggesting that "plateau experiences"—characterized by quiet
contemplation—were more important than emotional peaks. He also
expressed alarm that so many humanistic psychologists were turning to
untested New Age therapies and superstitions like the I-Ching, astrology and tarot cards. The audience responded to these comments with
shocked cries of "No! No!"

Their opposition was so fierce that Maslow decided to tone down
the language of the introduction he was writing for the second edition
of *Religion, Values and Peak Experiences.* The published version deplores
the growing influence of "fads and cults" as well as the prevalence of
"desacralized screwing." These were strong words coming from an academic, but probably made little impression on the average reader. If
Maslow no longer believed in "peaks," why issue a new edition at all? At
sixty-two, he may have been on the verge of publishing even stronger
warnings. But in August 1970, while jogging around his swimming pool,

a form of exercise prescribed by his cardiologist, he was felled by a massive and ultimately fatal heart attack.

If there was any consolation to be found in Maslow's early passing, he at least was spared witnessing the rise of therapy cults, and the transformation of his eupsychian dream into a malpsychian nightmare. Synanon, his favorite example of aggridance in action, proved to be one of the worst of the cults. In 1974, Chuck Dederich announced that Synanon had become a religion with a belief system that included elements of Taoism as well as the use of Ouija boards to channel the dead—who, when manifested, inevitably offered fervent testimonials to Dederich's leadership.

In 1977 Dederich further declared that Synanon had a mission to care for the abused children of the world. The overriding importance of this goal, it seems, justified drastic measures. Dederich ordered married couples inside Synanon to change partners every three years and turn over their own children to communal nurseries. Citing external enemies, he renounced his teaching of nonviolence and formed a security force, known to some as the "Imperial Marines." Disillusioned former residents and critical journalists became targets of punitive lawsuits and worse. The madness reached its climax in October 1977 when Paul Morantz, an attorney who had just won a $300,000 judgment on behalf of two ex-residents, was bitten by a four-and-a-half-foot rattlesnake that had been left in his mailbox. Two Synanon members, Joseph Musico and Lance Kenton, the son of bandleader Stan Kenton, were charged along with Dederich in connection with the attack.[14]

The original justification for Synanon was that addicts needed an all-encompassing substitute family to compensate for the socializing influences they had failed to absorb as children. By 1970, however, therapy gurus were beginning to offer similarly drastic programs for "normals." Arthur Janov's Primal Institute in Beverly Hills became the first such program to achieve a national reputation through celebrity endorsements. The handsome, charismatic Janov appeared on the *Dick Cavett Show* and was written up in *Vogue* magazine. But it was the institute's famous graduates, especially John Lennon and Yoko Ono, who did the most to promote Janov's approach. Endorsing the method in an interview in the January 1971 issue of *Rolling Stone,* Lennon credited his and Yoko's primal experiences with enabling them to get in touch with the raw emotional energy heard on their album *Plastic Ono Band.* The premise that there was something lacking in Lennon's earlier work, or that *Plastic Ono Band* represented a step forward, is one that many fans will dispute. Nevertheless, at the time, composure had come to be considered a form of psychological disability, and in the wake of Lennon's recommendation, Janov's institute was overwhelmed with applicants.

A clinical psychologist, Janov claimed to have discovered primal pain one day in 1967 when he heard "an eerie scream welling up from the depths" of a young patient who happened to be lying on the floor of his office. Soon he was helping other patients call up and release their buried psychic pain, a process that he touted as curative for a wide range of problems—from anxiety, nicotine addiction and homosexuality to speech impediments and persistent foreign accents. Although Janov patented the term "primal therapy," the underlying concept was hardly new. Inducing patients to relive old traumas, a process known as "abreaction," has been around for many years and repeatedly debunked as useless. Janov's emphasis on reliving the "trauma" of birth recalls, in particular, the theories of Otto Rank. Deliberately or not, Janov's theory also paralleled certain ideas of Carl Rogers. One source of psychic pain was said to be "parental denial," the frustration of the child whose family has failed to satisfy his basic needs for security and uncritical approval. Just as Maslow predicted, the Rogerian true self had morphed into the wounded inner child.

Newcomers to the Primal Institute signed up for three-week "intensives," during which they were expected to live in cheap motels and abstain from reading, watching TV, smoking, listening to music, chewing gum, talking on the phone and doing anything that might allay their anxieties or distract them from focusing on their inner selves. Group sessions typically began with Janov or a staff trainer asking, "Who's got a feeling?" This was the cue for one individual to step forward and begin reliving some traumatic incident from childhood, complete with tears and screams of "Mommy!" and "Daddy!" Clients exercised their emotions by pounding oversize pillows and, on occasion, attacking the walls with their fists.

One of Janov's more alluring promises was that the graduate of his program would never need therapy again. "Neither will he ever need to have any of his behavior interpreted by anyone," Janov added reassuringly.

Complete "clarity" could supposedly be achieved in six to nine months, but many patients stayed much longer. (One man I know was in primal therapy for four years. Despite this lengthy commitment, his problems were never resolved. Still, he defends Janov's theory and blames himself for failing to get to the source of his pain and have a genuine primal.) The promise of reaching an enlightened state beyond anxiety—and, indeed, beyond criticism from others—was obviously enticing. So, too, was the explanation that one's current problems could be traced to insults sustained in early childhood, if not indeed in the womb. If true, this meant that no one had any need to regret his own bad decisions or immoral actions.

With hindsight, perhaps the most curious aspect of primal therapy was Janov's vision of psychological health. Postprimal patients were said to be "clarified" of bad habits, neuroses and stress but, according to Janov, they were also less subject to ambition or strong passions. Their blood pressure, pulse and even body temperature were lowered, and postprimal women were capable of going through childbirth without anesthesia. This description would seem to contradict John Lennon's statement that primaling had enabled him to draw on raw emotional energy. Indeed, descriptions of postprimal man and woman often make them sound a little numb, even zombie-like, resembling the Apollonian Zunis of Ruth Benedict's imagination.

In his 1972 book, *The Primal Revolution,* for example, Janov scoffed at the notion that it is necessary to work at having a good marriage. "Normal people just are," he wrote, "and they let others be, which includes the spouse. Why should one have to work at any relationship?" Additionally, promised Janov, primal therapy could cure such delusions as the belief that military power, rather than the United Nations, was the key to preventing future wars. Further, it would rid people of their neurotic fears of "blacks, militants, youth, communism [and] socialism." Janov went on to describe a hypothetical character he called the Cold Warrior as the antithesis of postprimal man. The defining characteristic of the Cold Warrior is his belief that "things have to be tough to be good." In primal therapy, men and women achieve a higher state of consciousness and learn that a life of struggle is unnecessary. This protest against what Maslow called "the jungle outlook," the belief that the world is a place where people must compete against each other and toil for survival, was also the key to the humanistic vision.[15]

Quite a few of the basically healthy young adults who turned up on the doorstep of the Primal Institute were refugees from other therapies. Some were frustrated veterans of psychoanalysis, who found that after years of talking about their childhood experiences, their everyday problems were still unresolved. Others were seeking relief from the rage of the Rogerian true self, released during the course of encounter work, or from the overstimulated consciousness of the frequent LSD user. Primal therapy was supposed to be the final step in the journey, the last therapy they would ever need. But in due time, many veterans of Janov's institute would move on to still other corners of the human potential movement, including the notorious Center for Feeling Therapy.

"Feeling therapy" was the creation of Joseph Hart, a onetime assistant on the staff of Carl Rogers' schizophrenia project at the University of Wisconsin, who later wrote a book about client-centered therapy. After moving to the West Coast, Hart joined the faculty of the University of California at Irvine, where his popular courses delved into a variety of esoteric subjects including consciousness expansion, meditation and Senoi dream interpretation. Along with a former student, Riggs Corriere, Hart eventually went to work for Janov's institute, where he soon began to suspect that many of Janov's clients were not having "genuine" primals. People screamed because they knew it was expected of them, Hart thought, but there was little evidence of real progress.

Taking five other staff members with them, Hart and Corriere left Janov in August 1971 to form the Center for Feeling Therapy, with headquarters in a downscale Los Angeles neighborhood on South La Brea Avenue. Some of Janov's clients followed. The Center also accepted applicants who were unable to get into the Primal Institute, which was so popular that it had a waiting list.

Carl Rogers had talked about achieving "personhood," and Maslow's path to personal growth was supposed to make us "fully human." Arthur Janov promised "clarity." For Hart and Corriere, the goal was attaining "sanity." The truly "sane" had supposedly made a breakthrough to a higher state of consciousness. At home with their animal natures, they were as self-accepting as little children. They had also mastered the art of living completely in the moment, experiencing life as one unending peak experience.

In theory, getting sane should have been an easy matter since the

Center for Feeling Therapy made it a rule not to accept clients with pre-existing psychiatric problems or addictions. And, indeed, in the beginning Hart and Corriere created a relaxed atmosphere, joking with ex-primalers about the histrionics they had witnessed at Janov's institute. Living in the moment, however, turned out to require brutal candor about other people's shortcomings. Men and women in group meetings were subject to "busting," the Center's version of the Synanon "haircut." Another therapeutic exercise was "sluggo." As the name suggests, this was nothing more than a sucker punch, delivered by one of the staff counselors as a way of getting the client's full attention.

Even with such advanced techniques, getting "sane" proved to be an elusive goal. Before long, a core group of about 350 clients had abandoned their jobs and homes and begun living communally in rented houses in an unfashionable section of Hollywood, a short drive north of the Center's headquarters. Many went to work in Center-owned businesses, where their supervisors closely monitored them for signs of daydreaming or reflective thought, both forbidden deviations from life-in-the-moment. The inevitable breakup of family groups soon followed. Center therapists advised married couples and lovers to split up for their own good and assigned them to new sex partners, including members of the staff. Parents were ordered to send their children to live with relatives, on the grounds that they wouldn't be fit to take care of other human beings until they had become "sane" themselves. At least eight women were ordered to have abortions, by the same reasoning.

Carol Ann Mithers' 1994 book *Therapy Gone Mad* provides a harrowing and detailed account of how Hart and Corriere's impossible dream went sour. As Mithers points out, what happened at the Center for Feeling Therapy was a classic example of the phenomena of transference and countertransference. Patients in therapy tend to idealize the therapist, even fall in love with him. Having given up everything to follow Hart and Corriere, the Center's clients were all the more reluctant to entertain the suspicion that they might be less than perfect. Like the abused spouse who has become isolated from family and friends, they had no external reality checks, and they tended to assume that if therapy wasn't working, it must be their fault. Hart and Corriere, in turn, seem to have been genuinely surprised when their promises of blissful "sanity" went unfulfilled. No doubt they felt guilty, but in time they found a way to shift their anger onto the clients, blaming them for not trying hard enough.

Many of the "trust exercises" developed during the early days of the encounter movement were all too easily transformed into techniques for humiliation and social control. The Center's staff began to put women on starvation diets to keep them model-thin and commanded them to strip naked in front of the group for "crotch eyeballing." One woman who had been a devout Catholic was told to get down on her knees and "confess." While the therapist held a crucifix inches from her face, she was ordered to repeat the phrase, "I'm a cunt and I'm not sorry." A male client was assigned to wear a badge proclaiming himself an "All American Turkey." Another was ordered to don diapers and sleep in a crib.

Meanwhile, Hart and Corriere were even more effective than Janov when it came to marketing themselves. Joe Hart appeared on dozens of TV shows, including the *Merv Griffin Show* and the *Tonight Show* with Johnny Carson. Geraldo Rivera did a segment hyping Feeling Therapy's co-creators as the "Butch Cassidy and Sundance Kid of Psychology." While a group of Center residents devoted themselves to PR work, Hart's students at the University of California at Irvine were given course credit for writing admiring reviews of his books and placing them in professional and general interest publications. These promotional efforts were so successful that the Center soon became prosperous enough to move into new headquarters and begin holding public lectures and workshops for nonresidents. In time, it opened satellite centers in Montreal; Newport Beach, California; Brookline, Massachusetts; and Munich, Germany. A venture into employee training quickly snared a contract from the Los Angeles Water Authority. The same clients who were once promised that they could learn to live like carefree children were now goaded to work longer hours, dress for success and bring in as much income as possible. Hart and Corriere announced that the goal of personal evolution had been replaced by societal evolution—as good a way as any of avoiding having to explain why clients still weren't "sane" after years of intensive treatment.

This juggernaut came to an abrupt end in early 1980 when the charismatic Joe Hart abruptly left the Center with no explanation or goodbyes to the staff and clients who had idolized him for a decade. One story reported by Mithers is that Hart had chanced to read an article on the Stockholm syndrome and found it all too applicable to what was happening at the Center. Another possibility is that he was driven out by conflict with Riggs Corriere, who appeared to many of his associates to be in the grip of a manic episode. With Hart gone, Corriere became even more frantic and unpredictable. Finally, a group of senior staff members confronted him and told him that he needed a rest.

When the staff members explained their action to the Center's clients, admitting that things had gotten out of control, it was as if a magic spell had been broken. Suddenly free to speak candidly, clients discovered that companions they had lived with and worked beside for years had been harboring many of the same doubts. Submissiveness turned into outrage, and some disgruntled clients began telling their stories to the media. The *Herald* and the *Times* of Los Angeles both ran exposés, and the local CBS affiliate produced a documentary entitled "Cult of Cruelty." Nineteen former Center clients soon hired Paul Morantz, the attorney who had taken on Synanon, to sue for civil damages, and the California Board of Medical Quality Assurance began investigating more than fifty complaints of patient abuse. These legal repercussions took years to play out. The Center's insurance company settled with Morantz's group in 1986, but in the meantime the ex-clients were hit with a countersuit for defamation brought by some former staff members, which would not be resolved until 1992. The state licensing board, meanwhile, did not act on all the outstanding charges until 1989, when it revoked the licenses of Hart, Corriere and another Center therapist, Stephen Gold.[16]

Men and women who would not have been attracted to a religious cult had joined the Center in the belief that it represented the cutting edge of therapeutic practice. After all, the directors were licensed by the State of California. Hart had a respectable academic appointment and had worked in the past with the great Carl Rogers. His and Corriere's writings were reviewed in legitimate journals. Television hosts who were in the entertainment business and in no sense qualified to judge the claims of Joe Hart (or, for that matter, of Arthur Janov) were happy to give them a platform to address millions of viewers. In a decade when investigative journalists were hailed as heroes and were not afraid to take on the President of the United States himself, few took it upon themselves to question the claim that novel therapies held the answer to all human problems. Exposure came only when the Center had begun to fall apart and its victims delivered the story up to reporters.

The American Psychological Association, on its part, did nothing. Having failed to censure Leary and Alpert in 1965, the APA had missed its best chance to take a stand on the ethics of "revolutionary science." By 1970 the astounding growth of the human potential movement was creating new and sometimes lucrative opportunities for clinical psychology graduates. The APA was growing exponentially, and many of its younger members were doing some form of "therapy for normals." Unlike the American Psychiatric Association—the other APA—the American Psychological Association was not made up of medical doctors, bound by the Hippocratic oath. Moreover, "normals" were, by definition, not sick. While the Center's clients—not to mention thousands of others who submitted themselves to alternative therapies during this period— no doubt believed that their therapists were offering treatments to some degree vetted by the profession, it wasn't so.

Berkeley sociologist Richard Ofshe describes the 1970s as a period when "any two guys with an idea" constituted a school of therapy. Indeed, Dr. Perry London, a former director of the clinical training program at Harvard and a recognized expert on therapeutic ethics, testified in *defense* of Joe Hart and Riggs Corriere at their malpractice hearing in 1986, pointing out that the American Psychiatric Association recognized 417 schools of psychotherapy, at least 30 of which made use of confrontational techniques. Under the circumstances, London concluded, it was difficult to define an accepted standard of practice. In other words, things may have happened that fit the criteria of criminal assault, but London couldn't say for sure that they amounted to bad therapy.

Many of the novel therapies that have arisen out of the humanistic movement share a vision of the self as an empty vessel that gradually fills up with pain, a process that begins during the journey through the birth canal. Therapy consists of popping the cork of the patient's defenses and allowing all the poisons to drain out, leaving behind a purified self. In the case of the Center for Feeling Therapy, clients were ordered to live completely "in the moment" lest their brains begin to process more incoming pain messages from "society." Although the Center dissolved amid charges of coercion and assaults on patients, many variants on the basic theory of the empty self continue to thrive. To cite just one example, "rebirthing," pioneered by Leonard Orr, began in the mid-1970s when Orr started to practice yogic breathing techniques in saunas and hot tubs. A message on Orr's current website, quoting from his book *Physical Immortality*, explains that rebirthing involves methods "sometimes labeled by the medical community as hyperventilation syndrome." Properly done, they will lead to "the unraveling of the birth-death cycle" and, he promises, make you "master of your own consciousness."

Primal therapy also survives in many variants, all denounced by Arthur Janov, who insists that only therapists personally trained by him can be trusted. Janov, ironically, lost his voice as a result of surgery for a chronic throat problem and no longer stresses the importance of scream-ing. He also lost control of the Primal Institute during a contentious divorce from his first wife, Vivian. Along with his second wife, France, Janov moved to Europe, where the couple developed a considerable fol-lowing, but in 1986 they returned to California and established the Arthur Janov Primal Institute, which operates out of a storefront in the beach community of Venice. Janov also writes song lyrics—one of his numbers, "The Colour of My Love," became a hit for Celine Dion— but his real passion is proving that his version of primal therapy, and his alone, produces tangible results. According to Janov, research studies have charted long-term changes in the EEG patterns of his patients. The trou-ble with these findings is that many things, including meditation, med-ications and even quitting smoking, may alter brain-wave patterns. But where, one may ask, are the cadres of permanently "cleared" ex-primalers who live their lives without struggle or the need to work on their rela-tionships with others? John Lennon went on to use drugs. Robert A. Durst, a wealthy New Yorker who was in primal therapy during the same period as Lennon, was suspected of responsibility for the disappearance of his wife in 1982 and more recently was charged in the murder/decap-itation of an elderly Houston man.[17]

Oddly enough, from the vantage point of his beachfront Malibu home, Dr. Janov does appear to have achieved a plateau of serenity, which he maintains, in part, by inflicting aggravation on others. He warns potential patients away from all primal therapy practitioners not per-sonally approved by him, including those who work out of the original Primal Institute run by his ex-wife. Meanwhile, his latest book, *The Biology of Love,* tells mothers-to-be that their smallest actions—bad nutri-tion in the first few days of pregnancy, touching their babies too little or in the wrong way—will render their offspring vulnerable not only to stress but also to diseases like Alzheimer's in later life.

Margaret Thaler Singer, the Berkeley professor who helped the California authorities build their case against the Center for Feeling Therapy, is one of the small minority of clinical psychologists who have taken on the responsibility of helping the public separate good therapy from bad. In her book *Crazy Therapies* Singer lists a number of warning signs. One is what she calls the "Procrustean Bed"—an all-purpose diagnosis that can be stretched to fit any problem. "Unrealistic expectations" are another of Singer's danger signals, one that surely applies to therapies that promise to raise us to a higher plateau of consciousness, where we will no longer be bothered by the challenges of daily life.[18]

But unrealistic expectations were, of course, the whole point of humanistic psychology. Book titles like *On Becoming a Person* held out the possibility of dramatic transformation even while implying that those who clung to their old, traditional selves were not complete human beings. Americans have always been avid self-improvers, but the hefty fees and middle-class values of traditional psychotherapists were deterrents to young people who took their cues from the counterculture. Suddenly, as the 1960s drew to a close, novel therapies and religions were springing up everywhere. At the time, it didn't seem terribly suspicious that many of these groups purported to charge very little or nothing at all; on the contrary, the need to get paid was regarded as a sign of old-consciousness thinking.

Often, these groups were vague about their goals. It seemed almost a matter of chance which programs attracted which people. One woman I knew who wanted to be an actress joined the Fourth Wall Repertory Company in the East Village and disappeared inside its reclusive parent cult, the Sullivanians. Another friend, Barbara, the wife of a Harley-riding schoolteacher who worked with students considered too tough to attend regular New York City public schools, abruptly decided to follow Maharaj-Ji, the same guru who converted Rennie Davis. A month or so later I received a letter from her, mailed somewhere in Texas, saying, "God is even better than a double dip chocolate ice cream cone."

In 1970 a friend I'll call Suzy, who had recently been the maid of honor at my wedding, became involved with Fusion, billed as a Synanon-style program for "normals." Suzy was certainly no lost soul. A striking woman with long legs and a mass of red-gold hair, she had graduated from an exclusive East Coast college and was studying film at NYU.

When she told me that Fusion was helping her to bring her goals into focus, I took her seriously. My husband and I had met some other members of the program, who were living communally in a rented house a block from our apartment, and found them agreeably mellow—in retrospect, a little too mellow.

One evening after work, we agreed to attend a Fusion session being held in a funky commercial building in lower Manhattan. The leaders were a married couple who could easily have been twins—auburn-haired, tanned, untainted by self-doubt. Such creatures may not be out of place in Santa Monica, but by New York standards they were exotics. Under their direction, the meeting soon settled into a confessional, interrupted occasionally by deep-breathing exercises and group hugs. One of the first to speak was a youthful-looking woman who wore her red hair in perky pigtails and introduced herself as an actress. As her terrible secret emerged, her face turned blotchy and she wept inconsolably: She was thirty-seven years old! I understood that approaching forty could be frightening for an actress. Still, it also occurred to me that there were worse things than being thirty-seven and able to pass for twenty-three.

Another woman, the only one of us who had shown up in business clothes, may have been thinking the same thing. Politely but firmly, she questioned whether all this weeping and hyperventilating was really constructive. In an instant, the female half of the couple that I was by now mentally calling Our Fearless Leaders dropped her pose of California ease and unleashed a tirade, accusing the woman of being uptight, a source of negative energy and, generally, a person whose very appearance was repellent to anyone who was emotionally "clear." The verbal attack was so virulent and unexpected that the rejected "straight" fled the room. Fifteen minutes later, she could still be heard sobbing outside in the stairwell.

To my eternal shame, I did not go outside to console her. Instead, I stayed on, joining in another round of mandated hugging at halftime. During the second part of the evening, my husband became the leaders' favorite target, accused repeatedly of intellectualizing when he raised objections similar to those of the woman who had been expelled. Catching on a little faster than he did, I managed to volunteer a few acceptable "feelings" and was rewarded with cries of "Oh, you're so *clear*."

The next morning Suzy called. When I told her that my husband and I had no plans to return to Fusion, she reeled off a list of my shortcomings that was too concise and accurate to be spontaneous. *She* was not afraid to become a better person, she told me, and unless I wasn't either, we could not go on being friends. It occurred to me that she had rehearsed this speech, perhaps with coaching from the group leaders. I hung up the phone, and we never spoke again.

Brief as my experience with Fusion was, it taught me a lot about the power of the group experience. Thirty years later I still find it upsetting to think about. It also cured me of the temptation to believe that only lonely, weak-willed people are attracted to cults. Being bombarded by unearned approval had only made me uncomfortable. But sitting silent while others, including my own husband, were verbally abused had forged a strange bond of complicity between me and the rest of the group. On the one hand, I fantasized about showing up at the next meeting in order to expunge my guilt feelings by standing up to the leaders and telling them what I really thought. At the same time, a little part of me wanted to prove that I was superior to the people who had been the targets of the group's disapproval and capable of succeeding in the program if I really wanted to.

In its appeal to both good and bad motives, the cult's recruitment strategy is similar to the way a con artist approaches a mark. Most successful cons begin with what appears to be an opportunity to do a good deed. The mark is asked to help return lost cash or assist an undocumented immigrant in cashing a winning lottery ticket. At the same time, there's the suggestion that the good deed will also lead to a quick and easy profit. In the case of Fusion, the hook was not greed but egotism. I wanted to do the right thing, but also to look good doing it, win the admiration of the group and make Suzy regret the unkind things she had said to me on the phone.

Although the con artist analogy didn't occur to me at the time, I did have some experience with summer jobs in sales, and I knew that a prospective customer who feels compelled to argue with a salesman is usually well on his way to making a purchase. For every reason the customer has for not buying, the salesman can think of five reasons why he should buy. After all, that's his business. Unencumbered by mixed emotions or the desire to win the other party's approval, the seller has a psychological advantage. In the case of the Fusion leaders, they were also free to improvise new rules for the group as they saw fit. Winning an argument with them would have been impossible.

As obvious as all these observations may be, they do not seem to have occurred to the early promoters of the encounter movement. Too often, they assumed that merely by declaring the usual rules of social interaction to be in suspension, they could eliminate motives like the desire for power. Recalling the encounter sessions held with staff of the Immaculate Heart college, Bill Coulson illustrates how the desire to maintain control of the group could be rationalized in terms of the need to be authentic:

> Because we facilitators were in the group as persons, too, our wish to allow for self-direction among the college staff posed us with a unique dilemma. Clearly the groups should be what the people of the *school* wanted; in that sense, they were not our groups. But we *were* there. We didn't want to be silenced within the groups, just as we didn't want any of the members silenced, didn't want to do nothing, didn't want to withhold the contributions our own training and commitment prepared us for—didn't want, in a word, to be less than our real selves. . . . It was our irresistible temptation to see what the faculty were doing wrong and to model them for the correction.[19]

Naturally, the facilitators' attempts to be "real" were interpreted by college administrators as a bid for power, and the "nondirective" encounter groups that were a feature of the project led to bitterness, recriminations and institutional collapse. Nor is it surprising that the most successful transformational program of all was run by an ex-salesman well versed in motivational psychology and unburdened by any inner conflicts over his role as an authority figure. While Fusion disappeared without a trace, just one of many groups that did their bit to break down Baby Boomers' belief systems, Werner Erhard's "est" eventually touched the lives of an estimated five hundred thousand Americans, delivering a condensed course in the new religion of human nature.

As Erhard told the story, the idea for est came to him one day in 1971 when he had a peak experience while driving across the Golden Gate Bridge. A trainer of encyclopedia salesmen, Erhard devoured motivational literature as well as popular psychology. From his reading of Maslow, he had latched on to the basic tenets of humanistic psychology, especially the belief that the self is the seat of all values. However, Erhard's personal heroes were Gestalt psychologist Fritz Perls and Zen expert Alan Watts, whose houseboat was docked in Sausalito near his apartment.

Both men managed to live as they pleased, enjoying the delights of the flesh while attaining the status of counterculture gurus. Inspired by their examples, Erhard developed and began to market his own program, combining familiar humanistic rhetoric with elements of Scientology and borrowings from such motivational authors as Napoleon Hill, best known for the inspirational *Think and Grow Rich,* and Maxwell Maltz, the creator of Psycho-Cybernetics.

Even more than Chuck Dederich, Werner Erhard was the ultimate Maslovian aggrifant. He disdained the laid-back, nondirective style of Carl Rogers. Men and women who signed up for the est introductory seminar paid a hefty fee—$250 in the early 1970s—to sit on hard-backed chairs in a rented hotel ballroom listening to Erhard and his trainers revile them as "assholes" and respond to their questions with screams of "Don't give me your goddamn belief system, you dumb *motherfucker!* We're going to throw away your whole belief system! We're gonna tear you down and put you back together!" Bathroom breaks were denied, or at the very least severely discouraged, and attendees were subjected to rituals like the "danger process," in which they were paraded to the front of the crowded room a few at a time, where Erhard's assistants stood nose to nose with them and stared threateningly into their eyes.

The typical introductory session lasted 15 to 18 hours spread over two weekends. By the end of these harrowing lectures, trainees either "got it" or they didn't. But the nature of "it" was as elusive as the solution to a Zen koan. Essentially, "it" boiled down to the message that each of us creates our own reality and thus is responsible for everything that happens in our lives. If we are sick, it is because we have in some sense willed sickness. Erhard even told a couple who had survived the concentration camps that Hitler wasn't responsible for their suffering; they were.

Werner Erhard's own life was a testimony to the possibilities of reshaping reality. Almost every "fact" about his background and career comes accompanied by a counterfact that calls his official biography into question. Until 1960, he was a Philadelphia used car salesman named Jack Rosenberg. In that year, he deserted his wife and children to run off to California with a woman improbably named June Bryde. Though he hadn't divorced his previous wife, Rosenberg married June Bryde while using the alias Jack Frost. He began calling himself Werner Erhard after reading an *Esquire* article on the reconstruction of the German economy that included profiles of Werner Heisenberg and Ludwig Erhard. Both men had survived the Nazi era and were described by *Esquire* as emblematic of resurgent postwar Germany. Once Jack became Werner, June Bryde changed *her* first name to Ellen.

In 1971, the year Erhard had the peak experience that defined his future, he already held the San Francisco franchise for a self-help program called Mind Dynamics, whose mailing list provided est's first client base. The name est was said to stand for Erhard Seminars Training, though it also happens to be the title of a science fiction novel by L. Clark Stevens, in which the acronym signifies "electronic social transformation." As for Erhard's business interests, almost from the beginning they were protected by a maze of internationally based shell corporations structured for him by the tax shelter magician Harry Margolis. Erhard's financial dealings were so complex that even forensic accountants found it difficult to follow the money trail.

No fan of Maslow's ideas about aggridance, Carl Rogers once wrote that he approved of est's goals but deplored its authoritarian methods. The supposedly nondirective Rogers employed gentler methods, yet he had very specific ideas about the political implications of "personhood." For starters, the self-empowered human being would naturally be pro-environmentalist, antinuclear and suspicious of high technology in general. Erhard, on the other hand, cared nothing about turning out cadres of Birkenstock-shod liberals. He wore custom-tailored suits from Wilkes Bashford in San Francisco, drove a black Mercedes bearing the vanity license plate SO WUT, and served his guests the finest wines and Monte Cristo cigars. Erhard didn't tell people what their values should be, but his style implied that enlightenment was the key to power—personal, sexual and, above all, financial. Undoubtedly, this was the secret of his success. Hardworking people were willing to commit two weekends and endure verbal abuse pungent enough to make a drill sergeant blush if at the end of the ordeal they would be empowered for prosperity.

Erhard's refusal to guilt-trip trainees about money certainly accounted for his appeal to Hollywood stars, from Joanne Woodward and Cloris Leachman to Bert Reynolds and Diana Ross. John Denver's album *Back Home Again* carried a dedication to est. Actress Valerie Harper credited Erhard for her Emmy. Folksinger Harry Chapin and Yippie leader Jerry Rubin took the training. So did Yoko Ono—despite having previously attained "clarity" in primal therapy. Est was promoted by

Silicon Valley entrepreneurs, an influential executive at the Warner Brothers Studios, and Dr. Philip Lee, a former head of the University of California's medical school in San Francisco.

According to his biographer Steven Pressman, Erhard also made a special effort to target teachers, and during the mid-1970s an estimated 9 percent of the teachers in the San Francisco public school system went through est training. A pilot program for introducing est to second and third graders received funding from the Department of Health, Education and Welfare. Efforts to spread the est message in prisons were less successful, Pressman reports. Convicts, unlike teachers and other middle-class types, declined to sit still and voluntarily absorb abuse. Inmates walked out of est seminars in droves. During sessions at the federal penitentiary in Lompoc, California, the dropout rate was over 66 percent.

Motivational speakers do inspire people, at least in the short run. Throw in encounter group techniques designed to break down the trainee's psychological defenses, and the effect was especially potent. Many men and women left est training feeling exhilarated and empowered to attack their problems. By the late 1970s, however, Erhard had all but saturated the market for his programs and needed to reconfigure his message. In a move that soon backfired, he departed from his strict regime of self-interest, and in 1977 he announced the founding of the Hunger Project, with the goal of ending world hunger in twenty years. The initial response to the Hunger Project was enthusiastic. Veterans of est training signed pledge cards and made tax-deductible donations. Project activists John Denver and Harry Chapin were even appointed by President Carter to his presidential commission on world hunger.

In time, however, the press began to catch on that only a tiny percentage of the money raised was actually going to feed hungry people. In the universe of est, the hungry were responsible for filling their own stomachs. The Hunger Project's goal was simply to raise people's consciousness about the *problem* of hunger. Empathy and "caring" were virtues that made self-motivated people feel better about themselves. Actually getting together with other people to distribute food was at best problematic. If est graduates started to think that other human beings were incapable of feeding themselves, then they might conclude that they weren't masters of their own fates either.

The backlash against the Hunger Project was only the beginning of Erhard's escalating image problems. Rumors began to surface that he had a nasty temper and a mania for control. He had numerous affairs, but members of his staff who wished to have sex outside of marriage had to obtain his permission. Employees also complained of being interrogated for hours by "consultants" searching for evidence that they were harboring disloyal thoughts. Ellen Erhard sued for divorce, charging physical cruelty.

In addition to his divorce and suits by ex-staffers, Erhard was facing civil actions on behalf of people said to have been harmed by est training. One man had suffered a fatal heart attack during a "danger process" exercise. In a development reminiscent of claims in the literature on LSD, it also seemed that est training had the capacity to touch off manic episodes in individuals who had never been diagnosed as bipolar. Hospital emergency rooms came to expect a few est casualties in the wake of a visit by the program to their area, and Drs. Michael Kirsch and Leonard Glass reported on the phenomenon of est-related psychosis in the March and December 1977 issues of the *American Journal of Psychiatry.* It would prove difficult, however, to persuade juries that est had any financial liability for such negative outcomes. Ironically, because Erhard was not a psychologist and his trainers never claimed to be doing therapy, the program appeared to be immune from malpractice actions.[20]

Perhaps the greatest problem Erhard faced was that many est graduates were beginning to discover that their post-training euphoria didn't last. The belief that we have the power to create our own reality can be highly motivating. But when things go wrong, it can also lead to profound depression. This is exactly why Alcoholics Anonymous, the most successful self-help program in history, insists that its members acknowledge the existence of a higher power, however loosely defined. Newcomers often have trouble with this requirement, but in the long run it protects them from falling into the depressive's trap of obsessing about things that can't be changed. Some est graduates experienced a profound letdown over time; others simply began to look back on their former enthusiasm as vaguely embarrassing. Language that once had the power to shock became fodder for comedians' monologues. The turning point came as early as 1978 when the est practice of denying bathroom breaks was lampooned in the film *Semi-Tough.*

In 1985 Erhard regrouped again by creating the Forum, an upscale version of est geared to executives and professionals. He also ventured into business consulting through a firm called Transformational Technologies, which provided management training seminars for clients including NASA. Still, the bad publicity kept coming. In 1991, *60 Minutes* aired a devastatingly critical segment that included an interview with Erhard's daughter Deborah, who accused him of sexually abusing her. Erhard filed a libel suit against CBS, but never pursued the matter. Before the show was televised he had sold off his American assets and, apparently, left the country.

In the decade since, Werner Erhard's whereabouts have been a mystery. He is rumored to have a home in Costa Rica, though in recent years he has been seen in Mexico City and Toronto. In 1994 writer Dan Wakefield, an est graduate, caught up with Erhard in Ireland where he was leading, of all things, a training session for Roman Catholic clergy. Erhard vociferously denied ever molesting his children and blamed the Church of Scientology for orchestrating a campaign to discredit him. Strange as it seems, there was some truth to his complaint. As revealed by the *Los Angeles Times* in 1991, L. Ron Hubbard, the founder of Scientology, had been furious when he learned that Erhard had appropriated certain aspects of his teachings, including visual aids. Hubbard launched an anti-Erhard campaign that culminated in 1989 when the Church of Scientology hired a private detective named Ted Heisig to collect information to discredit Erhard and feed it to the media. Moreover, according to a 1998 article in *Time* magazine, Erhard's daughter later recanted her allegations of sexual abuse.[21]

Est's successor, renamed the Landmark Educational Forum, is a comparatively low-profile organization. Still, *Time* reports that three hundred thousand people took its introductory course between 1991 and 1998, and in the year 1997 alone Landmark had revenues of $48 million. Run by Erhard's brother Harry Rosenberg, the current incarnation of the Forum disclaims any connection with Erhard and takes pains to explain that its programs no longer make use of crude language or coercive tactics. The $350 introductory course even comes with a money-back guarantee to anyone who chooses to leave after the first few hours.

Judging by numerous reports from journalists and program graduates, the post-Erhard Landmark offers a kinder, gentler version of the old est, but with essentially the same message. An article by Alison Bass of the *Boston Globe* describes how the participants in her Landmark class spent a day and a half scaling emotional peaks and descending into dark valleys. Then, on the evening of the second day, came this key exchange:

"Consider that life is empty and meaningless," [the trainer] says. "There is no meaning. Life just is."

At first, people's faces crumple with bewilderment. Paula Houghton, the gift-shop owner from Maine is one of the first to get the point. "If life is empty and meaningless you can create anything you want," she says triumphantly.

Marisa Reilly follows her to the microphone.

"I feel so powerful," Reilly says. "I don't need to be a victim anymore. This is better than church. It's almost better than sex."[22]

Some might say that paying nonexperts to tell you to go home and solve your own problems is a sucker's game. On the other hand, if this were illegal, the consulting industry would be in serious trouble. *Time* cites scattered complaints from people who say that relatives were lured into spending thousands on Landmark courses or neglecting their own careers to serve as unpaid volunteers. But the Landmark Educational Forum lacks the classic features of a cult. Essentially, it's a marketing scheme whose product is a commercialized version of the peak experience.

The present-day version of the Forum even offers testimonial letters from Protestant, Catholic and Jewish clergy who have taken its courses. Interestingly, none see anything antireligious about the Landmark teaching that apart from the self, "life is empty and meaningless." Apparently this cut-rate existentialist message has become so ubiquitous in the culture that even priests, nuns, pastors and rabbis accept it as a truism.

During the 1990s, as the public became weary of discovering new victim classes, there was a renewed interest in the religious side of humanistic philosophy—this time emphasizing individual spirituality over the group experience. A spate of best-selling books instructed readers on how to locate the god—or goddess—within and develop a personal mythology based on Jungian archetypes, Native American myths, or prophecies channeled through contemporary mediums. Such books feed a real hunger in men and women who are looking for a way to be spiritual without actually believing in God. Psychologist Thomas Moore's *Care of the Soul,* a mega-bestseller, begins by cautioning that the soul "is not a thing." Moore then elaborates, "I do not use the word here as an object of religious belief or as something to do with immortality. When we say that someone or something has soul, we know what we mean, but it is difficult to specify exactly what that meaning is."

Since he is unable to locate the soul, or even define it as anything more than a quality that may be possessed by objects as well as people, Moore's advice on how to nurture the soul is predictably vague. He writes, for example, about the need to recognize our "mystery-filled, star-born" natures, whatever they may be. Moore seems to envision the soul as a neglected corner of the psyche, a sort of poor relative of the ego, once respected but now fallen on hard times. Like Blanche Dubois, it arrays itself in tattered finery and relies on the kindness of strangers in a pathetic effort to stave off despair.

Along with many psychologists in this tradition, Moore scorns hard science and what he calls the "intellect-oriented curricula of our schools." On the other hand, what he offers doesn't rise to the level of religion. Though he spent twelve years as a Catholic monk, that part of his life is obviously far behind him. His approach to spirituality mimics the ancient Greeks—indeed, the pre-Socratic Greeks—who tried to make sense of human behavior by studying the gods. The great attraction of Moore's books is that he recycles material from mythology and literature that was once a part of the heritage of every educated person, and he is not afraid to draw didactic lessons from them. But the lessons he draws are dubious. His prose is a river of soothing assurances, true and false, occasionally imaginative, often stupefyingly obvious. Hera is jealous, but also loving. Depression is a "rite of passage" associated with Saturn. We need to learn to "honor" Saturn and "abandon the monotheistic notion that life always has to be cheerful." There is, of course, no such notion in monotheism. Nor is it true, as Moore tells us, that schizophrenia "means 'cut off' or 'split' phrenes—lungs," or that the word "disease" means "not having your elbows in a relaxed position," though I wish that it did.[23]

While the search for private truths inspired a whole literature of New Age spiritualism, encounter group techniques that the counterculture tried and, for the most part, rejected have become entrenched in business, schools and government bureaucracies. More than 70 percent of major U.S. corporations now have some form of diversity training program in place, and the ubiquity of such programs on campus has been chronicled by University of Pennsylvania historian Alan Charles Kors.

Diversity training has become big business, its growth promoted by managers' fears that the lack of a diversity program may make their institution vulnerable to lawsuits or regulatory action. Defining diversity training isn't easy. At one end of the spectrum it can be as innocuous as a John Cleese instructional video. Trainers who say their goal is "managing diversity" usually focus on problem solving in the workplace and incorporate a minimum of heavy emotional content. At the other extreme is the antiracism school, which Massachusetts consultant Patti DeRosa, an advocate, calls "the heart and soul of the diversity movement." For more than twenty years antiracism programs have interpreted racism as a disease of Western civilization. More recently, the goal of antiracism work has broadened. No longer content to aim for political and institutional change, advocates speak of their mission as "transformative"—bringing about a fundamental change in human nature itself. In practice, this means personalizing their lessons by getting adults and children to play games like "blue eyes / brown eyes" or barring white students from certain elevators, restrooms and other facilities in order to give them a taste of what it "felt like" for blacks to live under Jim Crow laws. DeRosa quotes antiracism activist Vincent Harding as saying, "What we want is a new transformed humanity, not equal opportunity in a dehumanized one."[24]

Not all antiracism trainers are so idealistic. Privately, some joke about ROWing, short for "ripping off whitey." While few trainers acknowledge engaging in ROWing themselves, they may excuse the practice on the grounds that it merely makes up for past injustices.

The so-called "prejudice reduction" approach addresses a wider range of controversial issues, from race and gender to affirmative action, abortion rights, the death penalty and, recently, schoolyard bullying. Prejudice reduction traces its roots to the work of Gordon Allport, one of the founders of humanistic psychology. Allport's "contact theory" stressed that individuals overcome prejudice when they are able to work together as equals toward a common goal. (This observation explains the longtime popularity of "cooperative learning" in American classrooms, despite little evidence that assigning children to work in groups promotes achievement.) A more recent development in prejudice reduction theory holds that bigotry is a reaction to stressful experiences in one's past. Thus, prejudice reduction programs combine role-playing exercises with "emotional healing" based on sharing stories of childhood traumas. At my alma mater, Swarthmore, the 1998 freshman orientation week included an exercise during which students were instructed to line up by skin color, from lightest to darkest, and then testify one by one as to how they felt about their place in the line. Williams College's freshman orientation in 1995 featured "Feel What It Is Like to Be Gay" activities.

One of the leading marketers of prejudice reduction is the National Coalition Building Institute, based in the District of Columbia. The NCBI has run programs for corporations like Motorola and DuPont as well as at universities around the country. It also has branches abroad, addressing anti-Semitism in Switzerland and racial violence in England. It is especially active in Northern Ireland, where diversity training has been embraced as the latest solution to Protestant-Catholic tensions.

As a "healing" exercise, participants in NCBI programs are routinely asked to recall their most traumatic encounter with prejudice. During a demonstration workshop held in the Smithsonian's Experimental Gallery, for example, a seventeen-year-old girl told of her experience as the only African-American contestant in a music competition. After struggling through her harp solo she returned to the audience, only to hear the white woman sitting next to her hiss, "Who do you think you are? Why are you here?" This reaction is hardly typical of what whites think when they see a black teenager playing the harp. Indeed, it isn't even clear that the woman was not referring to the girl's ability level rather than her race. Still, it happened, and telling the story validated the girl's pain. In such situations, other members of the group who want to claim their share of attention and sympathy have no alternative but to search their memories for equally dramatic stories.[25]

A workshop for social service professionals held in Los Angeles, not long after the 1992 riots, showed off the expanding arsenal of prejudice reduction techniques. NCBI founder Cherie Brown and her Korean-American assistant, Unyong Kim, instructed participants to voice their "deepest negative feelings about their own group." Kim led off by unleashing a screed that began, "What I can't stand about you Korean-Americans is . . ." By the time her tirade ended, she was shaking and moaning. Brown, who is Jewish, then launched into her own monologue on the theme of

"What I can't stand about you Jews." Her denunciation of Jews for their insularity and lack of compassion was met with applause and hoots of approval, forcing Brown to remind the group that such internalized stereotypes are "not true," but "anything negative we feel about our group is a hurt that needs to be healed." While communities may have their own forms of dysfunction, she went on, to hold them responsible would be "blaming the victim." Having thus thoroughly confused what's false and what is simply politically incorrect, she then invited the trainees to come forward with negative "recordings" about their own groups.

The attendees at this particular workshop were all "human relations professionals," presumably used to discussing social issues in the course of their work. Still, their reaction to the workshop was divided. In the aftermath of the session, one woman, a lesbian lawyer, declared herself "transformed." Listening to another participant who was opposed to gay marriage try to work through his "bigotry" had been a "healing" experience, she averred.

Another member of the group, a Latino male, had managed during the course of the workshop to get in touch with his rage against white women like Cherie Brown. A comment Brown made about sexism had touched a nerve, causing him to fume that it "burns the hell out of me that I would be called racist and sexist." If the men and women present could change genders for just twenty minutes, he added, he would "take care of business" then and there. Months later, this man was still angry, complaining to a *Los Angeles Times* reporter who happened to be writing a follow-up piece on the workshop that he felt he had been "ripped off" by the facilitators' "pseudo-psychological" approach.

"He is wrong," the reporter editorialized in his article.[26]

Prejudice reduction specialists sometimes describe themselves as teaching a set of value-neutral communications skills, but clearly this is not so. Their workshops are based on the assumption that human conflict arises from our failure to live up to the all-important value of inclusiveness. Once participants are sensitized to the pain of the excluded, presumably they will give up their parochial habits and judgmental values in favor of a culture of universal acceptance. Group members may try to discuss problems from other perspectives—morality, social stability, fairness, even left-wing concerns such as economic power or the class struggle—but their contributions are little more than a distraction from the theme that "prejudice" is the root of all evil.

In the Los Angeles workshop, the lesbian attorney was surprised to discover that her opponent had no hostility to her personally. He was willing to listen to her views and explain his own. Still, nothing that occurred led her to question her belief that this man was a bigot. His openness was merely a sign that he was beginning the process of "working through" his prejudices. The Latino activist, meanwhile, was angered by the facilitators' attempt to equate their situations with his. If everyone is equally a victim, and equally a victimizer, then his own struggle was devalued.

Practically speaking, facilitators realize that their approach is unlikely to change the mind of anyone with strong convictions. That's why their enterprise is called prejudice reduction, not elimination. One goal of workshops is to mobilize participants who will continue to challenge "prejudice" in their communities. For the NCBI, this means establishing local chapters whose activities include circulating petitions in favor of hate-crimes legislation. Just how the criminalizing of thoughts and motivations will contribute to more open communication in the future is not apparent. Even the give-and-take of the democratic election process is viewed as a source of psychic pain by the NCBI. In North Carolina, following Jesse Helms' defeat of the African-American Democratic candidate Harvey Gant, one local chapter ran a workshop for Gant and a hundred community leaders, dedicated to helping the participants recover from the "divisive impact" of race on the campaign.

Unlike tolerance, unconditional acceptance of everyone by everyone else is an unrealistic goal, and continual focus on the psychic pain of prejudice inevitably generates new occasions for misunderstanding and increased anxiety. Even common English expressions are now fraught with controversy. One African-American woman wrote to the "On the Job" column of the *Washington Post* complaining that her office supervisor had reprimanded a co-worker for using the term "slave labor." Her problem was that the co-worker wrongly suspected her of lodging a grievance against him, and she had to deal with his resentment. The columnist's reply makes it clear that this woman was by no means the first to write in with this type of complaint.

Teenagers exposed to the prejudice reduction message have mixed reactions. Reporters interviewing students who have just completed prejudice reduction workshops have found a high level of cynicism about the tearful testimonials and mandatory rounds of applause. One girl laughed about a facilitator's insistence that she "jump up and down and say, 'I'm glad that I'm a woman!'" On the other hand, a New Jersey high school boy had reached the conclusion that "If people were prejudiced at all, they could be fined and put in jail." His classmate chimed in, suggesting that there ought to be places "like rehab centers" where the prejudiced would have go and "talk to a person of that race." Perhaps the most striking development was that a number of white students learned to see themselves as victims of prejudice, with their own grievances to pursue.[27]

One might suppose that getting people to unburden themselves of the pain of oppression would be a job for highly trained professionals. Not so. A quick survey of diversity training websites reveals that this is a market where the rule of *caveat emptor* applies. While some consultants list academic credentials, others summarize their qualifications with unspecific phrases like "twenty years experience in human resources." The head of one consulting company, which claims an impressive list of corporate clients in the United States and Canada, is described on her firm's website as "an outstanding leading edge thinker" who "has been studying transformational learning with many exceptional thinkers including Dr. Flores, Ph.D. Program Director of Linguistics, University of Berkley [sic]." However, there is no Dr. Flores on the linguistics department faculty at the University of California at Berkeley. A graduate assistant named Belen Flores, not a Ph.D., is in charge of the department's website and e-mail programs, not its educational programs.

In the name of attacking racism, prominent diversity trainers often disseminate ideas that are themselves racist. In an article entitled "Thought Reform 101" in the March 2000 issue of *Reason,* Alan Charles Kors draws attention to diversity trainer Edwin J. Nichols, whose firm's clients include the Internal Revenue Service, the Federal Reserve Bank, the Federal Aviation Administration, the FBI and the Naval Air Warfare Center, among other federal agencies. According to Kors, Nichols' programs incorporate material based on the science of "axiology," which teaches that different races have different "ways of knowing." For example, whites know things through "counting and measuring" while Asians learn through "striving toward the transcendence [sic]."[28]

Even where programs have been developed by psychologists with solid credentials, they are often carried out by facilitators with only a few days of training, such as employees of the client corporation's human resources department or, in the case of colleges and universities, graduate students who happen to be dormitory proctors. The NCBI, for example, gives a three-day workshop that qualifies trainees to lead both its Prejudice Reduction and Controversial Issues programs. The five-day NCBI workshop, at a cost of $795, also includes instruction in how to deflect criticism of the program and cope with group members who are "uncooperative and unwilling."

Dr. Roland Fox, a former president of the American Psychological Association, has been a consultant to major corporations and co-authored a book describing the elements of an effective corporate diversity program. Nevertheless, Fox views the field as a whole with wry skepticism, calling it a wide-open area in which "some people have made a lot of money." Many companies, notes Fox, have been burned by trainers who come in with their own political agendas and leave behind them a nucleus of disgruntled employees who have transferred their loyalty from the company to the facilitator. Often, he adds, the remedy has been to hire a second diversity consultant to undo the damage done by the first. As for the use of encounter-style testifying, Fox says simply, "It does go on and I don't think it's a good idea."[29]

Although Fox speculates that diversity training has been "kind of a fad" that has already peaked, there's no sign that behavior modification trainers are preparing to fold their tents and depart from the scene. On the contrary, since the market for antiracism programs appears to be saturated, consultants are finding new issues to address and developing programs that target the public at large. In May 2000, Dr. Antonia C. Novello, health commissioner of New York State, announced a $2.4 million pilot program to send "facilitators" into shopping centers, public plazas and busy sidewalks in order to confront individuals who are legally smoking and shame them into enrolling in smoking cessation classes. This program never got under way, but only because an alert reporter for the *New York Post* happened to hear of it and called the governor's office for a comment.[30]

Half a century ago, in his debate with B. F. Skinner, Carl Rogers questioned the ethics of allowing psychologists employed by corporations, universities and government to use behavior control techniques on a captive populace. Rogers worried that sophisticated advertising techniques and psychological profiling could turn Americans into docile consumers and faceless cogs in bureaucratic hierarchies. Ironically, in recent years Rogers' own methods have been widely adopted by the same institutions in the name of transforming America in accordance with his radical egalitarian vision. The encounter method is problematical under the best of circumstances, but when people are dragooned into taking part in a "transformative process" by facilitators with a pre-determined agenda, the only word for what goes on is brainwashing.

Since their motives are noble, liberal policymakers and educators have been slow to recognize any ethical problems with this form of attitude adjustment. They merely wonder why the target audience—Americans who persist in believing in old-fashioned concepts like tolerance and justice—seem to be increasingly distrustful of government and cultural tastemakers in general. Meanwhile, psychologists as a profession don't see these developments as their problem. A list of suggestions for a revision of the APA's code of ethics, posted on the organization's website during the summer of 2001, made no mention of the ethics of diversity training. When I called the APA's Office of Ethics, a spokesman told me that he could not recall hearing anyone raise the issue.

Dr. Fox explains, "The APA is a very large organization [and] this isn't the kind of thing they would get into." His suggestion that corporations and other institutions evaluate programs carefully before adopting them is well taken. Still, the fact that there are many, many doctors practicing a wide variety of specialties doesn't prevent the AMA from having opinions about the ethics and efficacy of the things doctors do. The APA's problem is that to ask about the ethics of value adjustment programs would open a Pandora's box. As James L. Nolan Jr. points out in his book *The Therapeutic State*, psychologists and psychiatrists have become our new priestly class. Happiness and unhappiness, good and evil are all increasingly defined through the prism of psychological concepts.

Psychologists want to enjoy their authority as "experts," but at the same time they want to be free to practice "revolutionary science"—trying out new ideas and expanding their list of treatable "conditions" and the range of their activities. But in time, every revolution runs out of steam and the age of accountability sets in. With the advent of HMOs this has already begun to happen in the realm of individual psychotherapy. Perhaps, as Dr. Fox suggests, corporations and employees, educators and students, and above all taxpayers need to begin to ask hard questions about why they allow psychologists to dictate their values through experiments in thought reform.[31]

Chapter 7

The Man
Question

In the late 1950s, when Abe Maslow was approached by a freelance writer who hoped to use his early research on female sexuality to rebut the Freudians, he did not have high expectations for her project. The study of 130 women that he had done at Columbia was twenty years old and had never attracted much attention. Moreover, the freelancer, Betty Friedan, wrote for women's magazines like the *Ladies' Home Journal* and *Woman's Home Companion,* publications hardly known for their intellectual clout.

In his youth, Maslow had been fascinated by dominant, high-achieving women. Ruth Benedict had been one of his original models of self-actualization, and other women, notably Eleanor Roosevelt and Jane Addams, were high on his list of heroes. In late middle age, however, Maslow read authors like Philip Wylie who were critical of modern American women, and he occasionally worried that they had become too overbearing—or, perhaps, American men were just too weak.

Though he had often thought about how his theory might apply to the female half of humanity in general, the complications seemed overwhelming. It seemed obvious to him that most wives and mothers—unlike, presumably, husbands and fathers—found it necessary to subordinate their search for personal identity to the needs of their families. As he told Friedan, "self-actualization is only possible for women today in America if one person can grow through another—that is, if the woman can realize her potential through her husband and children." And, he added, "We do not know if this is possible or not."[1]

Undaunted by this warning, Friedan went on to complete her book *The Feminine Mystique,* basing her arguments on Maslow's ideas. She succeeded so brilliantly that today the self-actualization model is the dominant view of female psychology, and it requires an effort of will to imagine how differently women were viewed a half-century ago.

Indeed, during the closing decades of the twentieth century, we got used to seeing fathers blamed for most of the world's ills. Novels, celebrity biographies and made-for-TV movies spread the message that every dad was a potential child abuser. News reports solemnly warned women that Super Bowl Sunday would trigger an epidemic of wife beating. Feminist theorists even begun to treat masculinity itself as a disease to be eradicated. When the Promise Keepers movement emerged onto the national scene, it was painful to watch the organization's leaders struggle for socially acceptable language to express their belief that a father is something more than a spare parent.

It is instructive to realize that when Freud reigned supreme, the situation was just the reverse. In the pre-Friedan era, everyone knew that maladjusted women were the chief cause of unhappiness in America. *Modern Woman: The Lost Sex,* a 1942 book by Ferdinand Lundberg and Marynia Farnham, a female psychiatrist, blamed higher education for "the masculinization of women with enormously dangerous consequences to the home, the children dependent on it, and to the ability of the woman, as well as her husband, to obtain sexual gratification." Helene Deutsch's two-volume tome on *The Psychology of Woman: A Psychoanalytical Interpretation* identified femininity with passivity and warned that women who were unable to "subliminate" their goals to those of their husbands or intellectual mentors suffered from a "masculinity complex."

Career women might be "masculinized," but those who stayed at home were hardly spared from condemnation. Cold, rejecting mothers were blamed for making their babies autistic. Clinging, seductive ones were said to produce neurotics, homosexuals and axe murderers. In a book entitled *A Generation of Vipers,* best-selling author Philip Wylie opined that modern labor-saving devices had rendered women beyond their prime childbearing years obsolete, turning them into parasites who had nothing to do but gobble chocolates, spend their husbands' money on junk, and join meddlesome volunteer organizations. Wylie's denunciations of the mom-goddess—"the brass-breasted Baal," he called her—made Hitler at Nuremberg sound measured by comparison. "I have researched the moms, to their beady brains behind their beady eyes and to the stones in the center of their fat hearts," he screeched. "The mealy look of men today is the result of momism, and so is the pinched and baffled fury in the eyes of womankind."[2]

Freudian thinking emphasized the mother's role as the dominant figure in the life of her infant—and, therefore, ultimately to blame for anything and everything that went wrong. Maslow's theory emphasized the ways in which men and women were alike. He said, for example, that the desire to use one's brain and do important work was healthy for both sexes. And in his 1939 paper "Dominance, Personality and Social Behavior in Women" he anticipated late-century feminists in pointing out that if high-dominance women sometimes seem "masculine," it is only because they exhibit traits such as leadership ability that are generally admired, and therefore judged by society to be "manly."

But Maslow had very little to say about family life. With hindsight, this was a glaring flaw in his view of human nature, one with sweeping implications for both sexes. The drive to reproduce, form families and provide for their welfare surely motivates more people than creative work and peak experiences combined. A devoted family man himself, Maslow understood this, but he also took it for granted. When he set out to identify self-actualizers, he was searching for the special factors that, in his opinion, lifted some individuals to a higher level of functioning. Thus, the models around whom he built his theory were the exceptions, men and woman who, for better or for worse, put other things ahead of family. As a result, the possibility that both men and women quite routinely achieve personal growth and satisfaction through the sacrifices they make for family did not fit into his thinking.

None of this troubled Betty Friedan at the time. A gifted polemicist, she saw that Maslovian psychology could be used as a blunt instrument to pummel the Freudians and pave the way for a new feminist revolution.

Betty Friedan—then known as Bettye Goldstein—graduated *summa cum laude* from Smith College in 1942 and began her graduate studies in psychology at Berkeley. A brilliant student, she seemed assured of a successful career. But like Ruth Benedict and Natalie Rogers before her, she was consumed with anxiety that a commitment to scholarship would blight her chances for marriage. In the spring of 1943, she was awarded the Abraham Rosenberg Research Fellowship, the most prestigious grant at Berkeley, with a stipend large enough to pay for her Ph.D. studies. According to Friedan, the reaction of her boyfriend at the time was, "You can take that fellowship if you want, but you know I'll never get one like it. You know what it will do to us."

For a young woman who thought she was in love and dreaded becoming "an old maid college teacher," these words were devastating. They triggered an asthmatic attack that sent Friedan home to Peoria to recuperate. Giving up on both the fellowship and the boyfriend, she decided to move to New York, where she found work as a reporter for the Federated News, a left-wing news agency with offices in Greenwich Village.

While at Berkeley, Friedan had moved in left-wing circles. Her boyfriend, presumably the same one who discouraged her from accepting the Rosenberg Fellowship, was David Bohm, a physics student who worked under J. Robert Oppenheimer and a member of the Communist Party. In New York, her boss at Federated News was Marc Stone, the brother of I. F. Stone, and her picture editor was Jean Roisman, the wife of leftist attorney Leonard Boudin. Her fellow writers included Virginia Gardner, who would later cover the Rosenberg spy trial for the *Daily Worker.*

Apparently, Friedan never joined the Communist Party, though she often agreed with its positions. When the 1945 defection of Igor Gouzenko touched off the first post–World War II spy scandal, Friedan penned an article charging that allegations of Soviet espionage were part of a "conspiracy" to place American nuclear secrets in the hands of industrialists. The article contributed to Marc Stone's decision that Betty was too radical for Federated News, which was trying to overcome the perception that it was a Communist front and maintain its relationship with the United Auto Workers.

Friedan's conflicts with Stone eventually led to her dismissal, and in 1946 she joined the staff of the official newspaper of the United Electrical, Radio and Machine Workers of America. The UE, as it was called, was a radical union, and Friedan covered women's issues from the perspective of a Popular Front feminist. Betty knew the issues, but she shopped at Bergdorf's and socialized with a smart set, which made her something of an anomaly. In 1947 she married Carl Friedan, a theatrical producer, and that summer they shared a vacation house with Jim Aronson and Cedric Belfrage, prominent leftist journalists who would soon found their own paper, the *National Guardian.*

Writing for the UE newspaper seemed to suit Betty's combative temperament, but the union itself was in decline. In 1949 it was expelled from the CIO for being Communist-controlled, and two-thirds of its members defected to a rival union. Three years later, Friedan was let go. There are varying accounts of how this happened, but one version of the story is that she was pregnant with her second child and the financially strapped newspaper, which had already given her a one-year pregnancy leave, balked at granting her a second one.[4]

By this time Carl was prospering in advertising, and in 1957 the Friedans moved to Grandview-on-Hudson, New York, where they occupied a picturesque if slightly ramshackle manse complete with gingerbread trim, a spring-fed pool and a commanding view of the Hudson River. Hardly typical of suburban America, Grandview-on-Hudson was in an area that was becoming a favorite retreat for writers, actors, artists and media types. Betty became active in a group called the Intellectual Resources Pool, which developed enrichment programs for local schools, among other projects. The heavily leftist cast of the Pool's programs aroused the resentment of many longtime residents, but Betty indignantly denounced their objections as anti-intellectual redbaiting.

Betty was also building her writing career. It was a good time to be a freelancer. The magazine business was less fragmented than today, and the mass circulation magazines paid well. Tailoring articles to the editors' requirements was a kind of low-grade torture for a woman whose politics and intellectual interests were hardly mainstream. Still, she was quite successful at placing her work.

Financially, at least, the Friedans were doing well. But the marriage had been tumultuous almost from the beginning. Guests at the Grandview-on-Hudson home witnessed volcanic quarrels that seemed to erupt out of nowhere. In her recent autobiography, *Life So Far,* Friedan suggested that Carl was physically abusive, a charge that prompted her now ex-husband to set up a website detailing his side of the story. Carl told of how Friedan once went on a rampage in the Fire Island summerhouse they had rented from writer Teddy White, breaking twenty-seven windows before her rage was slaked. On another occasion, he said, she attacked him physically while he was driving, shrieking—apropos of nothing—"You son of a bitch, you never took me to Europe!" Carl also claimed that a psychiatrist Betty was seeing once prescribed the antipsychotic Thorazine, but Betty refused to take it. Friedan's biographer Judith Hennessee writes, moreover, that she took amphetamines in an effort to control her weight. At the time, even conservative doctors were unaware that such "diet pills" could cause disastrous personality changes.[5]

Whatever fueled Friedan's explosive personality, years of therapy failed to resolve her problems. She was angry with her husband, furious at "McCarthyites," and also, for somewhat obscure reasons, often disgusted with her former allies on the left. Attending their ten-year reunion at Smith in 1952, she and a friend were appalled to find their former classmates chattering away about baby formula. Although most people do go to reunions to catch up with old friends, Betty presumably thought they should be circulating petitions denouncing anticommunism. Before her fifteenth reunion rolled around, she had designed a questionnaire asking her classmates things like, "What do you wish you had done differently?" Their answers would convince her that educated women in America were deeply frustrated with their role as homemakers. She began by calling this malaise "the problem that has no name." Later, she found a name for it—"the feminine mystique."

There was no question that Friedan was on to something. Social and economic trends during the post–World War II years simply didn't encourage women to capitalize on the political rights they had won earlier in the century. After the Great Depression and World War II, there was a desire to celebrate family life. The rapid growth of the suburbs, which placed married women far from job centers and relatives who might be available for childcare, discouraged them from having careers. By the late 1950s, many women who married in the years after the war were indeed restless. Their children were growing up, and they needed a challenge. More important, they had higher aspirations for their daughters, who were attending college in large numbers only to graduate into a world where corporations still pigeonholed women as secretaries and keypunch operators.

It was also true that Friedan's view of the situation was deeply colored by her own frustration level. As biographer Judith Hennessee observes, "She was finally coming to grips with the either/or choice she had made at Berkeley." Betty may have been steeped in Freud, but she was also well aware of the emerging school of humanistic psychology. She had studied with Gestalt psychologist Kurt Lewin as an undergraduate and with Erik Erikson at Berkeley, and she kept up with the writings of Maslow, Rollo May and Erich Fromm. The essence of Maslow, certainly, was his protest against the belief that the world was a "jungle," where human beings must struggle to survive. To put it another way, people shouldn't have to make such unfair either/or choices. If they did, it was a flaw in the social order that must be corrected. In the notes to *The Feminine Mystique,* which she began writing shortly after her fifteen-year Smith reunion, Friedan credits Maslow's teacher Ruth Benedict with her central insight: "It is not biological necessity, but our culture, which creates the discomforts, physical and psychological, of the female cycle."

Published in 1963, *The Feminine Mystique* was a polemic, as full of absurdities as the pop psychology books it rebutted. Friedan charged that editors of women's magazines promoted domesticity as part of a conspiracy with their advertisers to sell more home appliances—as if working women wouldn't buy at least as many washing machines and timesaving kitchen aids. She also claimed that the stay-at-home moms of the 1950s had reared a generation of passive teenagers whose under-developed egos gave them the affect of being "not quite 'real.'" This, of course, was a reference to the Baby Boomers who in 1963, the year her book appeared, were poised to demonstrate that they were anything but egoless and surely the most realness-obsessed generation America had ever produced. All this was in the venerable tradition of discovering an emergency that somehow had escaped the notice of everyone else. In Friedan's book the happy homemaker was transformed from villain to victim, but the prose used to describe her was often indistinguishable from Philip Wylie's. In this respect Friedan was a good pupil of Benedict. Since society itself is sick, the individual who best exemplifies its values is inevitably the sickest of all.

That said, *The Feminine Mystique* was indeed a groundbreaking book. Friedan simply took the self-actualization paradigm and applied it straightforwardly to women. (Maslow, who devoured the book in a single sitting, was impressed by her boldness, even though he thought she went too far in dismissing the importance of traditional women's roles.) Friedan's central message to women was a restatement of the principle of creative rebellion: Don't let anyone tell you that your ambitions are symptoms of some psychosexual disease. Take yourself seriously and follow your dream. If you want to go to work, just do it. You don't have to wait for the arrival of universal daycare, or government-sponsored family leave policies. Nor do you have to wait for sociologists to come up with a global solution to the woman problem. If enough women are seriously pursuing careers, then society will have to change to accommodate them.

This, in itself, was a revolutionary approach. Whole shelves can be filled with writing that starts from the premise that no one woman can possibly change her life until all of them do. And this, of course, can't happen until society itself is transformed. There was a long history of activist women being asked to consign their demands to the back burner until some more pressing problem—slavery, demon rum, capitalism—could be dealt with. Whether or not it's a matter of cause and effect, the prevalence of this kind of thinking on women's issues no doubt does have some relationship to the higher rate of depression among women—the assumption that no one problem can be solved until every problem is solved is a thought pattern that keeps depressives mired in passivity.

Of course, the enormous success of *The Feminine Mystique* didn't just happen. A passionate self-promoter, Friedan was ahead of her time in undertaking a national tour to publicize her book. Moreover, even though she had bitterly denounced the way Shirley Jackson and Jean Kerr were categorized as housewives-who-just-happened-to-write, this was precisely how Friedan chose to present herself in her public appearances. Her history as a committed leftist and radical journalist did not become part of the public record until 1998, when it was revealed by biographer Daniel Horowitz in a largely sympathetic biography. Horowitz's study came as a revelation to some, but Popular Front feminists were quite aware of Friedan's past at the time. In fact, she was often attacked as a turncoat for addressing her book to ambitious middle-class women. Friedan's roots may have been on the left, but she always wanted to be perceived as part of the mainstream.[6]

The leftist point of view was that poor women were already working, of necessity. These women had two jobs, at home and in the factory, and the priority was to find ways to help ease their burden. Worrying

about the petty psychological problems of middle-class college graduates was just a distraction. Moreover, it would ultimately hurt the cause,
since affluent women would just hire servants to take over the chores
they no longer had time to do. Feminists on the left had no objection to
poor women working as childcare providers in government facilities, but
they didn't want them to become domestics, where they would be largely
beyond the reach of union organizers and publicly financed benefit
programs.

On a more fundamental level, programmatic leftists were allergic
to Friedan's premise that individuals—even middle-class individuals—
acting in their own interests could be catalysts for positive social change.
This was contrary to their mode of operation, which called for intellectuals to get together to hammer out an agenda and then fight for it in the
name of "the people." Far better for everyone to suffer together than to
initiate changes that might not benefit everyone equally in the short run.

Friedan was more farsighted. In the 1950s the segregation of blue-
collar jobs by sex was often a matter of practical necessity. Men's work
tended to be hot, heavy, dirty and often dangerous. Women weren't
exactly clamoring to go to work in coal mines and steel mills, and even
if they were, integrating such facilities would involve monumental problems. When it came to professional and white-collar jobs, however, the
barriers were much more a question of custom. Friedan saw that on this
level of employment, enormous changes could come about very quickly.
Moreover, affluent women were trendsetters. Once they began to think
differently about careers, poor women would follow suit.

As it happened, the New Feminism won its greatest legislative victory
before it even got organized as a movement. Thanks in large part to conservative congressmen who believed they were exposing the fatuity of the
whole enterprise, the Civil Rights Act of 1964 included language that
forbade job discrimination on the basis of sex. Two years later, the National
Organization for Women was formed as an invitation-only lobbying
group to pressure the newly created Office of Economic Opportunity to
enforce the sexual discrimination provisions already enacted into law.
NOW's signal accomplishment lay in winning a ruling that help-wanted
ads could no longer be segregated by sex, a change with sweeping practical
and psychological consequences.

Friedan, who served as NOW's first president, certainly didn't think she had abandoned the left. NOW's statement of purpose endorsed such staples of the Popular Front agenda as a demand for "a nationwide network of child-care centers." But NOW's founding convention in 1967 also endorsed the Equal Rights Amendment and abortion rights, two positions that reflected its largely affluent, urban, Seven Sisters–educated membership.

Women in the labor movement tended to oppose the ERA because they believed that women in the workforce needed special legislation to protect their welfare. Most of the big unions eventually changed their positions and joined NOW in supporting the amendment, but working women in general were harder to persuade. Part and parcel of equal rights, as pointed out in NOW's statement of purpose, was ending the assumption that the husband bore the primary responsibility for supporting his family. As wonderfully egalitarian as this might be in theory, the practical consequence was that many women who had borne children thinking that their husband was obligated to be the breadwinner would now find themselves pushed into the workforce. NOW activists proved quite incapable of seeing that such women might have a legitimate gripe, and they dismissed the ERA's opponents as right-wingers who were trying to scare women by predicting negative outcomes that would never occur. In the end, the ERA was defeated, but most of the changes its opponents feared came about anyway, through piecemeal legislation and court decisions.

Abortion was another issue dear to the hearts of middle-class urban women. As a practical matter, career women, married or single, often found abortion a necessity. This was a dark secret that was hardly ever mentioned in public. When actresses missed work for elective surgery, they were routinely said to be suffering from appendicitis, and some quite famous stars of stage and screen were veterans of three or four appendectomies. On the other hand, many stalwart feminists, including Susan B. Anthony, had opposed abortion. For NOW, however, abortion rights became a touchstone issue, and anyone who disagreed was relegated to the status of "Uncle Thomasina," an enemy of her sex.

Friedan set forth the line on abortion in a speech she made in 1969 at the First National Congress on Abortion Rights. "Motherhood is a bane almost by definition, or at least partly so, as long as women are forced to be mothers. Like a cancer cell living its life through another cell, women today are forced to live too much through their children and husbands."[7]

Ironically, even as Friedan was defining abortion as the ultimate control issue, many of the conditions that had driven women to abortionists in the past were beginning to change. Birth control pills and other effective methods of contraception were becoming widely available. Women had more economic autonomy, and an out-of-wedlock pregnancy no longer made a woman a social outcast for life. Of course, unplanned pregnancies still occur, and some women do become pregnant as the result of rape. Moreover, there remain excellent libertarian arguments for believing that women should have control over their own reproductive capacity—or, more to the point, for believing that the government should *not* have control. Yet the plague of forced motherhood that Friedan bewailed in 1969 does not seem to be an issue in the twenty-first century. Nevertheless, abortion remains a question on which NOW can see no room for reasoned disagreement.

By making the ERA and abortion rights into threshold issues, NOW immediately alienated labor activists and churchwomen—two groups of women who had experience building large organizations as well as the will to devote their time and energy to the task. This didn't bother NOW's founders, since they had no interest in building a mass membership organization. Susan Brownmiller, in her memoir, *In Our Time,* tells how she tried to join NOW after receiving an invitation by mistake, only to be rebuffed. In the spirit of self-actualization, the founders were staunch individualists, to the point of being in denial about the need to have a structure at all. Like Abbie Hoffman, they were leaders who saw no pressing need for followers. From the outset, there was no real chance that the New Feminism would develop the sort of programs that build solidarity, from credit unions and insurance offerings to local chapters with a diverse membership.

By 1967, the New Left was already beginning to disintegrate as its focus on the Vietnam conflict gave way to separatist rhetoric about Black Power, American Indian Power and Third World Power. Not surprisingly, movement women began to wonder when it was gong to be time for Woman Power. When the male leadership found it impossible to take this question seriously, women began holding caucuses of their own.

These sessions often became highly emotional as women who had worked closely together for months began to share stories of nightmarish backroom abortions or babies given up for adoption. Out of these meetings grew the consciousness-raising circle, an exercise in group testifying that became the characteristic unit of the second feminist revolution.

The human potential movement was then at its height, and encounter groups were springing up everywhere. Radical women were certainly aware of the phenomenon. Ellen Maslow attended some early radical feminist meetings in New York City, and while she wasn't outspoken, she was invariably recognized and pointed out to those who didn't know her as a sort of celebrity-by-contact. Nevertheless, feminists who were there at the beginning deny being influenced by anything so typically American as a fad coming out of California. According to movement historian Karla Jay, the inspiration for consciousness raising was not the encounter movement but Maoist thought reform. The radical women, it seems, were influenced by William Hinton's book *Fanshen,* which describes how cadres descended on a Chinese village after the Communist victory and organized the peasants to denounce their landlords, a ritual known as "eating bitterness." Some early consciousness-raising groups actually carried out guerrilla actions, as when a cohort of women trooped to the offices of *Penthouse* aiming to embarrass the husband of one of them into quitting his job with the magazine.[8]

In spite of such forays, it's safe to say that most CR groups were practicing Maslowism, not Maoism, whether or not they realized it. Chinese thought reform did not exactly encourage the peasants to develop their own individual agendas, but consciousness raising was all about the search for individual self-actualization. Since the movement was so decentralized, it is difficult even now to generalize about what went on in CR meetings. One woman of my acquaintance, a social worker, used to say that when members of her circle started to debate whether it was necessary to kill male babies, she knew it was time to get out. Based on my own experience, most groups were much less creative. Where the members were mainly single, meetings often degenerated into the sort of "where are all the good men?" discussions that have been going on since women first gathered around campfires to stitch mammoth hides into winter robes. (Not that this was a frivolous question in the Sixties. Women's expectations were changing a lot faster than men's. For example, quite a few men hadn't yet figured out there were definite advantages to having a wife with her own income.) Married women, meanwhile, complained about their husbands and wished they could think of a plan for a fulfilling career.

Because CR groups tended to be made up of women from similar backgrounds, they were seldom a good place to get new ideas about careers or anything else. The tone of the discussion was not necessarily anti-man. It was just that there weren't any males around to speak up for themselves. The whole point of the groups was for women to encourage one another to take risks and maximize their individual potential. Motherhood might be a growth experience, but hardly anyone seemed to think that marriage could be. It was easy to advise a woman friend to shed a boyfriend or husband, much harder to justify telling her to compromise her goals or look for ways to mend a troubled relationship.

Without necessarily being aware of it, women who decided that marriage and relationships were dispensable were conforming to Maslow's model of the self-actualizer. As he explained it in 1954, self-actualized men and women are ruthless about terminating relationships that no longer serve their needs. Even when in love, "these people cannot be said in the ordinary sense of the word to *need* each other, as do ordinary loves."[9]

As inevitably happened in encounter groups, moral authority tended to flow toward the Greatest Victim. The woman whose husband beat her had a more interesting story to tell than the one whose mate merely sat in front of the TV eating pretzels. The marginalized person was always more worthy of attention, indeed more "real," because her very existence demonstrated the evils of "society." On the front lines of radical feminism, this principle proved enervating. Women who showed leadership ability, published books and managed their own lives with a modicum of success were inevitably accused of using the movement as a vehicle for self-promotion. Those with a history of bad judgment became icons. Thus, for a time, Valerie Solanis, whose claim to fame was that she had stabbed Andy Warhol and tried to kill him, was considered a heroine.

Another case in point was the movement's attitude toward my former Swarthmore classmate Jane Alpert. Jane had created what passed for a scandal at Swarthmore when she broke her back while climbing out of a window to avoid being caught in an assignation in one of the guest lodges. Since college maids and security guards regularly "caught" students breaking the rules and usually managed to look the other way,

Alpert's desperate escape attempt struck most of us as an overreaction, to say the least.

A bright woman, Alpert had a way of instantly adopting the enthusiasms of whomever she happened to be dating at the moment. After college she got involved with a self-styled revolutionary named Sam Melville, who influenced her to sell all her books, quit her job and take part in a conspiracy to plant bombs outside public buildings. In 1970, while out on bond on a bombing charge, she was converted to feminism and led a women's takeover of the underground newspaper *Rat*. Hailed as a heroine, she then jumped bail with the help of her new feminist friends. While living underground with a false identity, she joined a consciousness-raising circle and was converted to goddess-oriented feminism. Alpert then wrote an essay urging radical women to embrace their role as nurturers. *Ms.* magazine—which rarely published a dissenting voice, even on matters as trivial as lipstick and nail polish—printed Alpert's essay in 1973.

Feminists had no problem with Alpert as long as she was a fugitive from justice. She became controversial only in 1974, when she decided to turn herself in and do her time in prison. Left-wing feminists vilified her as a reactionary because she now condemned violence and refused to mourn Sam Melville, who died in the 1971 prison revolt inside the Attica penitentiary. Alpert was also accused—wrongly—of leading the FBI to another female fugitive, Pat Swinton. While Ti-Grace Atkinson and Flo Kennedy led the attack, others formed a Circle of Support for Jane Alpert, flooding feminist publications with letters and articles in her defense. Women who lived outside of Lower Manhattan could only look on in dazed bewilderment, wondering what any of this had to do with feminism.

In 1969 Carl Rogers published an article in *Psychology Today* warning of a troubling phenomenon: just as individual patients often decided that they were in love with their therapists, participants in encounter groups were falling "in love" with each other. Fueled by the group's atmosphere of artificial intimacy, such relationships were often inappropriate and they often ended badly, with troubling consequences for both parties. Coincidentally, 1969 was also the year when lesbians overcame their initial caution and began to identify themselves in feminist meetings and consciousness-raising circles. The result was an epidemic of conversions as women who had no history of homosexuality fell in love with other women and announced that they, too, were lesbians.

Women who had been homosexual before it was politically correct were often more than a little skeptical of these "political lesbians." But that didn't stop recent converts from exerting social pressure on their sisters in the movement. Susan Brownmiller writes of attending meetings of the New York Radical Feminists at which anyone who tried to speak from a heterosexual point of view was shouted down with cries of "Come Out! Come Out!" Brownmiller just couldn't buy the premise of a "lesbian utopia." Her skepticism on this score led to her being labeled a homophobe in some quarters.[10]

A group that called itself the New York Radical Feminists obviously wasn't even trying for mainstream appeal. But the wave of lesbian conversions inevitably spread to NOW just as it began to see its mission in broader terms. Here, too, a pecking order based on sexual identity developed. At a protest in Manhattan in December 1970, organizers passed out lavender armbands, asking all demonstrators to don them as a sign of solidarity. One of the few to demur was Betty Friedan, who took the issue public, warning that what she called the "lavender menace" would ultimately destroy the movement.

Many of the same women who criticized Friedan for projecting her personal middle-class problems onto all women had taken the "personal is political" approach much farther then she had ever dreamed. Friedan wanted a world made safe for ambition. She dismissed consciousness raising as "mental masturbation" and blamed lesbians and their radical allies for promoting a culture of victimization and an agenda that was not only "anti-man" but also anti-motherhood. She now began to emerge as a voice of caution and moderation, suggesting that the movement consider supporting female candidates even if they failed to endorse the entire NOW platform. Unfortunately, Friedan's notorious hair-trigger temper and tendency to see everything that happened as an FBI or CIA plot— including the rising numbers of lesbians in the movement—made it difficult to side with her even when she was right. After her term as president of NOW ended in 1970, her influence quickly waned.

NOW's 1974 convention was dominated by lesbian activists who promoted their candidate, Karen DeCrow, with the slogan "Out of the mainstream, into the revolution." This so-called Majority Caucus disrupted the proceedings by screaming, staging raucous demonstrations, picking fights and generally intimidating their opposition into silence. Female reporters on the scene downplayed the ugliness of the goings-on, apparently because they had agreed among themselves that the truth would make feminism look bad. Despite this journalistic wall of silence, even liberal pro-ERA women concluded that NOW had become off-putting and hostile.

It should go without saying that lesbians have a rightful place in a women's movement. But there should also be room for homemakers, senior citizens, Roman Catholics, evangelical Protestants and Republicans. A movement that considers the majority of female persons in the United States to be the enemy can't plausibly claim to be acting in the interests of women. But New Feminism never developed the capacity to reach out beyond its original base. Focused on discovering the issues within, it only become narrower, more dogmatic and more reductionist.

During the course of its troubled history, the New Feminism managed to expose all the contradictions of humanistic psychology—perhaps most notably its views on sex.

Abe Maslow had set out to liberate psychology from the heavy hand of moralism. In his 1949 paper "Our Maligned Animal Nature" he declared that the healthiest people in our culture "are most (not least) pagan, most (not least) 'instinctive,' most (not least) accepting of our animal nature." After Maslow gave up research on human sexuality, the task of defining what the natural human sexuality might be fell by default to Alfred Charles Kinsey.

Born in 1894, Kinsey began his career as a biologist, an expert on gall wasps. Supposedly, he was dragooned into the study of human sexuality when students at the University of Indiana demanded a course on marriage to replace moralistic, sex-segregated classes in "hygiene." Ignorance about the basic mechanics of sex was said to be a leading cause of unhappiness in marriage, and many at the time argued that sex education would reverse the steadily rising divorce rate. In reality, Kinsey's interest in the study of sexual behavior predated the marriage course and grew out of a desire to justify his own predilections for homosexuality, voyeurism and, most particularly, sadomasochism.

As James H. Jones set forth in his 1997 biography, the adolescent Kinsey was already experimenting with inserting foreign objects such as the handle of an old brush into his penis. As a young adult, Kinsey read Freud in an attempt to understand why he did such things, but rejected Freud's analysis as too close to conventional mores. By compiling the sexual histories of thousands of individuals, Kinsey hoped to overturn accepted definitions of normal sexuality and prove that sexual behavior branded as deviant was actually quite common. His early studies were supported by the National Research Council, the same group that funded Margaret Mead's fieldwork in Samoa, and by the NRC's director, primate specialist Robert Yerkes. But Kinsey's conclusions were largely fixed before his studies ever began. Like Mead and Maslow, Kinsey started from the premise that sexual problems were caused by civilization: "Most of the social problems and the sexual conflicts of youth are the result of the long frustration of normal sexual activities," he wrote in 1935. Three years later, in his first sex-education lecture, entitled "The Biological Basis of Society," Kinsey told his students that in chimps, gorillas and orangutans the family bond is based on mutual sexual attraction, and that "The anthropoid family breaks up as soon as the sexual attraction wanes."[12]

Far from exorcising his demons, Kinsey's studies emboldened them. His wife, his male associates and even his associates' wives were recruited to act out sexual scenarios on film. The informants he sought out for interviews were hardly typical. His samples were invariably skewed by the inclusion of large numbers of prisoners, sex offenders and female prostitutes. One of Kinsey's favorite informants was William Burroughs, whose sexual proclivities led to years of self-imposed exile in Tangier. Another was "Mr. X," an "elderly scientist" trained in forestry whose history included intercourse with seventeen blood relatives, among them his own grandmother, as well as six hundred preadolescent males and two hundred preadolescent females.

Little if any of this was known to Kinsey's contemporaries. He was secretive about his data and he cultivated the image of a wholesome family man. Even so, his methodology and sampling techniques were regularly questioned. In his published note on Kinsey's work at Brooklyn College, Maslow charged that 90 percent of the female students Kinsey interviewed were drawn from high or medium self-esteem groups, a factor which virtually eliminated women with traditional moral values from the sample. Margaret Mead, older and wiser than she had been during her Samoan sojourn, was appalled by Kinsey's attempt to reduce sexual contacts to "outlets" devoid of any emotional significance. Speaking at a symposium on Kinsey's book *Sexual Behavior in the Human Male,* Mead famously complained that it "suggests no way of choosing between a woman and a sheep."

When the follow-up volume, *Sexual Behavior in the Human Female,* appeared in 1953, reviewers in a wide variety of publications from *Cosmopolitan* to *Science* recognized it as more special pleading than fact. As the *Science* reviewer put it, Kinsey's arguments seemed to "culminate in propaganda for certain sociological views: that what is common in sexual behavior must be right; that the Judeo-Christian culture imposes undesirable restraints upon normal and natural sexual activities; that inhibition of sexual outlet, in some form or other, is biologically as well as psychologically unhealthy and unwise; that certain laws ought to be changed." James Jones notes that "apart from professional groups, Kinsey did not really have a vocal constituency."[13]

Summing up his subject's life work, Jones further writes, "By preaching the gospel of individual diversity, he hoped to strike a blow for diversity." Of course, it's one thing to tolerate individual variations on the norm, and quite another to have no norms at all. Kinsey claimed that no sexual activity was wrong as long as it was consensual and did not lead to any harm. But this was rank hypocrisy. People were hurt by the activities Kinsey sought to redefine as permissible, not least of all himself. Decades as a chronicler of bizarre sexual variations did not release Kinsey from his burden of guilt. On the contrary, he was as secretive as ever and suspicious of actual and potential critics to the point of paranoia. In 1954, when he was sixty years old, Kinsey had to be hospitalized for an infection of the testicles, caused when he hanged himself by his scrotum from an overhead pipe in his office.

After Kinsey's death in 1956, his mission was carried on by his former associates via the Sex Information and Education Council of the United States (SIECUS). One of the leaders of this lobby was Kinsey's longtime colleague Wardell Pomeroy, who argued that laws against child molestation were relics of the Victorian Age and that incest was just another outdated taboo, like adultery, homosexuality and sadomasochism. The latter claim was echoed by sociologist James Ramey, who wrote in the SIECUS newsletter, "We are roughly in the same position today regarding incest as we were a hundred years ago with respect to our fear of masturbation."[14]

Through SIECUS's efforts, many dubious statistics, rejected by scientists at the time of their publication, were upgraded to the status of "fact" by activists, journalists and the authors of popular books. For example, according to Kinsey, 69 percent of American men patronized prostitutes, 45 percent had committed adultery, and an astounding 17 percent had had sex with animals. As for women, Kinsey tabulated 7,789 interviews but not a single subject was reported as having given birth to a child inside wedlock. There were, however, 476 single mothers and 333 premarital conceptions. Moreover, out of the 1,075 women who reported having been sexually "approached" by a man as children, Kinsey found "only one clear-cut case of serious injury done to the child." Fully half of the female interview subjects reported that they slept in the nude, and Kinsey dismissed the custom of wearing a nightgown during marital sex as a "perversion." As independent researcher Judith Reisman has noted, this was a strange eruption of judgmentalism coming from a man who saw nothing morally wrong with sadomasochism or incest.[15]

Undoubtedly the most questionable segment of Kinsey's data involved observations of orgasm in children, some as young as two months old. Kinsey describes infants and young children responding to sexual stimulation with screams, writhing and tears—allegedly reactions indicative of pleasure. Reisman, a onetime segment producer for "Captain Kangaroo," was doing a study of sexualized images of children in the media when she became curious about Kinsey's published tables detailing child orgasms. How exactly had Kinsey gone about compiling this data? Who had stimulated the infants to orgasm while timing their responses with a stopwatch? (The answer, according to Jones, is that Kinsey relied on his informant Mr. X, who made a practice of taking notes on all his sexual misadventures. Kinsey, writes Jones, considered Mr. X a "hero.")

In 1981 Reisman used the occasion of presenting a paper to the Fifth World Congress on Sexology to call for an investigation of Kinsey's data on child sexuality. The reaction was an embarrassed silence. No one was prepared to defend the ethics of using pedophiles as research associates, but it was easier not to think about it. After some hesitation, the conference-goers closed ranks in defense of Uncle Kinsey, rationalizing that sexual contact between adults and children could be "loving." One Swedish sex educator even told Reisman that such activity could be "therapeutic" for the child.[16]

With the rise of humanistic psychology in the 1960s, the triumph of Kinsey's view of human sexuality seemed assured. Encounter groups celebrated the dark impulses of the "true self" and separation of "touching" from inconvenient emotional associations. Radical feminists eagerly adopted the premise that information would set them free. The Boston Women's Health Book Collective put together the perennially popular *Our Bodies, Our Selves*. (Older Americans who wonder how fellatio came to be regarded as a casual alternative to intercourse should consult the early editions of this volume, which sold one million copies in its first five years on the market.) Leading a more adventuresome wing of the self-help movement, a former teacher named Lorraine Rothman invented a menstrual extractor made out of a Mason jar, a syringe and plastic aquarium tubing. Known as the Del-Em, for "dirty little machine," the device could also be used for do-it-yourself early-term abortions. Rothman and her partner demonstrated the Del-Em to interested delegates during the 1971 NOW convention and then went on a national tour.

Roe v. Wade put an end to the do-it-yourself abortion craze, but the celebration of sexual freedom ended even sooner. It turned out that women in consciousness-raising circles talked about rape, sexual harassment, venereal disease and molestation—subjects that barely made the radar screen of Kinsey's study of female sexuality. The first anti-rape speak-out, held in January 1971 at St. Clement's Church in Manhattan, opened a new chapter of the feminist movement. Susan Brownmiller's book on rape, *Against Our Will*, appeared in 1975. The rediscovery of child sexual abuse and incest followed a few years later with a groundswell of books and articles by Diana Russell, David Finkelhor, Judith Herman, Florence Rush, Alice Miller and others.

Feminist theorists almost inevitably concentrated their attacks on Freudian psychology, whose influence was waning, if not yet quite dead. Occasionally they also took swipes against the "incest lobby," but these attacks seldom cut very deep and critics like Judith Reisman were dismissed as right-wingers. The problem was that the feminists basically subscribed to the Third Force celebration of unfettered sexuality as an expression of our "animal nature." If the results were sometimes harmful, the problem lay not with sex itself but with the way society perverted sexual relationships. Thus, rape was not really about sex but about power. (Of course, there was some truth to this axiom, though, surely, rape has *something* to do with sex.)

Disagreements about sex eventually splintered the New Feminism. Early on, feminists discovered that any challenge to the pornography industry provoked vicious counterattacks. After Susan Brownmiller, in *Against Our Will,* challenged the ACLU to stop defending pornographers, *Hustler* magazine printed a fantasy about her "naked breasts." *Screw* settled for printing her home address. Brownmiller went on to become a founder of a group called Women Against Pornography that aimed to clean up the Times Square sex industry and shame the purveyors of movies and advertising that glamorized violence against women. One early target was a film called *Snuff,* advertised with the slogan "Made in Latin America Where Life Is Cheap." The campaign against pornography had broad appeal. In addition to high-profile feminists, from Gloria Steinem and Bella Abzug to Grace Paley, Lois Gould and Letty Pogrebin, it initially attracted younger women, including writers, musicians and actresses who had no history of activism. As usual, however, the organizers pointedly declined to form alliances with mainstream and conservative opponents of commercial sleaze. Such people were obviously against porn for the wrong reasons.

Brownmiller ruefully recalls the feminists' "terror at being lumped with religious conservatives. . . . We honestly believed that radical feminists, with out deeper understanding of porn and our sophisticated knowledge of sexuality would succeed in turning around public opinion, where the old-fashioned moralists had not."[17]

The price of hanging on to their antipatriarchal rhetoric was that the anti-porn feminists were marginalized. They held conferences, watched one another's issue-oriented slide shows, and staged the occasional candlelight march. By 1982 the anti-porn feminists were themselves being attacked with that hated word, "conservative," by an emerging faction of pro-sadomasochism lesbians. The coming-out party for the new minimovement was a conference held at Barnard College in New York that April on the topic "The Scholar and the Feminists." Armed with props like nipple clamps, dog collars and dildos, and fluent in the jargon of academic deconstructionism, the lesbian sadomasochists were the baddest, scariest feminists imaginable. Even older lesbians were horrified.

Despite their off-putting rhetoric, the S&M lesbians had a point. They found the unisex utopian visions of the Sixties generation of feminists bland and unrealistic. It seemed obvious to them that sex and power were somehow related, and that sexual attraction was based on polarity—differences, not similarities, drew human beings to one another. Yet instead of testing these perceptions by having relationships with men, they preferred sex toys and (still more) conferences and manifestoes.

The tattered cloak of feminist solidarity was ripped asunder when anti-porn feminist Andrea Dworkin joined forces with legal scholar Catharine MacKinnon to draft legislation redefining pornography as a civil rights violation. The old principle that censorship should be based on community standards was now a dead letter. Thanks to the victories of the antimoralists, there were no community standards any more. Dworkin and MacKinnon proposed that women who were exposed to pornography and its social consequences could file civil suits, demanding damages and injunctions. Some old-line feminists had qualms about this tactic from the beginning. Still, Women Against Pornography supported the Dworkin/MacKinnon ordinance when it came before the Minneapolis City Council. They only became alarmed in 1984, when Dworkin and MacKinnon took their bill to Indianapolis, where it was supported by a coalition that included many conservative Republicans. Suddenly it dawned on the anti-porn women that right-wingers could also file civil suits, and the ordinance was so broad that it could be used to ban many of their own books.

In the end, the Dworkin/MacKinnon ordinance was twice vetoed by the mayor, and the Indiana version was ruled unconstitutional by a federal appeals court. The episode demonstrated that it was a lot easier to pick apart the American consensus on public values than to construct a new one. Even left-wing feminists, who presumably subscribed to the progressive values promoted by Abe Maslow, couldn't see eye to eye when it came to the specifics. By the early 1990s, what remained of the New Feminism was splintered into self-preoccupied cliques like the allergen-sensitive, who were determined to persuade the sisterhood that wearing perfumes and scented cosmetics was an act of aggression.

Even Gloria Steinem, whose cover-girl looks and business acumen had made her the most visible of all the New Feminists, was reduced to writing about her own struggle for self-esteem. When Steinem's book *Revolution from Within* appeared in 1992, the *Wall Street Journal* remarked that "having a serious leader like Gloria Steinem run around town talking about her low self-esteem is rather like having Lenin show up on 'Nightline' touting primal scream therapy." But such criticisms failed to recognize that the New Feminism, with its emphasis on consciousness raising, had been an offshoot of the personal growth movement from the beginning. Steinem's audience knew this, and they were on the whole quite pleased that she was sharing her personal life with them at long last.

The trouble with Steinem's book was that her advice seemed to be based on tag lines picked up during her own therapy sessions. She was a latecomer to self-esteem psychology and seemed to know nothing about its relationship to the movement she had helped found. Her advice about finding one's true "inner voice" was warmed-over Carl Rogers, mixed willy-nilly with snippets from experts who were in fact critics of Rogers.

It would be inaccurate to say that feminism had made American women unhappy. On the contrary, millions were happily taking advantage of new career opportunities and managing quite handily to juggle work and child-rearing chores. Still, there were also many thousands of women for whom the message that it was easier to shed unsatisfactory relationships than to stick with them hadn't worked out so well. Unlike Steinem, they didn't have a multimillionaire boyfriend and weren't living a glamorous life in Manhattan. Self-actualization is great when it works. But often, telling women to concentrate on their own needs in the short run left them in situations where they were all the more isolated, overburdened and depressed. In an ironic twist, the New Feminism had adopted its own version of the mother-as-martyr slogan, "I'd just as soon do it myself." Instead of holding men to their responsibilities as husbands and fathers, many women had kicked them out of the house, and were now enjoying "autonomy" at the price of carrying the entire burden of rearing a family.

Steinem also failed to identify the fundamental fallacy of self-esteem psychology. There is simply no necessary connection between psychological health and success. All of us are insecure at times, and successful people are often the most insecure of all. That's why they push themselves so hard. Even as she crisscrossed the country promoting her book, Steinem was starving herself to keep her famously lithe figure. At one stop she ate nothing at mealtime, and by the time she arrived at the airport for her flight out of town, she was so faint from hunger that a nervous tour escort was reduced to begging a snack for her from an airline employee. Steinem may have considered her stringent dieting something she could live with, considering the results. No doubt, also, many of the women who turned out to hear Steinem speak would have been happy to have her problems if it meant they could look like her and enjoy her celebrity lifestyle. This was only natural, but it has little to do with self-esteem.

It was the feminist therapists who were doing all the heavy lifting in the ongoing war against patriarchal values, and their arguments almost inevitably harked back to Ruth Benedict's claim that white heterosexual males are the true deviants of our society because they have most thoroughly internalized its values. Judith Herman, a clinical professor of psychiatry at Harvard, summed up the case against Daddy in her influential 1981 book, *Father-Daughter Incest:* "The sexual abuse of children is as old as patriarchy itself. . . . As long as fathers dominate their families they will have the power to make sexual use of their children. Most fathers will not choose to exercise this power; but as long as the prerogative is implicitly granted to all men, some men will use it."

In the short run, Herman advocated "consciousness-raising" in the schools to warn children that their fathers are potential abusers. Resistance to school-based sex education, she wrote, has always been strongest in "highly traditional, devout, authoritarian, and male-dominated families—that is, in families where children are at most risk for sexual abuse." In the longer run, Herman went on, the solution to the incest problem lies in dismantling the traditional family altogether by eliminating the sexual division of labor. Once males have been retrained to be "nurturing" and no longer insist on acting as authority figures, the exploitation of children will no longer be a problem.[18]

What basis did Herman have for her sweeping condemnation of the traditional family? Her primary research involved forty female incest victims who were psychotherapy outpatients in the Boston area during the late 1970s. Since these women were born in the late 1940s or the 1950s, one isn't surprised to learn that their parents had religious affiliations and adhered to the traditional division of labor between the sexes. If anything, it is worth noting that the mothers of nine of the forty patients worked outside the home. The molesting fathers in these families tended to be extremely controlling; they kept close tabs on their wives and daughters and discouraged them from making friends. Half were reported to be violent and over a third were described as problem drinkers. Moreover, in twenty-two (55 percent) of the families, the mother suffered from disabling illnesses, most commonly alcoholism, depression and psychosis. This is hardly the profile most readers would associate with the adjectives "highly traditional, devout, and authoritarian."

More recent studies show that girls are more likely to be abused by their stepfathers—and much more likely to be victimized by their mothers' live-in boyfriends. If no such cases showed up in Herman's research, perhaps it is because divorce and single motherhood were less common at the time her subjects were growing up. Or, possibly, daughters brought up in such homes were less likely to find their way into therapy.

The corollary to stigmatizing fathers was idealizing women and children as innocents. The 1980s produced cadres of mostly young, often female psychologists who believed, quite literally, that children don't lie, at least not about sex. Armed with anatomically correct dolls and their own preconceptions, they succeeded in eliciting horrific accusations that became "evidence" in a series of high-profile child abuse trials. Unsubstantiated charges of abuse were a ploy long used by some low-income mothers to gain leverage in divorce cases. As child abuse became a national preoccupation, middle- and upper-class fathers often faced similar accusations. When daycare employees were accused, as in the notorious McMartin Pre-School case in California, a male employee was often the initial target. Once the children capitulated and began "remembering" abuse, however, accusations against female teachers were piled on, and ironically, these charges tended to be even more lurid. Presumably, normal women wouldn't do these things, so female defendants were depicted in terms that implied they were insane or caught up in satanic cults.

The McMartin defendants were supposed to have buried a horse on the grounds of the preschool. Margaret Kelly Michaels, a junior teacher at the Wee Care Day Nursery in Maplewood, New Jersey, was convicted of 115 counts of molestation on the basis of evidence given by children, who told therapists that she made the entire class undress in the choir room and play "pile up," rubbed peanut butter onto children's private parts, urinated into a spoon and ordered her students to urinate on one another, and played "Jingle Bells" on the piano while naked. It is hard to imagine such things happening in busy daycare centers without being noticed by other adult employees or leaving behind some physical evidence. Rational people might have suspected that the children were confabulating, but the experts knew better. Eileen Treacy, the New York psychologist and child abuse expert who consulted on the Michaels case, opined that children use fantasy exclusively to empower themselves. "The only children who will fantasize to disempower themselves ... are severely disturbed children like those in institutions."[19]

How this relates to the child who imagines a monster hiding in the closet or a boogieman under the bed is unclear. But, of course, the charges against Michaels weren't children's fantasies, they were adult fantasies. In the Seventies, the disciples of Carl Rogers worked hard to break down social inhibitions about touching. A decade later, earnest feminist psychologists were writing curricula to teach children as young as four and five to distinguish "good touches" from "bad touches." Adults could no longer tell the difference, so we looked to children—their true selves uncorrupted by society—to tell us.

Meanwhile, some feminist psychologists had begun to specialize in helping women who don't recall being molested by Daddy to reconstruct their memories and get in touch with the inner victim. Authors Ellen Bass and Laura Davis, in the best-selling *The Courage to Heal,* offered a helpful checklist of symptoms indicative of past abuse. "Is it difficult for you to give or receive nurturing? . . . Do you find that your relationships just don't work out? . . . Do you often feel taken advantage of? . . . Do you have trouble making a commitment?" The checklist of E. Sue Blume, author of *Secret Survivors,* was even more expansive, including eating disorders, "avoidance of mirrors," headaches, arthritis or joint pain, "high risk-taking," and the kicker, "denial: no awareness of all."

It's easy to mock such all-purpose diagnoses, but for troubled individuals their appeal could be all but irresistible. Anyone who has spent time around toddlers has seen how they can be cooing with happiness one minute and bawling the next. Infants are gifted—and sometimes cursed—with the facility that the Rogerians so admired. They live completely in the moment. Most of these emotional highs and lows are quickly forgotten, but a few may remain alive in our memories, and it's tempting to try to reconstruct the horrifying events capable of reducing a toddler to inconsolable rage and grief. Unfortunately, the belief that calling up and "working through" childhood traumas—real or imagined—makes us healthier adults is more a matter of faith than science. The painful process that Bass and Davis call "making contact with the child within" may simply unravel the patient's existing relationships and plunge her into a deep well of anguish that will be difficult to climb out of. Substituting the word "survivor" for "victim" is just a matter of semantics.

For those who can't quite bring themselves to believe that all daddies are potential rapists, Alice Miller, in *The Drama of the Gifted Child,* cuts straight to the heart of the Third Force indictment of parenthood. For Miller, the crime of parenthood isn't sexual abuse; it is the parent's attempt to teach the child "value selection"—the lesson that some things are nice while others are nasty. Miller gives the example of a couple out strolling who purchase ice cream bars for themselves. Their toddler screams for an ice cream bar of his own, but Mom and Dad know it's too much for him, so they offer him a bite from one of theirs. Writes Miller, the child's "wish to hold the ice cream bar with his own hand was not understood.... He was faced with two giants who supported each other.... He had no advocate." The parents may believe they are being sensible and showing the child how to gauge his own appetites, but in Miller's eyes they are inflicting trauma. When a mother cannot accept her child as he is but expects him to "behave in a particular way," she has launched what Miller calls the "vicious circle of contempt" that creates "numb" adults.[21]

John Bradshaw, who was featured in a ten-part series on PBS, echoes Miller's analysis. Bradshaw not only blames authoritarian parents for the "soul murder" of innocent children, he holds them responsible for the rise of Nazism, the Mylai massacre and the cult deaths at Jonestown.

Hysteria over child abuse reached its peak in the mid-1990s. Since then, the issue has rapidly faded away. Perhaps the public simply grew cynical, but the catalyst for the turnabout was a series of malpractice suits filed by parents unjustly accused on the basis of memories "recovered" in therapy. Amazingly, once therapists faced financial and professional consequences for their actions, their conviction that "children don't lie" evaporated.

Ironically, by spreading the message that incest and child abuse are everywhere, feminist psychologists may have inadvertently paved the way for the resurgence of the pro-pedophilia lobby. Thanks to feminist scholars, there are now plenty of studies available that conflate serious abuse with milder incidents such as a glimpse of a flasher in a public place; but this equation can pull both ways. For example, Richard Gardner, a professor of psychiatry at Columbia University, argues that sexual abuse itself does not necessarily cause psychological problems; rather, it is the attitude of social disapproval surrounding the sexual acts that does lasting damage. Mary Eberstadt, in a pair of articles on "pedophilia chic," has chronicled the increase in favorable depictions of "man-boy love" in both mainstream and gay-oriented publications. Evidence that such views are on the ascendant includes the appearance of an article in the APA-sponsored journal, *Psychological Bulletin,* which concluded that boys don't necessarily suffer from being sodomized by older males. Kinsey, who made the same argument, would be delighted.[22]

The deconstruction of the family was an inevitable result of the triumph of self-actualization. After all, the goal of the new psychological paradigm was to create human beings who would undermine authority through creative rebellion and overturn the established norms of Western civilization. Supposedly, a new, more progressive value system would emerge to fill the void. But revolutions never go according to plan, and this one took some unexpected turns. Most people don't want to be lonely individualists, out there on the cutting edge of consciousness exploration. Even artists need a context, a sense of connection to an audience. Far from unleashing creative energies, self-actualization left both the arts and scholarship vitiated. Scholars confuse propaganda with original thinking. Artists see "pushing the envelope" as an end in itself, turning out "works" that are little more than rote gestures, the visual equivalent of thumbing one's nose at society. The breakdown of sexual norms was especially anxiety-provoking. In a world where people are free to reinvent themselves at any time, lasting relationships grow elusive. Childhood becomes the most dangerous time of life because children are subject to authority figures, now revealed as the ultimate source of dysfunction.

Despite miles of library shelves groaning under the weight of volumes of gender studies, the transition to the New Morality mostly takes place in the form of crude drama, played out in the headlines and on TV talk shows. On the *Sally Jessy Raphael Show,* a father complains that his son can't find a job because employers are scared off by his multiple facial piercings. "But this is me!" the son protests, "This is how I feel!" The audience looks appalled, but greets the statement with automatic applause.

Sex no longer has any meaning in itself but can become a moral issue when there are power relationships involved. Most of the time, this means that whether a sexual act is "nice" or "nasty," to borrow Alice Miller's terms, depends entirely on the identity of the actor. A heterosexual male who tells lewd jokes in the office is disgusting, but lesbians who distribute sadomasochistic sex toys to undergraduates at a college sex fair are serving the cause of liberation. The torture killing of a child by pedophiles is an aberration with no larger social significance, but the murder of a gay male by heterosexuals is a hate crime that, presumably, reveals the hidden agenda of mainstream America. (Never mind that millions of heterosexuals are home watching *Will and Grace*.)

Of course, sex and power have a way of getting mixed up together in confusing ways. This was never more evident than when the President of the United States, no less, was accused of being sexually serviced in his office by a female intern. A corporate executive or the manager of a government office in Peoria, credibly charged with such behavior, would know that his career was finished. However, since the President in question happened to be a proponent of abortion rights and the independent prosecutor investigating him, of all things, a professed Christian, it was clear that in this situation the President was not an authority figure but a designated victim. His wife duly came forward to defend him, telling an interviewer for *Talk* magazine that her husband's problems stemmed from his childhood, when "two strong women," his mother and grandmother, competed for his affection. "People need love and support," she added, evincing a perfect understanding of Rogerian psychology.

The significance of the Monica Lewinsky scandal was that it demonstrated how exempting private behavior from moral judgment inevitably undermines public morality as well. The President's defenders asserted that not only did he have a right to have sex in the Oval Office, he also had a right to lie about it under oath. Meanwhile, Miss Lewinsky, too young to recall when such things were supposed to be embarrassing, provided a narrative filled with the kind of details that even the most determined prosecutor would have been unable to extract from an unwilling witness. Two strands of the Third Force ethos had come into conflict: Clinton's right to take refuge in his private definition of truth versus Lewinsky's right to expose her true self in public. The sexual revolution that began in the Sixties came to a risible end the day that the President of the United States found himself unable to say, under penalty of perjury, what *is* is.

Margaret Mead and Ruth Benedict saw Western civilization as a grand mansion with many rooms. They imagined that they could chuck out unfashionable furnishings, redecorate, and even tear down and replace whole wings of the building without doing serious structural damage. They would always have a roof over their heads. The work of psychohistorian Dr. Lloyd DeMause suggests otherwise. DeMause spent decades studying original source material going back to ancient Greece and Rome in an effort to gain an overview of how children have been treated throughout history. He concluded that exploitation was the rule rather than the exception and "the further back in history one goes, the lower the level of child care." Even the incest taboo, he claims, is still regularly violated in some parts of the world. DeMause's conclusions are controversial. Others claim that societies from the earliest times have abhorred incest—though there is, of course, a difference between the existence of a taboo and the frequency with which it is violated. If DeMause is right, and the social disarray that exists in some parts of the world even today suggests that he may well be, we should honor the accomplishments of our civilization so far and think carefully before further weakening families in the name of a utopian faith in humankind's "animal nature."[23]

Chapter 8

The Malpsychian Classroom

In 1971, during a meeting called to evaluate their disastrous intervention with the Immaculate Heart schools, Carl Rogers, Bill Coulson and their research team discussed whether they would ever try such a project again. All agreed that they would not—or else if they did, they would not use the term "encounter groups." As Rogers put it, "I'd change the name just as fast as needed to keep ahead of the critics."[1]

Rogers said this jokingly, but as Coulson recognized, the remark captures, in a nutshell, the history of educational reform in America. Anyone who reads books and articles by critics of our schools is familiar with their frustration over the name-change game. No sooner is one misguided fad discredited than another, equally wrongheaded, pops up in its place. Still more confusingly, many ideas that sound promising— like outcome-based education—turn out to promote the very opposite of what their names suggest. This tendency leaves education critics wondering if they can ever get at the root of the problem. Charles J. Sykes, the author of *Dumbing Down Our Kids*, writes of battling "the hydra." Chester Finn speaks of "the blob." Kay Hymowitz identifies the problem as "anticulturalism."

Hymowitz comes closest to the nub of the matter. During the twentieth century, educational reform in America was largely in the hands of a group of intellectuals who romanticized children and disdained the heritage of Western civilization. G. Stanley Hall, the founder of the child study movement, said in 1901 that the first task of teachers was "to keep out of nature's way. . . . We must overcome the fetishism of the alphabet, of the multiplication table, of grammars, of scales, and of bibliolatry." A deeply learned man himself, Hall warned, "We are coming to understand the vanity of mere scholarship and erudition, and to know that even ignorance may be a wholesome poultice for weakly souls."[2]

No doubt some psychologist could write an intriguing study explaining why scholarly men and women, having made the choice to devote their lives to education, frequently exhibit a deep-seated animosity toward books. The short answer to this question is that the idealization of the natural child reflected the hostility of urban sophisticates to the stern virtues of what they liked to call American "Puritanism." American educators' fascination with early childhood development, a passion shared by Margaret Mead and Ruth Benedict, grew out of the belief that the very young need to be protected from their parents' efforts to inculcate bourgeois morals and manners. The argument that academic studies are elitist and irrelevant also masked the largely unconscious elitism of the educators, who found it difficult to imagine that the children of workers and the poor were capable of mastering challenging subject matter. By the 1930s progressive educators were already hard at work stripping primers and other schoolbooks of poetry, folk tales and literature in favor of written-to-order "realistic" material that combined a stringently limited vocabulary with content based on what its creators boasted were "modern theories of child psychology."

Carl Rogers, whose background was in the child study movement, staked out his position in a controversial talk that he delivered at a workshop on "Classroom Approaches to Influencing Human Behavior," held at the Harvard School of Education in 1952. Rogers' books were widely studied in courses on child psychology and counseling, and he had a reputation as a supportive teacher and mentor. Not surprisingly, the audience was startled when he confessed that he had "lost interest in teaching." The only learning that matters, he went on, is learning that "influences behavior," and all such learning must be self-directed. Otherwise, "the outcomes of teaching are either unimportant or hurtful. When I look back at the results of my past teaching, the real results seem the same— either damage was done—or nothing of significance occurred."

The implications of this conclusion were sufficiently radical to cause Rogers to "shudder a bit." Nevertheless, he went on to spell them out: It would be well to do away entirely with teaching, examinations, grades, degrees and, finally, "the exposition of conclusions." What would remain? "People would get together if they wished to learn."[3]

Much of this was not really new; G. Stanley Hall probably would have approved. The suggestion that schools themselves might be expendable was a bit jarring, however. It was one thing to do away with academic subject matter, quite another to lay off teachers. Over the next two decades, Rogers reassured his admirers that what he really had in mind was a new role for what Hall liked to call "the guardians of the young."

Teachers, Rogers stressed, must devote less (if any) time to dispensing "learnings" (his annoying term for lessons) and more to facilitating the personal growth of their students. Like clients in person-centered therapy, children must learn to accept themselves and formulate their own goals, rather than being taught to conform to "extrinsic" standards imposed by parents, schools and society. The key to this process was the teacher's ability to present himself as a "real person." As Rogers explained in a 1958 lecture entitled "The Implications of Therapy for Education," the teacher must be a facilitator who is "acceptant toward his own real feelings. . . . Because he accepts his feelings as *his* feelings, he has no need to impose them on his students or to insist that they feel the same way. He is a *person,* not a faceless embodiment of a curricular requirement, or a sterile pipe through which knowledge is passed from one generation to the next."[4]

By the time he came to write his book *Freedom to Learn* in 1969, Rogers saw releasing human potential as an "urgent" mission for teachers, one that must begin immediately because, otherwise, "our civilization is on the way down the drain." In this vision, teaching would become just another form of therapy for normals, and "the best education would produce a person very similar to the one produced by the best of psychotherapy." Of course, this meant specifically Rogerian therapy, which involves "an exploration of increasingly strange and unknown and dangerous feelings within oneself."

Rogers enjoyed playing the role of the lonely voice crying in the wilderness. Bill Coulson, who endorsed *Freedom to Learn* at the time of its publication, says that by 1972 Rogers was expressing alarm over the way his "tentative" statements were taken up by others and treated "as something that came down from Mount Sinai on tablets of stone." Like Maslow, he had assumed that authority would always be there, pushing back the tides of innovation. Nor, of course, did he imagine how far some students would go in releasing their "dangerous feelings." As Coulson observes, "The students caught on: if it's okay to *say* whatever they feel, then isn't it okay to *do* whatever they feel? And now we have shootings in school."[5]

Perhaps Rogers did have regrets. In reading his essays, however, one gets the feeling that he was of two minds. His prose is studded with words like "optimism" and "freedom." He even writes approvingly of Sylvia Ashton-Warner. One begins to believe that, after all, he just wants teachers to be more attentive, flexible and creative. At other times, Rogers plays intellectual terrorist, gleefully lobbing hand grenades into the laps of members of "the helping professions." In a 1978 essay entitled "Do We Need 'A' Reality?" Rogers sums up the "agreed-upon reality of values" in American culture with the phrase "a bigger bang for a buck." He then predicts that with the achievement of "full acceptance" of one another, we will no longer need to be limited to "a single culture-approved reality." Values like patriotism and nationalism are already passé, he notes, and in the future, we will see "the acceptance of millions of separate, challenging, exciting, informative *individual* perceptions of realty."[6]

There is something almost willfully childish about all of this. If there are to be millions of individual realities, and no one with the authority to say that one is better than any other, where does that leave learning? Where, indeed, does that leave civilization? Like Ruth Benedict and so many others, Rogers often seemed to forget that he was part of Western civilization—the very "culture-approved reality" that he was eager to scuttle.

Serious people have always found Rogers' thinking both superficial and troubling. Edgar Friedenberg, reviewing *Freedom to Learn,* writes: "Like that other American philosopher, Huckleberry Finn, Carl Rogers can get in anywhere because the draft of his vessel is so terribly shallow." Friedenberg goes on to describe Rogers' treatment of existential questions as so lacking in an "appreciation of the complexity of human conflict" that it is "almost eerie."

In spite of the scorn of academia and critics, Rogers enjoyed enormous popularity in schools of education. *Freedom to Learn* sold three hundred thousand copies in nine years and was required reading in many teacher training courses. Howard Kirschenbaum, Rogers' biographer, quotes liberally from papers on the book written by his students at Temple University. These future teachers not only liked *Freedom to Learn,* they felt that Rogers was addressing them personally. Kirschenbaum even shares his own fantasy of a "Rogers railroad train," moving through time with its doors wide open and new people jumping aboard at each station.[7]

Progressive education, with its anti-book bias, was already feeding on the roots of American educational theory. But the influence of progressive theories was contained to some degree because frontline teachers— at least those who did not have the benefit of a Columbia or Harvard education—persisted in thinking it was their job to turn out students who could find Ecuador on a map, solve quadratic equations and read *Julius Caesar* and *The Merchant of Venice.* Humanistic psychology altered the equation by effecting a fundamental change in the mentality of young adults, including those destined to teach. Whether they were influenced by reading Carl Rogers in the classroom, or had learned indirectly via the influence of Timothy Leary, Abbie Hoffman and Betty Friedan, the new generation of teachers believed that self-actualization was the goal of life. These young people had no desire to be "sterile pipes" or distant authority figures. They expected to find satisfaction in making their work as creative as possible, and they tended to think in terms of social goals. They wanted to raise the self-esteem of black children, promote sexual liberation, and save the environment from the depredations of big business.

Needless to say, all cultural changes are complex, and humanistic psychology was not the only source of antiauthoritarian thinking in the 1960s. Civil rights demonstrations had brought down Jim Crow laws that had stood for a hundred years. Baby Boomers, brought up on the permissive regimen of Dr. Spock, joined antiwar demonstrations and burned their draft cards with an alacrity that amazed New Left organizers and left them scrambling to keep up. The architects of Lyndon Johnson's Great Society, sensing that the moment for American socialism had come at last, promised to wipe out poverty in a decade. Newly minted teachers often arrived in inner-city classrooms directly from campuses riven by student demonstrations. It is hardly surprising that they found it difficult to identify with older colleagues whom they judged—harshly, though at times correctly—to be mediocre, self-satisfied and even racist. They wanted to be on the side of the children.

Such teachers were inspired by a spate of books written by angry, iconoclastic young Turks like John Holt, Jonathan Kozol, James Herndon and Herbert Kohl. Another influential manual was a British import, A. S. Neill's *Summerhill*. Neill described the operation of his Sussex boarding school, a temple to the "innate wisdom" of the child, where students were permitted to attend classes or not, according to their own whims. But first place in the utopia-now sweepstakes must be accorded to John Holt, who taught in a private school in Colorado and wrote under the influence of such icons of the humanistic pantheon as Paul Goodman, Lewis Mumford, Margaret Mead and Erich Fromm. Holt's influential *How Children Fail* appeared in 1964, but those interested in sampling his opinions at full strength would do well to peruse his third book, *Escape from Freedom*. Here, Holt advocates a guaranteed income for children along with full rights to vote, work, live where they please, attend school or not as they choose, use drugs, and control their own sexuality.

Holt envisions children hitchhiking on their own around the country, and he calls for distributing free birth control devices to girls as young as ten. As for the possibility that underage girls would be sexually exploited by adults, he writes, "In a society such as I propose, the dangers (to the daughter) of sex would be less.... If sex were not seen as dangerous, romantic and ecstatic, and at the same time dirty and disgusting, there would be less need to protect people from it." This, of course, proved easier said than done. The demystification of sex only sent people in search of thrilling, as yet unexplored byways. But the key phrase here is "in a society such as I propose." That such a society had never existed anywhere on the planet was immaterial. Holt passes on to his readers Paul Goodman's advice that "one good way to work for a truly different and better world was to act in their daily lives, as far as they could, as if that world already existed." Here is the philosophy of multiple realities in action: "Propose" a world that suits your fancy, then pretend to be living in it.[8]

While Holt was a creature straight out of Nowhereland, Herbert Kohl wrote about the very real problems of a sixth-grade classroom in Harlem. Born in the Bronx, Kohl graduated from Harvard a few years ahead of the first wave of Baby Boomers, did graduate work at Columbia Teachers College and was exiled to Harlem after being too outspoken during his first year of teaching in the New York City school system.

Kohl's *36 Children* still makes inspiring reading. Aside from his energy and commitment, Kohl's most impressive attribute was his ability to draw on his excellent liberal education to improvise lessons that captured his students' often wandering attention. When one boy in his class called another child a "psyche" (meaning psycho), Kohl took the outburst as a cue to retell the myth of Cupid and Psyche and introduce related vocabulary words like "psychology" and "cupidity." From there, he segued smoothly into a discussion of the evolving nature of language.

Perhaps inevitably, considering the times, Kohl also brought his own political and sociological baggage into the classroom. The year was 1962, a moment in history when it was becoming apparent that African-American children would have opportunities denied to their parents and grandparents, but Kohl was preoccupied with his own need to overcome what he called "my whiteness and strangeness." He suffered from a nagging feeling that the lessons he was teaching "came perilously close to a white perspective," and he objected to the approved history textbook on the grounds that it presented "a hopelessly dated and unrealistic faith in 'history's' capacity to solve human problems satisfactorily." It was important, he thought, to teach his kids the maxim that "one man's 'barbarian' was another's 'civilized' ideal."

Kohl reports that within a few years he lost touch with his best student, a girl he calls Grace. Grace won a scholarship to a prestigious New England prep school, and Kohl describes her as caught between two worlds, alienated from Harlem but not really accepted at her new school, where she is one of what he terms the "house Negroes." Grace's situation is hardly unexpected. An often wrenching psychological dislocation is the price that poor boys and girls have always paid for seizing the chance to broaden their intellectual and social horizons. This is unfortunate, but probably inevitable. The students Maslow taught at Brooklyn College in the 1940s were going through something similar. But the complex process of identity formation that Maslow saw as a response to alienation has been replaced, in Kohl's view, by the idea that Grace should have just stayed home. He is pessimistic about her future and uncomfortable with her "suppressed anger." He clearly prefers another girl, Pamela, who "knows who she is" and has gone on to become an activist with the community protest organization HARYOU.

One can't help feeling, with hindsight, that Kohl has done Grace a bad turn. Why make the effort to teach her Greek myths and awaken the love of language, if he can't honor her courage? Moreover, for Grace to suppress her anger may not be a bad thing. Middle-class children can often afford their moments of rebellion, but a teenager in Harlem is likely to pay a heavy price for such indulgence.

The year after the experiences described in his book, Kohl came under the influence of a colleague who advocated an Afrocentric education curriculum. Cautiously at first, he began to do less with Greek myths and more with black and Puerto Rican history. Three decades later, as a fellow of the Open Society Institute, Kohl is still hard at work developing multicultural curricula. His books include *Shall We Burn Babar?* in which he tells how he goes about disabusing third graders of their affection for Jean de Brunhoff's lovable elephant, showing them that Babar is a lackey of capitalism who recruits other little elephants into slavery by offering them sweets. The Babar books are suspect also because they celebrate a "power relationship" between Babar and the character of the Rich Old Lady, in which (horrors!) the human being has more power than the animal.

Kohl is also the editor, along with Colin Greer, of *A Call to Character: A Family Treasury,* an anthology of humanistic values that presents an interesting contrast to William Bennett's *Book of Virtues.* The problem with the "family treasury" is not its multicultural content per se. Kohl and Greer, who is the president of the New World Foundation, are obviously men of considerable intellectual attainment, and they have made some interesting choices. The difficulty they face is that humanistic values tend to be wispy abstractions. In the absence of specific ideals— based in religion, patriotism, love of family, a belief in the sacredness of human life, or faith in reason and scientific progress—"idealism" itself becomes a virtue, defined as "the ability to imagine a more perfect world or . . . to imagine future happiness." The anthology illustrates this concept with snippets from the Sermon on the Mount, Albert Einstein's *My Philosophy,* the *Diary of Anne Frank* (in the de-Judaicized Goodrich and Hackett version) and a passage from Ellison's *The Invisible Man,* which actually *is* about idealism. But we also find Emily Dickinson's "Tell all the truth but tell it skant" (idealism for politicians?), an excerpt from *Peter Pan,* and a retelling of the story about the little girl who wrote to Abe Lincoln advising him to grow a beard.

But, of course, some of the worst villains in history have imagined a more perfect world, Lenin and Stalin among them. No matter how open we may be to other cultures, some values are better than others, and identifying them is not child's play. In spite of this, Kohl and Greer caution parents not to draw definite morals from the selections they share with their children. Rather, they should allow the youngsters "to use their own judgment, make up their own minds about the moral issues at stake." They promise that perusing their anthology will be "a wonderful way for children and adults to come together on neutral ground." Perhaps Kohl and Greer simply mean that parents shouldn't be too heavy-handed. Still, it's hard to imagine how morality could ever be neutral territory in discussions between parents and children.

While Kohl was teaching a course in multicultural education at Carleton College in Minnesota in the spring of 1995, the campus was in turmoil over a scheduled debate on the subject of race and IQ between Charles Murray, author *The Bell Curve,* and Alvin Poussaint, an African-American psychiatrist. In his book *The Discipline of Hope,* Kohl writes that many African-American and Latino students found the mere prospect of Murray's presence on campus personally devastating. They felt the college was sponsoring an attempt to stigmatize them as "affirmative-action babies." One young man, a brilliant physics major, was so unnerved that he lost his ability to concentrate on his studies. The issue in Kohl's class wasn't Murray's right to speak. Rather, tensions flared when white students who had taken part in an anti-Murray rally said that they felt good about standing up for the cause of antiracism—and students of color were outraged. In Kohl's words, "They accused the white students of expressing liberal racist ideas, of believing that the university existed for the intellectual delectation of whites at the price of the dignity and self-respect of people of color."[9]

Intellectual delectation is, indeed, a purpose of higher education. But instead of helping his students to see that it isn't just a white people's game, a form of social one-upmanship, Kohl redoubles his efforts to raise awareness of multicultural issues. His students are asked to examine a list of statements such as "The 1950s were the best times in American history" from the perspective of various minorities. (Though, indeed, it isn't clear that any of them know enough history to compare that decade to others from *anyone's* perspective.) Kohl also encourages his students to drop their academic voice in favor of a personal one. He tells the class that "the important thing about what was happening at that moment was that the wounds of racism on campus were open and bleeding: since racism was a poison in the system we had to let the bleeding continue."

And continue it does. During one-on-one student conferences, white students object to Kohl's tendency to lump them together, and they insist that they see no reason to feel guilty about things that happened before they were born. Several confess to feeling "silenced" in class, each in a slightly different way. A Christian conservative complains that he often feels intimidated. A girl from a poor family resents the assumption that all whites are affluent. Blacks, Asians and Latinos, meanwhile, are variously angry and frustrated. Several, notes Kohl, express "exasperation at having to live with the constant presence of race and ethnicity as an issue. They wanted to be *students*."

Around this time, Kohl's efforts in behalf of multicultural awareness take an unexpected turn. In April, a bomb destroys the Murrah Federal Building in Oklahoma City. Muslim terrorists are initially suspected, not entirely without cause given the recent bombing of the World Trade Center. However, Irum, a Pakistani-American student, takes these suspicions as a cue to vent her anger at people who fail to accept her as a real American. "I'm from Des Moines, goddamit!" she screams.

As a result of this outburst, Kohl comments:

> We all had distinct and explicit proof of how the representatives of white culture manufacture and perpetuate racism. The challenge to everyone was to feel the world as Irum felt it at that moment, to understand what it was like to be a Muslim in the United States, to be of Pakistani origin in the United States and immediately become defined as the other, one of "them" rather than one of "us." There is no way of soothing those wounds.[10]

No wonder some students feel silenced in Kohl's class. Why risk being typed as a "representative of white culture," engaged in a nefarious plot to perpetuate racism?

Kohl's observation is nonsense, though nonsense with a very specific intellectual pedigree, traceable to the doyen of "otherness," Edward Said, the author of *Orientalism*. Sweep away Said's brand of academic conceptualism and one is left with the plain truth that people in Des Moines perceive Irum as different because she is different from most people in Des Moines. This may be a source of frustration and misunderstanding, and her outburst is quite understandable. Whether her wounds are so grievous that they can't be soothed, much less healed, is another matter. Kohl informs us that Carleton College—a representative of white culture, presumably—soon awarded Irum a diploma with *summa cum laude* and Phi Beta Kappa honors.

Kohl's vision of a homogenized society, in which distinctions of "us" and "them" have been erased, is not, in truth, very appealing. The only way to achieve it would be for people to give up the troublesome business of being Christians and Muslims, Pakistani-Americans and Swedish-Americans. They're unlikely to do this, and Kohl's campaign to reduce all learning to a kaleidoscope of multicultural perspectives certainly doesn't bring his dream any closer to realization.

Kohl seems to be an admirable man in many respects. He's a dedicated teacher who appears to work fearfully hard at his job. But he is also a casualty of the demand that teachers make themselves "real" in their dealings with students. He has taken his personal doubts about his role as a white authority figure for poor black children and projected them onto his students, who are expected to take on the burden of his psychic pain, of which he seems rather too fond. On the wall of his kitchen at home hangs a poster from the 1968 student uprising in Paris, bearing the slogan *La Lutte Continue*—"The Struggle Goes On." For Kohl it will always be 1968, a time as distant to his students as the Crash of '29 must have seemed to him when he was their age. One longs to take him by the shoulders, give him a good shake and shout, "You're white! You're part of Western culture! Just get over it!"

The quest for "realness" has claimed many casualties:

Joseph J. Ellis, a distinguished professor at Mount Holyoke and Pulitzer Prize–winning historian, invented a colorful past as a football hero and paratroop platoon leader in Vietnam in order to present himself as a man who had lived history instead of just lecturing about it.

The authorized biographer of Ronald Reagan, given unique access and cooperation, produced a book that is not about Reagan per se but about his own fantasies about Reagan.

Brian Hixson, a fifth-grade teacher from California, probably spoke for many younger educators when he complained in a *New York Times* op-ed column that increased emphasis on academics threatened his status as his pupils' friend and confidant: "My students like me. How can I jeopardize my place in their hearts by constantly admonishing them, even if gently, about the inadequacies of their best work?"[11]

When it's accepted that no one can learn from a "sterile pipe," all information must come prepackaged with a personal angle. But it is harder to challenge an idea that claims to come from personal experience—and it can be downright confusing when a biographer presents his subject through the lens of an imaginary friendship. For classroom teachers like Brian Hixson, the problem of self-presentation becomes a daily battle. It's difficult to be an authority figure when parents, the school board and the culture as a whole don't support that interpretation of your role. No doubt with the best of intentions, Hixson has opted to be a buddy to his students. But he may be doing them no favors. Emotional intimacy and learning don't necessarily mix well, as many people discover when their parent or spouse tries to teach them how to drive a car. Developing independent judgment, taking on challenging tasks and risking failure may all be easier to do when the teacher is not your pal.

Children have always been expected to learn many things that adults think they should know. The value of these lessons may not become apparent for years, even decades. Despite much talk about radical deschooling in the 1970s, this never really changed. What did change was the way educators thought about their students. Children used to be thought of as wild, exuberant creatures—strong, but in need of moral training and civilizing adult influences. This view of childhood is still current among children themselves, as is evidenced by the popularity of Bart Simpson. In the education schools, however, children came to be seen as bundles of unmet deficiency needs.

With hindsight, the change doubtless began with *Brown v. Board of Education,* the Supreme Court decision that outlawed school segregation. Integration was a worthy and enlightened goal, and there was logic to the argument that a segregated environment was inimical to learning. (On the other hand, it was ironic that the grownups expected children to bear the onus of social changes they weren't prepared to make for themselves.) In the years that followed, prominent educators argued that no child could be expected to learn unless he was provided with a nutritious breakfast and lunch. This, too, seemed sensible. No one wants children to go hungry, though some curmudgeons who survived the Great Depression may recall that they managed to learn quite a bit on an empty stomach. But the concept of deficiency needs kept expanding. Before academics could become "job one," to borrow a phrase from the advertising world, the schools would have to take on a succession of ever more expensive and controversial projects: mainstreaming the disabled, diagnosing and treating learning disabilities, establishing on-site health clinics, providing sex education and free condoms, teaching parenting skills, protecting children from sexual abuse, molding the attitudes that will lay the basis for the multicultural society of tomorrow. Of all these goals, none was more pressing—and more nebulous—than universal self-esteem.

The conviction that "extrinsic learning" must give way to the goal of raising children's self-esteem dates back to the mid-1950s, when Maslow's theory of deficiency needs was enjoying considerable influence. Beginning in 1959, Stanley Coopersmith, who had taken a master's degree at Brandeis before earning his Ph.D. from Cornell, launched a major study of self-esteem funded by the National Institutes of Health. Over a six-year period beginning in 1959, he and his associates studied 1,748 boys between ten and twelve years old in an attempt to identify factors that promoted high self-esteem, defined primarily as a propensity to take on more challenging tasks.

Summarizing his findings in a 1968 article in *Scientific American,* Coopersmith noted that proponents of self-esteem education argued that building the "constructive capacities" of children's personalities would protect them from future problems, just as vaccinations immunized them against polio or smallpox. Unfortunately, Coopersmith's findings did little to bolster Maslow's belief that children need material security and nonjudgmental love as preconditions for developing healthy self-esteem.

To his surprise, Coopersmith found that poverty was not a significant predictor of self-esteem. Boys from Jewish families scored somewhat higher than Catholics or Protestants, but family income level was immaterial. By far the most important determinant was parenting style. *Mothers and fathers who had firm values and set clear rules for their children were most likely to have sons with high self-esteem.* The most effective parents established "extensive and well defined rules" and imposed punishments that were sure and swift but not especially harsh. Coopersmith called these successful parents "benevolent despots." These findings upheld the commonsense belief that children respond best to adults who follow the rule of "firm but fair."[12]

Coopersmith's study received wide publicity, but his message that children need structure and support was not what advocates of "intrinsic learning" wanted to hear. The push for incorporating self-esteem lessons into the curriculum was temporarily stymied. In the meantime, however, radical reformers inspired by Carl Rogers, John Holt and certain experiments going on in British nursery schools had proclaimed the era of the "open classroom." By removing the teacher from her traditional place at the front of the room, the reformers hoped to deconstruct the educational experience, freeing children to move at will from one activity center to another and figure out for themselves what (and if) they wished to learn. Following the advice of experts like Charles Silberman, whose writing was supported by a Carnegie Corporation grant, a few school districts even invested in constructing open-plan schools that replaced classroom walls with movable partitions.

These experiments proved disastrous almost everywhere they were tried. But, predictably, open classrooms took their greatest toll on the children of the poor. Affluent, well-educated parents were better equipped to give their children the guidance they were no longer getting in school. Boys and girls who came from crowded, at times chaotic environments now had no one to insist that they learn self-discipline and good study habits. Often it was the poorest school districts that had spent heavily to build schools that were now white elephants.[13]

The heyday of the open classroom was brief. Anarchism as an educational method quickly lost its charm when teachers were faced with keeping track of students who were lounging in stairwells, racing through the hallways or smoking dope in the lavatories. Teachers' desks were restored to their traditional place of honor, though the teachers' authority never quite recovered from years of rhetorical assaults. Since grade school children now seemed to be less capable of sitting still, lining up in an orderly fashion and concentrating on their lessons, educators called for the expansion of Head Start programs, originally developed for preschoolers from the most deprived backgrounds. In a pattern that persists to the present day, educators responded to criticism of their methods by complaining that they just didn't get control of the children early enough.

Meanwhile, curriculum developers were applying themselves to the problem of helping children develop humanistic values. Perhaps the most popular approach was Values Clarification, developed by Louis E. Raths, Sidney B. Simon, Merrill Harmin and Howard Kirschenbaum. Although the charge was often denied, Values Clarification was essentially an adaptation of Maslovian motivation theory and Carl Rogers' ideas about person-centered therapy. Instead of being taught that certain things were right, others wrong, children were encouraged to "clarify" their inborn values. When students discussed hypothetical moral dilemmas in class, the teacher-facilitator carefully refrained from suggesting that one response was preferable to any other. Like shoppers in a market, children could select their beliefs from a dazzling array of possibilities.[14]

Values Clarification quickly became the target of fierce attacks from critics who saw it as a vehicle for promoting moral relativism. This was true only up to a point. Children could make their own decisions about lying, cheating and sexual activity because such things were seen as purely a matter of personal behavior. Moreover, it was taken for granted that the child's inborn nature would prompt him to see lying as wrong. On the other hand, the ability to adjust one's behavior to specific situations was a characteristic of self-actualized individuals. The high school students in the film *Cheaters,* based on a true story, show an innate understanding of situational ethics. After entering a prestigious academic competition, they reason that as students from an undistinguished high school they are at an unfair disadvantage. Therefore, by stealing an advance copy of the test they are just leveling the playing field.

When it came to progressive values such as antiracism, environmentalism or conflict resolution through understanding, however, no such leeway was allowed. Allegiance to these values, as currently interpreted, was assumed. Children were not asked to debate environmentalism, but to think up "ten things you can do for the environment."

Even the mantra that "we mustn't be judgmental" about other people's personal morals is hardly an expression of relativism. Nonjudgmentalism is more than just tolerance or a live-and-let-live attitude. It requires abandoning one's own ideas about morality. Values curricula in elementary and high schools may not always have been explicit on this point, but once students reached college, their duty became clear. One obvious example is the ubiquity of gay and lesbian sensitivity training on campuses. In many such programs students have been asked—indeed, badgered—to wear pink triangles as a gesture of solidarity with homosexual classmates. In their book *The Shadow University,* Alan Charles

Kors and Harvey A. Silverglate cite the experience of Patrick Mooney, a heterosexual student at Carnegie Mellon University in Pittsburgh, who was fired from his post as a residential advisor after he refused to don a pink triangle, as a matter of conscience. Mooney sued Carnegie Mellon, an action that was settled in his favor three years later, in 1994. Presumably, most students in this situation would go along rather than assume the financial burden and uncertainty of a lawsuit. Forcing people to wear pink triangles in the name of "sensitivity" is a bit of perversity worthy of the imagination of George Orwell. But it certainly isn't an expression of moral relativism. For one thing, it implies an analogy between the United States of America and Nazi Germany.

Values Clarification was destined to have a lasting influence on programs that aimed to educate American schoolchildren about drugs. The widely used Quest program was originally developed by Howard Kirschenbaum, and the even more popular DARE was developed by William Hansen of Wake Forest University in 1983 at the request of Los Angeles police chief Darryl Gates. In these programs, teacher-facilitators—or, in the case of DARE, specially trained police officers—were careful never to say in so many words that drug use was wrong. Students were supposed to discuss the facts among themselves and come to their own conclusions about healthy choices. All too often the long-term effect was to remove some of the stigma surrounding the subject and leave children with an unwarranted confidence about their ability to experiment safely.

As early as 1976, a study by Dr. Richard Blum of Stanford University found that children who completed such nondirective anti-drug programs were actually more likely to use drugs later on. Nevertheless, DARE continued to grow, expanding into some 70 percent of school districts nationwide. Some of the originators of the Quest program became disillusioned, as did William Hansen, who called for a complete overhaul of the DARE program in 1993. A few years later, Ellen Maslow opposed DARE's adoption in her hometown of Boulder, Colorado, declaring it a misapplication of her father's ideas. (Whether this is true or not, strictly speaking, is debatable; however, Maslow was capable of changing his mind when circumstances warranted and was often appalled by the dogmatism of people who claimed to be his followers.) Major studies emanating from the University of Kentucky and the University of

Illinois confirmed the program's failure to reduce drug use. There were also complaints that DARE presenters played on children's trust by encouraging them to turn in their own parents. Finally, in February 2001, DARE director Glenn Levant announced a $13.7 million grant from the Robert Wood Johnson Foundation to revamp the program. Even so, the replacement program will be phased in slowly.[15]

Values Clarification had many critics, from academic philosophers to parents and teachers, who objected to suggesting to students that cheating and stealing were options. Lawrence Kohlberg's theory of cognitive moral development was more subtle, and therefore destined to be more influential. Born to wealthy parents in 1927, Kohlberg grew up in Bronxville, New York, a community that in those days did not welcome many Jewish families. He attended Phillips Exeter Academy, graduating a bit too late to serve in World War II, but decided to pass up college and enlist in the merchant marine. A passionate Zionist, he served as second engineer on a tramp freighter engaged in smuggling Holocaust survivors through the British blockade of Palestine. Kohlberg liked to tell how he outwitted suspicious officials, persuading them that the refugees' mattresses lining the ship's hold were "banana beds," set in place to keep the fruit from bruising in transit. Another of his favorite stories concerned the rough-and-ready democracy practiced by the crew. In one port the sailors voted to deny themselves shore leave rather than risk compromising the secrecy of their mission. Passing the beer to celebrate their virtuous decision, they quickly got drunk, forgot their resolution and staggered ashore for a tour of the local nightspots.

In 1948, Kohlberg returned to the United States and entered the University of Chicago, where he earned his bachelor's degree in a single year and went on to do graduate work in psychology, studying the moral reasoning of children. His work drew on the theories of Jean Piaget, considered the gold standard in the field of child development. It also assuaged the anxieties of educators who worried that by teaching children to be disciplined and obey the rules they were turning out tomorrow's equivalent of the "good Germans" and loyal Communist cadres who blindly carried out the murderous orders of Adolf Hitler and Josef Stalin. Third Force psychologists saw the "authoritarian personality" type as the root cause of totalitarianism, and they wanted to train a generation of young people who would be fortified against its appeal.

In 1968 Kohlberg joined the faculty of the Harvard Graduate School of Education, which had become the energy center of the utopia-minded educational reformers. His engaging personality, combined with his belief that children could be liberated from deadening moral preaching, made him a charismatic figure. Kohlberg dismissed the notion that "moral character consists of a bag of virtues and vices" that we all carry with us throughout our lives, and he wrote scornfully of the "hidden curriculum" through which teachers—thoughtlessly, in his opinion—inculcated habits of obedience and neatness.

Kohlberg recalled the day his son, a second grader, confided to him that he didn't want to be one of the "bad boys" in school.

"Who are the bad boys?" he asked.

"The ones who don't put their books back where they belong," his son replied.

The professor was wryly amused that the teacher's "trivial concerns about classroom management" had been translated in his son's mind into moral imperatives.[16]

Kohlberg recognized that even radical schools like A. S. Neill's Summerhill had their own versions of the hidden curriculum. But studies had shown that people who may cheat in one situation don't necessarily cheat in others. And, of course, this is true. Many a salesman who filches pens from the supply room draws the line at embezzling from the boss or fixing up a purchasing agent with a hooker to win a contract. Kohlberg interpreted such research broadly to mean that habits learned over the course of a lifetime—our personal bag of virtues—are of little use when it comes to making important moral decisions.

Kohlberg identified six stages of moral reasoning, the sixth and highest being "universal ethical-principle orientation"—the recognition that certain "self-chosen ethical principles," such as the Golden Rule or Kant's categorical imperative, transcend man-made laws. The trouble with conventional moral training was that it was content to leave children on the lower rungs of the reasoning ladder. Very few people, even as adults, reached the stage of reasoning from universal principles. (According to Kohlberg, Ronald Reagan was stuck at stage four.)

To determine a child's level of moral reasoning, Kohlberg would pose a hypothetical scenario. For example: *A man named Heinz, who lives somewhere in Europe, learns that his wife has cancer. The only effective drug is available from a pharmacist who manufactures it for $200 but charges*

$2,000. Heinz is unable to borrow the money, and the pharmacist refuses to sell it to him on time. Heinz breaks into the drugstore and steals the medicine. Should he have done that?

In theory at least, Kohlberg wasn't primarily interested in the answer to the question, but in the reasoning behind it. In his schema, the child who answers that stealing is wrong because it's against the law is at a lower developmental level than the child who frames his answer in terms of universal principles like justice and respect for human life.

A large part of Kohlberg's appeal, which extended to many students of religion, was that he was emphatically *not* a moral relativist. He believed strongly that there were indeed universal moral principles, even if they happened to be interpreted differently by different cultures. Of course, as this implies, Kohlberg did believe that there were "right" answers to the moral dilemmas he posed. The trouble was, he couldn't define them—except vaguely—without accepting the existence of revealed truth. In order to get around this dilemma, both he and Maslow accepted the principle that the expression of values might differ at any one time and place, transcending the established laws and customs of any particular culture. Children had to be guided to the point where they could rely on their own moral reasoning. Paradoxically, the teacher, as a representative of the establishment, was not necessarily qualified to judge the student's conclusions.

One practical problem with this approach is that it reduces the quest for a good society to a problem in child development. Children are not philosophers, and their understanding of moral dilemmas is shaped by the attitudes of the adults around them. For that matter, most adults aren't moral philosophers either. Nor are we likely to do our clearest thinking on the day we learn that our spouse has cancer. Like Ronald Reagan—who earned Kohlberg's disdain for his criticism of civil disobedience by activists from UC Berkeley's Free Speech Movement—we tend to think that obedience to the law is a good rule of thumb.

Even Kohlberg's hypothetical situation is heavily influenced by certain cultural prejudices that happen to be not uncommon in places like Harvard's Graduate School of Education. In his example, the price of a lifesaving drug is controlled by the greed of a single profiteering store-owner. However, were it not for "greed," few lifesaving drugs would ever be developed and marketed. More importantly, the illness and impending death of a loved one is not a unique emergency but a situation that many adults will have to confront more than once in the course of their lifetimes. Even when drugs work miracles, they can at best postpone death.

Overall, the example of Heinz seems skewed to encourage youngsters to come up with sophistical rationalizations for robbing the drugstore. And, indeed, this is what happened. Some of Kohlberg's research subjects offered glib justifications based on the sacredness of human life and so on, but the quality of their underlying reasoning was appalling. (Children who reasoned that Heinz was likely to end up in jail, where he would be unable to care for his wife in the future, fell in the lower ranges of Kohlberg's scale, though of course they were right.)

By the 1970s Kohlberg had begun to question whether young adults were really capable of "stage six" thinking. "Perhaps all stage six persons of the 1960's had been wiped out," he wrote, "perhaps they had regressed, or maybe it was all my imagination in the first place." He began to think that it would be enough to get students to stage five, a level based on an appreciation of justice as defined by the social contract.[17]

In 1974 Kohlberg created the Cluster School in Cambridge, Massachusetts. The school was envisioned as a model "just community," which would be governed by town meetings where students, teachers and even maintenance personnel participated on an equal basis. Kohlberg had been impressed by a 1969 visit to an Israeli kibbutz, and he wanted to create an institution where everyone involved was committed to the pursuit of a higher standard of justice. Thanks to generous support from major foundations, the Cluster School enjoyed enviable advantages, chief among them a faculty of six teachers for just thirty students. Nevertheless, the experiment foundered. Petty theft and drugs were so rampant that it was closed after only five years.

This failure did nothing to deter school districts in Pittsburgh, Salt Lake City and Brookline, Massachusetts, among others, from adopting the "just community" approach on a larger scale. Lacking the vision that motivated the kibbutzim, most students, teachers and janitors were content to focus on their own work and let others run the school. They quickly tired of spending hours in aimless meetings that often came to resemble leaderless encounter groups. The students who were interested in the process were often the most discontented. In Brookline, for example, the school government came to be dominated by a handful of students who voted to ban pop quizzes and haul the most demanding teachers before a "Fairness Committee."

The demise of the Cluster School was just the beginning of Lawrence Kohlberg's problems. A generous and often lovable man, described by friends as "a sweet guy," he was no longer as productive or as engaged as he had been early in his career. His marriage failed and his resemblance to the stereotypical absent-minded professor became less amusing over the years as his work suffered and his appearance became more disheveled. Stories about Kohlberg's forgetfulness and eccentric behavior circulated among colleagues. For an expert in moral psychology, he was not always a good judge of character. He invited strangers into his home and trusted people who later took advantage of him. Friends and family blamed Kohlberg's decline on a tropical parasite that he had picked up while doing research in Belize in 1971. His chronic intestinal distress drained his energy and, at times, caused him public embarrassment.

In retrospect it is impossible to say whether other factors contributed to Kohlberg's problems. At any rate, by 1987 his brilliant mind could no longer cope with the challenges of daily living, and he entered Mount Auburn Hospital in Cambridge. One day in January he left the ward on a day pass while in what a police report later described as a "depressed state," and he was never seen alive again. His car was found four days later in Winthrop, a few feet from the edge of a tidal marsh, and on April 17 his body washed up at nearby Logan Airport. Suicide was presumed.[18]

B y the time of Kohlberg's death, his ideas were being challenged by his former student Carol Gilligan, who became the Graham Professor of Gender Studies at Harvard's Graduate School of Education. In her 1982 book, *A Different Voice,* Gilligan argued that women and girls were less likely to think in terms of Kohlbergian concepts like justice, and more likely to make moral decisions based on empathy and care.

Can it really be true that women don't think about morality as men do? The quality of Gilligan's research has often been questioned, and she has never released the data on which her conclusions are based. But if she's right, she has provided a scientific justification for the biblical injunction that wives must submit to their husbands, and know God through them.

This, needless to say, is not what Gilligan has in mind. She finds the female "ethic of care" less abstract, and therefore superior. But this is merely a matter of opinion and many would disagree. Empathy is an untutored emotion. How I feel about hunting depends on whether I empathize with Bambi or with the hunter's starving children. We tend to care most passionately about the people, animals or causes that make the most direct appeals to our feelings. In the absence of rational analysis and moral yardsticks like justice and tolerance, caring can be a wayward impulse, even a dangerous one. No one *cares* more than the suicide bomber.

Another problem with caring-based ethics is that it has to take into account the need to care for oneself. While Gilligan writes of balancing self-care and care for others, this is easier said than done.

Both Kohlberg and Gilligan hoped to construct a universal morality, freed from parochial notions of loyalty to religion, family and country. Kohlberg at least understood the difficulties involved, and he tried to overcome them by educating children to be pint-sized philosophers. Gilligan is just another utopian who chooses to believe that life needn't be a struggle. If we're faced with tough choices, ones that sometimes require us to fight for survival and the defense of our way of life, this must be the fault of civilization itself. "What if the equation of civilization with patriarchy were broken?" Gilligan asks, as if no one had ever considered this question before.

Gilligan's contribution to the religion of human nature is her theory that "our patriarchal society" harms boys and girls in slightly different ways. Girls suffer a crisis of self-esteem in adolescence when they are swamped by the "sea of Western culture," which does not honor their empathic insights. Boys run into trouble earlier, when their attempt to conform to masculine stereotypes alienates them from the nurturing influence of their mothers. White males especially grow up empathically challenged because the acculturation process rewards them for learning to become soldiers and free-market capitalists, capable of causing pain to others without (allegedly) feeling pain themselves.

The notion that we can end war and violence by taming the male ego is powerfully seductive—almost as seductive as the belief that eliminating capitalism would lead to universal prosperity and peace. No doubt this is one reason why gender studies are so lavishly supported by foundations as well as individuals like Jane Fonda, who recently donated $12.5 million to underwrite a gender education center at Harvard. Unfortunately, neither common sense nor independent research offers much support for the vision of a matriarchal utopia. The rising rate of single motherhood has demonstrated that separating boys from the influence of "patriarchal" males does not improve their adjustment. On the contrary, fatherless boys—not boys separated from their mothers—are more prone to violence and more likely to be incarcerated.[19]

Even if Gilligan turned out to be correct that dismantling masculine culture would make boys more "caring," this implies that women can just as easily overcome the socialization that makes them less prone to aggression. And in fact, in the twenty years since Gilligan published *A Different Voice,* they have begun to do just that. Today we have women who are fighter pilots, professional prizefighters, hard-nosed business executives and serial killers. A more androgynous America isn't necessarily a place less plagued with conflict.

Still, deconstructing Western civilization remains a central mission of the Harvard Graduate School of Education. Its professors regularly denounce Eurocentrism and competition, and students sign up for popular courses like Education for Social and Political Change. A recent conference on student research featured a panel discussion on the topic "Cuban Education: Our Role Model?" Up to a point, this may be a good thing. The openness of our culture to critiques from within is one of its great strengths. But it is far from obvious that our publicly funded schools and colleges ought to be testing grounds for radical utopian theories. Parents and taxpayers have never been asked if they care to support such a project, and after years of underwriting other people's agendas, many are now so frustrated that the future of public education is in doubt.[20]

The self-esteem movement that swept America in the late 1980s had diverse roots. Maslow saw self-esteem as a precondition to self-actualization and envisioned a broad range of social programs in order to ensure that every individual's esteem needs were satisfied. Rogers tended to emphasize the importance of enfolding people in a web of uncritical approval. A separate strain of thinking about self-esteem grew out of the Objectivist philosophy of Ayn Rand. In most respects, the Objectivists and the followers of humanistic psychology were opposites. Rand disdained "feelings" and glorified reason. A champion of capitalism, she attracted a totally different type of adherent from the laid-back followers of Rogers and Maslow, mainly upwardly mobile urbanites who dressed conservatively and enjoyed disputatious arguments. For an Objectivist, the very

idea that the government has a mission to make us feel good about ourselves was repulsive. Still, despite many obvious differences, the Objectivists and the Maslovians had one thing in common. Both believed that
there was such a thing as absolute values, but that the ultimate arbiter
of those values was the self. Therefore, self-esteem was a requirement. In
both belief systems, if you are depressed, insecure and confused about
values, you have no one to turn to for answers. You are sunk.

After being expelled from the Objectivist movement in 1968, Rand's
former lover and chief disciple, Nathaniel Branden, established himself
in California and began turning out pop psychology books that promoted his own take on self-esteem. Branden had almost no connection
to the promoters of self-esteem within academia and the schools of education, but his books sold well and did a great deal to popularize the
notion that self-esteem was the key to solving most personal problems.

On the humanistic side of the self-esteem movement, the best-
known voice was John Vasconcellos, the so-called "Johnny Appleseed of
Self-Esteem." The powerful chairman of the California Assembly's Ways
and Means Committee, Vasconcellos campaigned tirelessly to turn the
Golden State into a eupsychian society. By the early 1980s he had developed what he called the New Human Agenda, a comprehensive plan to
use the state's powers to achieve humanistic goals. Diane Dreher, the
author of an admiring profile of Vasconcellos, enthusiastically describes
his plan as "a vast political agenda incorporating all phases of human
development from birth to death—a stunning example of John's holistic, humanistic approach to politics."[21]

Born in 1932, Vasconcellos was, in his own words, "a good Catholic
self-abnegating boy." His overprotective mother discouraged him from
playing sports. His father, a math teacher and school principal, was a
reserved, devout man who rarely expressed anger and stressed the importance of service to others. The young Vasconcellos was a math prodigy
who attended Bellarmine Preparatory, a Catholic boarding school, and
the Jesuit-run Santa Clara University, where he was valedictorian and student body president. Stephen Early, one of his Jesuit counselors, recognized the gregarious Vasconcellos as a born politician and encouraged him
to enter public life. He joined the staff of Governor Pat Brown, and in
1966, having completed law school, he was elected to the state assembly.

That same year Vasconcellos began to receive counseling from
Father Leo Rock, a Jesuit trained in the therapeutic methods of Carl

Rogers. "I had been conditioned to know myself basically as a sinner, guilt-ridden and ashamed, constantly beating my breast and professing my unworthiness," Vasconcellos later wrote. "I had so little self-esteem that I lost my first election (running for eighth-grade president) by one vote—my own." With the help of Father Rock, he began a search for the "real me" that existed behind the façade of the "people-pleasing robot." Rock's humanistic therapy taught him that original sin is a myth. As Vasconcellos put it, "Neither money nor human nature is the root of all evil. The root of all evil is the *belief* that we're evil, and the resultant efforts which serve to make us so."[22]

Vasconcellos took to humanistic psychology with the same bearish enthusiasm that he brought to shaking hands with voters. In the year 1969 alone he attended encounter workshops with Abe Maslow, Rollo May, Richard Farson, Sidney Jourard, James Bugental and Bugental's wife, Liz, a former nun, among others. The results were the usual ones. Vasconcellos let his hair grow out into a curly mop and exchanged his suits and ties for multicolored shirts and bellbottoms. (His style has changed little over the years, and one commentator recently described him as dressing like "an Austin Powers garage sale.") Vasconcellos also stopped using capital letters in his correspondence, took up writing free verse and entered bio-energetic therapy to get "in touch" with his own body. Father Rock, meanwhile, introduced him to Mitch Saunders, the man described by Dreher as Vasconcellos' "dearest friend."

As invariably seemed to happen in Rogerian therapy, the discovery that human nature is inherently good also tapped a wellspring of rage. For several years Vasconcellos did not speak to his parents. When he reopened communications, he refused to call his father "Dad," much to the older man's distress. In Sacramento, he denounced fellow assemblymen as sellouts and cynics. After one outburst on the assembly floor, he was assigned monitors to keep him in line. In spite of his unpredictable behavior, "the touchy-feely legislator," as he was called, maintained generally good relationships with colleagues. He invited several, including future assembly speaker Willie Brown, to Esalen, where he introduced them to the famous seaside hot tubs.

In 1970, meanwhile, Vasconcellos met Carl Rogers at a "Freedom to Learn" workshop in Berkeley and quickly became a personal friend, often visiting Rogers at his home in La Jolla. Dreher calls the two "political partners," and she quotes Mitch Saunders as saying that Vasconcellos became Rogers' "political strategist." Over the following two decades, Vasconcellos would devote himself to promoting Rogers' radical antiauthoritarian ideas. Among his projects, to name just a few, were an Alternative Birthing Committee, a Task Force on Positive Parenting, and the California Human Corps. In 1979 he sponsored a Commission on Violence, which concluded that fighting alcohol addiction and child abuse, along with improving parenting skills, were the best solutions to the problem of rising crime rates. His 1986 "Peace Package" included funding for an educational exchange that sent the eighty-four-year-old Carl Rogers to the Soviet Union to consult with the minister of education on ways to foster individual initiative among Soviet students. Vasconcellos also brought spokesmen for minorities and environmental activists into the process of developing the state's water and energy policies, with results that have lately become apparent.

Vasconcellos gained a reputation as a man who never saw a social spending initiative he didn't like, a trait which in 1980 made him the Democrats' choice for chairman of the assembly's Ways and Means Committee. He used his leverage over the state's budget to champion a bill allocating a quarter of a million dollars for a statewide "Task Force to Promote Self-Esteem and Personal and Social Responsibility." Governor George Deukmejian vetoed the bill in 1985, only to find it on his desk again a year later. This time, Vasconcellos struck a deal to push the plan through, assuring the governor that the energetic promotion of self-esteem would ultimately shave millions off the state's welfare, criminal justice and health budgets.

California was already the self-esteem capital of America, and the California public schools had adopted policies in accord with Carl Rogers' dictum that emphasis on the teaching of skills actually harms children. In 1987, for example, they banished phonics in favor of the whole language method, which holds that children will learn to read and write "naturally" in their own good time, guessing the meaning of words and employing "invented spelling." Even bilingual education was justified in part by the fear that assimilation is a threat to personal authenticity.

Moreover, self-esteem-based programs like DARE and George Brown's "New Three R's" (one of the R's standing for "human Relations") were already implemented in schools in every county of the state. Another familiar figure in California classrooms was Pumsy, a hand puppet in the form of a dragon, who helped children practice relaxation techniques while urging them to banish their "mud minds" and get in touch with their "clear minds." (Pumsy also led youngsters in singing "I am special. So are you. I am enough. You are too.") Another popular program, called "Flights of Fantasy," employed meditation techniques to teach "internal seeing" and put children in touch with the "wisdom within."

Four years and three quarters of a million dollars later, the task force presented its report, entitled *Toward a State of Esteem.* The authors turned Stanley Coopersmith's speculation into a promise, writing that self-esteem "inoculates us against the lures of crime, violence, substance abuse, teen pregnancy, child abuse, chronic welfare dependency and educational failure." The report also took the position that there is no such thing as a bad feeling ("All feelings are honorable. . . . By themselves, feelings are neither good nor bad") and expressed regret that in America "indications of worth are based on production and achievements." References to the "spiritual" dimension of self-esteem left no doubt that the report's goal was to establish a secular psychology-oriented belief system, replacing traditional civic values.

Among the specific recommendations of the task force were requiring self-esteem mission statements from candidates for public office, the integration of self-esteem lessons with the "total curricula" of the schools, and mandatory self-esteem courses for all teachers. The latter recommendation promised to be a bonanza for entrepreneurs like Vasconcellos' friend Jack Canfield, the co-creator of the *Chicken Soup for the Soul* books, whose Santa Barbara institute already had government contracts to run self-esteem training seminars for everyone from social workers to welfare clients.

In conjunction with its report, the task force also published a book summing up the best available scientific evidence on self-esteem. The verdict was hardly encouraging. Stanley Coopersmith's research could now be shrugged off, since his subjects were all white males. But there simply was no evidence to show that enhancing children's self-esteem would help them avert problems later in life. As one of the volume's editors, Berkeley sociologist Neil Smelser, observed, "the associations between self-esteem and its expected consequences are mixed, insignificant or absent." The disparity between the task force's grandiose claims and the paucity of supporting evidence infuriated and baffled critics, but did nothing to dampen the spirits of true believers. Vasconcellos explained to a skeptical academic critic in 1995, "You can't measure love. . . . Self esteem is in that category. . . . We all know in our gut that it is true."[23]

California's endorsement of self-esteem had a snowball effect. In 1990 Bill Clinton, then governor of Arkansas, invited Vasconcellos to address a meeting of the Democratic Leadership Council. By the end of the following year, Maryland, Virginia, Louisiana and Kentucky, among other states, had set up self-esteem task forces. James L. Nolan estimates that by 1994, thirty states had enacted more than 170 statutes whose stated goal was enhancing self-esteem. The majority were education-related but some were targeted toward health care, welfare or the criminal justice system.[24]

During the early 1990s it was almost impossible to pick up a popular magazine or tune into daytime TV without getting a lecture on the importance of self-esteem. Were you overweight? Anorexic? Addicted? Codependent? Depressed? A mass murderer? Low self-esteem was undoubtedly at the root of your problem.

The zeal of self-esteem advocates proved to be their undoing. Fillips like celebrating "Self-Esteem Day" and naming February "Self-Esteem Month" provided inviting targets for satire. Garry Trudeau, the creator of *Doonesbury*, had great fun following the misadventures of imaginary task-force member Betty "Boopsie" Boopstein as she took part in "the first official study of New Age Thinking." Soon everyone from Charles Krauthammer, then of the *New Republic*, to actress/comedienne Tracy Ullman was taking swipes. Meanwhile, Chester Finn pointed out that a 1988 study by the University of Michigan found that 80 percent of graduating high school seniors had a positive self-image, yet in that same year only one-third of all seniors knew that the Mississippi River flows into the Gulf of Mexico.

Perhaps the most devastating critique of self-esteem came from Roy F. Baumeister of Case Western Reserve University. As part of his research for a book on violence, Baumeister and his assistants made an extensive study of the connection between violent behavior and self-esteem, later published as a lengthy article in *Psychological Review 5*. "People with low self-esteem are generally shy, humble, modest, self-effacing individuals." But:

If anything, high self-esteem is closer to the violent personality. Most per-petrators of violence are acting out of some sense of personal superiority, especially one that has been threatened or questioned in some way. I am not saying that high self-esteem, per se, directly causes violence. Not all people with high self-esteem become violent, but violent people are a sub-set of people with high self-esteem.[25]

This should not surprise anyone who recalls that Maslow used the term self-esteem as a synonym for dominance-feeling, the same drive that makes monkeys dominate others in their group. Maslow didn't worry that increasing self-esteem would make the world more violent because he believed that evolution had eliminated the drive to aggression. If war, violent crime and exploitation continued to exist it was because these things were cultural artifacts, products of our authoritarian society. Bring-ing this up again is not to berate Maslow but to point out how theory in the social sciences can be based on sweeping and totally unfounded generalizations. Long after these assumptions have become passé, the theory lives on as a justification for retooling our schools, government programs and civil society itself.

Ironically, the California self-esteem initiative proved to be a bless-ing. In 1993 the once proud public education system of the state of Cal-ifornia was humiliated when only Mississippi, Washington, D.C., and Guam had lower reading scores on the National Assessment of Educa-tional Progress. Since self-esteem was now official public policy, it wasn't hard to place blame. By 1999, the self-esteem movement was in retreat, and school districts were replacing "I Love Me" lessons with spelling and math drills.

Common sense appears to have triumphed, at least for the moment, but it's too soon to declare that the world has been turned upside down. A 1999 *Los Angeles Times* article headlined "Losing Faith in Self-Esteem" quotes Michael Furlong, a professor from the University of California at Santa Barbara who is engaged in training school psychologists. Fur-long agrees that self-esteem has been so debunked that "the only people who use [the term] are those who want to discredit the idea." However, as the article makes clear, that doesn't mean that Furlong has changed his mind in any fundamental way. His prediction that the same ideas will be repackaged under a different label recalls Carl Rogers' comment that it will be necessary to keep changing the name of the encounter group movement to keep one step ahead of the critics.

John Vasconcellos' attempt to mount a campaign for governor of California in 1997 fizzled, but the highly educated voters of his Silicon Valley district elected him to the state senate by an impressive margin. Vasconcellos has reinvented himself as an advocate of medical marijuana. His rhetoric seems almost libertarian at times, but he also promotes something called the "New American Politics of Trust." As one supporter defines it, the politics of trust means that we are entitled to personal freedom but "not the right to condemn others as 'evil' because their choices are different from our own. The mothers who throw away their children, and the children who attack other children, are not criminals. They are symptomatic of the disintegration of our society." Meanwhile, Vasconcellos' senate website calls for the government to undertake the project of "redesigning society to encourage development of healthy, self-realizing, responsible human beings."

The new buzzword in the values debate is "character education," essentially a return to old-fashioned methods that prevailed in the days before moral training was handed over to progressive educators and psychologists. As longtime character education advocate William J. Bennett points out, it isn't necessary to reinvent society or resolve vexing philosophical dilemmas before we can begin teaching children to behave themselves. Character education attempts to find a consensus by emphasizing self-discipline, personal responsibility, honesty and good citizenship.

The rapid adoption of character education, fueled by the availability of grant money from the U.S. Department of Education, means that psychologists and educators are hard at work designing new programs. On the grassroots level, however, many people who were running self-esteem programs a few years ago have simply switched hats. Their versions of character education would be all but unrecognizable to Bill Bennett. In December 2000, for example, parents from the Fort Cherry school district in McDonald, Pennsylvania, staged a successful revolt against a "character education" program called "Violence Free: Healthy Choices for Kids," taught by facilitators from a local women's shelter. The facilitators used role playing and other methods to teach children *not* to fight back against bullies. Rather, boys and girls were instructed to denounce the bullies by saying, "You're being unfair! You're bullying me!" Protesting parents also took exception to exercises in which children were asked intrusive personal questions such as, "If you could change one thing about your family, what would it be?"

Ultimately, children don't learn moral behavior from "programs." Nor can the job of defining virtue be delegated to psychologists, however well intentioned they may be. The humanities curriculum, which has been systematically devalued, needs to be restored to its former place of honor. And above all, we must recognize that so-called ordinary citizens—meaning people without Ph.D.s in psychology, education and the social sciences—have a right to participate fully in determining the way values are taught in the schools.

A few years ago, when the governor of Alabama was waging a fight to display the Ten Commandments in his state's public school classrooms, a young acquaintance of mine took his efforts as a personal insult. Why, she wondered, couldn't the school avoid offending atheists like herself by translating the commandments into secular form?

It is just possible that a randomly selected group of Americans could sit down over coffee at their neighborhood diner and come up with a reasonable secularized translation of the Ten Commandments—though, of course, the Diner Decalogue wouldn't have quite the same ring of authority. In real life, however, such tasks have tended to be assigned to experts like the faculty of the Harvard Graduate School of Education. And experience has shown that they couldn't do the job, even if they wanted to. Obviously, the HGSE people would begin by throwing out commandments one through three, since they assume the existence of a single deity and are offensive to atheists and Wiccans. The injunction to honor one's father and mother would need to be reworked, since rebellion against the patriarchy is a virtue. "Thou shalt not steal" would be out, since expropriating property may not be wrong under all circumstances, especially for members of exploited groups. Adultery, of course, is purely a private matter. And as for coveting . . . who really cares? "Thou shalt not kill" would probably make the cut, though it would likely be reduced to a condemnation of capital punishment.

No statement of public values could possibly be designed that would be congruent with the private beliefs of every single American. Despite humanistic psychology's goal of inclusiveness, the "religion of human nature," which assumes that each of us is a law unto himself, doubtless offends more people than the words "under God" in the Pledge of Allegiance. William Bennett is right when he says that we can't afford to defer the work of education until this conundrum is resolved, if it ever is. Nor need we. The task of defining America's civic values becomes easier if we recognize that they must be a reflection of our two-hundred-plus-year history and not a blueprint for some eupsychian society that may or may not come into being in the future.

Chapter 9

The Deconstructed Self

The years after his release from prison were not kind to Timothy Leary. The age of virtual reality initially seemed to be made for him, and he tried hard to reinvent himself as a cyber-guru, futurist and science fiction writer. His many projects included starting a company to produce CD-Rom "environments" and writing a novel illustrated with computer graphics about a bisexual black protagonist named Huck Getty Mellon von Schlebrugge. But Leary's nonfiction writings appealed to a limited audience made up of young people who knew what the word "extropianism" meant and found it fascinating to read about the four terrestrial and four post-terrestrial circuits of human consciousness. And for all his talk about connecting minds with computers, Leary acknowledged on occasion that electronic communication was mainly a medium for entertainment and education. It didn't take you into new worlds the way drugs did. Marginalized, he earned most of his income as a lecturer on the college circuit and through occasional acting work.

Jack Leary hadn't spoken to his father since 1976. Susan Leary Martino was a troubled woman whose personal relationships never seemed to work out. In January 1989, while her boyfriend Joel Chavira was sleeping on her living room couch, Susan shot him in the back of the head, for reasons unknown. Chavira survived, and Susan, twice found incompetent to stand trial for attempted murder, was remanded to Patton State Hospital, where she was often too withdrawn to speak. On September 6, 1990, while being held at the Sybil Brand Institute in Los Angeles following a court hearing, she managed to hang herself by a shoelace from the bars of her cell. She died two days later, at the age of forty-two.

Leary's fourth wife, Barbara Chase, filed for divorce two years later. Never a man who liked to be alone, Leary tried to make up for his single state by becoming a regular on the Los Angeles party circuit. His circle of celebrity friends included his goddaughter Winona Ryder, Susan Sarandon and Grateful Dead lyricist John Perry Barlow. He also mended fences with his third wife, Rosemary, who had resurfaced after living on the East Coast under an assumed name for twenty-four years. But these people all had lives of their own, and a lonely Leary often befriended young hippie wanna-be's, a miscellaneous assortment of cyber-geeks, alternative musicians and aspiring actors born too late for the Swinging Sixties.

For all his eagerness to be on the cutting edge of social and technological change, Leary was a curiously old-fashioned figure. He had championed the humanistic idea of a higher consciousness, but somehow he never bought into the Feelings Revolution. Indeed, one could argue that his decades-long search for other levels of reality was a way of avoiding the emotional complications of personal relationships in the here and now. In Leary's mind, sincerity was inevitably an indication that a person was taking himself too seriously. He preferred to amuse his friends with witticisms, tales of high adventure and self-deprecating humor. He could be great fun to be around, at least in the short run, but no one was really close to him.

Vicki Marshall met Leary at a computer fair in 1984. A few years older than most of his fans, she was not especially interested in Tim Leary the LSD guru and celebrity clown, but she admired his books and appreciated the kinetic intelligence that produced them. Hired on as Leary's editorial and personal assistant, she worked with him on many projects over the years and helped organize his personal papers, which gave her an opportunity to read his pre-LSD writings, including his Ph.D. thesis. "I loved his mind," Marshall says. "I considered him a consummate philosopher." Still, there were times when she wondered why he kept her on. His income was limited, and most of the things she did were tasks that he could just as well have performed for himself.[1]

During the fall of 1994, Leary consulted a doctor about an unusually persistent case of flu. The news was not good. A viral infection had been complicated by pneumonia. Worse, a complete physical revealed prostate cancer. Various treatment options were outlined, including surgery. But Leary told Marshall that he had "no intention of playing the Cancer Game." Once he had heard the diagnosis, he immediately understood what his ultimate fate would be. Now he wanted to show the world that death could be "a great experiment."

Leary soon elaborated on his plans in a conversation with an interviewer from *Psychology Today.* Ever conscious of his own status as a prophet-guru, he opined, "Divinity is something you have to work at, just like you work at any other profession."

During the course of this rambling and sometimes self-contradictory interview, Leary went on to share his advice for drug users in the Nineties: "Never take a drug that you don't receive from a dear, trusted friend." He apologized to fans of heroin and methamphetamine for all the years when he condemned "other people's drugs," and reminisced about how his own dear friend, British psychiatrist R. D. Laing had given him his first injection of heroin in 1979. (Apparently he had forgotten that in *Flashbacks* he describes injecting heroin in Switzerland in 1972.)

At other times during this conversation, Leary sounded more like his old libertarian self. He agreed with Carl Rogers that a behavior problem is not a disease, and scoffed at the new diagnosis of attention deficit disorder as just another strategy on the part of psychiatrists to control high-spirited young people with medication. As for dying, Americans who gave themselves over to the healthcare delivery system were simply acceding to "government-managed suicide." Dying shouldn't be controlled by priests or healthcare plans; rather, it should be a "team sport" for individuals and their loved ones. The Pope and Mother Teresa, he went on, were "two of the most evil people alive." But he approved of the families who called on Dr. Jack Kevorkian to help them manage their own deaths, free of state control. "One of the biggest political issues we have is self-dignified death, self-liberation."[2]

Turning his own death into a futuristic statement would be easier said than done. Exiting life while tripping on LSD would not be enough to guarantee Leary's status as a psychonaut. Aldous Huxley, after recommending the procedure in *Island,* had already managed this feat when his wife twice injected him with LSD as he lay on his deathbed in

November 1963. Leary's more ambitious plans included having his head removed and flash-frozen in liquid nitrogen within minutes of his death. The plan was that his brain could be thawed out and reunited with a viable body at some time in the distant future, when medical science had discovered the secret of immortality. Leary joked that when his turn for revival came, he hoped to be given the body of a seventeen-year-old girl.

The plan to cheat mortality through cryonics was nothing new. Back in 1988, while writing a book on futurism, Leary and some associates had begun to discuss, hypothetically, their ideas about their own funeral arrangements. After Tim talked of having his ashes scattered in the Ganges or, perhaps, shot into outer space, one of his part-time secretaries mentioned that she and her husband belonged to the Alcor Foundation, a group dedicated to cryonic preservation. Intrigued, Leary investigated Alcor and eventually signed up as a client. Whether he ever believed that cryonics might work for him is difficult to say; but he loved the concept. The brain, after all, was the hard drive of the human body. Save it, and at some point in the future perhaps all that data could be restored and put to use in a new system.

Leary was by far the most famous individual ever to commit to cryonic preservation, and for those who believed in the technology, his decision was a monumental development. In November 1994 he had a falling-out with Alcor, but soon struck a deal with a rival organization, Cryocare. Like Alcor before it, Cryocare slashed $20,000 off its usual $58,000 fee in the hope of garnering invaluable media attention. A clause in the contract gave Cryocare publicity rights, and Cryocare executive Charles Platt had an arrangement to write up Leary's last days for *Wired* magazine.

Vicki Marshall, who had visited the Alcor facility, learned that the freezing process destroyed brain cells, and she didn't see it as technologically feasible. Still, she understood why Leary was fascinated by the *idea* of cryonics, and since he wanted it, she was prepared to support him. When the contract with Cryocare was signed, she told its representatives that she had only one fear: "I don't want to see a photo of Tim's head in the *National Enquirer*," she said. They assured her this would never happen.

As his end drew closer, Leary began work on a book to be entitled *Soul Preservation,* which treated cryonics as a high-tech solution to the problem of mortality. When Marshall read over the manuscript, however, she had a philosophical objection. "You can't say that the soul is the brain," she told Tim. The brain might be the seat of consciousness, but after death it became just dead meat. Unless he could come up with a better definition of the soul and explain its relationship to the physical body, nothing he had written made sense. Leary worked on the problem sporadically, but his powers of concentration were even less than they had been in recent years.

As far as Leary's idea of dying as a "team sport" was concerned, the irony was that he had surrounded himself with a team of twenty-something groupies who couldn't take care of themselves, much less act as a team to care for an elderly cancer patient. Leary appointed one follower as his webmaster to create an Internet site that would monitor his decline, complete with daily updates on his drug regimen and links to futuristic graphics and music. One young fan volunteered to "babysit" for Leary so he wouldn't have to spend his evenings alone. Before long, he had moved in. Others followed suit, and soon Leary's home was a twenty-four-hour party scene.

The rented house high up in Benedict Canyon had always seemed to be floating in a time warp. A white shag rug and oversize hookah dominated the living room. Leary's books were stored on homemade block-and-board shelves. Psychedelic posters, movie memorabilia and a few good pieces of pop art hung on the walls. Everything was slightly dingy and in need of a good steam cleaning. With the addition of a coterie of mostly stoned young people, coming and going twenty-four hours a day, the resemblance to the old Newton Square commune was complete.

The new generation of Learyites sported purple hair, intricate tattoos and multiple body piercings. Some were well meaning, if ditzy. Quite a few had some idea, however unlikely, for profiting from their association with a faded celebrity. "A lot of people wanted a piece of him," recalls Marshall. One woman was planning to write a book putting forth her claim to be Leary's last girlfriend, which she wasn't. She brought a photographer into Leary's bedroom, plied Tim with Valium, and had herself photographed snuggling with him. Another individual took every opportunity to get Leary to autograph sheets of blotter acid for later resale. Others talked of film projects, CD-Roms and so on. It may well be that Leary encouraged some of these fantasies.

In January 1996, Leary went to the hospital for a round of tests. When the results came back, Vicki Marshall learned for the first time that his cancer had metastasized. Later, going through Leary's papers, she would conclude that he had been given the bad news months earlier, perhaps as long ago as January 1995. But only now, informed that a tumor was growing at the base of his spine, did Leary agree to radiation treatments. "I want to be a good boy," he told Marshall uncharacteristically. After the first treatment, he was so weak that he needed a cane to get around. After the second, he retreated to a wheelchair. Leary dreaded his visits to the hospital, and Marshall blamed his inability to tolerate the radiation for his rapid decline, which may or may not have been the case. After a while, she stopped insisting that he go on with them.

Leary had lost his appetite months earlier, and after the radiation treatments he scarcely ate at all. When Marshall was at the house during the day, she would coax him into drinking a can of Ensure, but the members of the ragtag entourage who were supposed to be caring for him at night rarely made the effort. They were happy, however, to share in the drugs that a friend was supplying for Leary's self-medication regimen. In addition to his cancer, Leary had tested positive for hepatitis C, a condition often associated with cocaine users and chronic alcoholics, and his doctors feared that heavy painkillers would cause further damage to his liver. Possibly, they were also reluctant to prescribe narcotics for a notorious drug advocate who was dosing himself with all manner of illegal substances on the side. At any rate, Leary was in excruciating pain, which he tried unsuccessfully to control with street drugs. He took frequent hits from balloons filled with nitrous oxide and consumed "Leary biscuits"—Ritz crackers topped with marijuana buds and dollops of cheese, then zapped in a microwave.

One day when Marshall arrived at the house, someone asked her, "Who are those junkies in with Tim?" She went into Leary's bedroom and found a group of strangers who had shot him up with drugs. Panicked, she feared that her fragile boss would overdose and slip into a coma. Instead, his eyes cleared for the first time in months. The drug, whatever it was, had been strong enough to release him from his pain. Realizing that something had to be done, Marshall turned to Cryocare executive Mike Darwin, who brought in specialists, including a world-renowned gerontologist, to examine Leary at the company's expense. The doctors found a patient who had lost at least seventy pounds and was in danger of dying from starvation before the cancer did its work.

Concluding that liver damage was the least of Leary's problems, they arranged a prescription for a Fentanyl patch as well as a supplemental supply of Dilaudid.

Cryocare also dispatched a nurse, but she resigned after a few days. Conditions in the house were so deplorable, she told a company representative, that if she stayed, she would be conscience-bound to file a report of patient abuse to the authorities.

Leary hadn't been able to work for a long time. His finances were in a sorry state and he had a houseful of people to feed. The only way Marshall could see to pay the bills was for him to start charging for interviews, as he had done at times in the past. The asking price for a sit-down with the dying guru was one thousand dollars. Leary made an effort to earn his pay by coming up with provocative remarks about his plans for a high-tech exit, but often he was just going through the motions. In one session with a local cable station, a barely coherent Leary was filmed in his backyard surrounded by the tall palm trees he called "my Lakers." In mid-sentence, his mind seemed to wander and he looked skyward, whispering the words, "Soon. Soon." When the footage was previewed at a special screening, some in the audience giggled at this. Vicki Marshall cringed. "The last daze of Timothy Leary," as she sardonically called them, had become such a media circus that even a dying man's longing for release was mistaken for shtick.

When not talking to anyone willing to pay for an audience, Leary held court for celebrity visitors, including filmmaker Oliver Stone, Yoko Ono, singer/actress Michelle Phillips and John Lilly, the man who talked to dolphins, among many others. His entourage, meanwhile, decided to raise cash by holding rent parties and open houses. A sign advertising "The Mother of All Parties" went up outside, and the paying guests streamed in—club kids from the Sunset Strip, ex-hippies, Rastafarians, cyberpunks and assorted others eager to visit the Timothy Leary death house, sample his drugs and perhaps catch a glimpse of the Acid Guru in the flesh, or what remained of it. There were people up and about at all hours, and Leary, who had trouble sleeping at the best of times, was exhausted.

A friend who supplied Leary with illegal drugs later estimated that the household went through eight hundred pounds of nitrous oxide in six months, as well as quantities of LSD, DMT and marijuana. Leary's possessions, including artworks, memorabilia and personal letters, were disappearing from the house at an alarming rate, later to turn up in pawn-shops or listed on eBay. When Tim confided to Marshall that he was thinking of writing some of his new friends into his will, she called in a lawyer to make sure this wouldn't happen, and got Rosemary Woodruff, an executor of the existing will, to remove his archives for safekeeping. "Quite frankly, I was the only sane person there," says Marshall.

There were old friends and members of Leary's extended family who genuinely cared for him, but no one who was willing to take respon-sibility for ejecting the freeloaders from the house and getting him to accept proper nursing care. He was the ultimate recalcitrant patient, sometimes incoherent but on other occasions canny and manipulative. The kind of people who would be inclined to lecture Tim about taking care of himself usually didn't remain close to him for long, even at the best of times, and some of those who remained his friends saw his deter-mination to party on until the end as a kind of heroism. A former employee of Leary's who lived out of state was asked by Cryocare to visit the house and see what could be done to help him. She reported back that she'd had a good time in spite of everything, but Tim was in a sorry state. "What he needs is a mom," she advised.

Vicki Marshall played the mom role when she could. But she was only an employee and had a private life of her own. For the sake of her sanity, she needed to get away from the house when her workday ended. As soon as she left, she became the target of intrigues on the part of the hangers-on, who saw her as their enemy. By now Leary could not hold onto any train of thought for long. He listened to the last person who talked to him on any given day, and when Marshall arrived in the morn-ing she often found that someone had put the idea into his mind that she had to be fired. "What is it that you do for me anyway?" Leary asked her one day. Marshall, who had been doing pretty much everything for Tim for months, bit her tongue and went to type up a list, but by the time it was finished he had forgotten why he wanted it. As much as she cared for Leary, there were times when Marshall suspected him of being the real instigator of the campaign against her. Probably, she was right. Leary's most enduring relationship was his love affair with drugs, and Marshall, not a druggie herself, represented a potential threat. On the other hand, as long as the house was filled with refugees from the Sunset Strip, Leary could feel confident that his supply would not be cut off.

Around the end of March, Marshall notified Cryocare that Leary was failing, and on April 1, 1996, its representative, Charles Platt, arrived with the high-tech freezer that was to be used to preserve Leary's severed head. The freezer was placed in the garage, where members of the entourage promptly began using it to store wine as well as a cache of Leary memorabilia, including the *Tibetan Book of the Dead* and his copy of the Beatles' *Abbey Road* album. Inside the house, Platt found a patient who was by no means hours away from death, as he had been led to believe, but pitifully weak and neglected-looking. When Marshall wasn't around, Leary was often at the mercy of stoned volunteers, incapable of remembering to change his Fentanyl patch, seeing to his hygienic needs or monitoring his habit of smoking in bed. On the night of April 15, Leary set fire to his bedclothes and was rescued only after someone belatedly noticed that his bedroom was filling up with smoke.

Platt had been in Los Angeles only a few days when he saw a *National Enquirer* story predicting that Timothy Leary would become the first human being to commit interactive suicide, broadcasting his death live over the Internet. Leary, indeed, was telling interviewers that when the time came he planned to swallow a "suicide cocktail." Meanwhile, Chris Graves, who managed the Leary.com website, was talking about videotaping Leary's final moments and, possibly, calling in a *Los Angeles Times* photographer.

Platt was shocked. While some might see cryonics advocates as part of the lunatic fringe, no one believes more ardently in medical science and in doing everything possible—and, indeed, more than is now possible—to preserve life. It was hard for the Cryocare people to understand why a man who cared enough about life to preserve his head for future revival would have passed up options like hormone treatments, which might have given him a reprieve of many months if started soon enough. As for suicide, the very idea was anathema. For one thing, a lethal dose of drugs would also cause damage to his brain tissue. For another, assisted suicide was illegal in the state of California. Platt had visions of being caught up in a criminal investigation. He worried that the police might decide to charge him as an accomplice or seize Cryocare's expensive equipment. At the very least, there could be an autopsy, which would make the cryonic preservation of Leary's head impossible. Disgusted, Platt withdrew the equipment from the house on May 3.

Leary's motley entourage was not sorry to see Platt go. Nor would he miss those he had come to think of as the "Joy of Now" people. "According to the Leary worldview," he observed, "they don't have to worry about building a career, they don't need that new BMW, they don't even need to bathe regularly or tie their shoes. They can just immerse themselves in the Joy of Now, just like their mentor." The trouble was, Platt added, the born-too-late hippies didn't grasp that this philosophy would never work as well for them as it had for Leary. Not one of them had Tim's intelligence, charm or sheer stamina.[3]

No matter how enfeebled Leary became, there was always someone willing to take him out for an appearance at Spago, his favorite restaurant, or to a trendy Hollywood party, even if they couldn't remember to bring along his pain medication or a clean change of underwear. Perhaps the people who arranged such outings honestly thought they were entertaining Tim, but they seemed to be driven mainly by their own need to believe that he was still having fun. On one such occasion, Leary was transported to a party in a Humvee, a rough ride for a man with metastasized cancer of the spine.

In one of his last evenings out, Leary showed up at the Beverly Hills Hotel, where someone had arranged for him to accept a Humanitarian of the Year award from the Association of Los Angeles Advertising Women on behalf of his friend Susan Sarandon. For some unknown reason, his companions on that evening had chosen to deck him out in a dog collar decorated with twinkling Christmas tree lights. Leary's wheelchair was also festooned with strings of colored lights. Looking as if he were on his way to a disco party for necrophiliacs, Leary made a dramatic entrance and was wheeled to his place at the head table.

Seated directly across from him was Art Linkletter. As everyone in Hollywood knew, with the possible exception of Leary's entourage, Linkletter's daughter had committed suicide while under the influence of LSD in 1968, and he had held Leary personally responsible ever since. The eighty-three-year-old TV personality was taken aback to see his old nemesis sitting three feet away and wearing an electrified dog collar. Still, he managed to hold on to his composure. "I feel sorry for Leary," he later told reporters. Leary, however, could not pull off his coup, if that's what it was supposed to be. Two or three sentences into his speech, he forgot why he was there and called out plaintively to one of his attendants, who fed him his lines: "Susan, we miss you.... Keep telling us what it is to be a human being."[4]

The embarrassing incident was written up in the L.A. papers, along with an account of Leary's appearance at Spago later that same night. Marshall was livid. "He had no business being out at that time," she says. One of the caretakers conceded that dressing Tim up in a dog collar had been an error in judgment, but, she shrugged, it had seemed like a good idea at the time.

During the final weeks of his life, Leary got scared. As Charles Platt saw it, he realized at long last that cancer wasn't just another of his faux-existential games. He began turning to longtime friends, especially John Perry Barlow. "He wanted Barlow to tell him how to die," says Platt. Like most of Leary's informal extended family, Barlow had never approved of Leary's desire to have his brain frozen, and he advised him to cancel his contract with Cryocare. Doubtless this was for the best, though it left Cryocare holding the bills for the aid it had provided and exposed Platt to the anger of cryonics advocates who felt that he had flubbed a chance to promote their cause.

Barlow, meanwhile, had his own take on dying. He believed in bringing "death out of the closet" and wanted his old friend to pass from the scene in a way that would refute what he called "the stupefying mass denial that causes almost 80 percent of America's health care budget to be blown on the last six months of life." In practical terms, this meant a continuation of the party-all-the-time mentality. One evening in May, Barlow, along with members of the entourage, rented wheelchairs and staged an impromptu parade down the Sunset Strip, ending with an evening at the House of Blues. The stunt might have passed for some kind of statement about access for the disabled, except that all the revelers save Leary were able-bodied individuals out for a lark. Barlow later drove Tim home in his rented convertible with two shrieking girls perched atop the trunk—a bit of whimsy that attracted the attention of a patrolman and nearly earned Timothy Leary one last trip to the slammer.[5]

After months of hinting at a dramatic finale, Leary's final moments on May 31 were an anticlimax. His ex-wife Rosemary and stepson Zach were at his bedside. There was no suicide cocktail and no live Internet broadcast. All that had been hype. A small portion of Leary's cremated remains was later shot into space as part of the payload of a commercial satellite. But far from sailing toward Alpha Centauri, as Leary once imagined, his ashes are expected to re-enter the atmosphere in a decade or so when the satellite self-destructs. Leary's travels in outer space will be briefer than his battle with the U.S. Department of Justice.

When the death was announced, tributes streamed in to the Leary.com website, many from Baby Boomers who remembered him fondly as a symbol of the magical mystery tour of the Sixties and their own youthful illusions. Even the obituary writers, for the most part, seemed eager to believe that Leary had once again fulfilled his role as guide to unknown regions of consciousness by showing us how to die a good death. His last words—"Why not?"—were solemnly recorded, and the *Washington Post* informed its readers that Leary had battled his final illness "with stubborn determination and a dazzling array of drugs." A columnist for *USA Today* said that by reneging on his promises of suicide, Leary had made "an affirmation of life."

Unfortunately, it wasn't so. For all his trips to the frontiers of consciousness, with and without the help of the *Tibetan Book of the Dead,* Leary had been completely unprepared for the real thing. Like his other projects, this "great experiment" had been conducted with plenty of flash, but no substance. A man who can't decide between suicide and a high-tech gamble on immortality—mutually contradictory strategies—is clueless about the big questions. Granted, Leary may have saved the healthcare system a few dollars by refusing treatment, but his sorry condition during his final months is hardly an argument in favor of bowing out of this world without a struggle. Most people can't recruit groupies to care for them in their final months—thankfully, considering the results. Far from bringing death out of the closet, Leary's friends had used him to perpetuate their own denial.

Afterward, the freeloaders stayed on at Leary's house until December, when they were served with eviction papers. The owner of the property then called in the bulldozers and had the premises razed. Meanwhile, within weeks of Leary's passing, Vicki Marshall was invited to a screening by Paul Davids, who had filmed interviews the previous autumn with Leary and various associates, including Marshall, Ram Dass and Ralph Metzner. Davids' insistence on having Leary sit for a life mask had seemed a little strange at the time, but he paid extra for the right to film the procedure and donated a copy of the cast of Leary's head to his archives. In the confusion of the moment, no one had interrogated the filmmaker about his intentions or paid much attention to his résumé, which included notorious footage of an "alien autopsy." As it turned out, Davids' "documentary" concluded with a shocking scene purporting to show Leary's corpse being surgically decapitated, followed by a gruesome shot of his "severed head"—actually a model made from the life mask.

"But don't worry," Davids assured Marshall, "it's very tastefully done."

When it came time for the film's release, a photo of the alleged "head" appeared in the *National Enquirer,* much to the distress of Leary's survivors. The duplicate cast remains boxed up in his archives where, according to Marshall, no one as yet has had the courage to look at it.

In contrast to his old friend Leary, Ram Dass believed that he had a sound philosophy about the problem of death. For some years he had devoted much of his time to what he called "The Dying Project," coaching AIDS patients and other hospice residents in a technique he called "conscious dying." Then, one night in February 1997, Ram Dass jumped out of bed to answer the phone and suffered a massive cerebral hemorrhage. At the hospital, doctors gave him a 10 percent chance of survival. Later he explained, "I'd always projected deep thoughts and profound experiences onto these people," but as he lay near death himself, "I didn't have any profound spiritual thoughts. I was looking at the pipes on the ceiling."[6]

Ram Dass survived and went through a difficult rehabilitation. He ordered his nurse to remove the picture of his Hindu guru that hung on his wall. Later, he regained his faith but emerged a humbler man. Instead of "conscious dying," he now teaches conscious aging, which amounts to accepting the inevitable slights of aging and decline with grace and good humor. God's truth may be absolute, he says, but "my understanding of truth can change from day to day."

Ram Dass's survival makes his public appearances inspirational for many stroke patients, and his advice about aging gracefully is well taken. Still, there is little in his message that one would be surprised to hear from a Unitarian minister or, for that matter, the Harvard psychology professor that Ram Dass used to be. Moreover, while Ram Dass preaches the benefits of meditation, he admitted to interviewer Sara Davidson that he personally finds pot a quicker way to achieve serenity. Marijuana can indeed provide an enjoyable and relaxing high, but finding nirvana in pot is no improvement over finding truth in a six-pack of Bud or a bottle of cabernet sauvignon. Four decades after the founders of the LSD revolution got behind Leary's slogan "Question Authority," it seems that the only cause that really matters to them is medical marijuana—the right of aging hippies to soothe their aches and pains with their herb of choice.

With hindsight, self-actualization was an enormously empowering creed for young people in a time of prosperity. The call to creative rebellion gave us Baby Boomers unparalleled confidence—justified or not—that we were wiser than everyone over thirty. For those with stamina and luck, the religion of human nature continued to be a serviceable philosophy well into middle age. While others were spacing out in communes, cults or treatment centers, they somehow got it together to finish their degrees, apply for grants and start successful careers. Despite much hand wringing about "selling out" the ideals of the Sixties, self-actualization had always provided a ready-made justification for looking out for Number One. Indeed, its first and most successful application had been in the corporate environment.

Once our generation began to emerge from its extended youth, humanistic psychology became a game of diminishing returns. It offered few clues about how to function successfully as a boss, teacher, spouse or parent. Having children was often the first life milestone that led Baby Boomers to question their antiauthoritarian principles. By the late 1970s we began to see the emergence of compromise positions. Social conservatives held fast to the old definition of liberalism but were unenthusiastic about identity politics and its consequences. Michael Lerner, the founder of the magazine *Tikkun*, proposed a "politics of meaning" in which the burden of achieving a utopia based on the value of "empathy" is to be left in the hands of government bureaucrats. Ironically, younger people were often more influenced by the pro-business, pro-individualist side of self-actualization. They tended to be cynical about government in general, though in practice they took for granted a level of government activism unheard of fifty years ago.

Many of the changes that Abraham Maslow advocated in *Religion, Values and Peak Experiences* have come to pass. Moral judgments based on Judeo-Christian ethics are routinely stigmatized as exclusionary. Other religions are often treated more sympathetically; they are protected by the mantle of multiculturalism and, at least presumably, there is no imminent danger that our elected representatives will try to translate them into public policy. Novel religions based on Eastern philosophies or New Age visions fit the new paradigm best. Indeed, Wicca—the religion of witchcraft—may be the most congenial faith for self-actualizers since it has no moral code beyond the dictum "do what thou will, but do no harm." The definition of what's harmful is entirely up to the individual.

As predicted by Aldous Huxley in his novel *Island*, psychology has emerged as the new arbiter of values. Making moral judgments is tricky, but we all think we know dysfunctional behavior when we see it. Of course, psychology is far from monolithic. All sorts of questions with enormous social implications are the subjects of ongoing debates as mysterious to outsiders as any papal convocation. The results of single experiments tend to be wildly overinterpreted by activists with social agendas of their own. Anyone who charted her life's course according to hot trends in psychology—from open marriage in the 1970s through confronting her parents with accusations of abuse based on "recovered" memories and bringing up children who were encouraged to "discover" their own values—has had a bumpy ride indeed.

In one respect both Maslow and Huxley were wrong. Organized religion did not wither away. On the contrary, evangelical and fundamentalist denominations grew stronger as Christians fled from liberal churches excessively preoccupied with values reorientation. Convinced, quite correctly, that they were the target of a campaign to brand them as ignorant hate-mongers, the religious right organized and began to flex its muscles politically. Thus began the culture war that continues to this day. For a time it seemed that the advocates of secularized, universalist values were destined to triumph. Americans believe in tolerance and, in general, they embraced the trend toward relaxed social standards and greater individual freedom. Moreover, the religious right probably did itself no favors by labeling their opponents as "relativists." This term hardly applies to Carl Rogers or to Abe Maslow, whose "religion of human nature" was based on the belief in inborn values and evolving levels of consciousness. A better term might be utopian, since many of the secularists' ideas would do quite nicely in a world without evil. At any rate, given a choice between relativism and absolutism, a term suggestive of Taliban-style fanaticism, many people would opt for the former.

In recent years, however, the secularist position has been losing ground. No doubt there are many reasons for this—the decline of the family and the failure of self-esteem education, frustration with the proliferation of self-proclaimed victims, a President of the United States who proved incapable of saying "what *is* is." Perhaps the overarching reason for this trend is that the Baby Boomers, whose generation embraced self-actualization so enthusiastically in the 1960s, are now entering the time of their lives when they begin to take stock. Humanistic psychology was supposed to unleash our creativity. A life devoted to accumulating personal growth experiences would enable each man and woman to construct a self that stands as a work of art, "the best self that we can possibly be." For many, this promise has proved hollow. The self-actualizers in Maslow's pantheon were supposedly so inner-directed that they could shrug off unsatisfying personal relationships without regret and improvise their own standards of ethics and value systems. Self-actualization taught us to regard friendship and love as disposable. Encounter groups put society in a confessional mode, erasing the old distinctions between public life and private, between deep relationships and shallow ones. Religion became a private matter, pursued through peak experiences, and humanistic books encouraged everyone to develop his or her own "personal mythology."

Taken to its logical end, the quest for truth through peak experiences led straight to that arid country known as Learyland, where life is reduced to a series of games played for one's personal amusement. Few people can abide in Learyland for very long. Most self-actualizers continued to search for love, and many tried to build an identity around belonging to one victim group or another, to the exclusion of the qualities that bind us together as civilized human beings—learning, tradition, loyalties, responsibilities, shared standards of behavior. Far from being enriched, the actualized self tends to be vain and radically deconstructed, bereft of connections to a larger sense of purpose or ideals, estranged from its past incarnations. It demands uncritical acceptance and, ultimately, an environment that is a mirror of its own concerns. If I'm a woman, then God must be a woman too; otherwise, what meaning can God possibly have for me? William Jefferson Clinton provided a textbook demonstration of the self-actualizer's approach to leadership during his eight years in the White House: instead of taking on the burden of the country's problems, he made the country take on the burden of *his* problems.

After the age of fifty or so, we begin to recognize that self-reinvention is a game that pays diminishing returns. No matter how hard we've worked on our careers, how many trips we've made to the gym, or how many mind-body workshops we've attended, the best we can hope for is maintenance. At some point in the not terribly distant future, "the best self we can possibly be" will be reduced to a heap of rotting bones and flesh or a container of ashes.

The contemplation of death has always been an occasion for human beings to look outward, focusing on the belief—or, for some, just the hope—that we're part of something greater than our fragile physical selves. Surely, contrary to the theory of Gordon Wasson, the origins of religion had less to do with mushroom-induced visions than with the inescapable mystery of mortality. Death, after all, makes the existence of a "god within" rather a moot point. Americans in the second half of the twentieth century were almost uniquely shielded from having to confront the reality of death. Thanks to modern medical science, many people could reach late middle age without having to confront the premature death of a loved one. Even the ravages of AIDS were concentrated within a small segment of the population, and the development of medication regimens soon offered at least some hope that the virus could be conquered.

Of course, there are exceptions. Many individuals do lose loved ones to devastating illnesses, accidents, or natural or manmade disasters. When tragedy strikes, psychologists have tended to medicalize its effects, redefining grief as "trauma." It is quite true that trauma can lead to long-term psychological problems, but trauma in itself is not an illness, just a fact of life. Unfortunately, grief, like guilt, is an emotion that makes self-actualizers uncomfortable. We accept that we can learn something useful from the plight of society's victims, but see little possibility of taking moral instruction from sinners or mourners. Their situations raise questions that we've already dismissed as having no good answers: Where does evil come from? Why must we die? The expectation that the grief-stricken will just get over it and return to "normal" functioning only leaves them feeling more isolated.

The banishment of religious references from the public sphere makes even talking about death a job for experts. It is a brave teacher who risks responding to her students' concerns about death without the guidance of an approved curriculum. Corporations and the media regularly call on trained specialists to advise us on how to cope with loss, and we have accepted the grief counselor as a fixture on the scene of every disaster. Only the occasional foreigner finds this development worthy of comment—like the Frenchman who lost a family member in the July 1996 crash of TWA flight 800. "Don't send us *psychologists!*" he exclaimed, according to the *New York Times.*

Nothing that follows is meant as a slur on individual grief counselors. Comforting the bereaved is a noble and often thankless calling, and those who meet the challenge seek to avail themselves of any techniques that may help. In fact, many certified grief counselors are clergy, healthcare professionals or dedicated volunteers who are required to have an academic credential. Still, psychologists have little to offer the grieving beyond a sympathetic ear and the obvious reassurances. When writers on grief theory try to go deeper, they typically assert the dubious premise that it is necessary to "work through" negative emotions lest they pile up inside and cause problems later on. Swiss psychologist Elisabeth Kübler-Ross popularized the notion that the grieving pass through five distinct stages: denial, anger, bargaining, depression and acceptance. Harvard's William Worden refined the list to four stages, ending with what the media now euphemistically choose to call "closure." Viewed from this perspective, mourning becomes just another mode of self-expression. Indeed, grief specialist Alan Wolfert of the Colorado Center for Loss and Life Transition has been quoted in *Time* magazine as calling grief an "art." Adds Wolfert pithily, "You have to feel it to heal it."[7]

During the first flush of enthusiasm over "grief work," as many as 10 percent of American school districts incorporated some form of "death education" into the curriculum, often as a unit of social studies, health or, strangely, home economics. Presented by teachers whose training may be limited to a one- or two-day workshop, such units are often nothing more than a series of conditioning exercises, designed to break down the cultural taboos surrounding the subject of death. Classes take field trips to morgues, funeral homes and crematoria, and in-class discussions revolve around sharing stories about the deaths of loved ones or, on occasion, the student's own suicidal fantasies. Junior and senior high school students are sometimes assigned to write their own obituaries, wills or even suicide notes.

Getting kids comfortable with the idea of death was supposed to enable them to think about it more sensibly, but it didn't always work that way. Jefferson County, Colorado, whose schools were among the leaders in adopting death education programs, began to question its approach when it experienced a wave of teen suicides—eighteen in a period of as many months, beginning in January 1985. In 1990 the ABC newsmagazine *20/20* aired a segment entitled "Death in the Classroom," which included an interview with Tara Becker, a former student of Jefferson County's Columbine High School, discussing how her own unsuccessful attempt at suicide came about after classes in death education:

"I had thought a lot about [suicide] as a possible option for several years," Becker said. "But I would never have gone through with it, never, because I wasn't brave enough. The things that we learned in the class taught us how to be brave enough to face death. We talked about what we wanted to look like in our caskets."

Nine years later, despite this early warning, Columbine High was still encouraging its students to imagine their own deaths. When eighteen-year-old Eric Harris submitted a paper for a psychology class describing a dream in which he and his friend Dylan Kleibold went on a shooting spree in a mall, his teacher, Tom Johnson, took no particular notice. After Harris and Kleibold acted out their murderous fantasies, killing thirteen people before turning their guns on themselves, Johnson was asked about the paper by a reporter who had heard it described by another student in the class. "I'm wondering, did I miss it as a warning sign?" Johnson mused. The paper hadn't struck him as ominous because, he explained, his students routinely fantasized in writing about antisocial or violent acts.[8]

After the massacre, Columbine High authorities decided that more grief work was in order. The National Association of School Psychologists sent in a team of volunteers who spent more than 1,500 hours counseling survivors in the first week after the tragedy alone. These sessions included group "debriefings," during which students were encouraged to share negative as well as positive memories of their murdered friends. Inevitably, some of the negative comments got back to victims' families, who were deeply wounded by them.

The belief that survivors need to work through their unresolved emotional issues with the deceased is one of the more questionable premises of grief theory. Surely, if there is any consolation in death it lies in the opportunity to forgive our departed loved ones all their shortcomings, and to extend that forgiveness to ourselves. Instead, patients in longer-term grief counseling are often urged to continue a one-sided argument with the deceased, an exercise that can set up a debilitating cycle of impotent anger and guilt.

Psychologists Roxane Cohen Silver and Camille Wortman were among the first to question publicly the assumptions of grief therapy, in a 1989 article entitled "The Myths of Coping with Loss," which appeared in the *Journal of Counseling and Clinical Psychology.* Their research found no evidence that working through the so-called stages of grief is a precondition of healing. On the contrary, the crucial step in recovering from trauma is the ability to "shape meaning" from the triggering event. Some people manage to do this fairly quickly, thanks to their pre-existing belief systems or attitudes. Others take longer.

Dr. George Bonanno of Columbia University Teachers College has also challenged the basic assumptions of grief theory. In one experiment, Bonanno studied widows and widowers and found that those who expressed positive emotions within a few months of bereavement were more likely to thrive over the next two years. Bonanno didn't know why this was so, though he speculated that upbeat people were more pleasant to be around and therefore got more social support from friends and acquaintances. He found no evidence that suppressing negative feelings—being "in denial"—caused serious problems to surface later on.

In a more controversial study, two Israeli researchers, Hanna Kaminer and Peretz Lavie, found that Holocaust survivors who suppressed their memories of the death camps enjoyed better health than those who did not.[9]

The belief that repression can be healthy is supported by studies of younger people as well. Jane Bybee of Northeastern University divided high school students into "repressors" and "sensitizers" as well as "intermediates" who fell somewhere in between these two extremes. The repressors in her study had better grades and superior social skills, and they were less likely to be depressed or anxious. Not surprisingly, Bybee suggests that students who are in control of their emotions are better able to concentrate on their studies and avoid acting out in socially unacceptable ways.

Such studies present problems for humanistically oriented therapists who believe that psychology has a mission to expose and correct social injustices. Testifying against a rapist may be the victim's civic duty, but how can a therapist advise a victim to come forward if she believes that doing so will prolong her psychological suffering? Therapists also worry that finding merit in repression presages a return to the 1950s mantra of adjustment for its own sake. Given the tendency of such principles to become oversold by zealous practitioners and pop psychology bestsellers, such worries can't be entirely dismissed.

The hottest movement in the field today is positive psychology, a term most closely associated with Martin E. P. Seligman, a recent president of the American Psychological Association and the author of a very useful guide to self-improvement entitled *What You Can Change . . . And What You Can't.* Seligman takes note of a phenomenon obvious to many social critics: the more we Americans talk about self-esteem and self-realization, the worse we feel. According to Seligman, diagnoses of depression have increased tenfold in the past fifty years. Depression is now so ubiquitous that it is considered "the common cold of mental illness."

The explanation for this epidemic of depression is not hard to find. We're all bombarded almost daily with the message that self-esteem is the key to happiness and success. But in reality, none of us is happy and successful all the time. We get laid off from our jobs, fail exams, fall in love with the wrong people, gain weight, lose money in the market and struggle through times when nothing seems to go right. On top of these problems, we're led to believe that they are a symptom of a fundamental inner flaw: low self-esteem. Werner Erhard, who managed to reduce self-esteem psychology to its crudest form, told audiences in so many words that all failure is willed.

In the past, literature, the arts, religion, the extended family—all reinforced the message that our petty personal problems were not important. What mattered was that each individual play his part, however humble, with dignity and honor. Modesty and caring for the needs of others were considered virtues. Today, they are more likely to be regarded as symptoms of a low self-image or codependency. Some therapists today even treat shyness as a disorder. The deconstructed self takes the epic of humanity and reduces it to a personal narrative, a one-man show. If the script goes wrong, the drama degenerates into soap opera, a saga of victimhood.

Seligman doesn't dismiss the idea that depression reflects a chemical imbalance in the brain. But he believes that much garden-variety (unipolar) depression is associated with negative thought patterns that he identifies as "learned helplessness" and excessive rumination. Women—and, one might add, sedentary intellectuals—seem especially prone to these styles of thinking, which may explain why they are more often diagnosed as depressed.

Interestingly, depressives don't necessarily have a distorted view of reality. In fact, they tend to be more realistic than their nondepressed counterparts. Therefore, according to Seligman, the best insurance against depression is to become the kind of person who reflexively sees the glass of opportunity as half-full, never half-empty. The idea that we can control our moods by thinking positively is certainly not new. Its history goes back to William James, the father of American psychology. Dale Carnegie and Rev. Norman Vincent Peale popularized variants of the method. Seligman insists that his positive psychology goes beyond just repeating nostrums "from the pink Sunday school world of happy events." Rather, it teaches specific skills designed to overcome negative thought patterns. This seems a bit unfair to James, who was hardly just a happy-talk merchant, and, for that matter, to Carnegie and Rev. Peale, whose ideas have helped millions.

Still, it may well be that Seligman is on to something. Positive psychology strategies are already part of many character education programs, and they certainly offer a vast improvement over self-esteem education. Instead of training children to become pint-size narcissists, the new curricula emphasize that happiness comes through practicing virtues like self-control, perseverance and gratitude.

Surprisingly, considering his harsh criticism of the self-esteem movement, Seligman has a great deal in common with Abe Maslow. A student of motivation theory, he wants to create an optimistic psychology, one that sees the human personality as more than just a collection of neuroses and psychological tics. Maslow started out as a behaviorist, studying primates. Seligman's roots are in cognitive psychology, the successor to behaviorism, and he began his studies by trying to discern the special qualities of his personal heroes, starting with Eleanor Roosevelt. Maslow called his models of psychological health "good human beings," while Seligman thinks of them as individuals who lead "good lives."

Despite these similarities, Seligman finds himself at odds with Maslow and humanistic psychology as a whole. His chief complaint is that Maslow and his followers abandoned rigorous science in favor of the pursuit of mysticism and New Age nostrums. But, one might point out, Maslow never set out to be unscientific. He began his studies of mysticism very reluctantly, and then only because he realized that he couldn't define psychological health without talking about values, and he couldn't explain values without taking into account the spiritual dimension of human nature.

Maslow admired the creative rebel, the outsider dedicated to "pushing the boundaries" and challenging social norms. As he himself recognized, there was often a fine line between heroic self-actualization and the manic phase of bipolar psychosis. By contrast, Seligman's model of the healthy personality as the striver who plays by the rules and is seldom discouraged, even to the point of being somewhat unreflective. Competitive athletes and successful insurance salesmen score well on his personality profile. Indeed, Met Life has already used the profile to identify candidates for sales positions. While it may be true that such people are unlikely to fall into depression, the prospect of a society filled with insurance salesmen is at least as dismaying as that of one dominated by depressed would-be artists and self-absorbed careerists. At a minimum, any model of psychological health must accept that a healthy society is made up of many different personality types. And even this is too simplistic. The real world is not a collection of types, but of individuals who may be dysfunctional and even deeply flawed morally but still make unique contributions. One thinks of the pioneering industrialist Henry Ford, who was also an irascible man and a notorious anti-Semite. Charles Lindbergh, who consulted with Ford on the design of the B-24, once wrote of him, "The world needs more men like him. More—but not too many more."

Much to his credit, Seligman understands that in the past, men and women of all personality types were insulated from depression by the values of their culture. Faith in God, country, scientific progress or the ultimate triumph of principles like justice and human rights gave them reason to be optimistic even when their personal circumstances were dire indeed. Seligman recognizes that the breakdown of belief has robbed Americans of "a context of meaning and hope." As he puts it, "When we need spiritual furniture, we look around and see that all the comfortable leather sofas and the stuffed chairs have been removed and all that's left to sit on is a small, frail folding chair: The self."

Unfortunately, as much as he longs for the "context" that values used to provide, Seligman is nervous about values in particular. He dislikes the effects of rampant individualism but has no desire to return to what he calls the old "Yankee self"—"the self our grandparents had," which "did little more than just behave." He also worries that the longing to recapture meaning is feeding "the current yearning for fundamentalist religion throughout the world."[10]

It is hard to see what American culture has done to deserve such dismissive treatment. Its core values, after all, are not just battered, over-stuffed sofas and easy chairs—inherited from our parents, presumably—that we settle into when we're worn out from pursuing our own interests. Millions of Americans still believe in these values and practice them in daily life. Christian fundamentalism may not be to Seligman's taste, but it seems to be remarkably successful at overcoming depression, alcoholism and addiction. Surely it is unfair, as well as a failure of curiosity, to dismiss it out of hand by lumping its adherents together with fanatics and terrorists. As for our American forebears, their "Yankee selves" did a lot more than just behave. These were the people who carved a nation out of the wilderness, established our constitutional democracy and fought a war to abolish slavery. It is quite true that the Yankee self routinely sacrificed its personal desires out of duty and obedience to a moral code that strikes many of us today as cruelly restrictive. But anyone familiar with historical documents and letters realizes that previous generations were capable of deep passions and florid outbursts of feeling that make contemporary Americans seem benumbed by comparison.

One month ago, even as I was writing the foregoing paragraph, my television screen carried the image of the north tower of the World Trade Center in flames. Later that morning, I stood on the roof of my apartment building and watched in horror as the south tower collapsed in a heap of smoke and ash. The days that followed put the question of individualism versus public values into a new perspective. Grief counselors had their place in offering comfort to the bereaved, but few people were turning to psychologists to explain the meaning of the tragedy. Instead, the sort of old-values people that the proponents of self-actualization psychology tend to scorn turned out to be the ones we looked toward to save us in a time of crisis. New Yorkers drew strength from the heroism of firefighters who gave their lives, rushing headlong into burning buildings in the attempt to save others. Catholics and non-Catholics alike were inspired by the story of Father Mychal Judge, the fire department chaplain who died while administering last rites at the disaster site and became the first officially identified victim of the tragedy. Prompted by our mayor, we thought about the example of Londoners who survived the Battle of Britain, and we knew that as they persevered, so could we. The Stars and Stripes were on display everywhere, even in some New York neighborhoods where one was previously more likely to see flyers for anarchist demonstrations and vegetarian communes. "God Bless America" became the unofficial anthem of the moment.

There were some who found these displays of community feeling ominous. For example, the "Letters to the Editor" section in the *New York Times* made it clear that a segment of educated opinion believed that the events of September 11 were just one more incident in a larger struggle between secularism and religion. One correspondent opined that not only "dogmatic religious movements" but also "political rhetoric" and "nationalism" are examples of "primitive emotions" that must give way to "revolutionary changes in how we think," based on the triumph of "reason"—as defined by people like himself, no doubt. Another argued that concerts of Christmas and Hanukkah music as well as holiday displays in department stores should be eliminated in favor of observances that give equal time to all the world's major religions.[11]

But surely, the lesson to be learned from the September 11 tragedy is just the opposite. Faced with shocking casualties and continued threats from enemies driven by hate, Americans sought to set aside their individual differences, at least for the moment, and unite behind symbols of our shared identity. At this time of crisis, the old-fashioned values of God and country proved to be far from obsolete. On the contrary, the deaths of police, firefighters and Pentagon employees, as well as civilians who took quick action to save others, demonstrated all too vividly how much we all depend on fellow citizens who live by these values every day and are prepared to risk everything for them at a moment's notice. The sacrifices willingly made by so many should make us skeptical of attempts to deconstruct Western values in the name of abstractions based on utopian fantasies of what human nature might be like in an ideal world.

Acknowledgments

The idea for this book came to me in 1987, shortly after John Alden Harvey, my boyfriend and life partner, was diagnosed with Parkinson's disease. In the decade that followed he suffered a series of neurological disasters, first depression, then slowly advancing dementia and, finally, death from a brain tumor. This private tragedy led me to take a jaundiced view of the constant drumbeat about the importance of self-esteem coming from educators, pop psychologists and the advice mavens. If a man who biked ten miles a day and ran the marathon in three hours could lose control of his mental faculties for no known reason, then there had to be something worth believing in that was larger than the self and its path toward fulfilling our "human potential."

With these doubts in mind, I dug out my tattered, yellowing copy of Abraham Maslow's bestseller, *Toward a Psychology of Being*. Older and more skeptical, if not necessarily wiser, I found that many of the ideas that were so exciting when I encountered them as a student in the 1960s now struck me as a virtual blueprint for the cultural ills of contemporary America—the pursuit of "truth" by way of psychedelic drugs and New Age nostrums, the need to undermine anyone who passes for an authority figure, the narcissistic preoccupation with our personal pain. After obtaining a copy of Maslow's posthumously published journals, I was surprised to discover that he, too, had doubts about the social impact of his theories. Although I would go on to write much that is critical of Maslow's ideas, I was always impressed by his intellectual honesty.

The search for more information on Maslow took me to the Archives of the History of American Psychology, located at the University of Akron in Ohio. In addition to the personal papers of Maslow and more than seven hundred other prominent American psychologists, this unique archive includes an extensive collection of films, photographs, journals and other materials. My thanks to the archive's director, Dr. David B. Baker, and his patient staff for all their help. Special thanks also to Dean Rogers of the Special Collections division of the Vassar College Libraries. During a period when the division was closed for extensive renovations, he assisted by locating the correspondence between Ruth Benedict and Abe Maslow.

Dr. William Coulson shared his reflections on his long partnership with Carl Rogers and provided me with much material, ranging from copies of his own numerous articles on the subject to the recording of Dixieland music cut by the Coulson Family Band. Vicki Marshall was unfailingly generous and candid in sharing her memories of Timothy Leary. Others who were especially helpful include Ruth Lewis, Gunther Weil, Herbert Kelman, Richard Ofshe, Dr. William E. Narrow, Director of the Psychopathology Research Program at the American Psychiatric Institute, Charles Platt, Roland Fox, Christina Hoff Sommers, Susan Brownmiller and Karla Jay.

Finally, thanks to my editor, Peter Collier, for having faith in this book and for his helpful questions and criticisms.

Notes

Foreword: The Road to Eupsychia

1. Irving Louis Horowitz, *C. Wright Mills: An American Utopian* (New York: Free Press, 1983), p. 4.
2. James Miller, *Democracy Is in the Streets: From Port Huron to the Siege of Chicago* (New York: Simon & Schuster, 1987), p. 322.
3. Edward Hoffman, *The Right to Be Human: A Biography of Abraham Maslow* (Commack, New York: Four Worlds Press, 1988), pp. 258–59.

Chapter 1: The Rise of Relativism

1. Franz Boas, "A Year among the Eskimo," in *A Franz Boas Reader: The Shaping of American Anthropology, 1883–1911,* ed. George W. Stocking Jr. (Chicago: University of Chicago Press, 1974), p. 55.
2. Boas, "The Background of My Early Thinking," in *Franz Boas Reader,* ed. Stocking, p. 41. Originally published by Boas as "An Anthropologist's Credo" in the *Nation* in 1938.
3. Boas, "Human Faculty As Determined by Race," in *Franz Boas Reader,* ed. Stocking, p. 226.
4. For more on Boas's ideas, see Melville J. Herskovits, *Franz Boas: The Science of Man in the Making* (Clifton, New Jersey: Kelley, 1973).
5. Du Bois wrote this in *Black Folks, Then and Now* (1939), quoted in David Droge, "Boundary Work in the Public Rhetoric of Intellectuals: Franz Boas' Atlanta University Commencement Address As a Refutation of White

Supremacists Science," available via University of Puget Sound website (www.ups.edu).

6. Boas, "American Nationalism and World War I," in *Franz Boas Reader*, ed. Stocking, p. 332. This essay was originally a letter to the *New York Times*, published 8 January 1916 under the headline "Why German-Americans Blame America."

7. Benedict's biographical account is found in "The Story of My Life," included in: Margaret Mead, *An Anthropologist at Work: Writings of Ruth Benedict* (Boston: Houghton Mifflin, 1959), pp. 97–110.

8. Mead, *Anthropologist at Work*, p. 119.

9. Ibid., p. 120.

10. Judith Modell, *Ruth Benedict: Patterns of a Life* (London: Chatto & Windus, 1984), p. 154.

11. Hilary Lapsley, *Margaret Mead and Ruth Benedict: The Kinship of Women* (Amherst: University of Massachusetts Press, 1999), p. 226.

12. Margaret Mead, *Blackberry Winter: My Earlier Years* (New York: Kodansha, 1995), p. 115.

13. Ibid., p. 80. For more on her reasoning, here with respect to Sapir, see p. 30.

14. Lapsley, *Margaret Mead and Ruth Benedict*, pp. 120–25.

15. Derek Freeman, *The Fateful Hoaxing of Margaret Mead: A Historical Analysis of Her Samoan Research* (Boulder, Colorado: Westview Press, 1999), pp. 230–31. In addition to reconstructing Mead's activities in Samoa, almost day by day, Freeman reprints her correspondence with Boas in full. This volume continues the argument begun in *Margaret Mead and Samoa*, later retitled *Margaret Mead and the Heretic* (Victoria, Australia: Penguin Books, 1996).

16. Mead's letter is reprinted in Freeman, *Fateful Hoaxing*, p. 231.

17. Mead, *Blackberry Winter*, p. 121.

18. Edward Sapir, "Observations on the Sex Problem in America," *American Mercury*, vol. 16, pp. 413–20; also, Lapsley, *Margaret Mead and Ruth Benedict*, pp. 191–93.

19. Lapsley, *Margaret Mead and Ruth Benedict*, pp. 144, 238.

20. Freeman, *Fateful Hoaxing*, p. 212.

21. Modell, *Ruth Benedict: Patterns*, p. 310; Lapsley, *Margaret Mead and Ruth Benedict*, p. 258.

22. Lapsley, *Margaret Mead and Ruth Benedict*, p. 140.

23. Modell, *Ruth Benedict: Patterns*, p. 310; Lapsley, *Margaret Mead and Ruth Benedict*, p. 259. Politics was a major source of the friction. Benedict's active participation in numerous Communist fronts was a principle reason why the department was named by John Dewey and Sidney Hook as a "Stalinist outpost," and during the period of the Hitler-Stalin pact, its reputation

as a nest of fellow travelers was a serious matter. Lapsley reflects Benedict's view of the matter when she calls Linton's grumblings about this problem "sinister" and accuses him of "a program of red-baiting" as well as "mud-slinging." Notwithstanding, when Benedict volunteered her services to the Office of War Information, she was denied a top-secret security clearance.

24. Ruth Benedict, "Anthropology and the Abnormal," *Journal of General Psychology,* vol. 10, no. 2, pp. 59–82.

25. Marvin Harris, *The Rise of Anthropological Theory: A History of Theories of Culture* (New York: Thomas Y. Crowell, 1968). "In its least flattering light," writes Harris, the message of *Patterns of Culture* can be summed up as "the observation that some cultures are different and others are similar." The discussion here of objections to Benedict's book draws on his discussion, especially pp. 398–407.

26. Modell, *Ruth Benedict: Patterns,* p. 177.

27. Ruth Benedict, *Patterns of Culture* (Boston: Houghton Mifflin, 1989), p. 277.

28. Ibid., pp. 271, 278.

Chapter 2: Fully Human

1. Richard J. Lowry, ed., *The Journals of Abraham Maslow* (Monterey, California: Brooks/Cole Publishing), vol. 2, p. 958. Additional information on Maslow's childhood and family was provided by Ruth Lewis, via letter. See also, Edward Hoffman, *The Right to Be Human: A Biography of Abraham Maslow* (Commack, New York: Four World Press, 1997).

2. A favorite story; see Larry Gross "Abe Maslow: The Mystery of Health," typescript, Maslow Papers, Archives of the History of American Psychology, University of Akron. Maslow also talked about his upbringing and early religious experiences to Dorothy Lee's class at Harvard. See transcript, Dorothy Lee's Freshman Seminar on Autobiography, Harvard, October 1960, Maslow Papers.

3. Larry Gross typescript.

4. Dorothy Lee's Freshman Seminar, pp. 23–24.

5. Undated correspondence, Maslow Papers, M1910, M399.1 & 399.2.

6. Willard B. Frick, *Humanistic Psychology: Conversations with Abraham Maslow, Gardner Murphy, Carl Rogers* (Bristol, Indiana: Wyndham Hall Press, 1989; first pub. 1971), p. 19.

7. Report to the Social Sciences Research Council, Maslow Papers.

8. Failing to find this paper in Benedict's archive, some have questioned whether she ever used these terms. Maslow explains in a letter to Weston LeBarre, dated 23 February 1967, that Benedict gave him her only copy of the lecture notes, which he later lost.

9. Maslow reported his discussion of the Benedictine Enigma to Ruth in a letter dated 20 December 1939, Ruth Fulton Benedict Papers, Section 32.8, Vassar College.

10. Formerly restricted correspondence, from Margaret Mead Papers, TR2, Library of Congress. Quoted in Hilary Lapsley, *Margaret Mead and Ruth Benedict: The Kinship of Women* (Amherst: University of Massachusetts Press, 1999), p. 262.

11. Quoted material in this section is selected from chapters eleven and twelve of Maslow, *Motivation and Personality,* 3rd rev. ed. (New York: Longman, 1987), esp. pp. 131, 132, 143, 154.

12. Frick, *Humanistic Psychology,* p. 42.

13. "In my innocence he taught me a great deal...." Maslow to Dr. Amram Scheinfeld, 29 April 1970, Maslow Papers.

14. Maslow, *Motivation and Personality,* p. 120.

15. Ibid., pp. 163–65.

16. See pp. xxxi–xxxii of Lowry's foreword to the third edition of *Toward a Psychology of Being* (New York, John Wiley & Sons, 1999). A version of Maslow's speech constitutes chapter six, "Cognition of Being in the Peak-Experiences."

17. Hoffman, *The Right to Be Human,* p. 207.

18. For more on the humanistic movement and its origins, see Roy Jose de Carvallho, *The Growth Hypothesis in Psychology* (San Francisco: EMText, 1991), pp. 16–17.

19. Hoffman, *The Right to Be Human,* pp. 247–48.

20. *Eupsychian Management* has been reissued as: Abraham H. Maslow, *Maslow on Management* (New York: John Wiley & Sons, 1998). See pp. 20–23, 72, 243.

21. Craig D. Rose, "Second Time Around: Latest Venture into Computer Making Is Therapy for Andy Kay," *San Diego Union-Tribune,* 16 September 1998, p. C-1. Also, "The Enlightened Manager's Guidebook," *Inc.,* 1 October 1998.

22. *Journals of Abraham Maslow,* vol. 1, pp. 32–33.

23. Ibid., p. 157.

24. Quoted in Marty Jezer, *Abbie Hoffman, American Rebel* (New Brunswick, New Jersey: Rutgers University Press, 1992), p. 22. My interpretation of Hoffman owes much to Jezer, one of the few writers on Hoffman to grasp the importance of Maslow's influence.

Chapter 3: Mushroom People

1. Timothy Leary, *Flashbacks: A Personal and Cultural History of an Era* (New York: Putnam's, 1981), pp. 110–11.

2. Lisa Bieberman, "The Psychedelic Experience," *New Republic,* 5 August 1967.

3. Edward Hoffman, *The Right to Be Human: A Biography of Abraham Maslow* (Commack, New York: Four World Press, 1997), pp. 265–66.

4. Abraham Maslow, *Toward a Psychology of Being,* 3rd ed. (New York, John Wiley & Sons, 1999), p. 120.

5. Ralph Barton Perry, *The Thought and Character of William James* (Nashville, Tennessee: Vanderbilt University Press), pp. 121, 266; Renee Tursi, "William James's Narrative of Habit," *Style,* vol. 33, no.1 (spring 1999), p. 67.

6. Howard M. Feinstein, *Becoming William James,* 2nd ed. (Ithaca, New York: Cornell University Press, 1999; first pub. 1984), p. 310.

7. As quoted in Dmitri Tymoczko, "The Nitrous Oxide Philosopher," *Atlantic Monthly,* vol. 277, no. 5 (May 1996), pp. 93–101. For James' description, below, see William James, *The Varieties of Religious Experience* (New York: Touchstone, 1997), pp. 395–96.

8. Richard M. Restak, M.D., *Receptors* (New York: Bantam, 1994), esp. pp. 36–37. For Gordon Wasson, see John W. Allen, *Wasson's First Voyage: The Redisovery of Entheogenic Mushrooms* (Seattle: RaverBooks, 1997).

9. Jay Stevens, *Storming Heaven: LSD and the American Dream* (New York: Atlantic Monthly Press, 1987), pp. 62–63, 173. Cohen's report was in the *Journal of Neurology and Mental Disease,* vol. 130.

10. Peter D. Kramer, *Listening to Prozac: A Psychiatrist Explores Anti-Depressant Drugs and the Making of the Self* (New York: Viking, 1993), p. 222.

11. Restak, *Receptors,* p. 55.

12. Leary, *Flashbacks,* pp. 24–27.

13. Leary's letter is quoted by Robert Forte in *Timothy Leary: Outside Looking In,* ed. Robert Forte (Rochester, Vermont: Park Street Press, 1999), p. 5.

14. Leary, *Flashbacks,* pp. 17–18.

15. Phone interview with Herb Kelman, 3 March 2001.

16. Stevens, *Storming Heaven,* pp. 132–33.

17. Richard Alpert, *Our-Story/My-Story/Your-Story/His-Story* (San Cristobal, New Mexico: Lama Foundation, 1970).

18. Maslow Papers, M433.

19. Timothy Leary, *High Priest* (Berkeley: Ronin, 1995), pp. 214–32; Leary, *Flashbacks,* p. 100.

20. For a reprint of the report that Smith wrote after the New Year's Day trip, see Huston Smith, *Cleansing the Doors of Perception* (New York: Jeremy P. Tarcher, 2000), pp. 10–13; for Walter Clark's comment, see Forte, *Outside Looking In,* p. 47.

21. Michael Hollingshead, *The Man Who Turned On the World,* ch. 1. Via internet, The Schaffer Library of Drug Policy, www.druglibrary.org.

22. Leary, *High Priest,* pp. 256–57.
23. Kelman interview. Brendan Maher's account is found in an editorial of the newsletter of the Massachusetts Psychological Association, undated, Maslow Papers, M433.

Chapter 4: Miracles

1. Timothy Leary, *High Priest* (Berkeley: Ronin, 1995), p. 295.
2. For first-person accounts of the day's events, see Huston Smith, *Cleansing the Doors of Perception* (New York: Jeremy P. Tarcher, 2000), pp. 99–107; and Jean Malmgren's interview with Mike Young, "Tune In, Turn On, Get Well?" *St. Petersburg Times,* 27 November 1994. Michael Hollingshead also gives a vivid, if factually garbled account in *The Man Who Turned On the World,* via internet, The Schaffer Library of Drug Policy, www.druglibrary.org. Hollingshead's narrative suggests that a second subject may have received Thorazine.
3. Rick Doblin, "Pahnke's Good Friday Experiment: A Long-Term Follow-Up and Methodological Critique," *Journal of Transpersonal Psychology,* vol. 23, no. 1 (1991), pp. 1–28.
4. Smith, *Cleansing the Doors,* pp. 1–7, 141.
5. *Journals of Abraham Maslow,* vol. I, p. 118.
6. Richard Alpert, *Our-Story, My-Story, Your-Story, His-Story* (San Cristobal, New Mexico: Lama Foundation, 1970).
7. Maslow Papers, M433.
8. Leary, *High Priest,* pp. 132–33.
9. Sybille Bedford, *Aldous Huxley: A Biography* (New York: Knopf / Harper & Row, 1974), p. 717.
10. Dana L. Farnsworth, "Hallucinogenic Agents," *Journal of the American Medical Association,* 4 September 1963; Jay Stevens, *Storming Heaven: LSD and the American Dream* (New York: Atlantic Monthly Press, 1987), pp. 182–83.
11. A few years later, it was revealed that the Society for the Study of Human Ecology, which had funded some of the early LSD research at Harvard, was a CIA front. Herb Kelman had received a few thousand dollars from the foundation to prepare the proceedings of a conference for publication, a project that had nothing to do with LSD. A leftist, Kelman was outraged when he learned that he had taken tainted money, and he contacted a reporter for the *Boston Globe.* On the basis of Kelman's interview with the *Globe,* Leary would later imply that Kelman was a CIA plant on the Harvard faculty. For the jealousy excuse, see Leary, *Flashbacks,* p. 266.
12. Brendan Maher, Newsletter of the Massachusetts Psychological Assn., Maslow Papers, M433.

13. Andrew Weil, *The Natural Mind: An Investigation of Drugs and the Higher Consciousness* (Boston: Hougton Mifflin, 1998), p. 201.

14. Art Kleps, *Millbrook: A Narrative of the Early Years of American Psychedelianism* (Austin, Texas: Neo-American Church, 1997; first pub. 1975).

15. Jim Chevallier, "Chez Jim: Ovum Visits Castalia," available on the Chez Jim website, www.jimcheval.com.

16. Kleps, *Millbrook*, ch. 3.

17. Lisa Bieberman, "Phanerothyme: A Western Approach to the Religious Use of Psychochemicals," Psychedelic Information Center, 1968. Available online through the Council on Spiritual Practices at www.csp.org.

18. Rosemary Woodruff, "Illusions," in *Timothy Leary: Outside Looking In*, ed. Robert Forte (Rochester, Vermont: Park Street Press, 1999), p. 337. Leary's account in *Flashbacks* suggests that he did hear, but didn't think it would be wise to stop on the bridge and pitch the box over the side.

19. U.S. Court of Appeals, Fifth Circuit, No. 23570, 1967 C05.643, 383 F2d 851, 29 September 1967, *Leary v. United States of America*.

20. The September 1966 *Playboy* interview is reprinted in Timothy Leary, *The Politics of Ecstasy* (Berkeley: Ronin, 1998). This edition contains just the first half of the chapters found in the 1973 book of the same title. The remaining chapters were reissued as *Turn On, Tune In, Drop Out*.

21. Cohen's testimony is quoted in Stevens, *Storming Heaven*, p. 279.

22. *San Francisco Oracle*, no. 7, available online at www.sirius.com.

23. Bieberman, "The Psychedelic Experience."

24. Paul Krassner's accusation is in "The Love Song of Timothy Leary," *Tikkun*, vol. 14, no. 6 (November 1999), p. 69; for Joanna Harcourt-Smith's rebuttal, see "Letters to the Editor," *Tikkun*, vol. 15, no. 2, p. 2.

25. *Outside Looking In*, ed. Forte, esp. pp. 54, 238.

26. "The Psychedelic Vision at the Turn of the Millennium: Discussion with Andrew Weil, M.D.," *Bulletin of the Multidisciplinary Association for Psychedelic Studies (MAPS)*, vol. 8, no. 1 (Spring 1998), pp. 28–37.

Chapter 5: Good Boy No More

1. Peter D. Kramer, M.D., Introduction to the 1995 edition of Carl R. Rogers, *On Becoming a Person: A Therapist's View of Psychotherapy* (Boston: Houghton Mifflin, 1961).

2. Biographical background on Rogers is taken from Rogers' essay "This Is Me," found in *The Carl Rogers Reader*, ed.Howard Kirschenbaum and Valerie Land Henderson (Boston: Houghton Mifflin, 1989). Also from Kirschenbaum's authorized biography, *On Becoming Carl Rogers* (New York: Delacorte Press, 1979).

3. Kirschenbaum, *On Becoming Carl Rogers,* p. 45.

4. For the Sommerville project, see E. Torrey Fuller, M.D., *Freudian Fraud: The Malignant Effect of Freud's Theory on American Thought and Culture* (New York: HarperCollins, 1992), pp. 168–69.

5. Rogers, *On Becoming a Person,* pp. 173–79. The Maslow quotation is from *Motivation and Personality,* 3rd rev. ed. (New York: Longman, 1987).

6. *Journals of Abraham Maslow,* vol. 1, p. 177.

7. Ibid., p. 157.

8. William Marra, "We Overcame Their Traditions, We Overcame Their Faith: An Interview with Dr. William Coulson," *The Latin Mass: Chronicle of a Catholic Reform,* January-February 1994.

9. William R. Coulson, *Groups, Gimmicks and Instant Gurus* (New York: Harper & Row, 1972), pp. 118–19.

10. Rosemary Curb and Nancy Manahan, eds., *Lesbian Nuns: Breaking Silence* (Tallahassee, Florida: Naiad Press, 1985), p. 13.

11. Ibid., p. 328.

12. Marra interview.

13. William R. Coulson, "Full Hearts and Empty Heads: The Price of Certain Recent Programs in Humanistic Psychology," expanded from an address at a conference on The Nature and Tasks of a Personalistic Pyschology, held at Franciscan University, Steubenville, Ohio, 20 October 1994.

14. Jonathan Freedland, "Sins of the Fathers," *The Guardian,* 21 December 1993, p. T8; see also, Larry B. Stammer, "Seminary's 'Terrible Truths' Are Detailed," *Los Angeles Times,* 1 December 1993, p. A3.

15. Coulson, *Groups, Gimmicks and Instant Gurus,* p. 4.

16. *Journals of Abraham Maslow,* vol. 1, p. 161.

17. Don Clark, *Loving Someone Gay* (New York: New American Library, 1977), pp. 268–72.

18. W. R. Coulson, "You Can't Do That: When Compassion Calls for Telling the Truth," Collected Papers from the NARTH Annual Conference, 29 July 1995.

19. Coulson, *Groups, Gimmicks and Instant Gurus,* p. 53.

20. Clark, *Loving Someone Gay,* pp. 133–37.

21. Harold C. Lyons Jr., *It's Me and I'm Here* (New York: Delacorte, 1974); for his arrest, see Sandra Boodman, "Extrovert or Exploiter? Federal Official Charged with Sex Offenses," *Washington Post,* 15 November 1981.

22. Quoted in Coulson, "Full Hearts and Empty Heads."

23. Carl R. Rogers, Ph.D., *Carl Rogers on Encounter Groups* (New York: Harper & Row, 1970), pp. 20–21.

24. This exchange was recorded in the 1976 documentary *Reflections,* released by the WBSI.

25. Kirschenbaum, *On Becoming Carl Rogers,* pp. 354–60.
26. Carl Rogers, *Carl Rogers on Personal Power* (New York: Dell/Delta, 1977), p. 164.
27. Ibid., pp. 220–33.
28. Carl Rogers, "Speaking Personally," in *The Carl Rogers Reader,* pp. 47–48.
29. Coulson, "Full Hearts and Empty Heads."
30. Rogers, "Speaking Personally," p. 48.
31. Natalie Rogers, "The Creative Journey," in *Positive Regard: Carl Rogers and Other Notables He Influenced,* ed. Howard Kirschenbaum (Palo Alto, California: Science & Behavior Books, 1995), p. 176.
32. Natalie Rogers, *Emerging Woman: A Decade of Midlife Transition* (Santa Rosa, California: Personal Press, 1980), p. 25.
33. Ibid., pp. 59–60.
34. Natalie Rogers, "The Creative Journey," p. 185.
35. Natalie Rogers, *Emerging Woman,* pp. 176–77.
36. Carl Rogers, "Speaking Personally," p. 52.
37. Ibid.

Chapter 6: Revolutionary Science

1. A. H. Maslow, *Religion, Values and Peak Experiences* (New York: Penguin, 1970), see esp. pp. 3–4, 28, 50, 76.
2. Phone interview with Gunther Weil, 17 October 2001.
3. *Journals of Abraham Maslow,* vol. 1, p. 440.
4. Ibid., pp. 528–29.
5. Abbie Hoffman, "Revolution for the Hell of It," excerpted in *The Best of Abbie Hoffman* (New York: Four Walls Eight Windows, 1989), p. 3.
6. Marty Jezer, *Abbie Hoffman, American Rebel* (New Brunswick, New Jersey: Rutgers University Press, 1992), pp. 100–1.
7. Abraham Maslow, "Critique of Self-Actualization Theory," in *Future Visions: The Unpublished Papers of Abraham Maslow,* ed. Edward Hoffman (Thousand Oaks: Sage Publications, 1996) p. 29.
8. *Journals of Abraham Maslow,* vol. 2, pp. 1162–63.
9. Jane Howard, *Please Touch: A Guided Tour of the Human Potential Movement* (New York: McGraw-Hill, 1970), p. 36.
10. Edward Hoffman, *The Right to Be Human: A Biography of Abraham Maslow* (Commack, New York: Four World Press, 1997), pp. 288–93.
11. Maslow to "Dave and Sue, Sonny and the others," 23 August 1965, Maslow Papers, M449.2. For the "no real 'knowledge'" comment, see the *Journals,* vol. 1, p. 577. For Maslow's views on aggridants in general see, for example, *Maslow on Management* (New York: John Wiley & Sons, 1998), pp. 167–76.

12. *Journals of Abraham Maslow,* vol. 1, pp. 584–86. Maslow later wrote "Synanon and Eupsychia," which appeared in the *Journal of Humanistic Psychology,* vol. 7, in 1967, and the program received a positive mention in the 1968 edition of *Toward a Psychology of Being.*

13. Hoffman, *The Right to Be Human,* pp. 315–19.

14. For more on Synanon and its enemies, see Dave Mitchell, Cathy Mitchell and Richard Ofshe, *The Light on Synanon* (New York: Seaview Books, 1980); also, William Olin, *Escape from Utopia: My Ten Years at Synanon* (Santa Cruz, California: Unity Press, 1980).

15. Arthur Janov, *The Primal Revolution: Toward a Real World* (New York: Simon & Schuster, 1972), esp. pp. 31, 220. For Maslow and "the jungle outlook," see Hoffman, *The Right to Be Human,* pp. 158–59.

16. For the history of the Center, see Carol Lynn Mithers, *Therapy Gone Mad: The True Story of Hundreds of Patients and a Generation Betrayed* (Reading, Massachusetts: Addison-Wesley, 1994). See also Doni Whitsett's review in *Cultic Studies Journal,* vol. 11, no. 2 (1994).

17. Carol Lynn Mithers, "The Silent Scream," *The Buzz,* August 1994.

18. Margaret Thaler Singer, with Janja Lalich, *Crazy Therapies: What Are They? How Do They Work?* (San Francisco: Jossey-Bass, 1996).

19. William R. Coulson, *Groups, Gimmicks and Instant Gurus* (New York: Harper & Row, 1972), p. 144.

20. L. L. Glass and M. A. Kirsch, "Psychiatric Disturbances Associated with Erhard Seminars Training," *American Journal of Psychiatry,* vol. 134, no. 1 (March 1977), pp. 245–47; and a follow-up by the same authors, vol. 134, no. 4 (Dec. 1977), pp. 1254–58. Also: J. Simon, "Observations of 67 Patients Who Took Erhard Seminars Training," *American Journal of Psychiatry,* vol. 135 (1978), pp. 686–91.

21. For biographical information on Erhard, see Steven Pressman, *Outrageous Betrayal: The Dark Journey of Werner Erhard from est to Exile* (New York: St. Martin's Press, 1993). For an interview with Erhard and a skeptical appraisal of *60 Minutes'* charges, see Dan Wakefield, "Erhard in Exile," *Common Boundary: Between Spirituality and Psychotherapy,* March-April 1994; and Robert W. Welkos, "Scientologists Ran Campaign to Discredit Erhard, Detective Says," *Los Angeles Times,* 29 December 1991.

22. Alison Bass, "Soul Training: At the Forum, a Retooled Version of the Controversial EST Movement," *Boston Globe,* 3 March 1999, p. F1. See also, Charlotte Faltermayer, "The Best of est?" *Time,* vol. 151, no. 10 (16 March 1998).

23. The Greek root of *phrenic* refers to the mind—as in schizophrenia, or split-mind; it can also refer to the diaphragm, not the same thing as the lungs.

24. Patti DeRosa, "Diversity Training: In Search of Anti-Racism," *Bright Ideas,* newsletter of SABES (System for Adult Basic Education Support), Adult and Learning Services, Massachusetts Department of Education, via internet at www.sabes.org.

25. Leonard Hughes, "The Pangs of Prejudice: Workshop Fights Bias by Facing Up to It," *Washington Post,* 19 September 1992, p. J3.

26. Itabari Njeri, "The Conquest of Hate by Turning Conflict Inside Out: A New Breed of Mediators Finds a Way to Bring Peace to the City," *Los Angeles Times Magazine,* 25 April 1993, p. 20.

27. Kirstin Downey Grimsley, "Sometimes 'Sensitivity' Is the Problem," *Washington Post,* 3 November 1999, p. E1; D'Vera Cohn and Ellen Nakashima, "Crossing Racial Lines: For Now, Anyway, a Tie That Binds," *Washington Post,* 13 December 1996, p. A1; Ellen Graham, "Students Recall First Brushes with Prejudice," *Wall Street Journal,* 10 April 1995, p. B1.

28. Charles Kors, "Thought Reform, 101," *Reason,* March 2000, pp. 26–34.

29. Dr. Roland Fox, interviewed by phone, 10 July 2001.

30. Frederic U. Dicker, "Gov Tells Cig Activists to Butt Out," *New York Post,* 19 May 2001, p. 7.

31. James L. Nolan Jr., *The Therapeutic State* (New York: New York University Press, 1998), pp. 2–4. Nolan has much to say on the question of how therapeutic values have come to dominate political rhetoric, the law and public policy.

Chapter 7: The Man Question

1. Betty Friedan, *The Feminine Mystique* (New York: Penguin, 1963), p. 285.

2. Philip Wylie, *A Generation of Vipers* (New York: Rinehart, 1942), pp. 184–204.

3. Judith Hennessee, *Betty Friedan: Her Life* (New York: Random House, 1999), p 36.

4. For Friedan's early career, see Daniel Horowitz, *Betty Friedan and the Making of the Feminine Mystique: The American Left, the Cold War, and Modern Feminism* (Amherst: University of Massachusetts Press, 1999).

5. Carl Friedan, "Living with Insanity," via internet.

6. Horowitz (*Betty Friedan,* p. 217) concludes that Friedan hid her radical past out of self-protection, because "she knew what happened to others with a past like hers." This may be true, but it doesn't necessarily follow that her "second narrative"—which attributes her discovery of the feminine mystique to her personal experiences as a woman and a writer—is a myth. The left didn't recognize Friedan's problem as worthy of attention, and her book probably came about more in spite of her leftist past than because of it.

7. Betty Friedan, *It Changed My Life: Writings on the Women's Movement* (Cambridge, Massachusetts: Harvard University Press, 1998), p. 160.

8. Karla Jay, via e-mail.

9. Abraham Maslow, *Motivation and Personality,* 3rd rev. ed. (New York: Longman, 1987), pp. 146, 157.

10. Susan Brownmiller, *In Our Time: Memoir of a Revolution* (New York: Dial Press, 1999), p. 173.

11. Abraham Maslow, "Our Maligned Animal Nature," *Journal of Psychology,* no. 28 (1949), p. 277.

12. James H. Jones, *Alfred C. Kinsey: A Public/Private Life* (New York: W. W. Norton, 1997), p. 327.

13. Ibid., pp. 579, 707, 710.

14. Judith A. Reisman, *Kinsey, Crimes and Consequences: The Red Queen and the Grand Scheme* (Arlington, Virginia: Institute for Media Education, 1998), pp. 164–65, 179.

15. Ibid., pp. 111–12.

16. Ibid., pp. xx–xxi. The October 1996 issue of *The Humanist* includes an interview with Kinsey Institute director John Bancroft by Gary Pool in which Bancroft dismisses Reisman as a "right-wing moralist." Bancroft can't say why Kinsey hid the source of his child orgasm data, but adds, "My hunch is he thought people would not take these data seriously enough. Although why it should make any difference whether it was one pedophile or three is debatable." In the end, Pool concludes, "Bancroft feels that the real impact of Alfred Kinsey's findings has little to do with the precision of his figures, but rather with the fact that he confronted people with a view of sexuality quite different from the one to which they had been accustomed." No doubt Bancroft is right, but this doesn't make it science.

17. Brownmiller, *In Our Time,* p. 307.

18. Judith Lewis Herman with Lisa Hirschman, *Father-Daughter Incest,* 2nd ed. (Cambridge: Harvard University Press, 2000), pp. 202–3.

19. Liaa Manshel, *Nap Time: The True Story of Sexual Abuse at a Suburban Day-Care Center* (New York: William Morrow, 1990), p. 167.

20. Ellen Bass and Laura Davis, *The Courage to Heal: A Guide for Women Survivors of Child Abuse* (New York: Harper Perennial, 1988), pp. 34–39. E. Sue Blume, *Secret Survivors* (New York: Ballantine, 1990), p. xxvii.

21. Alice Miller, *The Drama of the Gifted Child: The Search for the True Self,* rev. ed. (New York: Basic Books, 1994), pp. 88–89 and ff.

22. For an overview of these issues, see Robert A. Baker, ed., *Child Sexual Abuse and False Memory Syndrome* (Amherst, New York: Prometheus, 1998). The Gardner reference is in chapter two, Mary Sykes Wylie, "Shadow of a

Doubt." See also Bruce Rind, Philip Tromovitch and Robert Bauserman, "A Meta-Analytic Examination of Assumed Properties of Child Sexual Abuse Using College Samples," *Psychological Bulletin,* July 1998; and Mary Eberstadt, " 'Pedophilia Chic' Reconsidered: The Taboo against Sex with Children Continues to Erode," *Weekly Standard,* 1–8 January 2000.

23. Baker, *Child Sexual Abuse and False Memory Syndrome,* p. 13.

Chapter 8: The Malpsychian Classroom

1. William R. Coulson, *Groups, Gimmicks and Instant Gurus* (New York: Harper & Row, 1972), p. 155. For the background of this remark and Coulson's reflections, see John Neider's interview with Coulson, "Education That Harms Good Kids," *The Art of Family Living,* December 1993, available at www.aofl.org.

2. Quoted in Diane Ravitch, *Left Back: A Century of Failed School Reforms* (New York: Simon & Schuster, 2000), p. 73.

3. Carl R. Rogers, "Personal Thoughts on Teaching and Learning," reprinted in *The Carl Rogers Reader,* ed.Howard Kirschenbaum and Valerie Land Henderson (Boston: Houghton Mifflin, 1989), pp. 301–4.

4. Carl R. Rogers, "Significant Learning in Therapy and Education," reprinted in *On Becoming a Person* (Boston: Houghton Mifflin, 1995), pp. 279–95.

5. Neider interview with Coulsen.

6. *Carl Rogers Reader,* pp. 420–29.

7. Howard Kirschenbaum, *On Becoming Carl Rogers* (New York: Delacorte Press, 1979), pp. 378–80.

8. John Holt, *Escape from Childhood* (Cambridge, Massachusetts: Holt Associates, 1995), pp. 213, 216. On its original publication in 1973, the *New York Times* reviewer found Holt's ideas "astonishingly cogent."

9. Herbert Kohl, *The Discipline of Hope* (New York: Simon & Schuster, 1998), p. 313.

10. Ibid., p. 323.

11. Brian K. Hixson, "How Tests Change a Teacher," *New York Times,* 25 January 2000, p. A23. See also an article by Maryann Dickar, a white teacher of minority students in Brooklyn from 1988 to 1991. Dickar suggests that Kohl and Kozol err in teaching children that they can overcome racism through "individual effort." She calls for still more radical "discourses," presenting racism as a structural problem that transcends color. Dickar, "Teaching in Our Underwear: The Liabilities of Whiteness in the Multi-Racial Classroom," *The Researcher,* vol. 11, no. 2.

12. Stanley Coopersmith, *The Antecedents of Self-Esteem* (San Francisco: W. H. Freeman, 1967). Coopersmith's article "Studies in Self-Esteem" appeared in the February 1968 issue of *Scientific American.*

13. For an account of the movement's failure in Boston see Roland S. Barth, *Open Education and the American School* (New York: Agathon, 1972).

14. The key Values Clarification texts are Raths, Harmin and Simon, *Values and Teaching: Working with Values in the Classroom* (Columbus, Ohio: Merrill, 1966); and Howard Kirschenbaum, *Advanced Values Clarification* (La Jolla, California: University Associates, 1977). For a critique see William Casement, "Moral Education: Form without Content," *Educational Forum*, vol. 48 (Winter 1984), p. 181.

15. Sara Rob, "The Debate over DARE," *NewsBriefs*, May-June 1997; Richard Clayton, Anna Cattarello and Bryan Johnstone, "The Effectiveness of Drug Abuse Resistance Education Project (Project DARE): Five Year Follow-Up Results," *Preventive Medicine*, vol. 25 (1996), p. 307; James Bovard, "It Takes More Than Anti-Drug Slogans," *Washington Times*, 6 November 1996, p. A25; "Antidrug Program to Adopt New Strategy," *New York Times*, 15 February 2001, p. A1.

16. Lawrence Kohlberg, "Stages of Moral Development As a Basis for Moral Education," in *Moral Development, Moral Education, and Kohlberg: Basic Issues in Philosophy, Psychology, Religion, and Education*, ed. Brenda Munsey (Birmingham, Alabama: Religious Education Press, 1980), p. 18.

17. Quoted in Christina Hoff Sommers, "Ethics without Virtue: Moral Education in America," *American Scholar*, Fall 1984.

18. Catherine Walsh, "The Life and Legacy of Lawrence Kohlberg," *Society*, 1 January 2000.

19. Sommers devotes two chapters to Gilligan; see *The War against Boys: How Misguided Feminism Is Harming Our Young Men* (New York: Simon & Schuster, 2000).

20. Eric Adler, "What Fresh Hell Is This? A Guy Marooned in Women's Studies," *Women's Quarterly*, no. 27 (Spring 2001), p. 7; see also a report by a recent HGSE graduate, Robert J. Ortiz's "How Harvard School of Education Churns out Liberal Teachers," *Human Events*, 18 June 2001.

21. Diane Dreher, "Toward a Person-Centered Politics," in *Positive Regard: Carl Rogers and Other Notables He Influenced*, ed. Melvin M. Suhd (Palo Alto, California: Science and Behavior Books, 1998), p. 353.

22. Quoted from Vasconcellos' speech, "The Social Importance of Self-Esteem."

23. James L. Nolan Jr., *The Therapeutic State* (New York: New York University Press, 1998), pp. 177–78.

24. Ibid., p. 157.

25. Roy F. Baumeister, "Should Schools Try to Boost Self-Esteem?" via internet.

Chapter 9: The Deconstructed Self

1. Phone interview with Vicki Marshall, 3 October 2001.
2. Bill Moseley, "Still Crazy after All These Years," *Psychology Today,* vol. 28, no. 1 (January 1995), p. 30.
3. Phone interview with Charles Platt. For Platt's comment on the Joy of Now, see "The Strange Case of Timothy Leary," *Cryocare Report,* no. 8 (July 1996). For other views of Leary's last days see Richard Leihy, "On-Line, in Pain, an Apostle of Acid Prepares to Truly Drop Out," *Los Angeles Times,* 10 March 1996, p. F1; and Brian Doherty on Leary the libertarian in "The Transmigration of Timothy Leary," *Liberty,* May 1996.
4. David Colker, "Leary's Last Trip," *Los Angeles Times,* 3 June 1996; Sam Meddis, "A Cyber-Guru's Online Reincarnation," *USA Today,* online at usatoday.com, undated.
5. John Perry Barlow, "Timothy Leary's Dead," *Timothy Leary: Outside Looking In,* ed. Robert Forte (Rochester, Vermont: Park Street Press, 1999), pp. 21–23.
6. Sara Davidson, "The Dass Effect," *New York Times Magazine,* 21 May 2000.
7. Nadya Labi, "The Grief Brigade," *Time,* 17 May 1999, p. 19.
8. Jessica Koval, Ellen Yan, Thomas Frank, *et al.,* "The Colorado Tragedy: Deadly Omen," *Newsday,* 22 April 1999, p. A3.
9. Emily Nussbaum, "Good Grief! The Case for Repression," *Linguafranca: The Review of Academic Life,* October 1997, pp. 48–51.
10. Martin E. P. Seligman, *Learned Optimism: How to Change Your Mind and Your Life* (New York: Pocket Books, 1998), pp. 282–87. See also Seligman, "Building Human Strength: Psychology's Forgotten Mission," *APA Monitor,* vol. 29, no. 1 (January 1998); Seligman, "Teaching Positive Psychology," *APA Monitor,* vol. 39, no. 7 (August 1999); and Gregg Easterbrook, "I'm OK, You're OK: Psychology Discovers Happiness," *New Republic,* 5 March 2001.
11. See *New York Times,* 18 December 2001, p. A22.

Index